GIRLS FOREVER
BRAVE AND TRUE

GIRLS FOREVER
BRAVE AND TRUE

by Caryl Rivers

ST. MARTIN'S PRESS

New York

Library of Congress Cataloging-in-Publication Data

Rivers, Caryl.
    Girls forever brave and true.

    I. Title.
PS3568.I8315G57   1986   813'.54   86-3670
ISBN 0-312-32728-5

First Edition

10 9 8 7 6 5 4 3 2 1

To Alan, Steven, and Alyssa, with all my love.
And to Max and Esther, with love and thanks.

SCHOOL SONG (Unofficial Version)

Immaculate Heart High School

Immaculate Heart,
Immaculate Heart
Girls Forever Brave and True
They drink and they smoke
and they tell dirty jokes
But don't ever ask them to screw

GIRLS FOREVER
BRAVE AND TRUE

ONE

Kitty Cohen leaned back against the peach-beige cushion of the Mercedes as the chauffeur drove along Independence Avenue past the Rayburn Building, a pseudo-classical monstrosity that seemed absurdly grandiose for the rotund figure of Mr. Sam, who had been the Speaker for more years than she could remember. His most memorable words were not carved in marble on the frieze, but they should have been, because they described the way things ran on the Hill for a long time: "To get along, you go along."

Kitty looked up at a third-floor window. Mr. Henkling, South Carolina. He padded his campaign revenues with cash under the table from certain elements in the tobacco industry, and his wife on occasion slept with the tennis pro at Chevy Chase Club, a young man from Port Washington who had ranked fourth in collegiate singles at USC, but had suffered a nervous collapse from the pressures of the pro circuit and went to the same therapist as the ex-wife of the Secretary of the Treasury. The next window belonged to Mr. Grillo, New Jersey, whose second cousin was a minor Mafia chieftain in Bayonne.

"The usual route, Mrs. Cohen?"

Kitty nodded, and the chauffeur headed up the Hill past the House side of the Capitol, then turned to drive by the Supreme Court, where a group of tourists climbed the broad stairs so they could gape at the chamber where so many great battles had been decided. Mr. Justice Sourbine would be in his office now, having tea. He was something of an Anglophile.

1

He had set tongues to wagging last year when, at sixty-nine, he married a twenty-eight-year-old associate producer on the "Today" show; he had met her when he appeared on a special show for Law Day. She was pregnant and he was getting a hair transplant, which was taking root in rather sporadic fashion on his scalp. The attorney for a group of citizens suing a chemical company that had dumped toxic wastes into a reservoir nearly destroyed his case—not to mention his entire career—by giggling in the middle of closing argument. Every time he looked up at the wispy sprouts on Mr. Sourbine's head, the giggle crept into his throat, choking him. One good chortle, he knew, and the citizens of a small city in Ohio would spend the rest of their lives ingesting toxins, uncompensated.

Kitty smiled as the car moved on, finally turning onto Pennsylvania Avenue. She loved the scenic route home. It gave her time to run through some of the things she knew about the town—and it never failed to amaze her how much she did know. In a city where knowledge was power, this was a great comfort. She felt like a miser cheerfully counting the stacks of gold coin hidden in the attic.

She touched the button and let the window slide down halfway so she could inhale the crisp afternoon air. Washington was never more beautiful than on a day in early fall when the afternoon sun gave a pinkish cast to the marble. *Mausoleums*, some people scoffed, speaking of the city's edifices. Kitty loved them; they spoke to her. The Jefferson said, in a deep baritone softened by the gentle edges of Virginia, "I have sworn upon the altar of God eternal hostility against every form of tyranny over the mind of man." The Archives lectured, in the dry tones of a Yankee schoolmarm, "The past is prologue: Study the past." And the Lincoln, of course, in a nasal prairie twang, asked that the government of the people, by the people, and for the people not perish from this earth.

The voices that made Washington different from other cities, Kitty thought, were what so many people missed when they wrote about Washington. They wrote of the scent of corruption, sweet and sticky like resin, or the clash of giant egos large as mighty apes, or the acrid chill of betrayal as one deal after another was cut. All true, of course, but it wasn't all. The voices of the past spoke clearly, here, and men, and women too, were drawn to them, impelled by some deep urge to leave their own footprints on the shining sands of history. They came to serve, to do good, to find some great and noble deed. Even the worst of them, the ones who lied and cheated and stole and dissembled—even they, in their heart of hearts, thought that they had done some of God's work, and if they came out a little bit ahead by doing it, what was the harm?

As the car moved past the Executive Office Building in the direction of the State Department, Kitty saw a red slash of words sprawled across the side of a half-torn-down building. *US Out of Vietnam Now!* She frowned. The war. It was what obsessed everyone, now, it was what people talked about at their dinner tables, at the cocktail parties, in the offices and the wood-paneled legislative chambers, the war. It would not go away.

Richard Nixon had promised to "Vietnamize" the war, to begin pulling American boys home from a nasty, brutal battle half a world away that was tearing at the fabric of the republic. But it kept dragging on, and the promised light at the end of the tunnel seemed as dim as ever. Americans had turned, snarling, on one another. Now, in the fall of 1969, Washington seemed as divided as the rest of the country about Vietnam. Once, the war had seemed absurdly distant to Kitty; but now, with her son Jason in prep school, it had moved dangerously close. She had to keep working on Dan about the war. She was so sure she was right, and he was starting to come around.

She was thinking about what she would say to him when the car pulled into the circular driveway of the big house on Foxhall Road, the one to which she had come as a bride. She would have preferred something more modest, but Morris wanted to give her a palace, and he could afford it. She had come to love its quiet dignity, the lawns that spread out on either side, the stately elegance of the Georgian architecture.

She got out of the car and went into the house. She took the notes she had been working on out of the desk and sat on the modular couch in the living room, kicked off her shoes and stretched her legs out on the couch. Morris had always hated the couch; he had never sat on it when he was alive. A round couch was unnatural to him; it violated his sense of the sym-

3

metry of things. Once Morris made up his mind, there was no dissuading him.

She looked at the paper in front of her and sighed. A guest list used to be a simple thing, if you followed a few rules: Don't seat the Algerian ambassador next to the cultural affairs minister from the French embassy or the Israeli consul next to the Egyptian chargé. One or the other was bound to get the dessert fork stuck prong-deep between the shirt studs. In the old days, you could pretty much count on Americans being civil to each other, regardless of party affiliation. But with Vietnam turning everyone into hawks or doves, you never knew which species of bird would wind up garroting the other over the crudités.

And then, of course, there was the question of Dan.

It was no secret around town that the congressman from Nebraska was, as the kids would put it, shacking up with the widow Cohen. Some of Morris' old friends were not happy; they would have thought it appropriate for her to have performed an act of *suttee,* burning herself alive, if not exactly on his funeral pyre, perhaps on the sixth floor of the Morris Cohen Residence Hall at Brandeis. But dammit, thirty-eight was too young to pack herself in mothballs and wait quietly until she could rest beside Morris in her designated spot in Arlington National Cemetery. Morris had earned a spot in Arlington by serving on the USS *Lake Champlain* in World War II. The cemetery was getting so crowded these days that wives of veterans were being shipped off, upon their demise, to crypts with considerably less cachet. But Morris pulled strings and got Mr. *and* Mrs. Cohen a shady spot opposite a civil war artillery battalion. As Washington's biggest real estate dealer, Morris had a *thing* about location.

She sighed again and wrote "Len Fineberg" on the list. Dan was going to need the moneymen if he ran for the Senate, and if Len fell in line, the rest of the crowd would follow. And he would, because Len didn't want ex-Senator Rolvag to get his old seat back. Rolvag had voted against every arms deal for Israel, and Len was glad when Chet Hawkins knocked him off four years ago. But now Hawkins was dying of lung cancer, and the Nebraska seat was up for grabs. It was crucial that Dan make the run. Good for Israel—not that she'd say that to Dan. Morris had made a Zionist out of her. He was a tireless worker for the State of Israel, and she had expected to grow old beside him, smiling happily at his side as he cut the ribbon for this new wing or that research laboratory. He was such a big, strong man. He seemed as eternal as the pyramids. Once she had laughed at him when he said to her, "Kitty, if I die, I want you to remarry." Morris, die? The thought never entered her mind, even though he was nearly twenty years older than she. She was furious at him when he did die; one day she even marched herself over to Arlington Cemetery and yelled at him, under the ground, "Morris, this is a *lousy* trick, you have no right to do this, you hear me, Morris!"

But she was mortified as just then a busload of tourists passed by on the way to JFK's Eternal Flame, gaping at her. Thank God Maxine Cheshire at *The Washington Post* hadn't gotten hold of that little tidbit. People would have thought she'd gone dotty, and the caliber of her guest lists would have dropped several notches. She'd have had to settle for assistant press secretaries and members of the FCC, with an occasional drop-in from a hardening-of-the-arteries federal judge. She would not have met Dan Amundsen.

She thought of him and smiled, remembering the first time she had seen him, in this room, at the annual reception she gave for new congressmen. He had seemed so vulnerable, standing there with his sandy hair falling across his forehead like an unruly lawn, the Brooks Brothers suit cut right but the tie an abomination. Ever since Kennedy the look for bright young liberals had been windswept casual, but the truth was that to make it come out right you had to have an instinctive sense of style, which JFK had in spades. Otherwise, you just looked like an unmade bed; unkempt, not unconcerned. Dan knew what he was supposed to look like, but he just couldn't pull it all together. Her first instinct was maternal. This young man needed her *help.* She wanted to lace his shoes and put on his mittens, brush the hair back from his brow. When she started to talk to him, it was clear that he was very *very* smart, and a little bit scared. The Hill was an exclusive club, where friendships and connections were the routes to power, and Dan was smart enough to know very quickly how unconnected he was. He was an odd blend of sophistication and ignorance. He had read everything, it seemed, could converse passably in French, thanks to evening courses. But food was a vast unexplored terrain; he was always asking Kitty what some sort of food was—even something so unexotic as pâté. He could recite Wallace Stevens and Robert Lowell, but he drew a blank on Monet and Manet. He was like a canvas on which large areas were done in exquisite detail, while others were totally blank.

She could not, of course, resist playing Pgymalion. She sent him to Morris' tailor, and she was astonished at how fast he made the transition from off-the-rack to hand-cut British worsted. He was her star pupil. He soaked up information like a sponge, from the deployment of the Minuteman missile to the proper spoon to use for gazpacho. He did not remain unconnected.

Antonio, the houseman, came into the room and said that Constance Masters had arrived, and Kitty smiled and went in to greet her visitor. Kitty had been drawn to Con the first time she saw her, standing by the chocolate table trying to pretend she wasn't terrified. It was Con's first assignment as party columnist for the Washington *Press Herald*, and that alone would have been a plus for Con as far as Kitty was concerned, since the old columnist was an alcoholic with terrible breath who used to nearly knock Kitty over with the stench every time she asked a question. Con was wearing a black sheath with pearls—the outfit a woman chooses when she's not sure what to wear—and getting up her nerve to go talk to these people she didn't know but had read about. And of course, Con was so striking, with her dark hair and pale skin, and attractive people always interested Kitty. They started to chat, and soon Con was telling Kitty about her navy commander husband, and the fact that this was her first real job after spending fourteen years raising kids and following her husband around the country, trying to finish her college degree in installments. All of a sudden Con had laughed and said, "I don't even know you, and I'm telling you my life story. How did that happen?"

"I'm a very good listener, my dear."

"But there are all these fascinating and powerful people around. Why are you listening to me?"

Kitty looked over her shoulder. "The Chief Justice is talking about his hernia operation and the chairman of Ways and Means is bitching about alimony payments and the chairman of the FTC wants to pinch my ass. All in all, you're the best of the lot."

They had both laughed, and Con had become Kitty's closest woman friend after that night. The fact that they were both women trying to survive in the city that had once been a swamp was certainly part of the attraction.

"Kitty," Con said, breezing into the room, "the rumors are all over that he's going. Can I run with it?"

"How about 'almost certain.' He's still got his fingertips on the ledge."

"You think he can take it?"

"I think he can. If he really comes out against the war. It's a disaster, it's wrong, and so many of those boys are dying for nothing. I think people know it, Constance. I think if he says it, people will turn to him. I feel it in my bones."

"Nebraska isn't D.C."

"I know. It's a risk. But Dan is just about convinced that Vietnamization is a joke. I really think that it's one of those times when the right thing is also the smart thing, politically. Dan's popular. He's got good press. I think he could do it."

"There's a lot of backlash, Kitty. People saying the kids who protest are traitors."

"I still think that mothers and fathers want this war over more than they want some kind of victory. I really think that."

"I hope you're right. Hey, listen, I have a project for you. I'm bringing someone tonight. I want you to find her a man."

"Who is this person I'm supposed to find a stud for?"

"Not a stud. No lechers, drunks, sadists. Nobody married or gay. Somebody wonderful."

"You don't want much, do you, Constance?"

"Yeah, I realize I've just eliminated half the male population. But it's for my old high school chum, Peg Morrison."

"Peg Morrison? I know that name. Oh yes, she's the woman who won the Pulitzer prize. Six-Day War. I didn't know she was in Washington."

"Just back from Tel Aviv."

"You two went to high school together? Where?"

"Immaculate Heart in Crystal Springs. We were editors of the paper together. We were going to set the literary world on its ear."

"You must have been so excited when she won the Pulitzer."

"Hah! I wanted to bash her face with a frying pan. I heard the news on the radio when I was twisting yellow crepe paper over purple crepe paper for the officers club disco party."

"Oh dear."

"Well, it did do me some good. Here was Peg, doing what she always wanted to do, and I was farting around with crepe paper. I figured I'd better get my act together. I had this vision of my tombstone: Here lies Constance Wepplener Masters, beloved of her husband, her children, and the Schmertz Crepe Paper Company."

"That got you writing again."

"Yeah. So I owe Peg. She needs a man, not a suitcase full of clips. She has had the most *rotten* luck with men. First she falls absolutely head over heels for the most adorable guy you have ever seen. Sexiest green eyes."

"This is bad luck?"

"He became a priest. And she was bonkers over him. Then she went with an older guy. It was a mentor-type thing, but she was fond of him."

"He didn't go into the priesthood too?"

"No. Keeled over dead when they were having dinner at a Mexican restaurant. Face down in the flan. Heart."

"Poor Peg."

"Yeah, well, then she finally finds Mr. Right. They were going to get married and live in Paris. I really thought it was all coming together for her."

"It wasn't?"

"No. Remember Jeff Acker, the photographer?"

"Of course. He was here, once, before he went off to Vietnam. Was *he*—"

Con nodded. "When the med-evac helicopter crashed and burned, they had to use dental charts to identify him."

"Oh, the poor girl! How awful for her."

"Yeah, she's had a rough time. Find her a man. Preferably an atheist with no history of heart disease who's got a job where the biggest hazard is tripping over the rug."

"I'll try. By the way, I have some news for you. I hear the Halvorsen nomination is not a shoo-in. If you sniff around tonight, you might pick up something."

Con smiled. "Oh, that is a piece of news." She looked at Kitty quizzically. "Hey, how come you are always giving me these tidbits?"

Kitty chuckled. "To be truthful, you remind me of myself a few years ago. A lot of talent, a lot of chutzpah, no connections, and a certain raw hunger."

"Does it show that much?"

"My dear, in this town, it is like a small turd floating in the Potomac."

Con laughed, delighted. "Kitty, that is aptly put."

"When I was starting out, you can imagine what I was called. 'Social climbing Jewess' was one of the more polite phrases."

"They don't say that anymore."

"Of course they do. But quietly. They want to get asked back."

"Didn't it hurt, Kitty?"

"Oh yes, dreadfully. But my vengeance was to stay, and succeed. That's what is respected here, success. And of course the power structure changes so often that it's possible for people like me to buy my way in. It doesn't matter if it's old money or new money in Washington. You can be Catholic, Arab, or Jew. It's all very democratic, and rather savage."

"People can come here and be somebody, when they couldn't back home."

"Yes. Dan's a good example. His father was a mental case. But after law school, Dan got into politics, managed somehow to meet the right people, played his cards right."

"One of those cards was you."

"I've been a big help. But I'm no Girl Scout, Constance. Dan is going places. Together, who knows how far we could go."

"Am I hearing strains of 'Here Comes the Bride'?"

Kitty smiled. "Dan said something this morning he never said before. He said when he gets in the Senate, the people in Nebraska will have six years to get to know me. I'd be terrified, of course, but I think I could pull it off. He is younger, though."

"You're thirty-eight. He's thirty-four. Not such a difference."

"No. And I'm not really the mistress type, Constance. Too

9

uncertain. All right for the short haul, but a woman in this town really has to be married."

"Which reminds me. I'm going to call Peg and insist that she come tonight. She's been giving me some fake excuses."

Con dialed the number of the Washington *Tribune*, and Peg Morrison was startled when the phone at her elbow jangled. It was her first week in the city room, and hardly anybody knew she was back. It was going to take a while to get used to working in a room the size of a barn again. There were only two desks in the Tel Aviv bureau.

"You're going tonight, no excuses!" Con's voice announced.

"Oh, Con, I have to get my hair cut."

"Your hair is just fine."

"I have to finish painting the bathroom."

"Screw the bathroom."

"I don't really have a dress."

"Come naked. You'll meet men fast."

"You are going to *make* me go to this goddamn party, aren't you?"

"Be at my place at eight. Goodbye."

Peg sighed and hung up the phone. She looked around at the sea of strange faces hunched over typewriters. To most of these people she was just a byline, or a voice at the end of a long-distance line. She knew it was said of her that she was aloof, standoffish. The truth was that like many journalists who are fearless—even brazen—in their public roles, she was at heart a very private person, even a bit shy. She picked her friends—like her jewelry—carefully, and owned neither in abundance. But Con was right, she had to get out and start meeting people. Tonight was as good a time as any.

Which is why at eight-ten she was standing in Con's living room, zipping Con into a skin-tight silver sheath. Nine-year-old Lee junior looked up from the TV set and said, "Ma, are you going to another dumb party?"

"It is not a *dumb* party. I am working, Leezy."

"Daddy says they're dumb parties."

"Your daddy is wrong about that. I want you and Terry to behave for Mrs. Kessler. Don't wait up for Daddy, he'll be late. Is that up, Peg?"

"Yeah. I remember doing this a few times before."

"Except now it goes up easy. Would you believe *me*, a size ten? No hips."

"What happened to them, anyhow?"

"They went away when I had Terry. I think God did it."

"God?"

"Yeah, he always felt bad because he sent me a zit on my wedding day. When they gave me the Demerol I heard God say, 'Constance Marie Wepplener Masters, my good and faithful servant, arise and walk. You have no hips!'"

Peg laughed and looked at Con, thinking of how long they had been friends; since freshman year at Immaculate Heart High School. Peg had thought Con was the most sophisticated girl she had ever met. Con could recite all the dirty lyrics to Cole Porter's *You're the Top* and she knew about Penis Envy, she quoted Dorothy Parker at the drop of a hat, and most thrilling of all, she didn't want to be a virgin when she got married. Peg was sure she could learn from Con about how to stop being a nice, polite, good Catholic girl.

Con, for her part, found a soul-mate, someone who promised she would go to New York and share a garret in the bohemian wilds of the East Village, where they would be famous writers who said witty things just *all* the time and had lovers and lived lives of chic debauchery that would curl the nuns' hair. "We will be *immortal*, Peg!" Con would declare, at least once a week.

They shared their deepest, darkest secrets. Peg knew about Con's father, who drank and from time to time beat up Con's mother. It was why Con had always been a loner; people might guess. Con knew about Peg's hopeless love for a boy who did love her, but who loved God more. Together, they nourished the tender green shoots of their outrageous dreams, in an era when nice Catholic women made novenas and made babies, and that was about it.

They never did have a garret. Con met Lee, a midshipman at the Naval Academy, in her senior year, and they were married right after graduation. Peg went off alone to the University of Maryland to major in journalism. But the bond forged in adolescence lasted through time and distance. The letters flew as the two of them moved back and forth across the map, Peg to the world's trouble spots, Con to naval bases on two coasts. Now they were both home again, Con in a ranch house in Crystal Springs, a forty-five minute commute to the Pentagon for Lee, Peg newly settled in a redone Victorian house on Capitol Hill.

Peg studied her friend. Con had been pretty but pleasingly plump in high school. Her eyes had been wide-set and startlingly alive, but her face, then, was round and gave the appearance of being not completely formed. Now she was a beauty, with a new symmetry to her face since cheekbones popped out, and with her olive skin and dark hair there was a sultriness about her that would, Peg thought, draw men like moths to a flame.

Peg studied her own image in the hall mirror. "Is this too wrinkled? I dug it out of my trunk."

"It looks great. Blue always was your color."

"Me and the Blessed Mother."

"The BVM, Peg, always wore a bra."

"The pot calling the kettle black. Do you know what Sister Justinian would have said about that dress?"

"One-two-three," Con said, and she and Peg recited in unison: "A temptation to the animal lusts of men!"

"What's lusts?" Leezy asked.

"Never mind. In bed by nine, young man."

"Aw, Ma!"

"I don't want you waking up with a sore throat again."

"I won't. I promise."

"Nine. That's final."

Peg and Con walked out to the car, Peg tottering in her high heels.

"I am going to fall off these damn shoes," she grumbled. "I'm used to combat boots."

"When I was doing the car pool," Con said, "I used to imagine you in some exotic hotel someplace kissing some guy who looked like Omar Sharif."

"Mainly it was guys in fatigues spouting Marx. Let me tell you, Con, guerrillas do *not* smell great."

"So much for romance."

"The last trip I made is a blur in my mind. I couldn't remember if I was with the IRA, the PLO, the GNP, or the NFL. I knew it was time to get out when I was squatting in the bush in East Africa and this big snake came crawling up."

"Ugh!"

"I figured this was it, the end. The snake was going to bite me in the butt and they'd find me bare-assed with a snake in my drawers. I stood up, snake be damned, and I shook my fist at the sky, and I screamed, 'God, I don't want to be here! I want to be in a Hilton hotel with toilet paper and shampoo in little packets and color TV and room service.'"

"Not exactly the Apostles' Creed."

"It worked. Little plastic squares of Vidal Sassoon shampoo began to rain from the sky. Cured the whole revolution of split ends."

Con chuckled. "I'm glad you're back. You've got as fast a mouth as me."

"We always did get ourselves in trouble spouting off, didn't we? I remember the time you told Sister Immelda that Adam and Eve were gorillas because Darwin said so."

"Father Ryan said I could get excommunicated. My mother was very upset. So I said, 'Okay. No gorillas. Would you go for chimpanzees?'" Con pulled the car in a shrieking turn onto Colesville Road, knocking Peg against the door.

"You still drive like a maniac. It's a wonder we weren't both killed before we got out of high school, but we've come a long way since Immaculate Heart."

Con snorted. "I was going to write for *The New Yorker*. Doing 'Cocktail Capers' for the *Press Herald* is a long way from Rebecca West."

"Rebecca West had to start someplace."

"She did not start by writing up the hors d'oeuvres at the Liberation Day party at the embassy of the Republic of Bantu."

"How were they?"

"Pretty good. But I think they were camel pellets."

"Are you taking me somewhere I have to eat camel shit?"

"Not at Kitty Cohen's. She serves the best food in town. Her husband owned most of Wisconsin Avenue. Kitty got tired of doing volunteer work for Hadassah, so she started giving parties for pols. Lots of food and booze, and Kitty keeps her mouth shut about what she hears."

"But you don't."

"I certainly don't."

"How did you get this job, anyhow?"

"Sheer gall. I walked in to the managing editor and shoved

13

the stories I'd done for the base paper in Pensacola at him. I told him he had to hire me because I was a class act. He liked it. I started doing food copy. I made food an *art*, Peg. Know anybody else who could do the Ballad of Cracked Crab Salad and rhyme Chesapeake Bay with café au lait?"

Peg laughed. "You didn't."

"I did. How about *avocado* with *aficionado*. I tried *huevas patio* with fellatio, but that didn't make it. The Cole Porter of cuisine, that's me. Then I got promoted to religion, then parties. Hey, keep your eyes open tonight. Kitty is importing some single men."

"I'm not very good at parties, Con. My idea of small talk is 'Don't shoot! Don't shoot! Press! *Correspondente!*' She leaned back against the seat and looked out the window at the houses along 16th Street. "I don't know about this whole Washington business. I wonder if I made the right decision. I don't feel very much at home here. I guess the truth is that I don't feel at home anywhere."

"Not surprising. You've lived out of a suitcase for ten years."

"True. And after Jeff was killed I realized I didn't have any real friends, just people I'd meet in bars now and then and we'd talk about how it was a shame old so-and-so got himself shot in Rhodesia and where the next good war was going to be. I woke up one day, thirty years old, a tumbleweed. I figured it was time to come home and find out what my own country was like."

"Not a very happy place, Peg. The war is ripping it all up."

"I know."

They were driving through Rock Creek Park, the way they always used to come to take the copy for the high school paper to the printer. Peg had the sudden illusion that she had slid through some kind of crack in space-time; that she and Con were batting along in the '55 Ford, with the proofs in the backseat, and that a few miles to the north, in a cozy colonial home, her mother and father were sitting close together on the sofa, watching "Dragnet." And in the house next door, her best friend Sean McCaffrey was doing his homework, and Sean's brother Bill was getting ready to go to the gym for basketball practice. The sense of the past was so strong because she had been away so long from the scenes of her childhood that they seemed frozen in place, while she had moved on. So many things had changed, but here in the park the hand of time was invisible; the trees, the rocks, the road were so familiar. It was not hard to imagine that she would emerge from the park into a time that had vanished.

Peg shivered, and a sudden gust of desolation gripped her. She was a motherless child. A thirty-one-year-old motherless child. She had thought, once, that people simply outgrew their need for parents, peeled them off like flakes of sunburned skin. Why, then, this black hole that opened up sometimes at the center of her life? She felt suddenly like an astronaut, weightless in the void, around her only cold and uncaring pinpricks of light. There was an instant of terror; she gripped the car seat, inhaled. She was used to terror. It could be controlled. She had done it many times on her road to the Pulitzer prize.

The prize had been her Holy Grail. She had sacrificed the comforts other women sought to follow its spoor. Her daydreams wound around it. In them, always, her mother sat in the front row, smiling and applauding as her daughter accepted it, the Pulitzer. But her mother had been dead two years to the day when the news of the award came through. Cold in the earth, she could not smile or applaud. Peg was on assignment in Cyprus when the news flashed across the UPI wires. She had tried to call Jeff, but the lines to Saigon were hours behind. So she went to the hotel bar, alone, surrounded by strangers, and had a drink to celebrate the achievement she had first dreamed of when she was sixteen years old. She raised her glass and said, "Here's to you, Peg."

Back in her room she suddenly began to weep, furious at her mother for dying too soon.

"I did it. I did it and you'll never know. Oh Mom, why did you have to go and die on me? Why did you have to do that?" And then the winner of the Pulitzer prize for foreign correspondence threw herself across the bed and cried herself to sleep.

Con pulled the car out of the park, and then they were crossing Wisconsin Avenue, on the way to a party. Peg felt odd, disoriented, suspended between past and present. The last thing she really wanted to do was go to a party. But Con was probably right, she couldn't hide out in the city room forever. She shook her head, as if the gesture could dislodge the mist of memory. A Washington party. How bad could it be, anyhow?

TWO

Peg stood in the corner, watching people as they chatted in small groups around the elegant living room. Con flitted by and ordered, "Circulate!"

"Con, this is the dullest party I've been to since Emily Rudino gave one in the fifth grade."

"The one where no guys came and the girls had to play post office with each other?"

"I take it back. Emily's party was *better*."

"Talk to people, Peg, don't just stand there like a lump. I'll introduce you."

"In a while."

"Watch out for the guy in the gray suit. A married lech. The guy with the striped tie, over there, he likes threesies. But maybe you do too. It's been a while since we hung out together."

"Two women and one man?"

"Yeah."

"No thanks."

"Sister Justinian would be proud of you, an Immaculate Heart girl to the core. Go mix."

Con floated off and Peg looked around the room, at the understated elegance of the décor and the food and drink that flowed as if from some hidden spring. The affluence of America, the sheer abundance of *things*, had hit her with the sting of cold water in the face. Had it always been this way? Probably so. But her eye had grown used to sparser landscapes—the hot, bare expanse of the Sinai, the stunted greenery of parts of West Africa. The lushness and opulence of America struck her eye as obscene. She was aware of this sense of too *muchness* as she stood in the elegant room, watching the waiters bringing tray after tray of canapes. The men's bellies strained at the vests of their suits; the women were sleek, but it was a slimness born of discipline, not of want. She thought of the distended bellies of children she had seen in the Sudan; of the gaunt women with their burning eyes that spoke of the last stages of hunger and dehydration, and she felt once again the sense of being disconnected, in the wrong place.

Yet the opulence seemed to coexist with a sourness, a tiredness that had not been present when she had packed her bags for that first assignment in Jerusalem. John Kennedy had blown away the torpor of the Eisenhower years like an east wind, and the nation seemed hopeful and alive. She had been in a café on Dizengoff Street when the news flashed through the streets that John Kennedy had been gunned down in Dallas in 1963. She simply couldn't believe it. And then, five years later, it had been Martin Luther King, and Bobby Kennedy, and now the country to which she had returned was eating its entrails over Vietnam.

Vietnam. Where Jeff had died. Where he knew he was going to die.

She took a glass of champagne from a silver tray, and sipped it slowly. They had offered her Saigon, where the action was. But she had had this longing to come home, and so she did, but it wasn't home anymore, but a sour, angry, alien place. What was she going to do here?

"Aren't you Peg Morrison?"

She looked up to see a young man, very Brooks Brothers, a razor cut, shoes shined. State Department, she guessed. She turned out to be right. Indonesian desk.

"I read your stuff all the time," he said, and he proceeded to ask her a series of questions about the Middle East. She chatted with him, politely, noticing that he was attractive but feeling no inclination to do anything about that—though he gave out a distinct signal that he was available if she was. Finally, discouraged, he drifted away, and Peg looked for Con. She saw her in animated conversation with the senator from a Southern state. Con was obviously in her element; she seemed actually to glow. The color had risen in her face and she was leaning forward, listening. The flow of political gossip seemed to charge her, as if she were a toaster plugged into some unseen power source. Peg felt a twinge of envy; how long had it been since *she* had been that excited over a story?

Then Con was making her way across the room, grinning.

"Pay dirt," she chortled. "The committee isn't going to say yes to Halvorsen. They're going to torpedo him."

"You got that out of the senator?"

"Yeah. But no whispering to little birdies at the *Trib*, Peg. This is mine."

"I'm off duty. What did you say to him?"

"Branch water and bourbon makes him very mellow."

"Now I see why you wore that dress. Did you notice, he was staring at your boobs the whole time?"

"You bet. Boobs and bourbon and the senator spills his guts. They think if you're stacked you haven't got a brain. Or ears. They tell you *everything*. Come on, Kitty's dying to meet you."

Kitty Cohen greeted Peg warmly; she was, Peg thought, one of the loveliest women she had ever seen, with that ageless sort of face that is as arresting at seventy as at twenty-five. Kitty could wear clothes like a *Vogue* model—and did— but she lacked the angularity of a fashion model. There was real flesh under the Mainbocher gown.

Kitty smiled as she introduced Peg to the man standing next to her, Dan Amundsen. Peg groped mentally for the state. Idaho? No, Nebraska. Damn, she'd have to get it down if she was going to stay in Washington.

"I'm very glad to meet you, Miss Morrison. I read you all the time in the *Trib*."

He was a very handsome man, she noticed. He focused in on her as if there was no one else in the room. A happy facility for a politician. He had a way of making it seem something more than a learned talent. Peg found herself being flattered despite herself.

"You were in Vietnam, weren't you?" he asked her.

"Yes, a couple of times. But they were just quick swings through."

"What's your impression. Is there any light at the end of the tunnel?"

"Truthfully, no. I spent some time with the ARVN. There's

plenty of brave men in the South Vietnamese army, but the rot is at the top. I'd just come from Israel, so the contrast was probably all the more striking. Crazy as things get in Jerusalem, there's a real political structure, something that's going to stay."

"And not in Vietnam?"

"You know how, in certain situations, things start to go bad, and up to a certain point you can reverse direction, but after that point nothing you do is any good? That was my feeling about Vietnam. Not scientific, of course, but a gut feeling."

He frowned. "That's my feeling, too, but so many people want a win. After all the blood. The American blood."

"We could get a stalemate, I think. But we'd have to settle in for twenty years, like the French did. Would Americans agree to that?"

"No, Americans want a big bang. They want it fast."

"That they won't get."

Kitty walked up, touched Dan on the shoulder, and said, "Peg, dear, may I steal Dan away from you for just a moment? There's someone he has to see."

"Of course."

"Can we talk again?" Dan asked. "I think reporters have good gut instincts, as you call them. Let's have lunch."

Peg watched as Kitty and Dan walked across the room. She whispered to him, and steered him to a tall, balding man standing by the fireplace. Con had said that this was Leonard Fineberg, of Fineberg Industries, Inc. and Ltd., a big moneyman in the Democratic party. Kitty leaned in toward Dan as the two men spoke. Her eyes were cool, betraying no emotion, but Peg knew by her body language that something was going on there.

Damn!

It was a rule of hers, old Girl Scout Peg, not to move in on another woman's man. But talking to Dan Amundsen, she had had a wild urge to muss up his hair. Was Kitty a hair musser? Maybe Kitty wouldn't mind if she just *borrowed* Dan for a while, ran her fingers through his hair.

Then Con was at her side. "Having fun?"

Peg was still looking at Dan. "That is one sexy man, Constance Marie."

"Oh, no!"

"Are he and Kitty an item?"

"Touch him, and she holds your face in the Black Forest cake until you stop breathing."

"My luck."

"Oh shit, I think I am getting Leezy's sore throat. I left my cough drops in my coat. Did you see where the guy in the tux put them?"

"He went upstairs."

"Upstairs coat room. I'll get them."

"I'll go with you. I have to hit the john."

Peg went into the bathroom and peered at herself in the mirror. It was, she thought, an attractive but unremarkable face that stared back at her. Others would have disagreed. She had fair skin, a straight blade of a nose, almost patrician, and a long and graceful neck that was accentuated when she wore her hair swept up into a chignon, as she did tonight. But it was the eyes that drew attention to the face; they were the color of slate, alert, alive. They didn't miss much. She had trained herself to see in a way that most people did not. She scanned the small things about people and places, stored them in her brain cells for future use. People were amazed sometimes, when she recalled the color of a man's tie clip or the pattern of paper on a wall. There was no real trick to it; she just looked.

She dabbed lipstick on, carelessly—she had little time for artifice—then went out into the hall. She didn't see Con, so she walked down the hall, peering into rooms. Then she heard Con's voice, a hissing whisper, drifting from a doorway.

"Peg! Peg, is that you?"

"Where are you?"

"In here. Come quick!"

She hurried through the door at the end of a hall and was greeted by a truly astonishing sight. Con, clutching her box of cough drops, was sprawled face down on the floor, and lying on top of her was a very large, very naked man. He appeared to be dead. Or at least dead drunk.

"Good God, Con, what are you doing!"

"Oh Christ, Peg, that is a stupid question. I am lying on the floor with a naked man on top of me, it's my hobby."

"Who *is* that?"

Con wiggled to no avail. The man was a dead weight on top of her. "Don't you *know* who he is?"

"The ass is not familiar." Peg started to laugh. "Con, you look so funny."

"Stop laughing, you idiot, and get the Secretary of the Interior off my bones."

Peg walked closer. "It *is* him. John T. Cleggins. Isn't he the one who wants to save the white-breasted goshawk from extinction?"

"I know someone else who will be extinct if she doesn't *do* something. Get the son of a bitch off me!"

Peg tugged at the massive carcass of the secretary. "He's *heavy*. He's a big sucker."

"Peg, you've got to get him off!"

Peg clutched the secretary's leg and tried to drag him from Con's prostrate form. He wouldn't budge.

"I can't move him. Try to wiggle out."

"This dress cost me a hundred and fifty bucks. If it rips, I'll die. Try to lift him a little."

"Okay. I'll try." Peg put her hands under the man's chest and tried to lift him. "Oh Jesus, it's not working."

"I can't move. He must weigh three hundred pounds."

Peg put her shoulder against the man's torso and began to push. "Look, I'll try to roll him a little bit. I'll roll to the left and you wiggle to the right."

"Okay. Say when."

Peg pushed with all her might. "Now!"

"Uh, Uh, I'm coming, push harder, Peg, I'm almost, I'm almost—"

"Con, hurry! I can't hold him!"

"I'm out. Oh thank God, you are a friend, Peg." Con scrambled to her feet. "Shit, it's ripped under the arm. I knew I'd rip it."

"Look at me. I'm a mess. I'm sweaty all over. How did he get on top of you, anyhow?"

"I threw my coat on that chair and I was fishing in the pocket for my cough drops when I heard this strange noise and he fell out of the closet, right on top of me."

"He was standing in the closet with no clothes on?"

"I guess so."

"Constance Marie, what kind of a place have you brought me to?"

"Welcome to Washington, Peg."

They looked at the inert form of John T. Cleggins.

"What are we going to do with him?" Peg said.

"We? Who is *we*, kemo sabe?"

"He is an environmentalist, Con."

"Yeah, and those little goshawks *are* cute." She touched her ribs, gingerly. "Ohhh! If he fell on those damn birds the way he fell on me, he'd wipe out the whole species."

"Well, you go get Kitty. I'll stand guard."

Peg waited outside the closed door of the coatroom until Con came up the stairs dragging Kitty, who had a perplexed look on her face.

"What's this all about, Constance? Why are you being so mysterious?"

Peg said, "Mrs. Cohen, it's the Secretary of the Interior."

"Oh shit. He's passed out naked again. Did he fall on anybody this time?"

"Me," Con said.

"Does he do this a lot?" Peg asked.

"All the time. But he's a Cabinet member, so one can't *not* invite him. When he drinks, he gets this compulsion to take off his clothes and go in a closet. He hyperventilates, then he faints."

"This is the man who runs our national parks?" Peg said to Con.

"He's good, actually. He doesn't go to Yellowstone and pass out on the bears. Just in closets."

"We had better move him," Kitty decided. "I'll go get Dan." Peg and Con waited inside the room, and in a minute Kitty was back. Dan walked in behind her. His eyes widened when he saw the body on the floor.

"My God, who is it!"

"The Secretary of the Interior," Peg told him.

"He's *naked!*"

"Observant, isn't he," Con said to Kitty.

"My dear, in Nebraska they are fast on the draw."

"How on earth did he get like that?"

"He fell out of the closet," Con said.

"What was he doing in the closet?"

"Hyperventilating."

Dan looked at Kitty. "Kitty, this is very bizarre."

"Dan, love, I did not ask the man to do a nude swan dive in the cloakroom. The string quartet is enough entertainment."

"Well, we'd better get him out of here."

"The question is, how?" Con asked.

"We can carry him to the bedroom down the hall," Kitty said. "Come on, let's roll him over." The four of them tugged and hauled, and managed to get the Secretary on his back. They looked down at him.

"You'd think," Kitty said, "that for a man his size he'd be hung a little better."

"Kitty!" Dan said. "You are talking about the Secretary of the Interior!"

"Well, I can hardly help noticing. He is naked."

Peg picked up a flowered afghan that had been tossed over the arm of a chair in the coatroom. She placed the afghan over the secretary's private parts. "If you and Dan get his arms," she directed Kitty, "Con and I can get his feet."

With much effort, they managed to get the Secretary about two inches off the ground, and they carried their load out the door and into the hallway. As they struggled along, the bathroom door opened and a man stepped into the hallway. It was Leonard Fineberg of Fineberg Industries, Inc. and Ltd. His jaw dropped down to his bow tie.

"He passed out," Kitty explained.

"So we're taking him to the bedroom," Con said.

"It's the decent thing to do," Dan said.

"Yes, quite," said Leonard Fineberg, and he stepped over the flowered midsection of the Secretary of the Interior and proceeded down the stairs.

"Oh God!" Dan groaned. "This son of a bitch just cost me half a million dollars for my Senate campaign!"

"He's running!" Con said to Kitty. "I'm using it tomorrow."

"Don't worry," Kitty assured Dan, "I'll talk to Leonard." They dragged the Secretary through the bedroom door.

"It worries him enough that I'm Norwegian! Now I'm a Norwegian who drags naked men through hallways!" Dan wailed.

"As long as it wasn't Yassir Arafat, dear, we're all right." Kitty said.

After one try, they despaired of getting John T. Cleggins on the bed, so they put a pillow under his head and put a bedspread over him. "He'll sleep it off," Kitty said.

As Con and Peg walked down the stairs together, Peg said, "Remind me, when you ask me to go to another party, I have to wash my hair."

"Come on, Peg, I was the one he fell on."

"I think everybody in this town eats funny mushrooms."

"They don't have to. It's a weird place. But there's lots of men. Go meet one."

"My armpits are all sweaty."

"Lots of men like sweat. Turns them on."

"Maybe that's why they wouldn't let us wear sleeveless dresses at Immaculate Heart. Our sexy sweat."

In the living room, Peg saw Bill Forbes coming her way. She clamped her arms against her sides. State Department employees did not like sweat; the Pentagon, maybe. He was very nice, and very bright, and probably good in bed. At the State Department, they did things well. She tried to be interested, but wasn't. She didn't want to muss his hair.

On the way home she asked Con, "Are you going to write anything about this?"

"No. It would be a hell of a story, but I'd have to say who was *under* the Secretary, and that wouldn't get me to *The New Yorker* real quick."

"Are you going to tell Lee?"

"Are you kidding? 'Hi honey, I had a swell time. The Secretary of the Interior hyperventilated, then he fell on me naked.' He'd tie me to a chair and never let me out of the house."

"He's not exactly thrilled about your job."

"Not hardly. But he's been trying to get to sea and I said to him, 'What do you want me to do while you are out there on a boat for months at a time. Get so bored I'll be screwing the milkman?'"

"You're a good reporter, Con. You'll go far in Washington."

"Yeah, the party beat is a good way to make connections. And in Washington, access is the name of the game. I want to go to the Hill next. Hell, I've got lots of contacts now. I work hard to meet everybody. And I've done a few favors. You don't think the Secretary of the Interior is going to owe me one? I've got some chits I can call in."

"You're moving in fast company."

"I have a lot of catching up to do. Remember what a big talker I was in high school?"

"We are going to be *immortal*, Peg!" Peg said, imitating her.

"Yeah, but I was really scared, deep down. I was relieved, really, when I married Lee. I didn't have to put up or shut up. I didn't really know if I could do it."

"Now you do."

"Oh yes, I do. You've had a shot at it, you don't know what it's like when you haven't had it. Oh God, Peg, I've got to have my chance. I've just *got* to."

THREE

The Reverend Sean McCaffrey, assistant pastor of St. Ignatius Loyola Roman Catholic Church, Takoma Park, Maryland, rearranged his black raincoat so that it hung neatly over the erection under his black trousers. He'd been following the girl for two blocks and the panic inside him was growing along with his lust. He watched the back of her; the brown curls that fell in a cascade of ringlets and the neat globes of her buttocks undulating under the skin-tight jeans. What in the name of God was he doing?

It was, he thought ruefully, the beginning of some sort of inevitable slide toward the worst sort of depravity. How long would it be before he took to wearing only his collar, his raincoat, and tennis shoes, leaping out from behind trees to expose himself to teenage girls? He saw them, pretty little girls wearing plaid jumpers, and knee socks, staring in horror as the Flasher Priest struck again.

Or maybe not in horror. Teenaged girls were pretty blasé these days.

"Dig the pervert."

"Oh, that's only Father McCaffrey, the Flasher Priest."

"Weird. Why's he do it?"

"According to Kraft-Ebbing, it is a psychosexual disorder rooted in the tramautic damage to his id during childhood complicated by the repressive dementia caused by ten years of celibacy."

"Look, he's waving and pointing."

"Yeah, and he's pretty well hung. For an old guy."

Sean sighed. Even in his deviant fantasies he was giving himself Brownie points. Well hung. Why did men obsess about that? Even in the seminary, where you weren't even supposed to be thinking about stuff like that, the guys would discreetly eye each other at the urinals, checking things out. He was, he remembered, the best-hung seminarian at St. Lawrence the Martyr Seminary, and if that didn't rank up there with useless distinctions of the Western world, what the hell did?

He made a smart military right turn, deserted the tight jeans, and walked along F Street, feeling horny, grumpy and out-of-sorts. Father Barry was going to ask him to hear confessions when he got back, even though it was supposed to be the pastor's turn. Father Barry would hole up in his room with a bottle of Scotch and he'd be thoroughly plowed by ten P.M. Then he'd snore and cough half the night in the room next to Sean, puking his guts up at three A.M. He never said six o'clock mass. By six o'clock he was hung over and trying the sleep it off, the old bastard.

Sean regretted the thought instantly. Father Barry was to be pitied, a wreck of a man who could hardly function, whose only joy in life was bullying the assistant priests, Sean Mc-Caffrey and Brian Bryne.

"Lord, forgive my uncharity," Sean said.

The truth was that Father Barry scared the shit out of Sean. Was he the Ghost of Christmas Future? Sean saw himself, grizzled, unshaven, and his bowels not working right, looked over by a kindly old Irish housekeeper—Mrs. Slattery—who smelled of Lysol and lavender soap and who made stew with stringy, half-cooked lumps of meat in it.

"Eat up, Father, you'll be needin' your strength for the beano tonight," she would say, and he would wait until she left the room and then he'd pour cheap Scotch into a water glass and glug it down with the stew.

"Getting Irish again, McCaffrey," he said to himself. Not surprising; his genes were pure Irish, both sides, Kerry and Clare. The Irish had a gift for being morbid; they sang songs about their mothers dying and their fathers getting shot in the back during the rising by the Black and Tan. For his part, Sean had a long history of being morbid. As a kid he would lie on his bed and stare at the ceiling and imagine Being Martyred.

He'd picture every small detail, in technicolor and stereophonic sound.

Usually he was being eaten by lions or was tied to a cross being scourged to death. He'd grit his teeth and barely make a sound—other than a low moan—as the lion nibbled on his femur or the skin peeled off his back. Sometimes his mother would peer in and ask, "Are you feeling all right, Sean?" He'd say, "Yeah, Ma." He could hardly tell her, "Buzz off, Ma, I'm getting martyred."

In his daydreams, people were always standing around making admiring comments, like: "What a brave boy! He will be a saint!" As he died, a prayer on his lips, his tormentors— moved by his courage—saw the error of their ways and converted on the spot. They would fall to their knees and cry out, "I accept the one true God."

Sean climbed into his beat-up Toyota and thought about St. Lawrence the Martyr Seminary, and about Father Martin, who flogged himself three times a week to share the passion of Christ. Nobody thought that odd, at the time. In fact, some of the young men went to Father Martin's room to be beaten with a strap. He remembered his roommate, Dennis Coughlin, with angry red stripes across his back, gritting his teeth and trying not to cry out with the pain. Sean had offered to rub some ointment on his back, but Dennis said he wanted to offer up the pain for the sins of the world. Sean thought that admirable, but stupid. But then, Dennis wasn't too swift anyway. Sean noticed that the holiest seminarians were those who seemed to be somewhat deficient in gray matter. Sanctity, it seemed, rose in inverse ratio to IQ points.

Sean had known that he was smart—very smart—and the knowledge got him into trouble. It was a sin of pride to think you were superior to other people—and Sean thought he was smarter than all the other seminarians. (Brain power, fortunately, did not exist in inverse ratio to the millimeters of one's private parts.) So he would dutifully kneel down and examine his conscience and then apologize to God for pride, the sin of Lucifer. If anybody needed a flogging it was probably Sean McCaffrey, for thinking he was such a wise-ass. Still, he had stayed away from Father Martin. Masochistic daydreams of lions nipping at your nose were one thing, but real pain was something else. *That* Irish he wasn't.

Sean drove along 16th Street, then crossed over to 13th, across the district line from Washington into Takoma Park. The handsome brick structures that lined 16th were gradually replaced by older wooden ones, many of them showing the disrepair that is mute testament to the decaying of a neighborhood. The parish had once been prosperous—white, middle class, and largely Irish, but only a few of the old families remained. They had fled deeper into Montgomery County before the advancing tide of blacks, Hispanics, Asians, and even a few hillbilly whites. "St. Nasty's" was a well-known punishment stop for men of the cloth. To get there you had to be a drunk (Father Barry), a lecher (the former pastor, Father Riordan), a certifiable mental case, or a young, idealistic priest who runs afoul of some bishop.

Take a bow, Sean. Take a bow, Brian.

Brian had made the mistake of getting involved with the Black Panthers in North Jersey. He put together an ecumenical service with the brothers and the local clergy. Things went along smoothly until one of the brothers called the Very Reverend Matthew Mark Hannigan a motherfucker.

He did it conversationally, not with any malice, but the Very Reverend Matthew Mark Hannigan tended to regard his white-haired Irish mother as a candidate for beatification, and he took the remark rather more literally than it was intended. So it was St. Nasty's for Brian.

With Sean it was Boston and Stella Maris parish. Sean was very popular in the working-class neighborhood that bordered Logan International Airport, so much so that he got elected as a community representative to Massport, the agency that runs the airport. He started telling people like the presidents of Eastern Airlines and TWA that they were going to have to start shelling out big buckaroonies to soundproof the homes near the airport. Clerical eyebrows were raised higher than the new control tower, and Sean found himself on Amtrak with his press clips: "Priest-politician gets tearful send-off."

"It's my stupid mouth," he told Brian. "I was too quotable."

"At least you didn't call the cardinal a motherfucker."

"Not in public," Sean said.

Sean pulled the Toyota up in front of St. Ignatius, a massive stone building, and was careful to lock the car. The local dustheads would steal anything; they didn't care whether it belonged to a priest. He went into the rectory and sure enough, Father Barry confronted him.

"You are hearing confessions today, Father."

"I believe it is your turn, Father."

"My turn? Oh no, it is yours, Father. I checked the schedule and I am sure it is yours."

There wasn't any point in arguing, so Sean went over to the church and heard the confessions of the few people who turned up. Back at the rectory, he and Brian ate the housekeeper's meat loaf, and Father Barry said, "I must recite my Office," and retired to his room, where he kept the Cutty Sark. After dinner there was the AA meeting, and then family counseling, and it was eleven-thirty by the time Sean and Brian had a chance to relax in Brian's room and talk, as they often did. It was what saved their sanity.

Brian, a lanky young man with a shock of brown hair that kept falling into his eyes, looked more like a college sophomore than a priest. He had a plug-in refrigerator in his room that always had a supply of cold beer. Sean regarded it as only somewhat more miraculous than manna from heaven. He dropped wearily into a chair and told Brian about the meeting he had been to that afternoon.

"It's a good group, Bri. Clergy and Laymen Concerned. You know, the Prods are way ahead of us on the war. We're thinking about bingo and they're really doing something."

"You've seen Dan Berrigan with his bingo card lately?"

"I mean the rank and file. Us. We have to do more."

"Sean, you're trying to stop a highway that's coming through the parish. You going to stop the war too?"

"I think there is lots of potential to organize against the war in neighborhoods like this one. Whose kids are coming home in body bags? The Georgetown kids?"

"Where do you get your energy? Pushing for sainthood by thirty-five?"

"I am definitely not a saint. I proved it today." He told Brian about following the girl down the street. "I don't know what got into me. But my God, sex is all over the place these days. You walk down the street and you see girls with no bras and pants so tight you see—well, there's not much left to the imagination. How the hell are we supposed to ignore it, Bri?"

"We are heroic. Men of God."

"Men of God are not supposed to notice a nice ass?"

"Father McCaffrey, such language."

"Well, I won't scandalize you, at least."

"I'm still trying not to start every other sentence with moth-erfucker."

They laughed, and then sat in silence for a minute. Then Brian said, "Sean, do you mind if I ask you something personal?"

"No, go ahead."

"Well, I was—uh—I'd never had sex when I was ordained. Not since, either. What about you?"

"Not since."

"Before?"

"I had a best friend. Every summer I'd come home from seminary and we'd say, 'This is it, just best friends.' And the next night we'd be sleeping together again."

"How long did this go on?"

"Five years. Until I was ordained."

"Five years! Good God!"

"I was in love with her, Bri. And she loved me. You know, we lasted longer than some marriages these days."

"And you broke it off. Just like that?"

"When I was ordained, yes. We just stopped."

"Talk about heroic."

"Oh yeah. I offered it up. I walked around hurting for a long time. Every time I saw somebody who looked like her— but I stopped."

"And you've been celibate ever since?"

"Yes. But it doesn't come easy to me, Brian. Last year I went to one of those lectures on sexuality the Paulists run. Can you imagine, when we were in seminary, having a seminar on sex?"

"They'd just as soon have had a black mass."

"This Jebbe doctor was up there saying its okay to mastur-bate. That it's theologically sound if you do it just for health reasons. No prurient intent. I guess you are supposed to jerk off reading the *Journal of the American Medical Association*, look-ing at the centerfold of an enlarged liver."

"Oh God, talk about angels on the head of a pin. Some things in the church don't change. Want a beer?"

"Do I ever."

They talked for an hour, and then Sean felt the weariness coming over him, and he went into his own room, trying not to let himself get depressed by the seediness of it. The old lace curtains on the window were faded to a dull yellow, the furniture was mismatched and you had to kick the drawers in the bureau to make them work. He didn't mind having so little, only why did the few things he did possess have to be so tacky? He sighed. That was probably a sinful thought. Christ, when invited into the humble abode of a poor person, did not look around and say, "God, this place is *tacky!*" Not for the record, anyhow.

Sean switched on the light over his bed. The room didn't look quite as dreary that way as when the overhead light was on. He hoped maybe Father Barry was drunk enough to sleep through, tonight.

He walked into the bathroom, didn't switch on the light, and the young woman in tight jeans drifted into his mind. He knew she would. He used to struggle against it, take endless cold showers, lock himself in a titanic struggle with lust. But it had eaten up too much of his energy, hurt his capacity for work. Lately, he'd just done it the easy way.

He thought of her hair, tantalizing as it moved in the breeze. He imagined he could smell it, just a hint of the scent of shampoo still in it. He thought of touching his lips to the moving cascade of hair, of having it tumble across his face, against his tongue. He thought of touching the globes of her buttocks as she walked along, and his hand went to his own flesh and he felt the pleasure building at the core of him, as in his imagination he touched the body of the woman whose face he had never seen. The pleasure mounted, exploded, and he heard himself give a groan. He hoped Father Barry wasn't awake. His knees felt weak and he put his hand against the cold tile of the bathroom wall to steady himself.

"Forgive my weakness," he prayed. "Understand, and forgive."

The tension was gone. He could sleep now. Thank you, young woman. Your services to the Holy Roman Catholic Church and to the assistant pastor of St. Ignatius Loyola have been meritorious. He will be able to make it through another day at St. Nasty's without going berserk and trying to pick off parishioners with a .22 from the choir loft.

He felt, as usual, drained, dissatisfied. His palm was warm and sweaty against the cold dampness of the tile. You did not get a lot of afterglow with ceramic tile.

Then it came, as he knew it would, the desperate hunger to be held. He wanted to feel real arms around him, warm lips against his mouth, the solidness of flesh, not just a phantom as wispy as smoke. The craving was so bad it was a physical reality, like the body needing salt after you had sweated too much.

He walked back into the bedroom, stripped quickly and climbed into bed. It was the nights that were bad. Only at night did the loneliness get unbearable, a fog that drifted through the room until he thought he could feel the cold and the damp seeping into the marrow of his bones. He started to shiver, and he clutched his pillow, putting his arms around it, feeling foolish as he did so. A foam-rubber surrogate. What would a shrink think of that?

"Ah, Father, you say you—ah—hug your pillow every night? Very interesting. Now we will talk about your toilet training."

"Peg," he said, his face against the pillow. "Peggy."

She was the only woman he had ever loved, and he carried her about with him, like his luggage. She had inhabited all the bare little rooms of his decade as a priest, like a child's imaginary playmate. Sometimes he thought he could actually see her, her form changing according to his whim. At times she was about seven, the freckles marching like ducklings in a row across her nose; sometimes eighteen, with a mop of hair resolutely curled by Toni; often, as he had last seen her, at her mother's grave, a new sadness in those lovely gray-blue eyes. "I'm no stranger to death, Sean," she had said. "Not anymore."

He addressed his conversation to her from time to time, sotto voce, so as not to be dragged off to the Home for Demented Clerics. He had loved her so much, once, that it made his whole body ache, even his gums. Love was a mist with teeth in it. He might even have given up God for her, if she had asked him to. She never had. Loving God had been so pure, then, like ice, splintering silver light around him, refracting it from every surface, clean, cold, quick-freezing him with holiness. Now— No, he was depressed enough. Better

33

to pick through the memories like an old scrapbook, peering at one that might have yellowed with age, but could still give him pleasure.

So he thought of the Greystone, a dumpy, roach-ridden fleabag with no cross-ventilation in Ocean City, Maryland. It was a rendezvous for college kids with little money and a terror of getting caught, as well as a haven for a collection of people, who, one might say, had strange sexual habits, like the man who roamed the halls in a rubber suit. Peggy had been delighted with it. They had gone there twice the last summer he was home from the seminary.

"Oh Sean, this is exciting. A real hotel!"

He looked around at the lumpy bed, the broken chair, the one small window.

"Sodom and Gomorrah were probably cooler. While they were burning." He flopped down on the bed. "Jeez, this bed is full of lumps."

"It's just the old rats who died inside the mattress while they were eating it."

"Oh God, Peg, that's disgusting. Don't say that!"

She chuckled. "I knew that would make you want to barf."

"Shut up, woman!" he said, and he pulled her down on the bed and undressed her and nuzzled her breasts.

"Umm, I like that."

"So do I."

"Sean, do you like—perky?"

"What?"

"Perky boobs. That's what mine are. I mean, they're not humongous like Jayne Mansfield's."

"Perky is not the right word."

"What is?"

"Microscopic."

"Rat!" She punched him.

"Infinitesimal, minuscule—"

"I am going to put on my clothes and go home. If I can find my infinitesimal bra!" She started to scramble out of bed and he pulled her back, laughing.

"You have the most gorgeous boobs I ever saw and perky is just fine."

"It had better be!"

The Reverend Sean McCaffrey rolled over in bed and said,

"More than fine." In his empty room, holding his pillow, he thought of her body as if had been that night, translucent in the light spilling in from the boardwalk outside, her sweet, lithe body that had given him such pleasure. It was the last time they made love.

In the fall, he had gone back to the seminary and she to New York, to the Columbia Graduate School of Journalism. They wrote, every week, as always. In the spring he came to New York to tell her that he was going to go ahead with his ordination, that he did intend to take his vows. And he did; but there was a part of him that wanted, too, for her to try to dissuade him.

They walked along the Hudson, in Riverside Park, and he asked her to come to his ordination. She faced him, dry eyed, and said, "I can't, Sean. I'll be there in my heart, watching you, but please don't ask me to come."

Would he have given it all up if she had asked him? If she had said, "Sean, don't go, I need you!" would he ever have walked down the aisle in the cathedral, wearing the white robes? But she hadn't said it, and so he left her, offering up the greatest sacrifice of his life, giving his pain to God. The priesthood, purchased at such terrible cost, could be nothing less than glorious.

He sighed, and turned over in bed. Glorious? He had wanted to go to the missions to harvest souls like silver fish. *I shall make you fishers of men.* But Martin Luther King and the Civil Rights Movement opened his eyes to the fact that there was a ministry within the borders of his own country. He was not certain of what it was until Boston. It had all come together for him there—a way to serve and feel his life was of consequence. Christ walked the streets, defied the laws, rattled the pillars of the established order. Could his followers do less?

A most uncharitable thought about the cardinal crossed his mind. He said, almost as a matter of reflex, "Lord, forgive my uncharity."

He turned over again. He had real problems with two of his three vows: chastity and obedience. It had been a bitter blow to be ordered out of Boston. His spirit rebelled when he first saw St. Nasty's, the Devil's Island of parishes. Yet maybe some of the work he had started could bear fruit. If he could

35

just get things on track before they derailed him. But what if it happened again? If he upset the wrong people, roiled waters the hierarchy wanted tranquil. Could he do it again? Bow his head and meekly pick up his suitcase and go someplace where he couldn't make trouble?

He turned again, restless. He was a priest. He had taken vows. The problem was that Sean McCaffrey was still a wise-ass. But he was working on himself, trying to sculpt the mortal clay to the shining image of the Perfect Priest that existed in his mind. He said the words of the prayer he knew by heart:

"Oh God, let there be no more impatience, no more omissions in my duties or tepidity in Thy service; no more attachments to my own opinion and my own convenience. No more inordinate love for the esteem of others. I submit to Thy sweet yoke. Not my will, Lord, but Thine be done. Amen."

And finally, he slept.

FOUR

Kitty stretched, yawned, and looked over at Dan, asleep in the king-sized bed beside her. Just the sight of him made her start to feel itchy. Could this indeed be the former No Tits Titlebaum, virgin until age twenty-two, unsullied the day she walked down the aisle with Morris, relieved that with him beside her, men wouldn't try to pinch her tush? But here she was, eager to grope goyim flesh on the Porthault sheets (an anniversary present from her mother) transformed from a zipped-up Jewish widow to a slut. Her mother was pretending that she and Dan were just good friends, though of course she knew better, and Kitty figured she'd save herself a lot of grief and go along with the charade. Mrs. Leonard Titlebaum, life member of Hadassah, sponsor of so many trees in the State of Israel that she made Johnny Appleseed look like a weekend gardener, was terrified that her daughter wouldn't keep kosher in bed.

She smiled as she looked down at his sleeping face, so un-Semitic, down to the skin. His flesh even had a touch of gold in it. The hair on his chest was as pale as flax, like a Viking warrior's might have been.

Kitty sat up, fluffed her pillow and groaned inwardly. A Viking warrior? My God, where did that come from? Probably from one of the trashy books she read to ward off insomnia after Morris died. She didn't even know what the hell *flax* was.

The truth was, though, that Nebraska was as alien to her as Vineland might have been. Her images were golden: wheat-fields glinting in the sun, cheerleaders with real hair the shade of Clairol number six, cities rising from the plains, glowing like fire in the setting sun. That was probably absurd. Omaha was not Xanadu. But Dan was so—American, like the pictures of the smiling blond people who had inhabited the reading texts of her childhood. Kitty's people were Russian immigrants, and her father had been twenty-five when he came to New York, with four words of English and a fierce determination to suceed. They had ended up in an Irish neighborhood, and Kitty went to school with freckled little Kevins and Marys, and read about Protestant Dick and Jane (even Spot was tawny, and undoubtedly Protestant) and soon began to be ashamed of her dark, foreign-looking parents, who spoke so often in the words of the pale of settlement.

The shame clung to her, even after her father made three million dollars by parlaying his junk business into an empire, after they moved to Great Neck where Jews were *everybody*, and Kitty had her nose done by Dr. Dorfman and shopped at Bloomingdale's. Inside her head was a vision of America that Great Neck did not match, and of course she felt ashamed of her shame. One of the things that attracted her to Morris was that he was perfectly comfortable with who and what he was. Dan brought the old confusion to the surface again. When she and Dan first grappled naked on the Kagan modular couch, was her passion kindled by golden hair and white bread and amber waves of grain? Was it some vision of America unreachable to her that she was groping on the beige ultrasuede in the living room?

She pulled her knees up to her chest. Or, was she just a horny broad needing to get laid? Come on, Kitty, it's hormones we're talking about here, not "Oh beautiful for spacious skies." She had missed the sex she had with Morris—safe, regular, comfortable sex. To think of Morris doing something kinky was to imagine Moses in rubber undies. Dan was another story.

He turned, stirred, but did not wake. Dan had introduced her to practices she thought limited to the more debased members of the chorus line at Caesar's Palace. She still felt uncomfortable about some of it. She didn't feel very *Jewish* in black crotchless see-through panties. She could hardly imagine Mrs. Leonard Titlebaum, the Hadassah maven, slipping into a pair after she lit the Sabbath candles Friday night. And it was hardly something she could take up with her spiritual adviser. "Rabbi Mortensen, does it say in the Talmud anyplace about crotchless panties being *trafe?*" Kitty had giggled the first time Dan drew on her body with lipstick. She asked him if he could do God creating Adam, but he said, "Kit, this is sex, not the Sistine Chapel."

She wondered, idly, where he had learned all this stuff, out in Nebraska, for God's sakes. Did they dash about in wheat fields, smearing Revlon's Fire and Ice on their privates at harvest time? Was it some kind of homage to the fertility gods, ensuring that this year's Russian wheat crop would bomb again?

Dan stirred again and she reached over and brushed the unruly lock of hair from his forehead. Even fifty-dollar haircuts couldn't keep it under control. He opened his eyes and smiled, a smile that could melt your heart, all little-boy charm and big-boy sensuality.

She ran her hand across his chest and said, "Good morning, Viking!" and he said, "Good morning, Dark Lady," and pulled her to him. Before she knew it, he was ready and then so was she, and he pulled her on top of him.

Dan loved to be mounted, and at first that had made her feel like a fallen woman. Morris had been strictly missionary position—not that he was unadventurous—but he liked a sense of order in his world and *on top* was where he was supposed to be. If she'd said to him, "Roll over, Morris," he would have had a coronary right then, in the bed. But after all, one did have to keep up with the times.

"Ohhhhhhh!" groaned Dan, who was always noisy about orgasms, while Kitty was given merely to low, ladylike moans. Dan was a bit put out by that, but she was adamant. No way was she going to shriek like a branded steer. She still had *some* standards.

She cuddled next to him and he stroked her hair and then repaired to the bathroom. One problem with Dan was that after it was over he was eager to be up and away like a shot. Morris had been a cuddler, like she was.

He came out of the shower, his hair damp, and said, "Constance Masters had it in print this morning. I've really done it, haven't I? I can't go back now."

"The time is right."

"I know. Rolvag is out there, a screaming hawk, and I think you're right that people won't be with him long. But what if we're wrong?"

"We're not wrong. The junior senator from Nebraska, Dan Amundsen."

He grinned. "Oh, Kit, it sounds great, doesn't it?" Then he frowned. "Hey, did I do okay at the party? I was sweating, let me tell you."

"Nobody would have known it. You did fine."

"Did you talk to Leonard Fineberg?"

"Yes. He was quite amused, actually."

"Well, *I* wasn't, let me tell you." He sighed. "Kit, how am I going to raise two million dollars?"

"Bake sales are nice."

He groaned. "I don't know a *thing* about fundraising. I got into the House on peanuts. And Rolvag has the banks, the rich folks."

"Dan, you've talked to the Speaker and he's pledged his help. You've already talked to one of his moneymen. Don't play the little match girl with me."

He grinned, the grin that always made her forgive him. It said, "I'm naughty, but I'm so cute." He sighed. "Shit, Kitty, do you know *everything?*"

"Just about."

"The Jewish money. Why would they want to invest it in a Norwegian goy? This is big bucks, Kit. Am I worth it?"

"You think there's a Jake Javits in Omaha? Your vote on Israel is solid. You're just what they need. A blond goyim who votes right and looks cute in pictures with the head of the ADL."

"Well, I'm in it now. Whatever comes."

"By the way—I saw your picture in the *World Herald* with little Miss Cornhusker."

"You know what she is, Kit. A photo op."

"She was looking at you like you were a chocolate sundae."

"She's the daughter of a county chairman. Very sweet, but not too bright. The gossips like to make us an item. *You* know who my woman is, Kit."

"How would I play in North Platte, Dan? I can hardly pretend to be a Unitarian."

"Kit, stop worrying. You're smart, you're beautiful, you'll charm the socks off of them. You'd make the best wife a politician ever had."

"Would I, Dan?"

"Of course. Oh God, Kit, I nearly forgot, I have a hearing at ten. I've got to run. See you tonight, okay?"

He hurried off, and she frowned. Did he really have a hearing? Or did he just have an urgent need to be away, off to someplace, because he'd come too close to the subject of commitment. Dan always danced away from that one. What had he said, exactly? "You'd make the best wife a politician ever had." You *would.* Not you *will.* Not will you. Would. A statement of universal truth, or a proposal? Oh God, here she was, parsing his sentences, how utterly crazy. There were times he spoke as if it were a fait accompli, that they were as good as wed. Other times he seemed—vague. Not like Morris. You always knew where you stood with Morris. It was a hell of a lot easier that way.

Kitty had a meeting of the Mental Health Board that morning, and then she came back to wait for Peg Morrison, who was coming over to Foxhall Road for lunch. Con's tale had stirred Kitty's heart. A pretty woman with a tragic past was irresistible to a people-collector like Kitty. Of course, there was the ulterior motive. There was a chemistry between Dan and Peg, that was obvious, so it was hardly stupid of her to make a claim on Peg's friendship. Peg undoubtedly had enough of the Catholic schoolgirl left in her not to make a play for a man who had a brand on him.

Kitty dressed in a simple blue silk from Bill Blass, and went downstairs to greet Peg.

"Oh, I love your dress, Kitty," Peg said. "My favorite color."

"Bill Blass. He's a friend and a lovely man. Would you like to see some of his things?"

"Designer clothes are too rich for the blood of a working reporter."

"I can get a few things at bargain-basement rates. Let me see about it."

They went to the glassed-in porch, where Antonio served the veal. "To be honest, my dear," Kitty said, "I invited you over for more than chitchat."

Peg grinned. She liked people who got right to the point. "I figured as much."

"It's this damned war. I have a son in prep school, and a few more years—well, it could drag on. I've been trying to convince Dan that he can win if he takes a strong stand against the war. I really think it's the only way he *will* win. He's worried, but the feeling is just so strong with me."

"I haven't been back long enough to get a good handle on that, Kitty. But I'm convinced the war is lost. It's going to stain everybody involved with it. Lost causes always do."

"When you talk to Dan, would you tell him that? I think he respects your opinion."

Peg had lunch the next day with Dan at the Sans Souci. He wore a banker's gray suit with a quietly patterned tie, but Peg kept seeing a big scarlet K around his neck. At Kitty's luncheon, notice was served—along with the veal niçoise—that Dan Amundsen was taken. It was all very subtle; the message went down as smoothly as the wine. Peg began to see why Kitty had become a power on the Potomac.

"All right," Dan said, "let me play the devil's advocate. Vietnamization makes sense. We have to stay until they can fight their own war."

"Do you see us making much progress? We're getting deeper into the quagmire."

"These things take time!"

"I talked to Clark Clifford, after he had left the Defense Department. When Lyndon appointed him, he saw right away the whole thing was a disaster. I asked him why a lot of other people didn't. He said, 'History.'"

"History?"

"A lot of people staked their careers and their reputations on the war coming out right. So their instinct is to hang on, thinking that just another step down the tunnel, it will all come out right. They can't let go. That would mean they were wrong. History would say so."

"And in this town, most people have an eye on the history books."

"Leads to a lot of self-deception."

"Suppose you're right. Suppose *I'm* right, but my timing is off. What good can I do if I lose the seat to a hawk?"

"My guess is that the hawks have had their day. The Tet offensive was the turning point. The Vietcong nearly knocked off our embassy last year, right in Saigon. Our turf. It's coming apart."

"Kitty said they offered you Saigon, but you turned it down."

"Yes. Because of the body bags, really."

"The body bags?"

"I saw them stacked up, these green bags. The way you leave out the trash. It was so sad and pointless. I think it's going to end for us like it did for the French. Götterdammerung. Blood and death. I don't want to be there to see it."

When Peg got back to the office, there was a note for her from the editor, Tom Friedman, in his usual poetic style: "See me. Tom." She walked to his glassed-in office in the corner of the city room, wondering why in newspapers, the offices were made of glass. It gave office politics a special touch of paranoia.

"Enjoy your lunch with Dan Amundsen?" he said, leaning back in his chair and chuckling.

"Do you have spies everywhere?"

"This town is lousy with reporters. And you don't eat at the Sans Souci if you want to be inconspicuous."

"He wanted to pick my brains about Vietnam."

"He's a comer. That's what everyone says. Look, I have an idea for you. This isn't a command performance. You can say no."

"I'm listening."

"I think 1970 is going to be a real watershed year. I think society is changing beyond recognition. Oh sure, the pendulum will swing back again, but things will never really be the same. Some of the curmudgeons around here don't want to believe that, but it's happening. New voices, all over. Blacks, women, Hispanics, homosexuals. They don't buy the old rules anymore."

"The *Trib* likes the old rules. It wants to repeal the twentieth century."

Tom Friedman grinned. He was new on the job, a gunslinger from New York, a liberal, a Jew, a graduate of CCNY. The *Trib* had been founded by Virginia WASP's. He had made enemies at the paper, powerful ones. It still wasn't clear whether they were going to get him. But so far, circulation and ad linage were up.

"I'd like you to carve out a beat that might be called 'Dissent.' I want you to listen to those voices we usually try to ignore, here. The people raising hell."

"I like that idea."

"I thought you would. When the *Trib* covers these folks, we usually hold our white male Ivy League noses. I want somebody sympatico. Not an apologist, but somebody with feelings. Know what I mean?"

"I'm taking the job."

"It's not going to make you popular. A lot of people around here are going to hate every word you write."

"I've got a tough hide."

"You'll report directly to me. Any problems, I want to hear about them. Okay?"

That night, Con came over to help paint the bathroom, and Peg asked her about the word on Tom.

"Fair amount of resentment. He's from New York, not D.C., and Washington always sees itself as a little empire, really wired in. New Yorkers are outsiders."

"What the *Trib* needs. I can see that from here. Overseas, we didn't have to bother so much with office politics."

"Yeah, the *Trib* is good and gray, but that doesn't play anymore. The *Post* has just enough dazzle to make it lively, not enough to make it cheap. And Kay Graham is one smart cookie. Wouldn't surprise me if she hired Tom away."

A dab of paint dropped from the paintbrush onto Con's nose, and she sighed. "This is friendship, Peg. Standing in a crummy bathroom dropping paint all over myself."

"We're almost finished. And it looks so nice."

"Yeah, you can pee in style now. No snakes in your panties." She slapped another glob of paint on the wall. "Nothing else, either, if you keep up this hermit routine."

"I don't see how you can stand Washington parties. Nobody talks anything but shop."

"Washington parties are not for fun. They are for making contacts and picking up information. But you can meet men."

"Most of whom are married. I don't want that scene."

"Tried any of the singles bars?"

"God, no! I hate that. I feel like I'm back at the teen canteen at St. Malachy's, waiting for some kid with braces to ask me to dance."

"You didn't have any problems. Sean McCaffrey danced every slow dance with you. The whole seventh grade I got stuck with nerdy Frank Streep. He liked me because I had boobs. We didn't dance, he just leaned on me and breathed hard."

"Sean did the box step, that's all he ever learned. He was not the most well-coordinated kid in the world."

"How old were you when you met Sean, anyhow?"

"I was four when his parents moved next door. He was out in the backyard playing with a little red car. I went over and stomped on it."

"Why?"

"Because I didn't have one. Why should he?"

"Didn't he get mad?"

"Ripshit. Tore the arm off my favorite dolly. Then I smacked him, and he pulled my hair. Then we were best friends."

Con laughed. "If that's what you're into, I know this kinky bar in Georgetown."

"I'd go if they let me stomp little plastic cars. That really turns me on."

"Have you seen Sean since you've been back?"

"No. A letter caught up with me in Tel Aviv a few months ago. Sounds like he's doing great in Boston."

"*Was* doing great. They shipped him out after he got the cardinal pissed."

"Shipped him out? Where?"

"St. Ignatius Loyola. Takoma Park. A real shithole."

Peg stopped in mid-dab and turned to stare at Con. "Sean, here? He's here?"

"Close your mouth, you look like a guppy."

"It's just a—surprise."

"He's getting himself in trouble again. He's involved in antiwar demonstrations, and he's also got this group going, called Action. Interstate 80 is scheduled to go right through the parish, ripping up a lot of homes. He's fighting it. He's even got the blacks and Hispanics talking to each other."

"How does he—look?"

"God gets the best and the girls get the rest."

"Well, he's here. Well."

"Go see him. Cheer him up. That place is a dump. No, I take that back. See him, but with your history, do *not* cheer him up."

"Oh, that was a long time ago." Peg slapped another brushful of paint on the wall. "How is his brother doing? Sean told me in his letter that Bill was drinking."

"Yeah, he's a real lush. After Bill got out of Georgetown Law he started a firm with a couple classmates. They were making money hand over fist, a big office in Rockville. Then Bill started drinking and everything went down the tubes. Wife and kids left, he wound up in Shephard Pratt. When he falls off the wagon, Sean has to drag him out of the tank."

"Poor Bill. He seemed to have everything going for him."

"Yeah, that's what I thought. But who knows. Life is weird, Peg."

After Con left, Peg walked into the living room. The room was still stark and bare. She had only had time to pick out a few pieces of furniture, and the bulk of her things had not arrived from Tel Aviv. She had a bed, a sofa, a table. She could have rented a lovely furnished apartment on the top floor, but she was tired of living with other people's things. She wanted to buy rugs and drapes and what the hell, china. All the things she had never had time to own.

She'd ask him to dinner. Rectory food was always rotten. He was her best friend, after all. It figured that he was out trying to save the world. He always had.

She still remembered that day in Riverside Park, when he told her he was going to take his vows. When he left, she had felt numb, like she had taken novocaine. Feeling returned with a wrenching, awful hurt. It didn't go away, for weeks and weeks. She remembered sitting on the toilet in her apartment in New York, wondering how she could be the same person she was months ago, because that person didn't hurt all the time. She stared at the bathtub and prayed for the hurting to stop, but it didn't. She thought about killing herself. She wouldn't do it, of course, but she thought about it. She got a few moments of pleasure from thinking about how he would feel when he saw the headline in the *Daily News*:

JOURNALIST
KILLS SELF
OVER PRIEST

He would cry, and sob, but it would be too late. Then he would go into an order where they didn't talk for fifty years, as penance. Then he would die. His will would say that he wanted to be buried beside her, and they would be dead, but together.

It was a child's fantasy, but there was nothing childish about the pain. To banish it, she flung herself into her work. She lived for nothing but the job, there was a demonic fervor about the way she worked. Her star rose, quickly. She got a reputation for being cold, hard-nosed, and she liked that, because she was terrified of being hurt again. But Jeff saw through that, of course.

She went into the bedroom and looked at the odd things she had put on her bed. Her taste ran to hard-edged modern, but she had come home from Woodies with a log cabin quilt and a dust ruffle. Her parents' bed had had a quilt and a dust ruffle.

She ran her finger along the quilt. It looked familiar, and homey. She and Jeff would have lived in Paris, and they might have had a quilt, but never a dust ruffle. It would have made him puke. His photographer's eye for purity of line had no tolerance for dust ruffles. Paris pleased Jeff's eye, and that was why he had loved it so. Peg found Paris cold and dirty; she preferred London, because it was like the quilt, familiar and homey. Even before Jeff had died, a small voice inside her had been saying, "Come home." Now she was home. And maybe it was a mistake.

She felt more comfortable in Russell Square or in Dizengoff Street than she did on Connecticut Avenue. Washington had been a sleepy Southern town when she left. Now it was truly a world capital. And Crystal Springs had a skyline, steel-and-glass towers, vaulting upward. The place you grew up wasn't supposed to change that way; it was supposed to stay just the way it was when you were a kid, so you would know there was a symmetry to life. Your hometown was not supposed to sprout skyscrapers, dammit!

She crawled into bed and he drifted into her mind again. Sean.

The Reverend Sean McCaffrey. How long had it been? Four years. He had said the requiem mass for her mother, and afterward he stood with her at the gravesite, that lovely, cool spot under the trees. He had put his arm around her, just as he had done when they were eighteen years old and they had stood in the same place when her father had died. It was the first time she had really understood that people could die.

She had buried her father and her mother and then she had buried Jeff—whatever was left of Jeff—where he had wanted to rest, in a small cemetery outside of Paris he had once photographed for *Life*. Well, now there wasn't anybody left to bury. Thank God.

Home. Maybe if she said it often enough it would feel right. Home. Home-home-home. Nope.

Well, it would take time. She tried to say it again as she was drifting off to sleep but another word came into her mind instead.

Sean.

FIVE

"**D**on't frown, Morris," Kitty said to the portrait of her late husband, which hung over the bureau. It was a lovely portrait, by an artist who knew just what people who commissioned such works wanted; not such sychophantic flattery that a man like Morris would look like a vaguely Semitic Clark Gable, but not the sort of realism that couldn't bear to shave a centimeter off the nose or jowls. It was Morris on a good day, in good light.

It used to hang in the study, but when Morris died, Kitty moved it to the bedroom. It helped her sleep. She and Dan made love under Morris' benign eye. It didn't bother Dan at all, and after a bit Kitty got used to it as well. It would have been worse to turn Morris to the wall, as if she were doing something nasty. She had gotten into the habit of talking to him; it made the loss less real, somehow. Sometimes she thought she could see slight changes of expression as she chatted, which was doubtless her imagination.

"It's a new era, Morris. I am going off to Mickey Markowitz' private beach, and yes, I am going to swim naked. My God, Morris, they Do It in public these days. You're walking along the beach at Club Med and you actually have to step over people, screwing. Ellen Finestein says she was at a nude beach on St. Maarten with Herb, and they were sort of nervous, and guess who walks up? In his birthday suit. Their rabbi! There he was, Ellen said, his prick dangling right in front of her face. He was chatting away as if he didn't notice that his *puppick* was practically grazing her nose. She was trying not to stare at it, which was hard, under the circumstances. She changed temples, because after that, all she could see during the haftorah was curly pubic hair and a penis, and she didn't think that was quite appropriate for shul.

"I'll be nervous about this, I'll admit. But I have to keep up with the times. Even Mickey swims naked at their place in Aruba, and Mickey undressed in the closet for the first twelve years of marriage. But she asked me the weirdest question. She asked if Dan was circumcised. She said she would be nervous about having a foreskin on her private beach. I said, 'Mickey, you wouldn't be there to see it,' and she said, 'but I would know it was there.' She thinks if an uncircumcised penis were even to *touch* her sand, zap! the whole Markowitz family would be turned into Italians."

She sighed. "Oh Morris, I do miss you so. With Dan, it's like I'm on a merry-go-round, sometimes it's wonderful and sometimes it's awful, but it's never just—quiet, like it was with you. You knew what I was feeling, I didn't have to say anything. I'm the exact age now that you were when you married me. I'm doing it backward. I should have met Dan at twenty, had the roller coaster, and have had you to be quiet with at thirty-eight. I mean it's absurd, I have a son in prep school, and I'm flying off to roll naked in the sand with a lover. Who *is* circumcised, at least. Mickey doesn't have to worry about waking up at two A.M. with a craving for rigatoni.

"I'm holding it together, Morris. At first I thought I'd just quit, go back to doing Hadassah benefits. But I had to see if I could do it on my own, without you to lean on. And I can, Morris! What you told me is true, I'm smarter than most of the men out there. I can make things happen. And I like doing it. Oh, Morris, I *do* like it so much!"

Mickey Markowitz' private beach turned out to be lovely, white sand and azure waters, sealed off from prying eyes by a fence that would have kept out Alaric and his barbarian hordes. Kitty peeled off her suit, gingerly, and she and Dan swam nude and then stretched out on the beach to warm their bodies in the sun.

"I must say, Dan, after you get used to it, it doesn't seem so strange."

"You have a beautiful body, Kit. You should never wear clothes."

"I would look a trifle bizarre, luv, at a state dinner with my bazooms resting on the Eisenhower china."

"They are such nice bazooms."

"I didn't really have any until Jason was born. I was thinking of having them done before, but I didn't have to."

"Having them done?"

"Of course, darling. Money is wonderful. You don't have to settle for your great-grandfather's buns, you can have Warren Beatty's. God's work is a bit shoddy, sometimes."

"I never liked my ears."

"I'll get you new ones. Dr. Dorfman has a Chanukah special, two ears for the price of one. I don't know how much experience he's had, though. He has a very Jappy trade, and ears are not his big number."

Dan laughed. "It's a new world for a kid from Nebraska. Out there, the bull gets surgery before the kids do."

"Why would a bull care what his nose looked like?"

"Not his nose, you idiot, his testicles. A bull gets a blockage, there goes the farm."

"I would definitely *not* turn Dr. Dorfman loose on a bull. He'd take off an inch and turn it up a little, for a real goy touch."

Dan giggled and rolled over and kissed her ear. "You make me laugh, Kit, and I love it." He sat up, looked around. "Look at this place! How much does it cost to keep a place like this going?"

"Don't ask."

"I've never lived the way I do here—in Washington, I mean. It's so easy to get used to the perks. Can you ever go home again? I can't imagine going back to Omaha, practicing law, picking up my own laundry, just another face in the crowd. Being away from where the power is. I couldn't go back."

"You won't."

"But if I go for the Senate, and lose—"

"Cold feet again?"

"I guess." He sighed. "I wasn't going to talk politics, and look at me."

51

"Right, no more politics. We came to take the pressure off."

"Yeah, what, am I crazy? I'm lying here on a beach with a beautiful naked woman beside me, and I am talking about Omaha?"

He pulled her to him, and they kissed and touched and he said, "Come on. Let's do it in the water!" and she protested, "But, Dan, there might be sharks!"

"The thrill of danger!" he laughed, and carried her to the water and they made love with the warm water ebbing about their bodies. Afterward, they lay close together on the sand.

"Well, at least I didn't get eaten," she said.

"Oh?"

"Not by *sharks*, luv."

"You taste wonderful with salt."

"You are a terrible man."

"And you," he said, "are wonderful." They lay close together, letting their bodies dry in the sun. Dan was quiet for a long time, and when he spoke, there was a curious timbre to his voice.

"Kit, I don't think I've ever been as happy as I am right now. I really needed this."

She touched his lips with her fingers. "I'm glad, darling. I wasn't going to take no for an answer. You were exhausted."

"I don't know how to relax, Kit. I have this feeling that if I don't keep pushing—"

"What?"

"I have this dream. Had it for years, but I never told anybody about it before. Something good happens to me in my dream—like I win the race for the House, and I'm standing there as people cheer, and then I realize that my *dream* is a dream. I wake up, in my dream, and I'm my father. I'm lying in some loony bin someplace and I have no teeth. *I* am the dream, and I'm my father, dreaming me. See, sometimes, when I was a kid, and he'd have one of his crazy spells, he used to think he was me. He'd call himself by my name, and he'd play with my blocks. It was so crazy!"

"It must have been awful for you."

"After he snapped, we lost everything, the house, the car, everything. It seems everything I have is so—fragile. It can all go in a minute. We were middle class, secure—and then it was all gone. It can all just—go."

"Not me. I won't go."

"Kit, you're the best thing that ever happened to me. Don't ever let me lose you."

"You don't have to lose me, Dan. You don't."

"I can't believe it's okay to be happy like this. That some-body—maybe God—won't just come and take it all away, like he did to my father."

She had never seen him this way before; open, unfurled like a sea flower. The wariness that so often clouded his eyes blown away, as if by the Caribbean breeze. Her heart leapt, that he would trust her so.

"Dan, we can be happy. There's no reason we can't. We can do anything together."

"Right here, right now, I believe that."

"Not just here. Believe it."

"I can't fail, Kit. Oh God, you don't know what it's like, my dream. The worst thing is the teeth, isn't that funny? I actu-ally *feel* them getting loose, dropping out, and I'm trapped inside my father's body and nobody will believe I'm in there, and I want to scream, but I can't. It's worse than dying. A thousand times worse."

He shivered, and she pulled him into her arms and held him close until the shivering stopped. She had never loved him so much. She would never be a dream.

"I'm here, Dan. I'm real. I always will be."

Con hurried across the room to the table where Peg was wait-ing. They were meeting at their favorite spot for lunch, the Washington Roof.

"I'm buying," Peg said. "That was quite a coup, beating the *Post* on the story about Dan running for the Senate."

"Yeah, I'd love to have seen Ben Bradlee's face when he read it in 'Cocktail Capers.' But I never would have got it if the Secretary hadn't fallen on me."

"And I thought I did dangerous stories."

"Guess what, Peg? WTOP has asked me to do a segment called 'Washington People' on the morning show two days a week."

"You're going to be a star, Constance Marie."

"Just think, *me* on TV. I'm going to get Dan as one of my

first guests. I'm not telling *him*, but I'm joining Kitty's campaign."

"To get Dan to come out in a big way against the war?"

"Yeah. I've been talking to people. The doves. They'd love to see Dan going public, saying we have to get out."

"Why Dan in particular?"

"He's perfect. Middle America, hasn't got a reputation as a raving liberal, pretty middle of the road. McGovern's been vocal, but even though he's from South Dakota he's always been a maverick. If a guy like Dan Amundsen could be against the war, a lot of people would think twice about it."

"Constance Marie, you are becoming a power broker."

Con giggled. "We are going to be *immortal*, Peg!" She took a sip of her wine. "This is the way it's done. God, I used to believe all that shit in the civics books about the little boxes for the branches of government. But it's who you know, who you drink with—"

"Who you can manipulate."

"Right. And hell, why shouldn't *we* do it? The good guys can do it as well as the bad guys."

"You think Dan will go for it?"

"Yeah, he really is one of the good guys. He has the right instincts. And you know, I think once he gets a taste of the spotlight, he'll be hooked."

"You make him the next antiwar biggie and I'll write about him in 'Other Voices.'"

"Who are you doing first?"

"Vietnam vets. Then the Black Panthers. Gays after that. I can hardly wait to see the guys at the paper foaming at the mouth. Maybe I'll do a gay Black Panther, invite him to lunch in the cafeteria. 'Hi there, honky, you got great buns.'"

"I want to be there! Hey, guess who I saw on TV on Sunday? Sean. On one of those religious programs, talking about the war. Peg, he is really good. Cool as a cucumber. Have you been to see him yet?"

"No. But I will. Soon."

"I couldn't believe that the klutzy kid was this really smooth TV star. He could be big, Peg. Another Bishop Sheen. Oh shit, look at what time it is. I have to be on the Hill in twenty minutes."

Con managed to get a cab on 15th Street, and when she got

out at the Cannon Building she sprinted up the steps and ran down the hall. She got to the office of Clayton T. Firth at two exactly. She walked in through the huge wooden door and a young blond receptionist with a magnolia accent said, "Good morning. May we help you?"

"Constance Masters from the *Press Herald*. I have an appointment with the senator."

"Oh yes. One minute, please."

The blonde got up, rolling her hips, Con noticed, in a studied, Marilyn Monroe undulation. Senator Firth was known for hiring Southern beauty queens. If you could get yourself crowned in a contest named for an agricultural product or a motor vehicle part—Miss Soybean Curd or Miss Ball Bearing—you had a good chance of knocking down fifteen grand working for Senator Firth. The word was that you didn't have to understand complicated office machinery. If you could get a zipper down, that was good enough.

The blonde ushered Con into the inner sanctum, a corner office with a view. On the office walls were portraits of Stonewall Jackson and Jefferson Davis, as well as a series of photographs in which a number of presidents, starting with Franklin Roosevelt, draped in their arms over the shoulders of a progressively older Clayton P. Firth. The latest one was Richard Nixon, looking decidedly uncomfortable in a brotherly pose with the senator. But Senator Firth had a chairmanship that was important enough to make even Richard Nixon take time out from contemplating his many crises to drape a suit-jacketed arm over the bony shoulders of Clay (as they called him down home) Firth.

The senator, courtly as always, rose and stepped from behind his desk as Con entered. Clay Firth may have been the last of a dying breed, but he carried on the tradition with unmistakable panache. His full mane of silver hair, still luxuriant, touched his collar and curled, slightly. He wore a string tie around his collar instead of the currently chic Eton stripe, and his voice dripped with honey syrup. Actually, on his own south forty, the accent wasn't all that Southern. It sweetened and thickened with every mile he was driven north of the Mason-Dixon line by his black chauffeur in his white Cadillac Fleetwood. By the time he got to Memorial Bridge, Clay Firth sounded like Fred Allen's Senator Cleghorn.

The senator approached Con, took her hand in his and said, "Reporters are getting prettier all the time. What can I do for you, pretty lady?"

"Well, Senator, I thought we might have a little chat about Mr. Halvorsen."

"Why, yes indeed." He beckoned for Con to sit beside him on the leather tufted couch against the wall. Con sat down, wondering how much of Senator Firth's reputation as a ladies' man was real, how much skillful embroidery. He would not see seventy-five again.

She took out her notebook and said, "I hear Mr. Halvorsen had some *little* problems with his investments." She flashed him her most dazzling smile.

His eyes narrowed and he grinned, looking like an amused weasel. He enjoyed these little games of cat and mouse. And Clay Firth was always the cat—even when he decided to play at being the mouse.

"Did you hear that, now, pretty lady?"

"Yes, Senator, I did. Investments in Arab countries that are not—shall we say compatible—with U.S. interests."

She had put two and two together from a line she had heard at the party at Kitty's. A junior senator and a house whip were discussing Halvorsen, a private conversation, they thought. But Con was nearby, to all appearances intent on selecting a piece of choice beef wrapped in bacon and marinated in sake. She heard the senator sing a snatch of a ditty— "Into your tent I'll creep"—and she figured Halvorsen wasn't investing in Swedish meatballs.

Clay Firth chuckled. "Now, you are just as smart as you are pretty, aren't you?"

Con caught something in his inflection that told her she might get a story from him. Halvorsen had not treated Senator Firth with much respect at the hearing, making a few small jokes at his expense while the onlookers chuckled. A fatal mistake. Clay Firth liked to snare rabbits on his acres, in traps he made himself. Nothing fancy, but inevitably lethal.

"Libya, Senator?" It was a stab in the dark.

He moved closer to her, still chuckling. "An interesting country, Libya," he said. "I was there in thirty-eight. Very hot. Very dry. God-forsaken place." He let his hand rest very lightly, on her knee.

"It is Libya, then?"

His hand started to move, ever so gently, on her knee. Con thought to herself, How bad do I want this story?

He was quiet, rubbing. His eyes narrowed more and he had a contented smile on his face.

She made a decision. If the hand went up, she'd go with what she had. Maybe Libya, no confirmation.

The hand went down. The senator's palm curled around her calf, cupping it and rubbing.

"Libya," he said. He kept stroking her calf. He started to make a little humming sound in his throat.

"What kind of investments?"

Stroke-rub-stroke.

"Let's say oil. Yes, oil."

Rub-stroke-rub.

"American companies?"

His hand slid down to her ankle, up again to her calf. He was still making the humming noise.

"Dear me, no. Not American."

"European-Arab conglomerates?"

Down to the ankle, up to the calf.

"Mr. Halvorsen's favorite song is "La Vie en Rose.""

"French companies."

The hand went up the calf, then to the knee again. It rubbed, gently. The senator sighed. His hand felt like dry leaves rustling along her leg. Con thought, suddenly, of the moral guidance course she had taken back at Immaculate Heart High School. What would Sister Justinian have said about the ethical dilemma presented in the case of Catholic Girl Constance, who wants to get ahead in the rough-and-tumble world of Washington journalism, and is on the verge of a very hot story of corruption in high places? She is getting it because a high-placed senator is getting his jollies by feeling up her calf and achilles tendon. What should Catholic Girl Constance do?

Of course, Catholic Girl Constance should leap up, avoid the near occasion of sin by crying out, "I am a child of Mary!" and hurrying off, leaving the high-placed senator wondering what in blazes her mother's name had to do with anything. Senator Firth, being a Baptist, had little truck with the Blessed Virgin.

Catholic Girl Constance smiled and said, "Was he laundering the money?"

The senator had his eyes closed now, and was leaning back with a beatific smile on his face. He was stroking faster.

"Cleaner than a baby's behind," he said, and he stroked even faster, and then suddenly he shivered, gave a deep sigh, and his hand lay still on her knee.

She looked at him. He was very, very still.

Oh my God, Con thought, he died. I killed him with my calf. Could they indict a person for assault with a dangerous calf?

But then Senator Firth opened his eyes and smiled at her.

"You certainly are a pretty woman. Now, don't quote me, pretty woman."

"Reliable source close to the committee?"

"Unimpeachable source, my dear. That will suffice."

"Senator, you have been a wonderful help."

"Anytime, my dear." He closed his eyes and sat very still again. Con tiptoed out.

She went back to the paper and wrote the story, waited around until the managing editor called her in, as she knew he would.

"Who's unimpeachable?"

"Clay Firth."

He whistled. "Holy shit. We go page one with this one. Anybody else got it?"

"I don't think so."

"Eat your heart out, Ben Bradlee."

Con was elated all during the drive home; not even the traffic snarl on 13th Street could sour her mood. She was home before Lee, so she popped the meat loaf into the oven—a recipe left over from her "navy wife" days.

She had known, that first week at Great Lakes Naval Base, that she was going to hate being a navy wife. She had always felt disloyal about that. But the other wives had been nice young girls who chatted endlessly about clothes and hairstyles and bored Con to distraction. In desperation she joined a Great Books discussion group started by a few of the other wives who were outsiders—like Emma Fishman, who was Phi Beta Kappa at Vassar. Emma wore black stockings and ballet slippers and that alone was enough to put her beyond the pale. The fact that she was Jewish and quoted Emily Dickinson only made things infinitely worse.

Lee had talked to her about it, tentatively.

"Constance, hon, I know you like this group, but they are sort of—" He shrugged.

"Strange?"

"Yeah. Sort of."

"God, Lee, at least they don't sit around and talk about who served rancid tuna at the last luncheon."

"I know it's hard for you, here, but—"

"Oh, Lee, you don't want me to give up Great Books! I'm only halfway through Trollope!"

"Oh no, I don't want you to give it up, I know you like it, but well, it's just that some of the girls think you're stuck up."

"I'm not stuck up!"

"I know. But maybe you could—well, just go out of your way to be a little more friendly."

Seized by guilt, Con threw herself into an orgy of socializing. She hosted teas, bridge parties, little dinners. She even gave a Tupperware party. She wrote to Peg about it.

"God, can you imagine me, giving a Tupperware party? I always thought Tupperware was the small town in Ohio Sinclair Lewis wrote about. Peg, we spent *hours* with Tupperware. Did we want round Tupperware or square Tupperware? Did we want salad Tupperware or meat Tupperware? Three hours we spent! I felt I was in a novel by Kafka, that I'd never get out of this little room full of people having orgasms over plastic bowls. Peggy, write me a letter. Tell me what Maryland U. is like. Do the professors really make fun of Catholics and make them Lose their Faith, like Sister Justinian said they would? Are fraternity parties orgies where everybody screws on the floor, like Sister Justinian said they were? I will be *soo* disappointed if they aren't. Write me! Write. Don't use the word Tupperware, though, even in jest!"

And Peg wrote back, "Con, I've been waiting for somebody to try to make me deny my faith, but nobody gives a damn whether you're Catholic or not. They only want to know what sorority you pledged. If I said I was a member of the Sodality of Our Lady, they'd ask if that was the brick house next to the Tri Delts. I'm on the *Diamondback*, and Con, I've got a shot at an editorship next semester. I do mostly the slug work, but it's a start. I had to interview a home ec teacher, and we talked about stoves. Can you imagine going to college to learn how to make fudge? All the home ec girls only want their Mrs. degree anyhow. Making fudge and making out, that's about it. Oh, we have a sex ed. course and it says masturbation is perfectly normal. Sister Justinian would *faint*. The kids call it Sucking 101. But frat parties are terrible. People fall on the floor but they're too drunk to screw. Fraternity men are crashing bores. Their idea of a good time is to take you out and buy you a pizza and talk about themselves for three hours. They wonder why you're not so thrilled when they stick their hand up your dress. By then, they've forgotten your name. I hang around with the guys on the staff, but I'm not really dating anybody. I had a letter from Sean. He has to use code words in his letters, because the priests open their mail. He said they hoped they'd read his last letter, because he said the seminarians were doing satanism and screwing a goat in the back of the chapel on Thursday nights. Same old Sean! Oh, oh, I have to go, I have a chem final and I don't know a molecule from a proton. Write soon. Love, Peg."

Con tossed the potatoes into the oven and sighed. She had tried to be a good navy wife; at least she hadn't gotten him exiled to some awful place, like Guam. He'd just been unlucky, getting stuck behind a desk. He wanted to go to sea, and except for one brief assignment, he'd been on shore the whole time. He did his job too well—and so every day, his dream seemed to be moving further away.

When Lee came home, Con told him about the Halvorsen story, and he nodded politely and said that was nice. Lee had always loved history, read as much of it as he could. But ever since she had been covering politics, he avoided the subject like the plague.

At dinner he said, "I got a letter from Sam. He's getting his own command." That was the third of his friends who had written to tell him their good news, and it seemed to make Lee more desperate than ever. He didn't talk about it. He drank, quietly. Lee thought it unmanly to complain. His father, good old Midwestern Protestant farm stock, had taught him that a man buttoned his lip and took what came, and Lee seemed to regard that as Sacred Writ.

Lee looked at his plate and said, "No vegetable?"

"Potatoes are a vegetable."

"I mean a *green* vegetable, Con."

She decided it wasn't worth arguing about. At least she didn't have a party to cover tonight, so she could feed him a hot meal, not just leave it warming in the oven. Lee ate quickly, and as Con was doing the dishes, she heard Lee and Terry arguing.

"Where is your retainer, young man?"

"It's around, Dad. I'll find it after I finish my homework."

"No you won't. You'll find it right now. If you lose another retainer, you are going to pay for it."

"It's not lost. And if it's such a big deal, I'll pay the damn seventy-five dollars if it gets lost again."

"Don't you open up a foul mouth to me!"

"I only said damn. That's not dirty. You should hear what the other kids say."

"I don't care about the other kids."

Con went in to mediate, as usual.

"Constance, this child is totally irresponsible. Spoiled rotten. A good year at the Naval Academy would straighten him out."

"I don't want to go to the damn Naval Academy," Terry said.

"That's it, young man. You're grounded for the weekend."

"All I said was I didn't want to go to the Naval Academy."

"The *damn* Naval Academy. I never said a curse word in front of my father in my life. I had respect for my father!"

"I didn't say a curse word. You should hear—"

"Terry!" His father glared at him.

Con said to her son, "Terry, go upstairs and find your retainer. Then finish your homework.

"But, Ma—"

"*Now*, Terry."

"Okay."

She turned to Lee and said, "Let me get you a cup of tea. You're all wound up."

"Dammit, Constance, you let these kids ride roughshod over you."

"Lee, I don't. But if you think they're spoiled, then you come home earlier at night and deal with the boys."

"How many nights are you out at those damn parties?"

"Lee, let's not go into that again."

"That's right, we won't!" he said, and he grabbed a copy of *Newsweek* and marched off into the den.

Con went back to the kitchen. It used to be, when they'd quarreled, they'd make it up later in bed. Tonight, they wouldn't. Once, she would have thought it was another woman, but now she knew it was the job, the sea slipping further and further away, and probably the alcohol. He always said one or two drinks at night weren't a problem, but it worried her. Sometimes it was four, or five. She wished she could help. But he wouldn't let her.

The Halvorsen story just might get her to the Hill, she thought. Let the old farts take this story and stuff it. Then let them call her "the dame who goes to parties." The Hill. It was where she ought to be. Constance Masters, congressional correspondent.

It did have a ring to it.

SIX

Father Barry grabbed Sean as he was going upstairs to recite the prayers of the Office, a daily duty. The older priest gripped his arm with talonlike fingers, his eyes glittering.

"Father McCaffrey, you are spending too much time away from the parish. Marching in the streets. The business of a priest is not politics."

"Father, I carry out all my assignments. I run the AA group, the drug group, I do pastoral counseling. I take little time for myself, Father."

"Yes, you are—an ambitious young man."

"No, Father, just a priest who does the work required of him."

"Ah, is a priest required to be on television?"

Sean reddened. "It was a religious program. I was invited. Television can be part of a ministry too."

Father Barry snorted, a display of disapproval. "I believe," he said, "that attendance at the beano is down. Have you been announcing it at Mass?"

Father Barry hovered over the Wednesday night bingo-beano franchise like Pierpont Morgan over his stocks. Who could blame him? They were the only things that kept St. Nasty's afloat. The games were Irish inventions, cultural artifacts eagerly assimilated by black and Hispanic Catholics. It appealed to their sporting natures, and if there wasn't the possibility of the big win you could get with the numbers, the odds were better.

"Father," Sean said, "why don't we advertise in the Montgomery *Journal?* I bet we'd double the house that way."

Father Barry's whole face brightened. "Yes, yes, a good idea. Do it right now, Father."

With a sigh, Sean postponed his prayers and looked up the phone number of the newspaper. Beano. Bingo. Words that were not mentioned in the litany of the Holy Office. He wondered what would happen when he went to face St. Peter with his list of priestly accomplishments.

"Ah, Father McCaffrey. And what did you do on earth in the service of the Lord?"

"Well, I got beano attendance up from forty-five to two hundred and fifty."

"Beano. I don't recall anything about beano in the Gospels."

"Look, I made a two-grand profit on beano in one month and that ain't—you should pardon the expression, sir— chicken shit!"

"Two grand! My goodness. Proceed, Father McCaffrey, into the company of the Elect."

A half hour later Sean finally got upstairs to start his prayers. He had barely begun when the housekeeper knocked on the door.

"Call for you, Father McCaffrey."

He went downstairs and picked up the phone. It was his father on the line.

"Sean?"

"It's Bill." He knew, from the inflection in his father's voice. "He's been drinking for three days. Sean, I try to talk to him, I do, but—"

"Do you want me to go over there?"

"Oh, Sean, I hate to ask you."

"It's okay, Pop."

"They have this new place in Ellicott City, they'd take him if you could only persuade him to go."

Sean got in his car and drove over to the Westminster, an elegant condo on New Hampshire Avenue, with units eagerly snapped up by the young professionals who were moving to the Washington area. Washington was a major city now, a place of money and power, and the nearby suburbs in Maryland and Virginia were sharing in the affluence. Hence, the Westminster. Sean's father had used most of his life savings to buy it. It was a haven for Bill, a place he could live when he wasn't someplace drying out.

As he pulled his car up in front of the condominium complex, Sean tried to fight back the familiar anger. Bill had always been the fair-haired boy. Sean grew up in his shadow like a scrub plant trying to catch some rays of his father's love through the sheer bulk of the figure that loomed above him. Bill did it all; all-city forward, all-star halfback for the CYO, big man on campus at Holy Cross. Life was handed to Bill on a silver platter, and he had somehow managed to fuck it up.

But he always managed to get his father's attention, didn't he? First by success, then by failure. It was what occupied Liam McCaffrey's waking hours, all Sean and his father talked about. How was Bill doing? Is Bill hiding booze in the laundry hamper? Has Bill been to see his kids?

Bill.

The sour taste of resentment rose in Sean's throat, the residue, perhaps, of Friday nights. Every Friday after practice the McCaffreys had the varsity over for hot chocolate and TV. There was laughter and horseplay and high spirits. Sean would sit in the living room as his father slapped players on the back, told jokes, talked about pass plays. Sean, then in his sci-fi period, would sometimes try, by the sheer force of his mind, to get his father to look at him. "I'm here, Pop. Look at me. I am Zabor, from the planet Urf, I command your mind to turn and look at me."

After all these years, the Reverend Sean McCaffrey had no more luck than Zabor. It was always Bill, even as a lush. Small, nasty, evil thoughts about Bill crept into his mind, unworthy thoughts for the Perfect Priest.

"Oh God, meek and humble of heart, make my love like Thine. Heart of Jesus, inflamed with love for me, don't let me hate my brother."

He got into the elevator—carpet and Muzak—and went up to Bill's apartment. Using his own key, he stepped inside and looked around. The place was a mess. Old, half-eaten food was turning rancid on the table. A soiled pair of underpants lay on the floor. Sean thought of how Father Barry told him that new curtains at his room in the rectory were out of the question, and the anger flared in him again.

Sean walked into the bedroom and found Bill sitting on the

bed in his pajamas, unshaven, drinking from a bottle of bourbon and grinning at him. It was a defiant grin, as if he got a perverse satisfaction from flaunting his abasement in his younger brother's face.

Looking at them, one would not suspect they were brothers. Bill was a large man, running now to flab, though in his football days he had been a solid wall of muscle. Sean favored his mother's side of the family; he was wiry, well-muscled, but slender, and he had never been able to match Bill's athletic prowess. Sean's hair was dark and curly, his eyes a deep green; he had the sort of Irish looks that spoke of the Mediterranean, or the Semitic. Bill's hair was sandy and straight, his face square and his skin so reddish-fair that he burned after a few minutes in the sun. His eyes were blue, often mild, intelligent. Now they were alight with a sardonic malice, giving him the air of a large, evil leprechaun.

"Ah Father, come on a corporal work of mercy?"

Bill had perfect pitch; he could mimic anyone. Now he was doing Barry Fitzgerald in *Going My Way*.

Oh, God, Sean prayed, *don't let me hate my brother*. He said aloud, "Come on, Bill, I'll take you someplace where you can get help."

"Fuck off, Sean," Bill took another drink.

"I've made the arrangements. You can come in my car."

"No thank you, *Father*. I'll just sit here and drown in my own swill, thank you very much."

"I'll pack your clothes."

"Fuck you, Sean."

"Where's your suitcase. Closet?"

"You really get a charge out of calling the old man and telling him I'm on a toot, don't you."

"I didn't call him. He called me."

"You holier than thou little shit. What gives you the right to judge me?"

"I'm not judging you. I just don't want to see you flush your life down the toilet."

"What the hell do you know about life, Sean? You live off the Big Tit, Mother Church." He took another defiant slug of bourbon. "When did you ever work one day in your life, when did you ever make a buck?"

Sean took the bottle away from him and put it on the bureau. "This is no answer."

"Ah, and you'll be making a novena for me, then, Father. I should get that, along with the lecture, boyo."

Sean flushed. Bill always had the knack for making him feel foolish; sanctimonious.

"I just know you're not going to solve your problems with a bottle." He used his priestly tone for that one, cool, just an edge of condescension to it, the twelve o'clock mass inflection. He felt the warm thrill of vengeance in using it on Bill.

Bill laughed. "Using the *voice*, again, Father. The one they taught you in seminary to make the peons fill the collection plate?"

Bill always caught him at it. Vengeance faded. "Look, dammit, I know you have problems—"

"Oh, a few, boyo. My wife left me, she took the kids. I'm bankrupt, and my partners are trying to screw me out of what I do have left, and on top of that, I can't get it up anymore. You don't know about that, do you, Sean? You don't ever have to get it up."

"We're leaving."

"You lock yourself away from life and the old man thinks you're hot shit. But I know why you did it, Sean. Because you couldn't make it anyplace else."

Sean felt the blood heating his face. "That's not true!"

"Got you, didn't I? Do you keep your little pecker tucked away safe for God? Do you holy men do it to each other? I always wondered if you were a fag, little brother."

Bill's eyes were glowing with hatred; the force of it made Sean dizzy. Had it always been there? *Why does he hate me so?*

"I remember little Peggy next door really had the hots for you. I'll bet you didn't even fuck her. You didn't do anything, you sanctimonious little shit!"

"Just shut your mouth!"

Bill laughed again. "The holy man has a temper. Isn't that a sin, Sean?"

"I'm sick of you. Just shut up!"

"Wanna make me? Wanna make me shut up, little brother?" Bill lumbered off the bed and stood facing Sean. "You never could fight. Always ran home sniveling."

"I'm not going to fight with you. I'll just call the police and they'll haul you out."

"You shit!" Bill slapped Sean on the face, so hard that Sean's head snapped around.

Sean stared at his brother. Bill had never hit him. Even when they were kids, they would wrestle playfully sometimes, but Bill was always aware that Sean was no match for his size and strength.

"Turn the other cheek, *Father*," Bill said, the contempt thick in his voice. Then he slapped Sean again, even harder.

Sean felt blood warm inside his mouth and a stinging pain on his cheek. He just looked at Bill, unbelieving.

"You shit!" Bill said again, and he hit Sean so hard that the blow knocked Sean off his feet; he hit his head on the edge of the bureau as he went down. He scrambled to his feet and faced his brother. The blow triggered something inside him that had nothing to do with a heart inflamed with Divine Love. He dropped to a crouch and smashed his fist squarely into Bill's face. Bill reeled, then it was his turn to gape, astonished. Sean had taken self-defense courses in the tough neighborhood in Boston where he worked. He thrust his fist into Bill's midsection, expertly. Bill made a little *whoosh!* as the breath was forced out of him. A bloody veil fell over Sean's senses and he hit his brother again and again, savagely. A rivulet of blood trickled from Bill's mouth and Sean aimed for it; the blow landed, true, and Bill crumpled to a heap on the floor. Sean, standing over him, heard himself saying, "Get up and fight, you coward! You lousy drunk, get up and fight."

Bill got to his hands and knees and tried to struggle up, but then he collapsed on the floor and began to weep, the blood and saliva from his mouth pooling on the green shag rug.

As quickly as it had dropped, the veil of Sean's irrational fury deserted him. He saw himself, blood staining his knuckles, standing over a defenseless drunk who was groveling on the floor. Horrified, he dropped to his knees and put his hand on Bill's shoulder.

"I'm sorry. Bill, dear God, I'm sorry! Forgive me!"

"Sean," Bill said, his breath coming in huge sobs now, "I didn't mean to hit you. I didn't!"

"I know. Oh god, I know. I'm sorry."

"Help me, Sean. I don't want to be like this. Help me."

Sean helped Bill to the bed, then went into the bathroom, his hands shaking, and soaked a washcloth and gently wiped the blood from Bill's face. Bill, docile as a kitten, let Sean help him dress and lead him to the car. He slept, like death, in the backseat on the way to the sanitarium and did not wake when attendants put him on a stretcher and took him to a room in the east wing.

Sean stood, watching his brother sleep, his breathing deep and even. Then he drove back to the rectory and went straight to Brian's room.

"Brian, will you hear my confession? Now?"

"Sean, your face. You're cut!"

"Brian, please!"

Brian picked up the purple cloth signifying the power to grant absolution and draped it over his shoulders. Sean kelt before him.

"You don't have to do that."

"I want to."

"Go ahead, Sean."

"Bless me, Father, I have sinned. I—I hit my brother. Hurt him. And he was drunk and couldn't defend himself. I don't know why I did it, I—" he stopped, inhaled, not knowing what to say next.

"Sean, what happened?"

"I enjoyed hitting him, I really *enjoyed* it. I feel so filthy, so low—"

"How did it start?"

"He was goading me. It was the booze."

"What did he say?"

"Called me a sanctimonious little shit. Said I went into the priesthood because I couldn't make it anywhere else. Then he hit me, and I—I just went crazy."

"Your face is cut. He must have hit you pretty hard."

"He was drunk. And he's my brother!"

"You have a right to defend yourself."

"No, I beat him up, Brian. Knocked him down, made him bleed. Why did I do it?"

"Was there—something in what he said? A germ of truth?"

"Oh yeah, of course there was. I always wanted to be like him. Big and handsome and a jock. And he was my father's favorite, of course. Jeez, Brian, it's all so banal."

"Make your act of contrition, Sean."

"Oh my God, I am heartily sorry for having offended Thee—"

And then he got up and dropped heavily into a chair. Brian got him a beer and Sean couldn't help grinning.

"This is a hell of a penance, Father. A Miller High Life."

"The new church. We make religion *pleasant*. What else did your brother say, Sean?"

"That I was on the Big Tit, couldn't make it anywhere else. Talk about a raw nerve. I do wonder, Bri, how would I do out there."

"He wanted to hurt you, Sean, because *he* was hurting. Drunks always know the vulnerable points."

"Why didn't I see it? I *counsel* families of alcoholics, but I snapped at the bait just like anybody else. And when he started to cry, I felt like dog shit."

"I know what you're feeling. My father used to do the same thing, when he got to drinking. Go at me until I'd lose control and then I'd lash out and he'd cave in and I'd hate myself. It was a pattern. It took me a long time to understand, to forgive myself."

"I hated him, Brian. Really hated him."

"I know. But he needs you, Sean. You're going to have to distance yourself from what he says. If he can drag you into his sickness, he's not so alone."

"You think he wanted me to hit him?"

"In some way, yes. He suckered you in. But it'll tear you apart to get drawn into the trap."

"I've said that to people, Brian. It's so easy to say. I *knew* it all, in my head, but—"

"Yeah. It's different when it happens to you."

Sean shook his head. "I should have known."

"Don't eat yourself up over this. What you did was human. You're a man, not a saint."

Sean smiled, ruefully. "I have a hard time with that. I do expect myself to be perfect. As Father Peter told me a hundred times, 'You are proud, Sean McCaffrey. Humble thyself.'"

"And did you?"

"I tried. But I'm not big on humble, Bri."

"Me either. Get a good night's sleep, Sean."

"Fat chance. But thanks."

He went back to his room and took out the book of Devotions to the Sacred Heart his mother had given him on his ordination, the year before she died. He flipped to the heading "Humility," and knelt by the bed.

"Oh God, Thou knowest my evil inclinations, the vicious habits which make me wander from Thy law. Change this hard and stubborn spirit, this obdurate heart of mine. Humble me, O Lord. Let me submit myself to Thee."

He closed the book with a sigh. He had tried to mean the words. In seminary, he said them with a blazing passion, and he had felt in his bones the hunger to lie prone at the feet of the Living God, to drain the vessel of his selfish soul and fill it only with the love of God. Why, lately, had his spirit rebelled? If it was only God who filled him, where was Sean McCaffrey? Who was he? Was drowning oneself in God holiness, or simply a way of not having to discover the lonely landscape inside yourself? Once he had burned for God, blazed with love. Love? or infatuation? Who could sustain that passion, and not be consumed by it? He had thought that the fire of God's love tempered men, made them strong. But so many older priests seemed flaccid. Why? Because they had not made decisions, assumed control of their own lives?

He got up, heavily, thinking that there were so many questions and he had so few answers. He undressed quickly and fell into a deep and dreamless sleep. He woke up feeling curiously refreshed. He hadn't even heard Father Barry barfing. Terrific, he thought, beating up my brother is better than Valium. What the hell was the world coming to?

Later in the week, he went to see his father and was glad to find him more chipper than he had been in a long time. Dr. McCaffrey had lost a great deal of weight since his heart attack. He had once been a big, solid man, like Bill, but now his sleeves and collars were too big, giving him an air of frailty that made Sean sad. I do love you, he thought. It's all right if you love Bill more.

Dr. McCaffrey had been named Catholic Layman of the Year in 1956, cited for his endless battles against the plunging neckline and the condom. "The Nemesis of Smut," the *Catholic Herald* had called him. But now, kids were taking the pill and going to movies where people did oral sex to each other and didn't wear any necklines at all, and it was too much for Dr. McCaffrey to comprehend. He withdrew from the field, an old soldier whose battles were fought and forgotten. But today, there was a hint of the old sparkle in his eyes.

"I saw Bill yesterday. Oh, he seemed so much better!"

"Yes, he does look better."

"You know, he got so drunk he fell down and hit himself on the table. His face is all bruised."

"That's what he told you?"

"Yes. And he said you were so good to him. Half-carried him to the car. You're a good brother to Bill."

He wanted to say to his father, "Pop, I had to half-carry him because I beat the shit out of him because he was drunk." He didn't say it. His father wanted to believe in the Perfect Priest almost as much as Sean did.

Sean shrugged and changed the subject. He and his father chatted for a while—about Bill—and then Sean pulled on his jacket and walked out to the front porch. As he did, he saw a blue car pull up in front of the Morrison house next door. Funny, Emily Morrison had been dead six years and he still thought of it as the Morrison house.

The car slowed down, then sped up again. As it went by, he saw a familiar figure at the wheel. Inside his chest, his heart took a convoluted little hop; he could actually feel it. After all these years, it could still happen when he saw her.

The blue car turned at the end of the street. He got into his car, and following a hunch, made the turn into Sligo Creek Park. Sure enough, the blue car was parked there, by the swings. He saw her, walking by the creek, her hands in the pockets of her trench coat. He wondered, as he watched her, if the kids from the Catholic high schools still thought of this as their favorite place to neck, the way he and Peg had made out in his father's Cadillac. Or did kids neck in cars anymore? Probably just went to the nearest motel to screw like bunnies. He suddenly felt very old.

He walked up behind her. She was so deep in thought that she didn't hear him approach. He stopped right behind her and said, "Hi. Wanna neck?"

She turned around and her mouth made a little O of surprise, and then she threw herself into his arms and he hugged her as hard as he could without knocking the wind out. The feel of her in his arms was dazzling, flooding him with memory. He thought, suddenly, how nice it would be just to stand, forever, with his arms around her like this. The thought made him drop his arms to his sides.

"Sean! Omigod, you're a sight for sore eyes! Look at you! It's true, God gets the best and the girls get the rest."

He laughed. "Don't believe that one. We're all rejects and basket cases."

"You don't look like a basket case. You look wonderful! Where's the Caddy?"

"Sorry. Only a Toyota. Vow of poverty, you know."

"So much for necking. I don't fit in a Toyota."

She was, he thought, even lovelier now than she used to be, but of course, he was biased. There were small lines at the edges of her eyes, which made the eyes seem more vulnerable, appealing. And they were glowing with pleasure at seeing him.

"We have a lot of catching up to do," he said.

"Tell me all about how you got kicked out of Boston."

"A fat mouth. And one too many headlines in the *Globe*."

"You *are* having a problem with obedience. Didn't I say you would?"

"Oh yeah, I keep getting into trouble. Listen, do you have time to be taken out to dinner by the Hero Priest of the Amazon?"

She laughed, delighted. "Remember, I was going to write that story and make you more famous than the Pope? But Sean, you never did go to the Amazon to save souls. Cost me a *great* story."

"I guess the Hero Priest of Takoma Park doesn't cut it."

"I had it all planned. It was going to be the big moment in *The Peg Morrison Story.* I was going to throw myself in front of you and save you from a poison dart."

"You were?"

"Yeah, but now we'll have to rewrite the script. I'll just throw myself in front of a mugger."

"Lacks drama."

"Yeah, in the other movie I died. In this one I just lose my American Express card and get a footprint on my back."

He laughed and she said, "Oh Sean, best friend, I am so *very* glad to see you."

"Best friend, are you settling down for a while? No more globe trotting?"

"I'm going to stay put. The legs are going."

"Not so's you'd notice."

"Let the kids get their asses shot at for a change. The old gray mare is going to stay where it's safe for a while." She grabbed him by the arm and began to tug him in the direction of the cars. "Come on, if you are going to feed me, do it now. I'm starving." He followed her, noticing that she still walked the way she did as a kid, with a quick long-legged stride that had its own awkward grace. He had followed her to all sorts of places—she was fearless—even on a five-mile hike through the storm sewers when they were seven that could have drowned them both. Following her seemed *very* familiar.

They went to a small place on Georgia Avenue for veal parmigiana, and he told her about Boston and she told him about Jerusalem and the Sudan and Rhodesia and a quick foray to the Mekong. She said that one local chieftain in the Sudan had been so taken with her blond hair that he had offered two camels. When the photographer tried to explain that the Washington *Tribune* did not barter the flesh of its employees, he went up to three.

"Knowing my cheap publisher, one more camel and I would have been in big trouble."

"What would you have done with a tribal chief?"

"Taught him a jump shot and signed him up for the NBA. His name was Abdul already, he wouldn't have had to change it. That sucker *was* tall."

"Are you really going to stay home for a while?"

"I think so." She was quiet for a minute. "It was fun, a lot of it, chasing around to all the fires. But no way do I want Vietnam. To see the kids dumped into the body bags for the flying coffins? No way."

He paused and looked at her. "Peg, I was so sorry to hear about your fiancé."

"I know. I still have your letter. It helped."

"From what I read, he must have been quite a guy."

She smiled. "A lot like you, actually." She shook her head, still smiling. "Why do I always fall for guys who want to change the world?"

"He did the picture of the little girl with her leg blown off, didn't he? The one that was on all the front pages?"

"Yes. He was—a witness, I guess. He always felt he had to drag people's eyes to the horrible things war did. Hold their noses in it. He never made it glamorous."

"That's a noble calling, Peg."

"Yes, but there was a dark side to it. He had to keep going back to look over the edge. It got to be a sickness. Like people who survive some terrible tragedy, and they feel guilty to be alive. I think all those people he photographed haunted him."

"He couldn't stop going back?"

"No. He carried all sorts of things with him, as if they had some magic power to keep him alive. A baseball card. Sam Dente, would you believe. But he knew their power was going to run out. I was going through his things—I never told anybody this—and he'd left a poem on the top of his desk. 'I have a rendezvous with death, at some disputed barricade.'"

"Maybe it was just something he had been reading."

"No. It was a message to me. An apology, I guess. 'I will not fail that rendezvous.' He didn't. He got there right on time. Death was my rival. And he went to her."

"Oh damn, Peg, I am so damn sorry."

"Sometimes I think that if I had been different, he would have stayed. Or for a different woman."

Sean shook his head. "I don't think so. That kind of obsession blots out everything else."

"Maybe."

On impulse, he reached over and put his hand on hers. "It wasn't your fault."

"I kept running it over in my mind. Could I have smashed his cameras? Dyed my hair? Did I *not* say something? But there's no point. None. He's dead." Suddenly, she shook her head, as if to dislodge the thought. "Oh Sean, I'm not going to ruin your dinner by crying into my beer."

"It's okay. What are best friends for?"

"Oh Sean, I knew I had something to tell you. I was down at the Dead Sea, last year, and this group of tourists comes by. You won't *believe* who was with them?"

"Who?"

"The lesbians. From the Greystone. The very same ones!"

"The two fat ladies who had the room next to us? They were real nice. Are you sure they were lesbians?"

"With crew cuts and beige slacks, Sean, they were not Sisters of Charity."

"And the guy in the rubber suit wasn't into scuba diving."

"The guy across the hall? No, he wasn't."

"He did give me a strange look when I met him going to the john and I asked him where he took lessons."

She laughed, a full, warm rich laugh, and her hair tumbled across her face. He wanted to knot both his hands in it, keep them there for hours. "Oh Sean," she said, "we did some crazy things!"

"I always knew nobody would ever stop you. Damn, you even got the Pulitzer prize! How many people get the thing they dream about?"

"It wasn't as wonderful as I dreamed it would be. Reality can't touch dreams. But it keeps me off the obit desk. And I still love what I do. Most of the time."

"How many people can say that?"

"Can you, Sean?"

"I'm not sure. In Boston, I was really helping to change the system. I was part of the machinery that makes things go. And you have to be, if you want real change. You can't do it from the sacristy."

"What about Action? Con told me about it."

"I don't know if we have a prayer of stopping the interstate, but we're going to try."

"How about a story in the Washington *Tribune?*"

"We're going to pull La Raza into the coalition soon, and that would be a great time."

He told her about how he had put the group together, bragging just a bit, enjoying the admiration in those blue-gray eyes. It was why he had always done the dumb things like hiking through sewers, to see that look in her eyes. Suddenly, he remembered something.

"Oh shit. The goddamn beano. I have to run it tonight."

He walked with her to her car, and she said to him, "I really bent your ear, didn't I? I guess there was a lot of stuff in there that I needed to get out."

"Anytime, Peg. I mean that."

"I'd like to see a lot of you, if you don't mind." She saw the look on his face and she added hastily, "Friends."

He nodded. "I think maybe we both need a friend right now."

He kissed her lightly on the forehead and walked to his car. As he drove along Georgia Avenue, he found himself singing, something he never did. "Oh sweet and lovely, lady be good. Oh lady, be good to me."

He felt, he realized, uncommonly fine. Why did the night seem full of promise, with shimmering, wonderful things floating just beyond his grasp? Why did he feel, as the cool, sweet night air seeped into the car, that he was seventeen years old again, that everything was possible?

The sensation was so sharp that it took his breath away. Why did he never feel that way anymore? Was it just getting older? And oh, he had missed it so!

But then he frowned. He had grown used to examining his feelings, inspecting them for flaws. Was this a near occasion of sin for him? Would he want to knot his hands in her hair whenever he saw her?

Shit.

"What's all this sin crap? You had a nice dinner, a glass of wine with an old love. You haven't felt this good in a long time. Feeling good is *not* a sin. For Chrissake, stop trying to get martyred!"

He turned the car toward Takoma Park. Even the thought of the combined forces of beano and bingo couldn't spoil his mood. He sometimes envisioned hell as this large room in which a loudspeaker kept saying over and over again: "Under the O, thirteen; under the Eye, twenty-seven."

"I am so lonely, misunderstood," he sang. "Oh lady be good—to me."

SEVEN

"I'm speaking at Georgetown Wednesday," Dan said to Kitty. They were lying in the big bed, having a brandy. "Political Science Association. Time to take the plunge."

"You're going public? On the war?"

He nodded. "Something Peg Morrison said stuck with me. History's going to deal harshly with those people who didn't see it. And history's catching up, fast."

"Yes, I think it is. I'm glad you're doing it, Dan. I know you feel it."

"More and more. But God, it's risky. History is mainly a matter of timing. I hope I'm calling it right."

They were silent for a minute and then Kitty said, "Dan, did you study history in college? You know so much about it."

"No. I was an English major. I wanted to be a college professor, once. After my chaotic childhood, it seemed like a nice, safe life. But I had a teacher who got me interested in history—and politics. Once I got a taste of politics, I knew that lecturing to kids at Prairie Normal U. about T. S. Eliot would be way too tame." He paused. "Listen, Kit, I think I want Adam Crabtree."

"He's good, no question about that."

"Expensive."

"We can afford him. If you want him, get him."

"He's quick out of the gate."

Kitty frowned.

"Problem, Kit?"

"Just what I hear. Adam Crabtree would peddle his

mother's tush in Times Square for three points on the Harris Poll."

"I need someone who works fast. Adam went into Joe Rains' Senate campaign a month before the election. Rains was twenty points behind Ralph Cotter, and they pulled it out."

"Because Adam Crabtree found out that Millie Cotter spent Thursdays screaming naked in the woods. I still remember the press conference where she was trying to explain that sexual scream was really legitimate therapy. And the look on Helen Thomas' face when Millie said 'multiple orgasm.' Helen nearly swallowed her pen. And she wasn't the only one. Roger Mudd nearly choked."

"Kitty, even in this day and age, holding hands bare-assed and yelling like banshees in the Green Mountains is a little strange."

"Dear little Millie Cotter. She was such a naif, poor thing. The day she had her first orgasm, she announced it at a brunch for wives of the Democratic Study Club."

"She did?"

"Yes. People had just started talking about the failure of détente when Millie popped out with it. She was very excited. She hadn't had one in thirty-seven years."

"No wonder she was excited."

"Yes. She told everybody about sexual scream. Unfortunately, Mrs. Senator Nolan was there. Edith Nolan was screwing Jimmy Harrington, who was the AA to Senator Dents, but a couple of weeks later he left Dents to go work for Adam Crabtree. So Adam heard the sexual scream story from Jimmy, but Edith regrets she ever did Adam any favors, even indirectly, because he was handling her husband's campaign and he told Jimmy he couldn't sleep with Edith during the campaign. So Edith was miserable—her husband is impotent, because he's a souse—but a good chairman when he's sober—and Jimmy took up with a woman whose husband was a D.C. cop and broke Jimmy's arm in three places."

Dan laughed. "Kit, you know everyone's business."

"Yes I do. But I don't hurt people with what I know. Poor Millie Cotter's in a rest home. I hear she's so zonked out on drugs she can't even *think* about orgasms. Adam Crabtree didn't have to make her a laughing stock."

"His man was twenty points behind. You use what you can get."

"But what difference did it make to the destiny of the Republic that Millie screamed in the woods, bare-assed or not? That was her private business."

"She was married to a man in public life. It's a fishbowl, Kit."

"It was cruel, what Adam did. That TV spot—just a ten-second shot of a forest, with a faint howl in the background. That *killed* Ralph Cotter."

"It *was* funny. It's considered the most brilliant political ad of the past twenty years—that and the one they used against Goldwater, the little girl with the daisy getting nuked."

"Adam Crabtree has ice water in his veins. The word is out that he wants to be the kingmaker of the next Democratic president."

"Good Lord, I'm hardly in that category."

"He sees your potential, Dan. Just don't let him sell you a bill of goods."

"I won't. I'm my own man. By the way, you were right about Len Fineberg. He's a gem."

"It's *Len*, now, is it?"

"A man gives you half a million dollars, you should call him by his first name. I owe you a lot."

"I just opened the doors. If you'd been a turkey, Dan, my help wouldn't have meant *bupkus*."

"Do you suppose I could think of a way to show my gratitude?"

"Knowing you, I'd say the answer was yes."

He slipped his hand under her gown, and began to caress her. Then he lifted her, and put her down on the rug at the foot of the bed. Dan had a *thing* about floors. She felt deliciously wanton, about to have sex on the rug, something that would have horrified Mrs. Leonard Titlebaum. The Hadassah maven would never have made love on the rug, because the dog peed on it; it was certainly crawling with germs, despite the Lysol the cleaning man sprayed.

And then they were thrashing about on the rug, hang dog pee, and Kitty felt the desperate hunger that Dan's body was able to draw from her own. She had not known that sort of fever existed, certainly not in proper Jewish matrons. She would have died for his touch, and he knew it, damn him. But then there was no room for thoughts, just the lovely swirl of sensation that blotted out the world, and she heard a voice—could it be her own?—crying out, "Yes, Dan! Yes! Yes!"

When it was done he touched her hair and said, "Kit, my dark lady, you are so wonderful!" and then he kissed her and was gone, leaving her body sated but another place inside her curiously empty. It was always this way—except that time on the beach in Aruba. She had all of him then, every part of him opened to her, a snail crawling from its shell. It would happen again. When they were married, the part of him she so rarely seemed to find would yield under her gentle touch.

She got up, slithered into her clothes, wondered if she should make the daily duty call to the Hadassah maven. "Hi Mom, I've just had brandy for breakfast and screwed on the rug with a Norwegian." And her mother would say, "On the *rug!* The *germs!*" Dog urine ranked higher in her mother's pantheon of germ-causing agents than Norwegian semen.

She decided, instead, to ring up Peg Morrison and see if she was free for lunch on Thursday. Peg touched something maternal in Kitty; perhaps it was the sadness that seemed to coil sometimes inside those blue eyes. Peg would be animated, talking, and then suddenly she would look as if she were listening to music no one else could hear. Peg had seen so much of death. Kitty realized it one day when Peg had talked about Vietnam. She had only mentioned Jeff's name twice—each time gingerly, as if the word were a bruise.

She dialed Peg, and when she heard her voice, Kitty said, "Congratulations, my dear, on 'Other Voices.' It's marvelous."

"Thanks, Kitty. There do seem to be so many of them now, with the war and black power and the women's movement. It's as if a wall of silence suddenly came crashing down. Around here, though, people think the barbarians are at the gates."

"I can imagine. Oh Peg, I want to let you know that Dan is speaking at Georgetown Wednesday. He's finally coming out against the war."

"I'll tell Ben Stark, our congressional guy. I know he'll want to be there."

"I think Dan was really influenced by some of the things you said. I really appreciate that."

Peggy was smiling when she put the phone down, having made a date with Kitty, whom she was getting to like more and more. The smile vanished in the next instant.

"Morrison!" Buck Stollmeyer called out across the city room. "Where the hell is Morrison?"

Peg shook her head and walked into the assistant managing editor's office. She and Buck Stollmeyer already hated each other's guts. He was a large, beefy man who liked to throw his weight around. The kind of man, Peg thought, who would back down from a real fight. Most bullies did.

"Christ," he said, looking at her copy, "a whole story fully of bellyaching."

"A man who got his legs blown off in Vietnam says he's against the war. That's not bellyaching."

"What is this series, anyhow?"

"It's on dissent. People who want to change things."

"Whiners. And sex and race shit. Complaining broads."

"If you don't like it, talk to your boss. Tom Friedman *assigned* me to this story."

"I think it's shit."

Peg felt her temper rise, but she controlled it. Instead, she said cooly, "I disagree. Argue with Tom, not me." He always tried to goad her, and she wasn't going to give him the satisfaction.

Back at her desk, she looked around the city room, realizing she would have few allies if things went to the wall with Stollmeyer. The room was still unfriendly turf. Abroad, there had been a we're-all-in-this-together comaraderie that had often transcended the competitive nature of the job. Here, she had the sense that everyone was watching her, warily. The young reporters on the local staff were too awed by her Pulitzer to talk to her in the friendly, teasing way they bantered with each other. There were a few reporters she had started out with who were still on cityside, but they avoided her, as if she were a token of their failure to move beyond the district line. The editors weren't sure how to treat her now that she was no longer on the other end of a telex. Buck Stollmeyer resented her, probably for getting the one thing in life he wanted. A returning female holder of the Pulitzer prize, it seemed, made *everybody* uncomfortable.

She also had the sense that she was viewing Washington differently than most of them. At first she thought it was just because she was seeing it with a fresh eye, but there was something else as well. She was more conscious now of being a woman than she had ever been.

Once, she'd tried to be just like the men. Now, she noticed that most of them, from the bureaucrats to the bureau chiefs, had a peculiar way of—what was it?—*sanitizing* things. The words they used, the way they defined reality as a series of bloodless "issues" seemed absurd to her. They believed they could control things, from the broad lanes of Pennsylvania Avenue to the paddies of the Mekong. It was why they couldn't see what was happening in Vietnam, because life was messy and emotional and scattershot, and that didn't fit in with the game plan. She talked to Con about it.

"When I was on that half-track in Sinai and we hit a mine, I got thrown to one side and had a sore ass for a week. The man sitting next to me had his head blown off. I knew, then, I couldn't control things. People here think everything can be managed. Listen to them. Strategic hamlets and sanitary bombing and all those words that don't mean anything. But they believe it."

"Know what they need, Peg? A couple of days in a day-care center. Women take care of all the messy things in their life. No wonder they think things are under control."

"Do you ever get the feeling that they're seeing things in black and white and you're seeing it in color and they think it's *you* who's crazy?"

"Women always see things that way. But we're only women so it doesn't count."

"I feel like I'm caught between a rock and a hard place. I'm doing stories now on people who say all the rules, everything we learned, is wrong. And I think they're right, a lot. I don't want to be an imitation man anymore, but I don't want to be an outcast, either. A Mae Craig with her funny hat, and everybody thought it was cute when she asked a question at the presidential press conference."

"A dippy broad."

"So how do I win? If I try to be macho, flaunting my nonexistent balls, I'm a bitch and a castrating woman. I can't get into the old boy network, but God forbid if I bat my eyelashes to get lunch with an undersecretary. They say I made it on my back. If I admit I actually *feel* something about a story, I'm an overemotional broad. How do I win?"

"If you find out, let me know. I've broken some important stories, but I've broken them in the wrong place. At parties. I work damn hard to get my sources, and a lot of the guys who look down on me sit on their asses and rewrite handouts. The bastards. But at least you got the big P. They can't take that away."

"Yeah, but I got it for writing what it felt like seeing somebody's head get blown off. About guys peeing in their pants. About people being sick and scared. Me included. Know what Andrews at the *Post* said? This got back to me. He said, 'If all it takes to get the Pulitzer these days is writing about guys crapping in their pants, that's what I'll write.' The s.o.b. never got three feet away from a general."

"Andrews doesn't have to write about shit. What he writes *is* shit."

"I feel like a square peg in a round hole, here. No pun intended."

"Like I felt in the navy."

"I figured you weren't the perfect navy wife."

"I had to be so nice to so many stupid men. Peg, some of those guys were so dumb they'd have flunked the Head Start entrance exam. Where do these guys get off thinking they're so great, just because they have balls?"

"Yeah, you'd think they have to dip 'em in ink to write their second-day leads. I can write and think rings around most of them, and I don't even *have* balls."

"You'd look pretty weird in your pantyhose if you did."

"They'd promote me to assistant managing editor. Balls must be the only requirement for that job. Brains sure are not."

The waiter brought them more wine and Con filled her glass, saying, "Hey, I saw Sean at WTOP yesterday. He's doing more TV than Milton Berle. He tells me you are feeding him."

"Oh yeah, the slop they give him at the rectory is awful. Meat loaf. Irish haute cuisine."

"You're doing it again, Peg. Trying to take care of him, a little mother hen. You always did cluck over him. He's a big boy now."

"But he seems lonely."

"Oh God, this conversation is *soo* familiar. Do not, I repeat, do *not* go getting yourself involved with a priest. I know you, Peg. Sean is your blind spot."

"We're just friends, Con, that's all."

They were quiet, and then Con said, "I never asked you right out, but I read between the lines."

"Oh yeah, every summer when he was home from seminary."

"And after he was ordained?"

"No."

"Was he good in bed?"

"Yes, he was—lovely. Sensual. Not wham-bam."

"I had an affair when we were in Hawaii. It was so damn hot and nobody wore clothes anyway."

"How was it?"

"Typical navy. By the book. I never could figure out how a guy who could tie thirty-seven kinds of knots could be so clumsy. Cute, though."

"Lee know about it?"

"He was having a fling of his own. Bad time."

"Lee seems so tense, Con. All wound up. Doesn't laugh much, and he used to."

"He's miserable at the Pentagon. Stuck at a desk, not old enough to retire. Really frustrated, and takes it out on the kids."

"But he adores the boys, Con. You can see that."

"Oh he does. When they were little they were very close. But Terry's a teenager now and he's always challenging Lee, and Lee tries to pull the navy 'I'm in command here' crap and it doesn't work. And he drinks too much."

"Lee?"

"Yeah, the straight arrow. Would you believe he gets plastered a couple nights a week?"

"Like falling down drunk?"

"Oh no. If you didn't know him, you wouldn't know he'd had a drink. His words slur a little, that's all." She sighed. "But back to more interesting things. Has Sean been celibate?"

"He told me he has."

"How the hell does he do it, Peg? He's a gorgeous man, looks healthy, how the hell can he not have sex the rest of his life?"

"It was his dream, ever since he was a kid. To be a priest. It means everything to him."

"And you're not attracted to him anymore?"

"I wouldn't say that, exactly."

Con looked at Peg sharply. "And what would you say, exactly?"

"Oh shit, he makes my hormones do the twist. But it is strictly hands off, Con, Girl Scout oath."

"If it isn't, Peg, you'll be the one who gets hurt. You've had enough hurting, I think."

Peg sipped her wine, slowly, then she nodded. "Ain't that the truth."

EIGHT

Sean walked up the driveway to the door of Transition House in Ellicott City. His father said Bill was doing better than he had done anyplace else. But his father had been optimistic before; was he grasping at straws?

Sean walked down the antiseptic, modern hallway and knocked on Bill's door. Bill opened it and motioned him in.

"Hi, Sean. Welcome to D wing. The color scheme here is pink and gray. That's for drunks. The schizophrenics get blue and green. You always know where you are."

Sean laughed. Bill's sense of humor had come back, that was a good sign. His eyes were clear, his movements more fluid, not lumbering like when he was drinking. The bloat was gone from his face. He was starting to look like the old Bill, the handsome man who was his older brother.

"Pop said you were doing great. Looks like he was right."

Bill nodded and sat down on the bed, and Sean sat in a chair next to him.

"Pop," Bill said. "I've been talking a lot about Pop. To a shrink. A woman, yet. Would you believe that?"

"I think it's a good idea."

"At first I said no way. But I was so goddamn bored after a while I said what the hell. So I have this shrink. She's pretty good, actually."

"And you're talking about Pop."

"Yeah, now there's a can of worms I never wanted to open. Lots of things I never realized, little brother. I never was as good as he thought I was. He thought I was the best, the brightest. He thought I was so smart. But I wasn't."

"Come on, Bill, you were all-star everything."

"Yeah, I was good at sports."

"Outstanding senior at Holy Cross wasn't just for being a jock."

"Sports was easy, so I guess I thought everything should be that easy. I had this feeling that I was swimming over my head, that my feet were never touching bottom. And I could never fuck up because he was counting on me so much. I just kept on swimming, getting deeper and deeper."

"And what happened?"

"One day, I panicked. I had this big case, and I knew I couldn't handle it. And I went down. He said, 'You'll be back on your feet in a few days.' He didn't understand. I crashed. I went down far and I went down hard."

"Yeah, I understand."

"Do you?"

"No, I guess I really don't."

"I envy you. You have a niche. A place to go. You don't have to invent yourself as you go along. God, there are times when I'd love to have that collar."

Sean touched his neck. "Three bucks, it's yours."

"The man will cheat his brother on his deathbed!" Bill said, doing Barry Fitzgerald with a grin. Sean laughed.

"Let me tell you, Sean, this therapy is one of the toughest things I've ever done. Have you even been shrunk?"

"No."

"It's like stripping naked and looking at yourself."

"I don't know if I'd want to do that."

"Well, I have to. Figure out if there's any point to being alive."

"Bill, you've got two beautiful kids, for starters."

"Rene doesn't let me see them anymore. I came over there drunk one night, made them cry. Hell of a thing, my own kids."

"Things will change when you stop drinking for good. Believe that."

"Will you pray for me, Father?" The irony in his voice was gentle, but unmistakable.

"If you want me to."

"Sure, why the hell not?"

"You don't think much of what I do, do you? You think I hide from life."

"That was just booze talking. I get mean."

"Do you know what I do every day? I see junkies who'd kill their mother for a fix and thirteen-year-old girls who are knocked up and people who are dying. It's not all twelve o'clock mass and bingo."

Bill nodded. "I guess I don't give you enough credit. But he thinks you're so perfect. Some kind of saint. He always throws it up to me, Sean this, Sean that. It makes me want to puke."

"Shit, Bill, I spent my whole childhood trying to get him to notice me. It was always, 'Bill made the team. Bill's in *Who's Who*.' I had to get *ordained* to get noticed!"

His own words surprised him. He knew they were true, but he had never put it quite that baldly—to himself or anyone.

"So there it is, little brother," Bill said. "How many years has that been floating around inside there?"

Sean shrugged. "Hell of a long time, I guess."

"He was our father," Bill said. "And look at what the hell he did to us!"

"He didn't mean any harm."

"Oh sure, take his side. I expected that from you!"

"He loved us. Still does."

"Christ, don't you know what he did to you? He shoved priest, priest, down your throat until you turned into one. Or did God whisper right into your ear, 'Pssst, Sean, it's Me!'"

"Don't make fun of me, Bill."

"Don't lie to yourself. That's what I did. I told myself so many lies I didn't know what the truth was. And now maybe it's too late."

"No, don't say that!"

"You're such a goody two-shoes. You think you can sprinkle a little Holy Water around and make everything right, like the goddamn animals you tried to patch up. They died, Sean, despite a gallon of Holy Water."

"Not all of them."

"Believe what you want, Holy Water, pixie dust, hell, who cares?"

"*I* do, dammit! Yes, I think I can change things. I have. I'm going to turn this highway thing around, and I won't use pixie dust. I'll work my ass off."

Bill laughed. "You think the church really cares about those niggers and spics you work with? You'll just get your ass in a sling again and they'll send you off to another church in another stinking hole. Grow up, Sean."

"I don't want to grow up if it means I have to be a cynic like you, thinking everything is shit except Jack Daniels."

"Thank you, Father, for the corporal work of mercy. Comfort the afflicted."

"Oh Christ, I didn't mean that."

"Seems we have a real *talent*, Sean, for gouging each other. Pop's boys."

"No. I—I love you, Bill."

"Crap. Stop talking like a priest. You hate my guts because you think he loved me more than you."

"Okay. I hate your guts. No, *hated*. But you're my brother. I want to love you."

"Well, maybe we'll get there someday, little brother. I doubt it. But maybe."

For the next few days, Sean thought often about Pop's boys. How had it gone so wrong? His father did love his sons; he had meant well. He wanted the best for them. The best for whom? How early had his father started talking about the priesthood for Sean? Fifth grade? Early.

I had to get ordained to get noticed.

The day of his ordination, his father had stood on the steps of the cathedral, put his hands on Sean's shoulders, his eyes shining with tears of pride. "Father McCaffrey. Oh it sounds wonderful. Your mother and I are so proud of you."

He shoved priest, priest, *down your throat until you turned into one.*

Sean stomped on the thoughts, forced them away. He had enough to do without plunging into the morass of family history. There was a meeting of Clergy and Laymen Concerned, and Action was coming along nicely, but there was a lot of walking on eggs to do there. La Raza, the citywide Hispanic coalition, had brought numbers and energy to the group, but it made some of the blacks edgy. A few wrong words and the whole thing could blow sky-high, and the neighborhood would be a superhighway before he could get it together again.

They had come close at a meeting Tuesday night. Estella Sanchez and Chuck Washington went at it, after Chuck used the word "spic" in what he assumed was a humorous way. Estella didn't see the humor in it, since she had been called just that thirty minutes earlier in the checkout line at Food Barn. Sean patched things up, barely. He kidded them, hummed a few bars of *West Side Story*.

"What have we got here, the Sharks and the Jets? Save it for the enemy."

"Okay," Chuck said, with a grin. He was a huge man, six-foot-six, who wore his head clean shaven and sported a dashiki. He looked terrifying—especially to suburban whites—but he was actually a humorous, gentle man, who was trying to keep the trucking business he had started from going under. "Tell me, what do I say?"

"Hispanic!" snapped Estella, giving the word a Latin trill. She was a widow with two children, a quick, ready wit and a temper to match. Sean had spotted her early on, figuring she had the capacity to be one of the leaders of Action. He had been right.

"Well, then, *"we* want to be Afro-Americans."

"Well, ah'll be damned," drawled Randy Walters, just up from Richmond and unemployed, "if ah'm gonna be white trash."

"How about working-class hero?" Sean suggested with a grin.

"Yeah, I like that."

"Sounds pinko," said Chuck.

"They think we are all communists," complained Estella. "Some kind of crazy radicals, for wanting to save our homes."

"Yeah, we can call ourselves anything we want," Randy agreed, "but the rich folks up county see us coming and you know what they'll say? Here come the spics, the niggers, and the white trash."

"And their commie mick priest," Sean added with a grin.

"Now if we can just get the kikes and the Polacks, we have a shot," Chuck said, and they went back to work at the business at hand, the testimony before the transportation committee in Annapolis. They had Congressman Backman on their side, and Joe Tydings was leaning, but it would be the governor who would be the key to Interstate 80. He was the one who could pull the plug. To convince him, they needed an environmental impact statement, pronto. Sean had been trying to rustle one up, and he got in touch with one consulting firm with a liberal bent. He was told the cost would be fifty thousand dollars.

"Fifty thousand! Listen, some of these people are living on food stamps! Don't you guys do pro bono?"

"Sorry, Father," he was told. "We did our charity for this year!"

Sean slammed down the phone. *Charity!* He resented being a beggar, resented being treated like some kind of wino who had his hand out for a quarter for a pint of Muscatel.

Blessed are the meek, he thought, and snorted. Meek might be fine for evening prayers, but in the real world it got you absolutely no place.

He slogged through the week, trying to work on the legislative package, the draft of a proposal for Clergy and Laymen Concerned, run the AA and drug meetings, say mass, hear confessions, and keep his temper when Father Barry carped at him. But Friday night lay ahead, a beacon in the fog. Peg had invited him to a cocktail party at Kitty's to meet Dan Amundsen.

"He's a good contact for you, Sean," she said. "Now that you're in politics, might as well mingle with some of the pros."

He dressed in his good black suit, fussed over his hair; he was nervous, he had to admit. Hobnobbing with high society was not his usual pastime. Bocce and Chianti back at Stella Maris weren't exactly the prelims for Foxhall Road. He admitted his worries to Peg when she came to pick him up at the rectory.

"This is a bit out of my league."

"You'll do fine, Sean. Just be cute and Irish. They'll love it."

"I speak Spanish. I can be the token spic, too."

"Now don't get huffy. Just be yourself and relax. It'll be fun."

"Oh, no! My whole childhood, whenever I heard that line from you, it was total disaster."

"When?"

"The time you made me hike through the storm sewers and you got a nail in your foot and I got dysentery."

"It wasn't dysentery. You're exaggerating."

"It was too. Amoebic dysentery. For a whole month, every time I went to the bathroom, it was green."

She giggled. "Okay, but that was only once."

"The tree house? I said we couldn't make one, but you insisted."

"We had a lot of fun in the tree house."

"*You* were not in it when it fell out of the tree."

"That was quite a scream you let out."

"When you are plunging to the earth at eight hundred miles an hour in a tree house, it is a natural human reaction to scream."

"It was three feet, Sean."

"It *felt* a lot longer, going down."

"But I let you eat all the Twinkies."

"Big deal. My wrist was in a cast for a month. I only ate the Twinkies because you felt so guilty. Twinkies make me want to vomit."

She laughed, and he grinned. He had always loved the sound of her laugh; that was another reason he had done a lot of dumb things as a kid, to hear it. It had a peculiar sound, somewhere between a rasp and a tinkle, and it made him feel warm all over.

"Sean, you make it sound like you were always doing what *I* wanted. What about the year you decided you were Zabor, from the planet Urf, and you let me be your zort."

"You were a good zort."

"It was a whole *year* before I found out a zort was a little green warty reptile."

"That's because zorts are not quick on the uptake, Peg."

She reached over and pinched his ear.

"Ouch! I had forgotten about *that*."

"Just because you're a priest, you think I won't pinch you? Zorts pinch *anything!* Oh, turn here, Sean, this is it."

They went inside, and Peg introduced Sean to Kitty, who took his arm and began to introduce him around, taking great care to put him at ease. She saw to it that he and Dan had some time alone in a corner to chat, and then she hurried back to Peg.

"He is just adorable, Peg. Is he a full priest? I mean, like he—uh, doesn't—"

Peg laughed. "He's celibate, Kitty."

"I don't mean to offend your religion, dear, but what a waste of a natural phenomenon. Like putting plywood across Old Faithful."

Peg giggled. "There's a Freudian image, if ever I heard one."

"Freud did not approve of celibacy. Jews are *very* big on sex, but of course we have to feel guilty about it."

"Catholics feel guilty *thinking* about it. Especially Irish Catholics."

"Makes me rather glad I'm Russian Jewish. The pogroms were a nuisance, but at least one could *think* about sex." She looked over at Sean and Dan, deep in conversation. "They do seem to have hit it off."

In the corner of the room, Sean was trying to be subtle about popping the mouth-watering hors d'oeuvres into his mouth as he answered Dan's questions. With all the other impressive people in the room, Dan seemed focused only on him, which made Sean feel very important indeed.

"You've been quite active with Clergy and Laymen Concerned, haven't you, Father?"

"Yes, I have, Congressman."

"Call me Dan, please. What got you involved?"

"I guess it's because I've been mainly in working-class neighborhoods. I found myself doing a lot of funerals. It's the kids from East Boston and Takoma Park who are coming home in coffins, not the ones from Newton or Chevy Chase. Cannon fodder. It isn't fair."

"But it's in the blue-collar neighborhoods where they still fly the flag. I have a lot of them in my district, in Omaha."

"A lot of guys there, World War Two vets, they remember the good war. But it's changing. They're seeing too many of their kids dying."

"You think they'd respond to a call to bring the boys home? Even if we don't win?"

"Yes. But it has to be done the right way. There's a class thing going on, a perception that the antiwar movement is full of rich college kids telling people what to do. Your average working stiff, he gets his back up over that. I think he has to see more of *his* type people saying the war is stupid."

"You mean the hard hats demonstrate not because they love the war, but because they resent the class thing?"

"That's a lot of it, yes. Which is why I want to be active. I've been on the streets for ten years, I know these folks. They're smart, and it's a mistake to talk down to them, to lecture them."

"Father, I'm putting my campaign together, and I wonder, is it—" he grinned—"kosher—if I talk to you from time to time. You know a lot about the people I want to reach."

"It's kosher," Sean said, also grinning.

"Listen, I had a call from the producer of 'The Advocates' on PBS. They are doing a show about the clergy and the war, and they want good people. Do you mind if I give them your name?"

"No, not at all."

A woman came by and latched onto Dan's arm and said, "Excuse me, Father, but can I borrow Dan for a few minutes?"

Sean found his way to Peg, who was happily stuffing herself at the chocolate table. She popped a bonbon into his mouth and said, "Oh Sean, this is so good you could die."

"Listen, Peg," Sean said, his mouth full of brandied mint chocolate, "there's going to be a speak-out tomorrow in Lafayette Park. Bishop Cooke asked me to talk. Want to come?"

"He's the Episcopal bishop, isn't he?"

"Yes. A very impressive man. I wish he was ours."

"You don't like Archbishop O'Toole?"

"You mean one of the great minds of the fourteenth century? Christ! He thinks condoms are the big moral issue of the day."

"Sounds like your father."

"Even The Nemesis of Smut is resigned to the pill. But it did take a while."

Peg picked Sean up at the rectory the next day, and they drove downtown. There was a large crowd gathered in the park by the time they arrived, a typical crowd: kids in jeans, suburban housewives with kids in tow, tweedy-looking men from local universities. Every weekend in the city there was some kind of antiwar activity going on, and a massive march was to be held the end of November. A speakers' platform with a mike had been set up in the park, and Sean and Peg walked over to it. Peg looked around at the gathering; a good turnout for a sunny Saturday in September, when people could be off doing other things. Then she saw, across the park, a peculiar sight. She grabbed Sean's arm and pointed.

"My God, Sean, look over there!"

"Oh yeah," he said. "It's Commander Blanton and his Thunder Troopers. They're always around."

A group of twelve men, wearing Nazi-type brown uniforms and caps, stood near a huge banner bearing a swastika that had been planted in the ground. Their commander, Raymond Blanton, stood next to the flag, his arms crossed across his chest in a studied imitation of Benito Mussolini. Under the Nazi-style cap his blond hair was cropped in a fifties-style crew cut, and deep lines creased his cheeks and forehead. Five D.C. cops stood nearby, keeping a sharp eye on the Nazis.

"It's been *years* since I saw him. My God, he's still at it."

"He's got to be a masochist, Peg. He's been hit more times than Rocky Marciano."

"He does look the worse for wear," Peg said.

"Yeah, but he's in good shape. It's a healthy outdoor life, being a Nazi. Nobody invites you *indoors* except the folks at D.C. jail."

The Thunder Troopers had become almost as familiar a sight to the natives as the Washington Monument. Commander Blanton and his crew had a decided flair for the dramatic—such as invading the House chamber during a voting rights debate dressed as Stepin Fetchit and doing jive talk as the honorable members gaped. They were on hand when the House Un-American Activities Committee hauled in the kids from the Progressive Labor party after they cut cane every summer in Cuba. At some point in the proceedings, one of the troopers would try a flying tackle on a witness, making the Senate caucus room resemble the forty-yard line. The Nazis said atrocious things about gas chambers and lynchings, of course, but no one seemed to take them seriously. They had become local color, something for the tourists to gawk at when the cherry blossoms palled.

"Mommy, who is that man?"

"He's a Nazi, dear."

"Can I take his picture?"

"Yes, sweetie, but hurry, we have to do the Lincoln and the Eternal Flame before lunch."

The crowd grew steadily larger, and the program began, with a well-known folk singer playing "Blowin' in the Wind." A professor from GW started things off, and then Bishop Cooke stepped to the microphone to say a few words to the crowd. He had become one of the foremost voices in the religious community against the war. As Peg listened, she made a mental note to do a piece on him for "Other Voices." Dovish clergymen really made the bile in Buck Stollmeyer's stomach rise. She thought of him, belching and tasting the sour residue of his tuna sandwich as he read direct quotes from the bishop. The thought gave her a warm feeling inside.

The bishop ended his talk and Sean said, "I'm on," and climbed the steps to the podium as the bishop introduced him. Sean began to speak, his voice clear and firm, but his tone informal. A silence fell across the park as he spoke.

"I knew a kid named Richie Dano. He was a big kid, right tackle on the team at Dom Savio in East Boston. He dropped out of school to enlist because he thought it would be an adventure. On his third day in Nam he got his head blown off by a mine. I said the funeral mass. His mother came up to me afterwards, and she said to me, 'Father, tell me, did Richie die for nothing? Did he?'"

The feeling in Sean's voice was obviously real, not faked. The crowd was hushed. He had them in the palm of his hand. Amazed that he was so good, Peg felt a rush of pride. This was her best friend, *her* Sean; she had known him all of his life.

"I lied to her. I said, no, Richie was a *hero*, his death wasn't a waste. She knew I was lying. It was *her* kid. And then I lied to some other mothers and fathers, saying all the right comforting stuff. None of it true. Finally I decided I'd have to stop lying. For me, there have been too many Richies. I don't want to bury them anymore. I don't want to say words over their coffins, I want my words to be used to stop this war. I want to bring the Richies home so they can grow up and live and have kids and get to be old men watching their grandchildren. To die for your country when it is in dire peril is a sacrifice; to die for a misguided, mistaken political adventure is a crying shame!"

He finished, and there was a moment of utter stillness before applause burst across the park. Bishop Cooke put his hand on Sean's shoulder; as he came down the steps she saw it in his eyes, the sense of power. He had done well, and he knew it.

"You were fantastic!" she said, as he walked up to her.

"It went okay?"

"You know it did."

He grinned, then, for an instant, and she took his hand and squeezed it. As she did so, she saw that one of the Thunder Troopers had left the pack and was walking up to them. He was a scrawny, pimply-faced young man, an unlikely Aryan superman.

"You commie," the young man hissed at Sean. "You commie faggot priest!"

Sean ignored him. Peg stared at the boy. His coarseness, following Sean's eloquence, offended her sense of propriety. "Keep your mouth shut," she snapped at him. "Twerp."

The boy looked at her, and his mouth twitched. "You sleep with the commie faggot priest. Commie slut."

"Oh, be quiet," Sean said.

"Commie slut, sleeps with a priest," the boy said again, his voice rising. Heads started to turn.

Sean, annoyance flashing across his face, said, "Just go away and be quiet."

The boy stuck out his lip belligerently. "I'm an American, buddy, and nobody tells me what to do. Not some commie priest!" He shoved Sean on the shoulder, not really very hard.

Sean stepped back and said, quietly but firmly, "Don't do that."

"I'll do what I want, *Father*," the boy said, mockingly.

He stepped forward as if he was going to shove Sean again. Seeing the motion, Peg reacted exactly the way she did when she was six years old and somebody tried to threaten her best friend Sean. She curled her right hand into a fist, pivoted, and gave the boy a roundhouse right, square in the jaw. The blow had all the force of her hundred twenty-nine pounds (after the chocolate table, hundred thirty-one pounds) behind it.

The blow staggered the boy, but it was hard to tell whether the expression on his face was pain or sheer astonishment. He was as scrawny as a plucked chicken; his lean body didn't offer much wind resistance. As he struggled to keep his balance, his heel caught in a patch of wet mud and he went down hard, on his back. Four D.C. cops—who had been waiting for the chance—leaped in, grabbed him, and dragged him to his feet.

"I didn't do nuthin'!" he protested.

"Tell it to the judge, Lester," one of the cops said. "Heil Hitler."

"*She* attacked me! That crazy broad!"

"You're hallucinating, Lester."

"You saw it, she *hit* me!" Lester screeched again.

"Oh, did the mean little girl give the big bad Nazi a boo-boo?" said one of the cops. "Okay, Lester, wave bye-bye!" and he was hauled off to the paddy wagon, still protesting. The other cops surrounded the troopers, daring them to try anything.

"Go ahead, Ray, we're waitin' on ya," one said, smiling.

But Blanton was not eager for another fun weekend at D.C. jail. Most of the inmates were black, and a Nazi plunked down in their midst could not expect the welcome wagon from the brothers. Discretion, he decided, was the better part of valor. No blitzkrieg today.

Sean, who had been watching the whole scene with what could only be described as open-mouthed horror, blanched as dozens of eyes turned to gawk. He grabbed Peggy's wrist and started to hurry away. One of the cops stopped them, and he said, with a big grin, "Lady, that was one hell of a right cross."

"Thank you," she said, as Sean tugged at her, trying to disappear into the crowd. "God, Peg, you hit him right in front of the Episcopal Bishop of Washington!" he moaned.

"I thought he was trying to hurt you," she explained as she tried to keep up with him.

"Peg, we are supposed to be nonviolent. That is the whole *point!* Oh my God, in front of the bishop!"

"Oh dear, I really did embarrass you, didn't I?"

"Episcopalians think Irish Catholics just drink and brawl. You did not change any minds back there."

"I didn't think. I just smacked him."

"Peg, you are thirty-one years old. I thought you had outgrown hitting people."

"I thought so too."

"You gave Brian MacNamara three stitches in the fourth grade when he was only trying to get the geography homework."

"I know. I thought he was stealing your book." She sighed. "I do have this habit of acting before I think. People say I'm brave, but that's not it, really. *I* move before my brain does. You can say you don't know me. That I'm just this drug-crazed hippie who leaped out of the crowd."

He laughed, suddenly. "For a drug-crazed hippie, you do pack a punch."

"I really decked him, didn't I? Course, he was a runt. God, I hope nobody at the paper finds out. I'm persona non grata already."

She stopped walking and began to laugh.

"Just what is so amusing?"

"Oh Sean, it *was* fun, wasn't it?"

Sean looked up at the sky. "If you hadn't written 'Thou shalt not kill' in *stone!*"

She started to laugh and couldn't stop, and as he tried to hurry her away from the park she was nearly doubled up with laughter. To a young man in jeans who looked at them curiously Sean said, "Drug-crazed hippie," and the man nodded solemnly and said, "Heavy, man." That made Peg laugh all the more. It wasn't until they were on the far side of Pennsylvania Avenue, nearly to 15th Street, that she was able to control herself.

"I can't take you anyplace," he said.

"Oh Sean, I'm sorry." She tried to look contrite, but she was still grinning. "I'll make it up to you."

"How?" he said.

"Your zort will cook for you."

"Twinkies in gravy?"

She put her arm around his shoulder. She was wearing some kind of perfume that made him think of the woods near Sligo Creek in the spring, and it mingled with her own warm woman-scent. It made him suddenly dizzy with memory.

"Veal in a sauce of cider, light cream, and brandy. And wild rice."

"Really?" He groped for an image to replace the one forming in his mind. He tried to concentrate on the face of the Sacred Heart on the stained glass above the altar at St. Ignatius, but all that filled his mind was the memory of her lying close to him, her face buried in the hollow of his neck, her breasts bare against his chest, and the smell of spring flowers in the woods near the creek.

"A Riesling, 1959," she said, "and afterwards, orange Cointreau cheesecake."

With a superhuman effort, he banished memory. He looked at her and smiled. "Oh Peg, those are words to live by. Do you mean it?"

"Yes, it's in the fridge. Forgive me?"

"*Ego te absolvo*," he said.

NINE

Kitty walked out of Garfinckel's and looked at her watch; out of the corner of her eye she saw a couple rounding the corner of 14th Street. She would not have given them a glance if there hadn't been something familiar in the gait of the man. She looked.

It was Dan, walking, laughing, with a young blond woman whose face stirred a memory. A secretary on the Hill? Why did she know that face?

Miss Cornhusker. The "photo op" from Nebraska. Kitty watched her, intrigued. A shock of blond hair, right from a bottle, that bobbed as she walked. Home job, probably, too brassy to be a good salon job. Heels too high, too much ass in the walk, an echo of the fifty-yard line and tubas. Kitty had seen a thousand like her, pretty, eager young women who hopped into bed with powerful men, not knowing that bed was as far as they'd get. She'd play fine in Omaha, but she'd be out of her class on Foxhall Road. But she was pretty. And so young.

Damn.

Kitty had supposed that Dan slept with other women, back home. He was a single man. A woman friend had once told her, about John Kennedy, "With Jack, sex is like dessert. He likes it, but it doesn't have to mean anything." Dan was the same way, she suspected. She could tolerate casual infidelities, as long as his heart belonged to her. She had never asked him about his past loves, and he had never volunteered. She wondered what sort of sex things he had been into. Orgies? She could see Dan at an orgy, *leading* the damn thing, like it was "The Farmer in the Dell." "The farmer takes a cow, heigh-ho the dairy-o, the farmer takes a cow."

Kitty felt a sudden throb of anger, watching Miss Cornhusker shaking her tush down 14th Street. This was *her* turf. She never asked Dan what he did in Omaha, but to bring Miss Cornhusker to Washington was a violation of their unspoken agreement. It was gauche. And it hurt.

She watched them as they disappeared around the corner, just as her chauffeur pulled up. She told him to forget the manicure—no way was she going to sit and get her nails painted while she seethed inside. She went home, took the dog, Mitzi the wolfhound, for an unaccustomed romp, fussed over the fall blooms that didn't need tending. By cocktail time she was quite calm. When Dan arrived, he moved to kiss her hello, but she offered him only a marble-cool cheek.

"Kit, what's wrong?"

"Interesting, the sights one can see on 14th Street," she said.

He sighed. "You saw Joyce and me."

"It's Joyce? I never knew her name."

"She works for the Chamber. They're in town for the annual trip, so I took her to lunch."

"Scotch?" she asked, and she made him a drink and handed it to him. "I'm not the jealous type, Dan, but I am rather—territorial."

"Kit, she's going back Thursday. I'll see her at the reception Wednesday night, that's it."

Kitty poured herself a sherry. "Do you sleep with her?"

He shrugged. "I have. Now and then. It doesn't mean anything."

"Broads. Easy come, easy go."

"I didn't mean that."

"You're a single man. I never asked you for any commitment. But maybe I ought to find out where I stand. I had the impression—correct me if I'm wrong—that I was a bit more than a photo op."

"You know you are. Don't say that!"

"Just how *do* you feel about me, Dan? We're good in bed, is that all?"

"Dammit, Kit, you know it isn't."

"No, I don't, Dan. I don't know. It's hard getting near you. You run away."

He looked down into his drink. They were both quiet, and then he said, "It's hard for me to trust people. Other people are—uncertain. You never know."

"Can't you trust me?"

"I want to. You're the first woman who—I don't know how to put this—could make me lose control. Sometimes I need you so much it scares me. I don't know if I want to need anybody like that."

She was quiet, sipping the wine. "I understand. But I can't live on the end of a yo-yo. Not knowing, from day to day, whether you care. Some nights, if you're late, I say to myself, 'Is this the night he's not coming at all?' And if it is, I guess I could live with it. But, Dan, I have to know."

She was composed, but she couldn't disguise the tremor at the end of the last word. She wondered what she would do if he just turned and walked out the door. She thought she just might die. But of course, respectable Jewish matrons did not die of broken hearts. That was for *goyim*.

He didn't turn to leave, just took another sip of his scotch.

"We are good together, Kit. You're the first person who made me believe in happiness. I used to think it was all a crock. But with you—" He let the end of the sentence trail off.

"I could make you happy, Dan." The words slipped out, and she felt vulnerable, exposed. She hoped there wasn't too much pleading in her voice. She had not felt this way since seventh grade, when she had walked up to David Cantrowitz in the school cafeteria and asked if he wanted to go to the Halloween dance. Standing there in her white angora sweater and padded bra, keeping her lips together so the braces wouldn't show, she prayed to God, "Don't let him say no, God of Abraham, of Ruth and Esther, Lord God of Yisroel, don't let David Cantrowitz say no!"

Dan's eyes were clouded, she could read nothing in them. And then he said, quietly, "I love you, Kit."

She came to his arms and he was saying, "Oh God, Kit, I do love you," and they went, holding hands, upstairs to the bedroom. They made love in the big bed, not with the itch of new-minted lovers, but with a tender languor. It was different than it had been. Married love, she thought.

He sighed, a deep, contented sound, and drew her to him. He didn't leap up but stayed, restful, by her side. It's going to be all right, she thought. It's going to be.

"We're going to have to make plans, Kit," he said. "After the Senate campaign, time to settle in. I never wanted it before. Now—we'll have time, Kit. All the time in the world."

Con put her feet up on the Danish teak coffee table (stained by airplane glue) and popped off the top of a Schlitz. She was intent on her current campaign, getting Peg a man.

"This guy is neat, Peg. Covers federal court, single, went to Duke, and has the cutest little drawl. A little young—twenty-six—but what the hell. There's a party Saturday night and he'll be there."

They were sprawled out on the couch in Con's living room. Lee was working and the boys were upstairs studying.

"Saturday? On Saturday Sean and I are going to watch *Now, Voyager*. Bette Davis, Paul Henreid. Three boxes of Kleenex. I'm doing beef Wellington."

"You're spending an awful lot of time with him."

"We laugh a lot, and I really need that. And Sean knocks himself out to entertain me. It's nice."

"That's fine, but you have to look around for a guy—unless you and Sean have gone beyond the brother-sister thing."

"No, it's very platonic. Relaxing."

"I can remember when you two couldn't keep your hands off each other."

"Ancient history."

"You can't tell me there aren't any sparks."

"Not on his side. We can even joke about sex, about the fact that he's celibate. He seems to have that worked out."

"Peggy, men do not have that 'worked out' unless they are dead or somebody cuts it off."

"One neat thing about you, Con, is your delicacy."

"I just do not believe that Sean doesn't feel anything for you sexually."

"Well, he doesn't. You can tell when a man's bells do not ring for you. He's been celibate for ten years. I guess you get out of the habit."

"That's depressing. Let me ask you something. Supposing,

in the middle of Bette Davis' big scene, Sean threw you down on the couch and jumped on your bones?"

"Con, that is not going to happen. It just is not in the cards. Besides, I don't want to mess up a good friendship."

"Friendship is fine, but you need a man."

Peg was silent, and Con said, "It's been more than a year since Jeff was killed. How long do you plan to keep yourself in cold storage?"

Peggy smiled. "Con, you're not going to ship me off to the frigid ward, are you?"

Con laughed. "I did mangle poor Sigmund Freud, huh? You didn't believe that!"

"Of course I did. I was terrified that I was going to end up on the frigid ward with tubes up my nose. Where did you come up with that anyhow?"

"I made it up. It sounded sort of logical."

"Oh Christ, I should have known."

"If you don't start going out with guys who haven't taken a vow of celibacy, Peg, I *will* find a frigid ward. And I will make you go there."

"Do you believe in the vaginal orgasm?"

"About as much as I believe in the Virgin Birth."

"I wonder if I would like sex with five guys?"

"Christ, I can't get her to go on a date with a guy who hasn't sworn off screwing, and now she's thinking orgies. You do go from one extreme to the other."

Peg laughed and said, "Times have changed since we were maidens, haven't they? Now people are screwing each other like jackrabbits. But I don't think I'd like sportfucking. I think I am sort of old-fashioned."

"Right, Peg, just an old-fashioned girl who wants five guys at once. Waiting for Mr. Right, Mr. Right, Mr. Right, Mr. Right, and Mr. Right."

"I remember something else you told me when we were in school, and I believed it *forever*."

"What?"

"That if you look at the size of a man's feet, you can tell the size of his penis."

"Absolutely true."

"Says who?"

"Sigmund Freud."

Peggy threw a pillow at Con. "Sean and I played doctor when we were six. I thought it was adorable, all pink and little and cute. But then, I thought it was pretty cute when he was eighteen, too."

"How big are Sean's feet?"

"Humongous!" Peg said, and they both giggled like school-girls.

"Have another beer, Peg."

"Don't mind if I do. Hey, let's drink a toast to your Halvorsen story. UPI quoted you."

"Yeah, it got good play."

"So when are you going to the Hill?"

"The managing editor wants me up there, but I know some people aren't happy about it. I haven't been at the paper a year, and it would be a big jump."

"You've earned it. Two exclusives in a row. You beat the whole damn pack."

"I know. That Halvorsen story, I put that together piece by piece. It wasn't just my sexy knees. Peg, I want it so bad I can taste it. But I'm trying to be cool. Say, what's the reaction on your series? I hear a lot of talk about it."

"I get more bags of mail than Santa Claus. Most of it demanding I be drawn and quartered on the East Lawn."

"Are you getting heat inside the paper?"

"Oh sure. But Tom has backed me all the way. And a few people have come up quietly and congratulated me. The *Trib* has been so damn hawkish. Oh, I'm doing Sean in next week's 'Other Voices.'"

"He was really good on 'The Advocates.'"

"He has done one hell of a job, Con, between his antiwar work and Action. He put that whole coalition together from scratch. He is a *very* good pol. He keeps putting himself down, though. Doesn't know how good he is. Or doesn't want to know."

"I used to feel sorry for Sean, being Bill McCaffrey's little brother."

"Yeah, but he's in his element now. He just might pull off the highway thing."

"It's a long shot."

"Yeah, and he needs the governor. My story ought to help. And I called Bill Janes at the Baltimore *Sun* and he's going to do a piece. They need an environmental impact statement, and that costs a pile."

"Peg, Kitty has friends with tons of money. And she thinks Sean is darling. Let's get their heads together."

"Con, that is a *great* idea!"

"I'll set it up. Could you get Sean to flirt a little? Kitty loves to flirt."

"Sean used to be very good at it."

"Oh Peg, this is exciting. I love being a power broker! A year ago I was running the PTA bake sale, and now I'm building empires. Oh, I am *magnificent*."

"And modest."

"That too. But enough of *moi*. Back to penises. Does Richard Nixon fuck?"

"Yes, but only small Asian countries."

"Ah Peg." She raised her beer can. "To us."

"To us. Girls Forever Brave and True."

They both joined in the chorus:

"Immaculate Heart
Immaculate Heart
Girls Forever Brave and True
They drink and they smoke
and they tell dirty jokes
But don't ever ask them to screw."

They both started to giggle, and a voice from upstairs floated down: "Ma, you and Peggy are making so much noise we can't study!"

"Okay, Leezy, we'll behave."

Peg looked at her watch and said, "Oh I have to run. Sean is stopping by tonight to pick up some stuff on highways I read for him."

"You're not only feeding him, you're doing his homework. When are you getting pinned?"

"He works so hard. I like to help."

"Five minutes ago we were talking orgies, and here she goes off to spend the night with a guy who's taken a vow of chastity."

"And poverty. *I* have to buy the booze."

"I give up. You'll be mothering that man until he's in the old priest's home."

Peg grinned. "I probably will."

TEN

She walked into her apartment and snapped on the light.
It was starting to look like a real home; furniture, paintings on the walls, new china in the cabinets. Sean had
brought over a few of his albums from his father's house and
had helped her hang Jeff's pictures on the walls. She had finally been able to do it. She chose the happy ones—French
children, Paris at sunrise.

It helped to have Sean beside her when she hung them. She
told him about Jeff; for the first time she was able to speak of
him without the jagged edge of pain whirring in her gut. In
some way she had clutched at the pain—it seemed disloyal
not to hurt for him. Would she lose the part of Jeff she still
had, when the pain went? But Sean had said no, the pain was
a cloud; she would see the past better when it was gone. And
he was right.

It was good that they had resumed their friendship, good,
too, that he no longer felt desire for her. When she had put
her arm around him in the park, she had sensed no response
at all. At first, her vanity had been wounded. No woman
wanted to think she couldn't dredge up a memory in an old
love. She certainly remembered. In the jeans and sweater he
wore the night she went to the Action meeting she could see
the outline of his body clearly. It was a man's body now, no
longer a boy's, still lean, but heavier in the chest and shoulders. The boyish awkwardness had vanished, and he was indeed beautifully male. She remembered the eagerness with
which he had discovered sensuality; how playful he was at

times, how fierce at others. Odd, that he could cut off that side of his life so completely, like a faucet stopped with a turn of the wrist. Had sensuality become for him only an echo, like the sound of the wind in the trees when the windows are sealed shut?

And they were sealed, she thought, with a pang of regret. No, better the way things worked out. Now they could be good friends, nothing more.

He arrived, right on time, and she said, "I've got the stuff. I went through the highway report and typed a summary."

He walked in and dropped heavily into a chair. "Peg, this is above and beyond the call."

He looked exhausted. There were shadows under his eyes. When he didn't sleep, it showed on his face.

She gave him a beer and he drank it, thirstily. "How was your trip?" he asked.

"Exhausting. Four cities in a week. Oh Sean, this is such a different country than the one I left. You get a sense of what it must have been like in the Civil War. Brother against brother."

"And it keeps dragging on. Nixon isn't doing zilch."

"Can I read you something, Sean?" He nodded, and she pulled a piece of paper from her typewriter. "The dominoes are falling. As I have traveled around this country, from which I have been absent for a decade, I hear them. The sounds reverberate on the banks of the Sandusky River in Ohio, along Route 1 in Georgia, in the town halls of New Hampshire, and along the broad lanes of Constitution Avenue in Washington. But they are not the dominoes we expected. They are our national will, our purpose, our concern for one another, our sense that we are one nation from sea to shining sea. No matter what the war in Vietnam is doing to that country, it is tearing this one apart."

"Peg, that's wonderful! Not what you'd expect from the Washington *Tribune*."

"Not hardly. I will catch a lot of shit for this one. I really drop the mask of the objective reporter and let it all hang out. It's a little scary."

"Because you're vulnerable."

"Yeah. That's me, Peg Morrison, talking. They throw the

brickbats at *me,* not at the Panthers, or the women's movement. That's scarier then getting shot at."

"You're doing that more, lately, I notice. I see more of you in your stories than I used to."

"Yes, I don't want to just collect facts and put them in baskets anymore. I want to use what I've learned. European journalists do that a lot more than we do. I think American reporters are trained to be clerks. Clerks of fact. I don't want to do that anymore."

He looked at her and smiled. "You are quite a woman, Peggy Ann Morrison. Did I ever tell you that?"

She smiled. "Not in a while. It certainly is nice to hear. Oh, how's it going with Backman's people?"

"Great. They're solid. But the clock is ticking. Brian has a friend at the chancery who says the Montgomery Chamber of Commerce is starting to get worried. A couple of local construction guys are big givers to the archdiocese. They could lose a bundle if the interstate gets stopped."

"I hear Backman's guy, Halloran, is tight with the archbishop. He thinks you are hot shit."

"Me?"

"I talked to him for my story. He said that if half the guys on the Hill had the political skills you have, a lot more would get done."

She saw a small smile flit around the corners of his mouth, but then he shook his head. "I've learned a thing or two, but I doubt if I could hack it on the Hill. I'm just a two-bit parish priest."

"Come on, Sean, I've covered these guys. I see guys up there making forty grand who haven't got half the brains you have."

"In the circles I've been moving in lately, there's a lot of temptation for me. To start feeling self-important. I am only the vessel of God's will."

"Oh bull-puckey. God's will doesn't get done if some nerd tries to do it."

"Bull-puckey?"

She laughed. "I heard that in Georgia. Sean, it isn't a sin to know your capabilities."

He sighed. "Bill says I spend my life on the Big Tit. I've always had a safety net under me."

"Under you! More like the one they throw over you when they haul you away."

"That too." He leaned back in the chair and closed his eyes. She had a sudden impulse to go to him, to pull his head into her lap and stroke his forehead, the way she used to do in the backseat of his father's Caddy. She might have done it, but he was wearing the black suit with the collar. Was that deliberate? A signal to her to keep hands off? Did he really think she would try to seduce him, when she knew that was the last thing he wanted? She felt a throb of anger, that he wouldn't trust her more.

He opened his eyes and said, "Peg, without me, Action might not make it. I'm not being—boastful, it's just that I hold things together. If they pull me out—Jesus, I do have trouble with that vow of obedience."

"Would you go? If they ordered you out?"

"What choice would I have?"

"Stay, and run Action."

"Leave the priesthood?"

"If they try to take you away from your work."

"Peg, I'm a priest. I don't want to fail at it."

"Just a thought. Come on, have another beer."

"I can't. I have a ton of reading to do. And I have to get up for six o'clock mass. Father Barry's orders."

"Sean, you have antiwar meetings and Action meetings at least three nights a week. How much sleep do you get?"

"Four, five hours a night. But I don't need much sleep, I have a lot of energy." He got up from the chair and went to get his coat.

"Look at you! You've got bags under your eyes. You're exhausted. You are going to lie down and take a nap. You're out on your feet."

"I don't have time—"

She took his hand and began to lead him to the bedroom. He followed her, docilely. "Okay, but wake me in a half hour."

"I will. Lie down, now, come on."

He took off his jacket and his collar and he stretched out on the bed. She started to untie his shoes, then slipped off his shoes and said, "If you aren't asleep in five minutes, I will come in and brain you with a tire iron."

He smiled, then closed his eyes and she went into the kitchen and made herself a cup of coffee. When she came back to the bedroom he was fast asleep, his breathing deep and even. She pulled a blanket up over him and stood watching him for a minute. Sleep seemed to peel away the years, and she saw in the sleeping form so clearly the little boy who used to fall asleep in her arms in the sandbox when they were six years old. She knelt down beside the bed and wound her finger lightly around a curly lock of his hair. No matter how hard he tried to keep the curls under control, they had a will of their own. She bent over and kissed his forehead, her lips just brushing his skin. He sighed in his sleep.

"Zabor from the planet Urf," she whispered, "your zort does love you so."

She stood up and left the room, picked up the phone and dialed St. Nasty's. "Brian? It's Peg Morrison. Sean was over here and he looked awful. I got him to take a nap and he's sound asleep. Do you think you could take the six o'clock mass tomorrow? I think he'd sleep through if I don't wake him."

"Sure, Peg, let him sleep. He needs it."

Peg pulled her sleeping bag out of the closet and tossed it on the couch. She put on a nightgown—the flannel, not the black lace—and climbed into it, remembering with a twinge that the last time she had used it she had camped out with Jeff in the south of France. Jeff and Sean; how alike they were. She was attracted first to Jeff because he looked like Sean, even moved in the same way, had the same dark curly hair. But the resemblance was more than physical. Jeff was a worrier, like Sean. A carer. He could never just snap the shutter and then erase his subjects from his brain. They stayed, engraved on his brain cells as they were etched on his film; hounded him, in the end, to his death.

He had always worried about her, always made her take what he considered good airlines, made her promise not to take foolish risks. She was drawn, it seemed, to men with a wide paternal streak, running through their natures like a skein of ore through the earth. She wanted a man who could care, and feel other people's pain. The macho power-driven types bored her silly. And she was not very good at casual sex, despite a few charming interludes. Sex for her was bound up with all her other feelings; she never gave only half her heart, which was why, of course, it got knocked about. But to settle for a life of catch-as-catch-can amours, encounters in a hotel here, somebody's apartment there, seemed the equivalent of eating only pizza and tacos, a junk-food love life. No, what she wanted was to pledge herself fully to one man, who could risk, as she was willing to, the hazards of commitment.

But she had the desolate feeling, sometimes, that no such man existed for her, and that it was her fault. Was there some blemish, some crack in her psyche, that would always send a man hurtling away? It was odd; she had seen so many women who seemed to be able to hang onto men. She saw two hundred-pound women, with greasy hair and bad complexions, moving along the street with men hanging near them like pilot fish. The world moved in twos. But not for her.

She remembered Jeff's face as she had seen it the last time, at Orly. He seemed to be looking beyond her into some invisible dimension; she herself felt invisible. He had not deflected from that last, fatal trip, just as Sean had not veered from the path that led to ordination. They had both loved her, but not enough; in the end, with both of them, she had turned invisible. Maybe she just wasn't *lovable*, there was the truth of it.

Since she was having no luck at sleeping, she decided to compose a personal ad for herself:

"White female, 31, seeks man for lifelong commitment. (No marrieds, gays, S-Mers, foot fetishists) I am five-feet-eight, one hundred and twenty-nine pounds. I have only one cavity, a nice collection of pre-Columbian grave figurines, and the Pulitzer prize. I have an excellent jump shot and I can, under duress, handle a Thompson submachine gun and drive a land rover. I have a good sense of humor and perky boobs. I am loyal and kind."

Loyal and kind, just like Lad, a dog. If a man wanted *that*, he could get a collie.

She sighed, closed her eyes, and turned over. She hoped the dream wouldn't make an appearance tonight. She never knew when it was going to come; it ambushed her, like the land mine buried in the sand. The half-track would move across the sand, slowly, inexorably, only this time she knew what would happen. She would try to scream but her vocal cords were frozen into silence, and then it would be there— the head, lying on the sand. It would not help Sean's beauty sleep to have her shrieking in the living room. He would go back, gladly, to his barfing pastor. She would probably have to put an addendum to her personal ad:

P.S. I wake up in screaming nightmares, but only several times a month. But I am not too noisy and just a little sweaty, and I do make a lovely *canard à l'orange*.

Finally, she slept, and did not dream. When she awoke in the morning, she looked in on Sean, and found him fast asleep, in the same position in which he had fallen asleep. She smiled and went into the kitchen and called Country Caterers, around the corner, and ordered juice, croissants, and for Sean the mushroom and ham omelette. It came on a tray with the food in little wicker baskets with white-and-blue checkered napkins.

She took the tray into the bedroom, and as she walked in, he opened his eyes, sat up, and looked around, disoriented.

"Peg? What time is it? I—"

"Stay in bed. Don't you dare move."

"Six o'clock mass, jeez—"

"It's eight-thirty. Brian did the six. And you are having breakfast in bed."

His eyes focused on the tray. "Breakfast? Oh my God, Peg, did you do that?"

"Sure, Sean, I stayed up all night weaving the baskets."

He laughed, and she set the tray down on the bed and propped the pillow behind his back.

"Wow. What's the occasion?"

"In Bavaria, the natives always bring the village priest breakfast in bed on the feast of St. Mathilhide the Martyr."

"You are making up saints again."

"I'm not. St. Mathilhide died in 1421."

"How?"

"Hit a turn on the autobahn doing ninety."

He picked up a croissant and took a bite. "Oh, this is good! This sure beats the last breakfast you brought me in bed."

"The Greystone, I forgot all about it. I did bring you breakfast."

"Cotton candy. For breakfast. I thought I was going to barf."

"It was all I could find on the boardwalk. Remember the bed? The one with the rat bodies in it?"

He choked on a bite of omelette. "Now I *am* going to barf. I should have known you were going to say that."

She laughed and sat cross-legged on the bed, tucking her nightgown under her toes. He was eating the omelette, and she leaned over and picked a piece of ham out of it. He slapped her fingers.

"Stop that! You always did that!"

She laughed. "It used to drive you crazy."

"Still does. You'd say you weren't hungry, then you'd eat all my food. You haven't changed, Peggy Morrison."

"Do you realize we've known each other all our lives?"

"Yeah. And you can pick at my food if you want, with your dirty, germy little fingers."

They ate the omelette together, cleaned the tray until not a crumb was left. Then Peggy went to the closet to get a bath towel for him. He was standing by the bed when she came back into the room.

"Peg," he said, "this has been a very special morning for me. I won't forget."

"It'll be a tradition. Every St. Mathilhide's day."

She leaned over to give him a sisterly peck on the cheek, but he put his lips to hers and kissed her full on the mouth. She felt his body pressing on hers, the muscles in his chest hard against her breasts. Her mouth opened under his and suddenly, she felt his tongue in her mouth. The soul kiss, her favorite in the backseat of the Caddy. Old friend, welcome home.

Then he drew back, surprise on his face. "I'm sorry," he said, "I didn't, I—"

She smiled and shoved the towel at him.

"Go take your shower, Sean. Before the Kissing Priest gets carried away."

He grinned at that. It was the name he had conferred on himself the night in his senior year she and Con had got him drunk and he started kissing both of them. "Will do, best friend."

He walked into the bathroom and she gripped the edge of the dresser, hard, physically weak in the knees with desire for him. The frigid ward had lost a patient.

She heard the shower running, and she wondered what he would do if she peeled off her nightgown and got into the shower with him. She could tell him she just wanted to go to confession.

"What sins do you wish to confess, my child?"

"Well, this one."

"Oh my."

"And this one. And of course, this one."

"I see. That's it?"

"Yes, Father."

"Kneel, my child, for your penance."

"Oh, you just reminded me of another one. And Sean, while you're giving me absolution, would you mind soaping my back?"

Oh Peggy, girl, keep your hands off him. He doesn't belong to you. He never did.

She went into the kitchen and was reading the *Post* when he came in, his hair damp and shining from the shower. He looked fresh and rested.

"I feel great! Peg, you've made a new man out of me."

"The old one wasn't so bad."

"I have to run. My junkies await."

She walked over to him and this time kissed him gently on the cheek. Her hand was on his shoulder, and she felt his whole body shiver at her touch. She stepped back.

"Bye, Sean."

For an instant, something fluttered in his eyes, but she wasn't able to read what it was.

"Bye, Peg. Are we still on for dinner Thursday?"

His voice was light and cool, as if nothing had happened between them. But she had felt him shiver.

And then he was gone. She walked back and sat down with the *Post*. Her heart was thumping inside her chest. She wanted to laugh like a little child. She wanted to turn hand-springs.

"Dumb, Peggy Ann. Really dumb. D-U-M-B." She heard Con's voice, "You're the one who'll get hurt, Peg. And I think you've had enough hurting."

When Sean had gone off to the seminary, she had tucked her damaged heart away someplace safe—behind the pancreas, possibly—someplace dark and quiet where it could heal. For a long time, no one touched that buried heart. And then there was Jeff, who was so much like Sean. Even then, it took her a long time to dare to love again. He was patient with her. Finally, one day, she realized the heart was healed, the fissures repaired, the cracks filled in. And then Jeff went to Saigon.

She knew right away what it was when Stan Pavlik walked into the bureau that day; she only had to look at his face. She just said, "How did it happen?"

"Chopper. It crashed."

"How many died?"

"Everybody. Oh God, Peg, I'm so sorry."

After the funeral she went right back to work, because she knew if she didn't work she would go mad. She supposed that maybe someday she would want to live again. Sean's letter helped more than he knew.

"Peg, I've been praying for you, hurting for you, ever since I heard. You have to hang on, Peg, for all the people who care about you. I think you have important things to do. Miles to go. Promises to keep. I believe in you. I love you. I wish I could help."

How many times could a heart get battered? A heart was not a Midas muffler, you couldn't just pop in a new one when the old one went bad. And hers had all those cracks in it. How strong could it be?

Be smart, Peg. Be careful.

But still, when she got up to rinse out the cup, she was humming. She never hummed in the morning, only coughed. Bad sign. Very bad.

So why did she feel so good?

ELEVEN

"How do I look?" Con asked. She had a curly red wig plopped on her head, and she was wearing a tight red dress with black mesh stockings and high heels.

"Like Orphan Annie when she grew up to be a hooker," Peg said. "Con, you aren't really going to wear that."

They were in Con's bedroom, and Con was admiring her image in the full-length mirror.

"Sure. I might run into somebody I know. It's a disguise."

"Why did I let you talk me into this?"

"Come on, it'll be an adventure. Could be a good story."

"Is this place a high-class whorehouse, or what?"

"No, private home. The owner runs a chain of discount drugstores. The tip I got says the parties are just sex things."

"And politicians go?"

"So I hear. There's always a supply of girls on hand."

"Pros?"

"Could be. But I think its more like G-girls who get a charge out of screwing the high and mighty."

"So we're supposed to look like G-girls?"

"Yes. You are going to be a GS three at the General Accounting Office. No, you look too classy for that. Make it the Commerce Department."

"And you?"

"I am definitely the Pentagon typing pool. Hi there, I'm Connie!" She looked at Peg. "You don't look slutty enough. This is not a press conference. Try more rouge."

"I don't do slutty real good."

"Yeah, you look about as much like a slut as St. Theresa."

"We've both had the same amount of experience."

"St. Theresa stayed in a convent and prayed for fifty years."

"The way my love life is going, she is a real tramp compared to me."

"Curls. I have fake ones. Dynel, and really ugly." She pinned a tangle of fake curls to Peg's head and said, "Oh yeah, really tacky. And I have a pair of pantyhose with *seams.*"

Peg struggled into the pantyhose. She was wearing her blue dress with the low neckline, and when she displayed herself for Con's approval, Con frowned.

"No, Peg, you're still too classy. I know. I have an old push-up bra. Remember those?"

"God, I haven't seen one of those in years."

"Get it on."

Peg wiggled into the bra and then zipped up her dress again. The bra pushed her breasts up so high that there was a distinct cleavage line visible above the neckline of the dress.

"This is not very natural, Constance Marie. I look like I'm ready for the casting couch."

"Yeah, the elevator scene."

"What's that?"

"Going down."

"This is one of the crazier things you have made me do."

"Stick with me, Peg, I'll bring adventure back into your life."

"Constance, adventure is exactly what I was trying to get *away* from."

They drove, in Con's car, to a large old home in a fashionable section of Arlington. There were quite a few cars parked outside, and when they walked to the door a man in a tuxedo took the invitations Con handed him.

They walked into the foyer. The living and dining room were already crowded with people, and a cash bar was doing a brisk business. There did, indeed, seem to be a large number of unattached women present. Some of them stood in pairs, or threes, and men seemed to be cruising, looking over the crop.

"Ha!" Con said. "Pay dirt. See that guy, the one in the gray suit, with the Bloody Mary? He's the AA to Senator Kirkland. And look, in that corner, the two guys talking to each other. The one on the right is Congressman Wylie and the other guy is a lobbyist for the meat packers."

"So how does this work? They use the bedrooms upstairs?"

"If they like, I'm told. Or they pick out what they like and leave. See the guy going out with the girl in the miniskirt? You can bet they didn't come together."

"Does money change hands?"

"My source says that for some of the regulars it does. She can't prove it. But it's mostly amateurs."

"Aren't these guys afraid of getting caught? Especially the elected ones?"

"Nobody writes about this stuff. Everybody knows it goes on, but unless a guy gets caught in a public way with a floozie, mum's the word. But this stinks. I plan to write about it."

"What the hell do the women get out of this? The amateurs?"

"Look around, Peg. A lot of these girls are from hick towns in Nowheresville, USA. This is really the big time. Who knows? They figure they might just snag one of these big fish. Marry him. Be somebody."

"Fat chance!"

"Yeah, at least the pros get paid. The amateurs will get used, then tossed away. Women are like small change in Washington, passed from hand to hand. There are plenty more where these came from, waiting to get on the bus."

"What does the guy who runs these things get? Favors?"

"Probably. And he gets to hang around with powerful people. This town runs on power, not sex. Sex is just the stuff you use to lubricate the tires."

A man, middle-aged and well-dressed, asked Con if she would like a drink. Con refused, politely. Then another man approached, and she smiled and shook her head.

"I wonder," Peg said, "if I smell?"

"I told you you looked too classy."

"Con, I would be turned down in Hong Kong brothels because my clothes were in bad taste."

"Oh shit, there's a guy I know, let's go to the other room."

They made their way slowly into the living room. Con spotted another congressman, leaning against the mantel, talking to a young brunette.

"He's married and he has five kids. Oh, wouldn't the folks back home love to get a look at this. He's very big on morality. Good stuff."

"What can you write about this?"

"I'll have to use a lot of blind stuff, say that high-ranking officials were on hand, use the stuff my source gave me about the night she was here. It's going to be tricky."

"Can you use the name of the guy who owns the house?"

"We'll have to lawyer this one. We could get some young girls to come in and see if they get money or a proposition out of someone."

"That could be entrapment."

"I know. But I hate the hypocrisy of this. These are the same guys that yell for law and order, talk about getting pimps and prostitutes behind bars. Hey, would you look at that! In the corner."

A tall distinguished-looking man, graying at the temples, was deep in conversation with two young girls in the corner of the room.

"Know who that is?" Con asked.

"Sure. Senator Cale Canavan. The Voice of the Third World."

"Talk about radical chic. I didn't expect to see him here."

"You think leftists aren't male chauvinist pigs, Con? They are the *pits*."

"Yeah, bleed for the oppressed masses and tell the wife, 'Do the goddamn dishes!' "

"Canavan is one of those real knee-jerks. When some right winger sticks electrodes in somebody's privates, it's torture. When a leftist does it, power to the people!"

They floated around the party for a while, watching as many of the men and women would pair off, go up the stairs, and not be seen for a while. Many of the women were young; they looked like teenagers. It was clear the men were not looking for deep conversations about the balance of trade.

Peg walked up to the bar to get a cold drink, and as she did so, she realized that something was pulling around her thighs. Con's pantyhose. They were too small and they were working their way down her hips. In a minute they would be around her knees. But both bathrooms were occupied, so she told Con, "I'm going to find a place where I can get these damn pantyhose off before they fall off."

"If you use one of the bedrooms, make sure it's empty."

Peg went upstairs, found a bedroom with an open door an peered in. It was empty, and she pulled the door most of the way shut and began to wiggle, quickly, out of the pantyhose. She had her dress up, sliding them over her toes, when all of a sudden she felt a hand on her rump.

"Ahhhhh!" she said, giving a startled jump. She turned around to discover she was staring into the face of the Voice of the Third World, Senator Cale Canavan.

"God, what legs!" he said.

"How the hell did you get in here?"

The senator giggled, exhaling a cloud of bourbon that nearly knocked Peggy on her face. His eyes were glazed. The Voice of the Third World, she realized, was definitely plastered. He pushed the door shut and grinned at her.

"Let's fuck."

"I was just leaving."

"Oh doll!" He grabbed her wrist and flipped her onto the bed. He fell on top of her and began to nuzzle her breasts, slobbering just a bit as he did so.

"Oh God, what tits!"

"Is that what you say to Jomo Kenyatta?"

The line, however, was lost on Senator Cale Canavan, who started to rub her thigh.

Great, Peg thought, I make a scene and I blow Con's story. I don't make a scene and I get pawed by a great humanitarian. What a choice.

As his hands groped at her thigh, she said, "Senator, stop that!"

"Not Senator! I'm Frank. Oh doll!" He tugged at her panties, trying to pull them down, all the while breathing such fumes into her face that she thought she just might throw up all over him.

"Oh doll, great legs. Oh!"

"I'll *kill* Con."

"Con? Who's Con? Bring him in. Let's share."

Peggy pulled his hands away from her panties.

"Just stop that, Senator."

"Oh, I'm Frank. Oh, I want to fuck you!"

The senator reached down, unzipped his fly, and pulled out his private parts; he rolled over slightly to display them to full advantage.

"Oh doll, all for you. That's all for you!"

"I've seen bigger balls on a Ping-Pong table. Now will you please go away and leave me alone?"

"Ohhh, fuck me. Please fuck me!"

"I am not going to fuck you. You support the PLO."

"I love your tits. Ohhh. Ohhh!"

Then Peggy heard, from the hallway, a voice calling her name. "Peg! Peg, where are you?"

"Constance Marie, I am in here!"

The door opened and Con peered in. She looked at the scene on the bed and said, "Oh my God, the Voice of the Third World!"

"Unfortunately," Peg said.

"What is it saying?"

"Fuck me! Fuck me!" wailed Senator Cale Canavan.

Con walked in, sat on the bed, and put her hand on the Senator's thigh. "Hi theah!" she drawled, in a fake Southern accent.

The senator rolled over to look at her. "Oh, you have nice tits too."

"We're going to be very nice to you, Senator," she promised, as Peg slid out from under him.

"Two," the Senator giggled. "Both fuck me!" He lay back and closed his eyes; his private parts, exposed, were still standing at attention.

"Con?" Peg said. Con just grinned.

"Now close your eyes, Senator," Con cooed. "This is going to feel *soooo* good." She picked up the glass of scotch that he had set down on the dresser. It was ice cold.

"Constance Marie, I like the way you think," Peg said, straightening her dress.

"Fuck me!" said the Voice of the Third World.

And Con turned the glass over and poured the ice-cold scotch right on the senator's crotch.

As they ran down the hall, they could still hear him screaming.

* * *

Sean hurried up the steps of the Rayburn Building and walked down the hall to the door that said, Mr. Amundsen, Nebraska. Dan was waiting for him.

"Hi Sean, come on in. I'm going back to the state this weekend, and I have to speak at a big Knights of Columbus breakfast."

"Life in the fast lane."

Dan laughed. "I did want to ask you what you can tell me on the Catholic position on the war. I don't know much about it."

"Well, there isn't any official position, but some people are arguing that Vietnam is not a just war, and as Catholics they can morally refuse to serve."

"A just war?"

"Yes. The Church isn't against all wars, but a war has to be fought for good and moral reasons to be justified. The flip side of that is that Catholics should oppose an unjust war."

"What are the things about Vietnam that could make Catholics say it's an unjust war?"

"Our policy of bombing civilians. Using weapons like antipersonnel bombs and napalm. You could argue we are conducting a war of terror against civilians."

"Yes, you could. Anything else?"

"The nature of the government we are supporting. It's corrupt, doesn't have the support of the people, and suppresses religious freedom."

"What if a Catholic had a bishop who was for the war? Like Cardinal Spellman. Would a Catholic have to follow his lead?"

"People have the idea the Church is pretty authoritarian. But in fact, one's own conscience is primary. If you read what the Church says carefully, you find that the bottom line is that the individual *has* to follow his own conscience."

"Even if the Church disagrees?"

"Yes. Bishops don't noise that around, of course. And 'the Church' is a very big, very diverse institution."

"Well, this 'just war' idea. One way to reach the World War Two vets might be to say that *their* war was a just war but this one is not?"

"Yes. And point out that you aren't saying that our fighting men aren't brave. But the politicians made a mistake putting them in a situation in which they can't win. And which is wrong."

When he left Dan's office, Sean swung by the Longwood Building to see Halloran, Backman's man. The first time he had come to the Hill, he was intimidated by all the marble and the oversized wooden doors. Now, it was familiar turf. There were many good people here, he had learned, who wanted to use the mechanism of government to make the Republic a more just, more peaceful place. If only he could spend all his time here, not in some jerkwater parish running beano games, he could really do God's work.

Father Barry's voice sounded in his ear. "You are an ambitious young man."

Was it true? His pride had always been his weakness, he knew. He had battled it, all the years he had been a priest. Ambition had no place in his image of Sean McCaffrey, Perfect Priest, who was humble, submitting to God's sweet yoke; who was tranquil of soul and at peace with himself.

Of course, the kicker was that Sean McCaffrey thought he had to be the Perfect Priest because he *could* be one. Even in his submission, he thought wryly, he was arrogant. Father Peter had been right.

"Sean, the real danger to your vocation is your pride," he had said shortly before Sean's graduation from seminary.

"I have tried not to be proud, Father. I took the job of scrubbing the bathrooms for the past six weeks because I hate it so."

"And yet, on your hands and knees, you still think you are better than others. More humble."

"No, I—"

"Be honest, Sean. Did you not feel more holy?"

"Yes, Father."

"It is what you must banish from your heart. The sin of pride. You must tear down your arrogance. I will tell you what you must do. You will kneel, wearing sackcloth, at the feet of your brothers, and beg their forgiveness for your conceit. Then perhaps you will be fit to be a priest."

So he stood naked in his room while Dennis wrapped a piece of gray cloth round his loins. Wearing nothing more, he walked in front of his classmates in the dining hall. He was supposed to feel humbled; but the truth was that instead of feeling that he was sharing in the passion of Christ, he was really thinking how absurd he must look in this getup. An Irish Catholic version of Sabu the Elephant Boy. He had a terrible urge to blurt out, "Sabu say this is *really* dumb, white men!" but he figured that would really blow his vocation all to hell. Dutifully, he knelt on the stone floor and touched his forehead to the stone and said to them, "I confess my pride. I confess my arrogance. May God humble me and cleanse my soul of sinful pride." And he beat his fist hard against his breast, saying, "Through my fault, through my fault, through my most grievous fault."

His classmates walked by him and each one touched his head, a sign had they accepted his penance. When he rose, he felt a marvelous, cleansing sense of humility wash over him. They were his brothers and he was the least of them, not fit to bathe their feet.

But the next day he was back to thinking that Dennis was a birdbrain, Kevin Mulcahey was a pompous bore, and Jordy Farrel was a wimp. Humility did not take well on Sean McCaffrey. He produced antibodies against it.

"Oh Lord, forgive my arrogance. Humble me, Lord," he prayed, and then he started to think about the Action meeting he was going to. It was his defense against troublesome thoughts, to simply outrun them, to keep so busy he had no time to think.

At the meeting, he coached Estella on her upcoming appearance before the Maryland House of Delegates. She was getting cold feet.

"I am so afraid, my knees will knock. They will say, 'Look at her, the spic can't even talk English.'"

"You'll do just fine. When were you ever at a loss for words?"

"Oh, at a meeting in the neighborhood, yes, I can open up a big mouth. But Father Seanito, to go before Congress!"

He laughed. Father Seanito was the nickname he had picked up among the Hispanics. "It's not Congress, Estella, just the Maryland House of Delegates."

"I forget the statistics. They go out of my head—poof!"

"Never mind statistics. Just go up there and give them a

show. You're a woman fighting for your home, your bambinos. Pull out all the stops."

"I work hard, señors. By day I labor in a factory! At night I go to school to lean the language so I can be a good American. But where will I go if the bulldozers come? I am a widow, my babies and I will be in the street. Shall we go to a condo for seventy thousand dollars? Tell me, señors, where will we go!"

"Wonderful. Do it just like that. We'll make the six o'clock news for sure."

"I should not tell them that one of my *bambinos* is eighteen and makes six-twenty an hour on construction?"

"Absolutely not. In fact, maybe we ought to give you Lucia's baby to hold in the hearing room."

"Father Seanito, I have never met a priest like you."

Sean grinned. "Dishonest, you mean?" He laughed. "I wonder if Chuck should wear his dashiki. I wouldn't want him scaring those guys in Annapolis—especially the Neanderthals from the Eastern Shore."

"Ah, Chuck. In a dashiki he would look—exotic. In a shirt and pants like an ax murderer."

"Good point. Actually, he wouldn't harm a flea."

"So I have discovered. I do not get upset anymore when he calls me a spic. And I call him *negrito*."

Sean shook his head. "America, America."

After the meeting he had to go on a somewhat mysterious errand. Chuck said that his neighbor, Claudia Brown, had to see him, but he couldn't say why. Sean had an idea. There was a warrant out for her son, Elmore—Elly for short—on a murder charge. He had been a member of a group of Black Panthers in Baltimore. There had been some trouble—a shootout of some kind, and one man died. Elly Brown had been on the run for four months.

Claudia Brown lived in a neat, well-kept brick row house. She was a widow who worked as a domestic, and her only son had been a student at a junior college in Baltimore when he had gotten involved with the Panthers.

"Let's go out on the porch, Father," Claudia Brown said nervously when he arrived at her house. "The FBI was here, looking for Elly."

They stood on the porch, in the cold and dark, and she said, "Elly has to get to somebody in the press. To tell his side. He saw that story about you in the *Tribune*. By that woman."

"Peg Morrison."

"He has to tell his side, Father. And if she's a friend of yours, Elly would trust her. I know you could get in trouble, but, Father, somebody has to listen to him."

"He's accused of a very serious crime, Mrs. Brown."

"I know. But the lies they've told, Father. This is America, and the police lied. It isn't fair!"

"I can talk to Peg Morrison. But I can't promise anything."

"I know, Father. Please call me at Chuck's, not here. The FBI—Father, I don't feel safe, here."

Sean was bone-weary by the time he and Brian had a chance to talk, in Brian's room.

"I don't know, Brian, I'm getting to like the attention. The TV, the speeches. Maybe Father Barry has me pegged. An ambitious young man."

"Sean, did anyone ever tell you that you were *scrupulous?* Why do you beat yourself over the head all the time?"

"Do I? It's just that—my idea of a priest is not a guy who goes on TV. You know, my hero when I was a kid was Damien the Leper."

"It's hard to get leprosy at St. Nasty's. Hepatitis, VD sure."

Sean laughed. "You know what I mean. I wanted my life to be hard. I wanted to suffer for the glory of God. I wanted a challenge. I hated the life of the suburban priests I saw, driving their Buicks, playing golf, getting fat."

"You were born in the wrong century, Sean. They don't crucify Christians anymore."

"You're telling me I have a martyr complex?"

"I think you have extraordinary talents. You're a born leader. You keep thinking you ought to want to be in some monastery someplace, on your knees twelve hours a day. Accept your gifts, Sean. Don't hide them under a bushel."

"For a long time, Bri, I knew I was a fraud, wearing this collar. The respect was for the collar, not the man. But at the same time, even when I was a snot-nosed seminarian, I had this feeling I was something special. The other day, when I spoke at that rally, I *had* that crowd—" He held out his hand, curled it into a fist—"thousands of people there were *mine.*

And I didn't think about God, I thought about *me*. There's a temptation for me, Brian."

Brian shook his head. "Oh God, there's nothing like Irish Catholic guilt. I'd envy you your talents, except I know that you just *can't* enjoy them. Listen, Sean, would you hear my confession?"

It was a weekly ritual. Sean heard Brian's confession, and then he confessed to Brian, the usual sins; pride, arrogance, uncharity (toward Father Barry), and, finally, acts of impurity. After he made his act of contrition, he admitted his doubts about the last one to Brian.

"It doesn't make any sense, Brian. Why do I confess it?"

"We are priests and we are supposed to abhor sin. But we sin all the time. So we confess."

"But for a confession to be valid, you have to have the intention of avoiding the sin in the future."

"And you have the intention. At the time."

"No I don't. I know I'm going to masturbate five or six times a week."

"Confessing, Father, or bragging?"

Sean grinned. "You know what I mean. The drive was put there for a reason. Okay, so I'm not making babies. But the drive is good. Natural."

"It can be used for evil. Rape, for example."

"I am not running around raping people, Bri."

"I hope not. We already have a lush, we don't need a rapist." Brian cast his eyes up to heaven. "Lord, forgive my uncharity."

"It's a scientific fact that a man's body has to ejaculate regularly to work right. It's not a sin to keep your body working. It's wrong not to."

"But do you cooperate with sexual thoughts when you ejaculate?"

"How can you *not* cooperate? It's impossible to slice your body off from your mind like that."

"But we have to try to be closer to the suffering of Christ than other men, Sean. That's why we chose the hard path. Even if we fail. And we fail all the time."

"I know that. But to tell you the truth, Brian, I think my sexuality makes me a better priest. A woman came into confession the other day and said she couldn't afford another kid, but her marriage would crack if she and her husband couldn't touch each other most of the time. And I understood, not in my head, but in my gut. You can't just turn sexuality on and off like a light bulb."

"What did you tell her?"

"I gave her the name of Dr. Martin G. Dyer, a good Catholic doctor. I told her to do what he said."

"He'll find some medical reason to put her on the pill."

"Yes."

"Isn't that a bit hypocritical?"

"Come on, Bri. The church is already starting to change on that. Telling people they either have to have baby after baby or give up sex is crazy. Maybe criminal. And don't tell me rhythm works. It doesn't."

Brian sighed. "Sean, I don't have the problem with sex you have. I have the opposite one, in fact. I never told anybody this before, but in some way I'm relieved I don't have to deal with it."

"Relieved?"

"Yes. I can go for weeks without thinking about sex. Maybe it's a good thing I'm not a married man. I wonder if I could—perform—when I had to. And that makes me question my vocation sometimes. Am I hiding out?"

"It's all gotten so complicated, hasn't it? Is it just because we're getting older, or because the world has changed? It was so much easier in seminary."

"Maybe it's better that it's all up front, now. At least we have a shot of working out our problems. When it was all—buried—I think there was a lot of quiet desperation."

They were silent for a minute and then Brian said, "Sean, Peg is a good friend of yours, isn't she?"

"The best. Like the sister I never had."

"I never had a close woman friend. How do you manage it, without—you know—the other stuff getting involved?"

"Well, I just don't think of her that way. I just don't." But he shifted his eyes away from Brian's as he said it.

He finished the beer Brian had given him and went back to his room. "Lord, forgive my untruth," he prayed.

Why had he lied to Brian? Well, it was partly the truth. The women in his fantasies were carefully constructed to be as far away in physical type from Peggy Morrison as possible. The last was a long-haired Asian. At the rate he was going, trying to put distance between himself and Peg, he'd wind up fantasizing about Ho Chi Minh.

He had tried to tell himself that his sexual feelings about Peg were merely embers of memory, never again to blaze. The kiss in the bedroom disabused him of that notion. He had been so proud of his control: macho priest, keeping his prick under the dominion of his will. He wondered what he would have done if she had asked him to to make love to her. He thought of the feel of her lips against his, the gentle pressure of her breasts under the nightgown, her lovely, soft, *perky* breasts, and then he found himself with an erection.

Damn.

Macho priest was not doing very well. So far it was prick 2, macho priest 0.

He had already jerked off once today, and for a man of the cloth, twice was excessive. You could not justify twice on health grounds. Cold shower.

He gasped as the cold needles of water hit him, and he came out of the shower shivering but flaccid. This was getting ridiculous. He was sliding closer to the Flasher Priest every day.

As he shivered in the cold air of the room, it came—the need to be touched, held. This time the loneliness was not an ache but a bone-rattling pain. He had the sudden wish that he had a pet—a golden retriever, perhaps—something warm and alive that he could hold against his flesh. He shivered again. A dog, just the ticket. The Flasher Priest who sleeps with his dog. At least that would keep Brian awake during confession—indecent exposure and bestiality.

Sean walked to the dresser and picked up his book of Devotions to the Sacred Heart. He knelt by the bed.

"I know I ought to have the purity of an angel. Pardon my sensuality and the little guard I have kept over my senses. I sacrifice those eager desires I have to be esteemed and loved by others. Let me live, oh God, only for Thee. Fill me, body and soul, only with Thee."

In the seminary, when he asked God to possess him, God had complied. He felt an exultation that seemed to lift him from the ground; he was giddy with God, drunk with Him. It had been so wonderful.

A line from Shakespeare flitted across his mind. "I can call spirits from the vasty deep. / Why, so can I, or so can any man. But will they come when you do call for them?"

What was it he had conjured, that nineteen-year-old boy? The Living God? Or his own romantic illusions? Whatever the truth, Sean McCaffrey could no longer command God to fill him and expect Him to obey.

"Dear God, I'm so alone," he prayed. "I'm so confused and tired. Help me to go on. Help me."

And then he climbed into bed and went to sleep, not knowing whether his prayer would be answered.

TWELVE

"How was your weekend?" Con asked Peg. They were having lunch at their regular spot, the Washington Roof.

"I did veal marngo for Sean and Brian and we watched Errol Flynn kill Japs."

"There's two of your five guys. Just call St. Bernadette's and round up a few deacons."

"You are incorrigible. But you know, I think Brian has a little crush on me. He's adorable."

"Sounds like you're striking sparks with the wrong priest."

Peg sipped her wine quietly. Con looked at her.

"The edges of your mouth are curling. Out with it."

"It's nothing."

"Peg!"

"He kissed me. I was wrong about the engines being shut down."

"And afterwards?"

"He went home. Nothing since. I think it should stay that way."

"It won't, Peg."

"I'm not going to seduce him. If he comes to me—" she shrugged.

"Oh Peg, you know what's going to happen. You two little moths are going to flutter around the flame for a while and then zap, right in. Then what?"

"Who knows?"

"There are a thousand eligible guys in this town. Bill Forbes has been asking about you. A lot of guys would come running if you only showed some interest."

"I can get laid, Con. Anybody can get laid. I can't get *loved*. I only loved two guys in my life, and they both left me."

"Jeff *died*. That is not like running off with his secretary."

"I know. But I couldn't stop him from going to Vietnam. Funny, all the men who were important in my life left, one way or another. My father died, Jeff died, and Jack Goldman had a heart attack right in front of me. Sean went to the seminary. So you can see why I'm leery of starting out with some new guy."

"Oh Peg, you really did get clobbered, didn't you? At Immaculate Heart, I was sure you'd be the one who'd get carried off by Prince Charming, and I'd be the one without a man."

"And you turned out to be the first girl to get married. You met Lee, and bingo!"

"Are you still in love with Sean?"

"I guess I never stopped loving him, one way or another. Hell, we played doctor when we were six, he gave me my first kiss, he was my first lover. That's a lot of history."

"History reminds me, my mother says hello."

"Oh, how is she?"

"She will outlive us all. I go over for my weekly visit to the shrine of Saint Frank Wepplener, AKA my father. Strange how he has achieved beatification since he died from too much booze in the liver."

"Did he ever stop beating her up?"

"Never. Till the day he died, he was Joe Louis and she was Max Schmeling. I swore I'd never go back to that house, remember? I didn't, until he died. And now she keeps talking about what a happy family we were, what a good husband he was. It makes me crazy."

"Maybe she's happier that way, repressing it all."

"She's pissed at me because I'm working and I don't have much time to nip in for a little ancestor worship."

"The women's movement came thirty years too late for her."

"Oh, she's against it. She says, 'These women just need good husbands, like I had.'"

"Jesus Christ."

"Yeah, can you imagine? Just what Gloria Steinem wants in

her Chrismas stocking, the late, sainted Frank Wepplener, middleweight."

"Our mother's generation really did get messed up, didn't it?"

"Home, hearth, and kiddies, and nothing else. That was me too, for a while. If I hadn't gone to work, Peg, I would have ended up nuts. Not that I don't love Lee and the kids, but God, I was so bored. And now things are going so great for me and so badly for him. I wish he'd just get out of the damn navy."

"Think he will?"

"No. But I can't be good little navy wifey anymore. I don't hang around with navy people. Time for *me* to retire from the service, at any rate."

"Fourteen years. You earned your stripes."

"Yeah, but Lee got used to my being there, cheering him on. And now I think it's my turn. He says he understands, but I don't hear any cheering."

After lunch, Con was thinking about her friend as she drove to Foxhall Road. Con remembered the day she had officially adopted Peg, when Peg had written her first story for the *Messenger*. Even then, she had felt years older than Peg. She smiled as she remembered the mop of curly hair, those eager blue eyes, the vulnerability. She had introduced Peg to Edna St. Vincent Millay, Dorothy Parker, and the mangled version of Sigmund Freud. They had agonized together through all the adolescent crises; Peg was the only one who knew about her father, battling Frank.

And here it was, fourteen years later, and she still felt like tucking Peg under her wing. Maybe it was all those years riding in jeeps, but underneath the Pulitzer prize-winning globe-trotter was still the girl with the blue eyes who was so goddamned vulnerable. And then there was Sean, thirty-one going on seventeen. Ten years as a celibate, and now he was undoubtedly falling head over heels again for the only woman he'd ever been to bed with. The two of them belonged on "Romper Room."

Con sighed. The politics of men and women were *very* familiar to her; fourteen years in the navy had ensured that. She had watched as the women and men jockeyed for position, how they flirted and postured and sulked and gossiped, and how certain affairs turned out to be good for moving up, others kept you in Guam forever. It was enough to make a cynic out of Mary Poppins.

She had had two affairs herself. One was just to chastise Lee for neglecting her, but the other had been a dazzling, passionate fling. It had to end; two careers would have been wrecked, not to mention two marriages. But it was wonderful, for a while, the scent of danger adding to the spice. She had felt so alive.

And now she felt that way again, but it wasn't a man, it was her work. She wanted to share her excitement with Lee, but she'd see his eyes glaze over when she started in. He seemed to be closing her out, drawing up into an airless world of his own. But she didn't have time to agonize over it. All marriages went through good times and bad.

She pulled into the driveway at Foxhall Road, pleased to be seeing Kitty again. Kitty was smart, she liked using power and she wasn't afraid to admit it. A Washington hostess could be a person of considerable influence if she played her cards right. And Kitty knew how to deal.

Kitty greeted her warmly and said, "Well, Dan's really in it now. Oh Constance, I was so sure, but now—what if he loses?"

"That's always the chance you take, when you run for office."

"But I was the one who pushed him to take a stand against the war. He can blame me if it backfires."

"He won't do that. He knows you're in his corner."

"Yes, but this means so much to him. I wonder if I shouldn't have just kept my mouth shut."

"And then what if he'd lost? You'd blame yourself."

"Yes, but he wouldn't." She sighed. "Oh well. You wanted to talk to me about Father McCaffrey's group?"

Con explained about the funds Sean needed and Kitty listened attentively. Then she said, "Father McCaffrey is a very handsome man, Constance."

Con chuckled. "I figured you would notice."

"Is Peg in love with him?"

"Now how the hell did you know that?"

"Something in the way she wrote about him. And I remembered you said she had been in love with a man who went into the priesthood."

"Yeah, it was Sean. The two of them are big buddies now."

"Is that smart?"

"Not for Peg. She's a total idiot where he's concerned."

"Certain men have that effect on one, Con dear."

"Speaking from experience?"

"How did you guess? Congratulations, by the way, on the Halvorsen story."

"Thanks."

"Did Clay Firth put his hand on your knee?"

"Kitty, are you psychic?"

"No dear. Clay Firth put his hand on my knee, and I got a big donation to Hadassah Hospital. You don't think Senator Firth gives a damn about sick Jews, do you? Tell me, when are you going to bring that handsome husband of yours over here again?"

Con found herself telling Kitty all about Lee's troubles at the Pentagon, how he wanted to get to sea.

"Constance, let me make a few inquiries."

"You wouldn't mind?"

"Of course not. What are friends for? By the way, Senator Billington has been asking me quite a few questions about you."

"About me?"

"Yes. He seems quite taken with you. That is a friendship that could be useful. The presidential talk is already heating up."

"What, exactly, is *taken*?"

"He enjoys the company of bright, attractive women. Not always a let's-go-to-bed situation. Not that he's averse, if the woman is willing. But my dear, he is a civilized man, enjoys the company of women, bed or no."

"Isn't his wife ill?"

"Yes, she's been mentally ill for years. In and out of hospitals. George has been quite decent about it. They stay married, but only in name."

"So you think I ought to cultivate him?"

"Yes. I do have an ulterior motive, dear. He could do Dan a world of good. George is going right to the top. I am a good spotter of talent, Constance. Oh, I do miss a few. First time I met Ted Agnew I said he was a parvenu who'd never get out of Baltimore County. But there's no accounting for tastes."

Con made it a point, at a party at Kitty's the next night, to sidle up to George Billington. He was a tall man, well-built, with a receding hairline and an aquiline nose; he looked as if he could have posed for the bust of a Roman senator.

He had a manner, too, that she rarely encountered in men in politics. Old money and breeding had tempered the edge of ambition until it seemed only a faint aroma, like a subtle after-shave. Unlike so many men, he didn't need Washington to define him. His family hadn't come over on the *Mayflower*— that was for riffraff—but at the invitation of a royal governor who wanted to give his somewhat bumpkin colony a touch of class. And Kitty was right. He did enjoy the company of women, and he was not the sort who would push you up against a file cabinet while trying to get his pinkies under your pantyhose. They chatted about the hot topic of the moment, Henry Kissinger.

"The problem with Henry," George Billington said, "is that he thinks it's 1870 and he's Metternich. He adores jetting about and using the world like a chessboard. He is fairly good at it. But, of course, when Metternich slipped up, a few armies just blew the shit out of each other on a hillside in Prussia. Now we could all go up in smoke."

When George said "shit" in his elegant Connecticut tones, it sounded like the king's English.

"He's short," replied Con. "All short men want to be emperors. Napoleons."

"Yes, he'd like Henry the Great."

"No, that's much too mild. Henry the Magnificent would be acceptable."

"Yes, when he comes to the Hill, I always have the feeling he would not think it inappropriate if we prostrated ourselves on the floor of the Senate Caucus Room."

Senator Cale Canavan drifted over and said, "I hope I have your vote on the UN resolution on Israel, George."

"Sorry, Cale. If we throw out the Israelis for roughing up prisoners, half the Third World would have to go. Cale, this is Constance Masters, from the *Press Herald*."

Senator Canavan looked at her quizzically and said, "Have we met before?"

"I don't think so, Senator." She smiled, demurely.

Canavan drifted away and George Billington muttered, "Pompous prick."

Con said, "Actually, we did meet before. The last time I saw him I was pouring Scotch and water on his crotch."

George Billington looked at her, raised one fine patrician eyebrow, and said, "I think this is a story I want to hear."

The late afternoon sun turned the lawn on Foxhall Road a warm gold as Kitty greeted Peg, Sean, and Con and invited them into the living room, where she served canapés and a good white wine. The wine was a nice touch. It might have been taken as a hint of anti-Catholicism to just bring out the Jack Daniels and plonk it on the table. One wouldn't do that for a rabbi. Sean, Con noted, really did look handsome in the black suit with the turned-around collar. He was flashing those green eyes at Kitty for all they were worth.

"You have an interesting life, Father. Stopping wars and stopping highways."

"Rabbi Hillel said it was the duty of those who serve God to move beyond the narrow walls of the temple, Mrs. Cohen. I happen to agree."

The edges of Kitty's lips turned up, just perceptibly.

"I am not intimately acquainted with the works of the great Hillel," she said. "Unfortunately."

Sean smiled. "Actually, it was really Martin Luther King who changed everything for me. I had planned on a career in the foreign missions. Dr. King made me realize how much work there was to be done here."

His eyes were bright, Con noticed, as he spoke of King. He means it, she thought, he isn't just bullshitting.

"Dr. King taught all of us that the political process can be used by people who never used it before. There's a lot of talent, a lot of energy, out in those neighborhoods that look so run-down."

Peggy was beaming at Sean like a proud 4-H kid watching the judges pinch her prize heifer. And Sean was putting on a good show: an adroit mixture of boyish charm and political savvy. Kitty was leaning back against the cushion of the white Haitian cotton sofa, appraising him with that languid feline grace of hers. She would have regarded a Giacometti—or one of Michelangelo's heroic male nudes—with precisely the same degree of esthetic interest. Kitty was never overt when she found a man sexually interesting. You could tell only by a certain glint in those cool hazel eyes. Con wondered if, at this very instant, Kitty was entertaining a vision of Sean, stretched out on the lime-green imported Porthault sheets on the big bed upstairs, naked as the Florentine David. Kitty would never strip a man in her imagination merely to peer at his prick. She would compose a suitable artistic setting, the lighting of a Turner and a few strains of Bach—and *then* she'd peer at his prick.

Sean was leaning toward Kitty, listening intently as she spoke. He was, Con thought, a man aware of his own sensuality, and at the moment he was not above using it to get his environmental impact statement. She remembered, with a sudden clarity, the boy of eighteen, handsome, but tentative, and so klutzy he was always falling over his own feet. He was not uncertain now. There was a sureness about him that surprised her. He would make a good politician indeed.

"I understand you had some dificulties in Boston, Father," Kitty said.

"Call me Sean, please."

"If you'll call me Kitty."

"Well, the cardinal got annoyed when I said to the president of Eastern Airlines, 'What doth it profit a man if he gains the New York-to-Atlanta run, but loseth his own soul.'"

Kitty chuckled. "You said that in public?"

"Yes, at a Massport meeting on airport noise. It made the six o'clock news. The cardinal didn't laugh. I learned to confine myself to innocuous Biblical quotes."

"Such as?"

"If a man have ten goats he should bring them on the mountain, but if he have two goats, he should bring them to the stream."

Kitty laughed, appreciatively. She collected people who amused her, and Sean had definitely joined that group. Sean flashed Peg a quick smile.

He is showing off like crazy for her, Con thought. Strutting like a rooster.

Kitty suggested that Sean and Peg take a walk around the garden to see her late fall blooms, and she and Con watched through the window as the dark-haired young man and the fair young woman strolled along the cobbled walk.

"Tell me," Kitty asked, "is he as ingenuous as he appears? Or did he check a book on Hillel out of the library yesterday?"

Con laughed. "Sean is a smart cookie. But the idealism is real."

Kitty's eyes followed Sean. "I'll call my friend Phil Bernstein at Systems, Inc. He owes me a favor." She paused. "He is a bit vain. Just a bit."

"Sean?"

"Yes. Look at the fit of his suit. Tight in the ass and neat across the shoulders. He's had it altered. Most clergymen bag in the seat."

"I love to see the gears turning in that mind of yours. What else?"

"He is ambitious. I suspect that makes him uncomfortable. Moody, too, I bet. Black Irish, not the ruddy peasant sort. Irishmen like that usually end up as poets or IRA gunmen. Or drunks. But witty ones. Brendan Behan types."

"This is fascinating. Go on."

"Sex. That is a very sexual man, celibate or not. No wonder Peg's in love with him. But I do worry about her, Constance."

"I do too."

"There's something fragile about her. When I read her stories, I can almost feel her reaching, growing. She's peeling layers off things, and in doing that, she's revealing herself. She hasn't quite found her voice yet, but I think it is going to be one of the really interesting ones. If she doesn't get cut down in the process. This can be a vicious town, if the dogs turn on you."

"Yes, Peg's a tough lady in one way. She'd go any damn place. But there's a part of her that's very vulnerable, she's been hurt so much. My hide is a lot tougher."

"Constance, my dear, you be careful. To be an ambitious woman in Washington is like walking in a mine field. Don't get cocky."

"Noted. And I'll remember."

It was late that night before Con considered her day finished. She got dinner for the boys, warmed it up for Lee when he came home, and put the finishing touches on a story while

Lee went over papers he had brought home from the Pentagon. It was after eleven by the time she went into the study to join Lee. It was *his* study, even though she worked at home often, using the kitchen table. She would not have thought of using the lovely rolltop desk in the study. The desk was a symbol of the fact that it was *his* job that was the important one.

He was sitting in the Barcalounger, his Father's Day present, having a Scotch. The bottle was open on the desk.

"Hi hon," she said. "How was your day?"

"Lousy." His speech was fuzzy around the edges, more so than usual after he had had a drink.

"Can I get you something to nibble on? Cheese and crackers?"

"No." He was silent, sipping his Scotch. He was still as trim as he had been in his Academy days. He took good care of his body. The face, though, had changed. Lines were etched in his forehead and the blue eyes, which had once been merry, were duller and darker now. It was more often anger than laughter that flickered in them. Something had gone very wrong today, she was sure. She could read his expressions, after fourteen years, like the morning headlines.

"Do you want to talk about it?"

"No."

"Honey, you can't just keep everything inside like this."

"I don't want to talk, dammit!"

"Lee, don't shut me out!"

He stood up to pour himself another shot, and stumbled as he did so. He was drunker than she had ever seen him, and he was a man who could hold his liquor.

"Don't have any more, please."

"Are you saying I'm a drunk?" he snapped.

"Of course not. You've just had a little too much."

"Big shot reporter, on TV and everything, you really like to stick it to me, don't you?"

"That's not fair! I never criticize you. You've gotten nothing but support from me, Lee. It's not fair!"

He laughed, bitterly. "You don't have to *say* anything, Constance. I see it in your face."

"You are imagining things."

"Who are you going to bed with?"

The question startled her. "What?"

"You looked like a whore the other night, flashing your tits around in that dress."

"You used to like that dress. And I was not, as you so quaintly put it, flashing my tits around."

"Who's grabbing them? Some stud over at the TV station? Or maybe some pansy from Foggy Bottom?"

She looked at him, astonished. The anger fairly crackled along his skin. Was this Lee, who kept everything under control? She had never seen him like this.

"Lee, I am not sleeping with anybody."

"Don't lie to me. I know you're putting out for somebody, and it sure as hell isn't me."

"You're the one who's asleep when your head hits the pillow, not me."

"Now you're saying I can't get it up?"

"Dammit, I did *not* say that, I just said—"

And then he slapped her, hard across the face, with the palm of his hand. She just stood, stunned, looking at him. He had never hit her; in fourteen years of marriage he had not so much as raised a hand to her.

"You slut!" he said, and he doubled his fist and punched her hard in the stomach. She sank to her knees, wondering if she was hallucinating. This couldn't be happening.

"Oh you slut!" His words slurred badly. He reached down and grabbed her by the hair and punched her in the face. Her senses began to blur. He punched her again, in the stomach. She found herself lying on the floor.

It isn't happening!

And then he kicked her, once, twice, three times, in the ribs, viciously.

A jet of anger washed across her and she got to her feet panting, and ran into the kitchen, holding her stomach. She heard his footsteps as he came after her. She fumbled with the kitchen drawer, yanking it so hard it fell out and the utensils scattered all over the floor. She reached down and picked up the knife Lee always used to cut the roast. A starburst of white-hot hatred ignited in her brain, blocking out the fear and the pain.

He came in the room and walked toward her, both fists in a

knot, his face white, his eyes those of some animal. She held the knife out in front of her.

"If you come near me, I'll kill you, you bastard!"

He stopped, saying nothing.

"You lay another hand on me, and I'll stick this in your rotten heart, do you hear me? I don't care if you *are* my father!"

His mouth opened in surprise, and he turned and walked out of the room. She stood, trembling, the knife in her hand. *What had she said? What was it she had just said?*

She stood absolutely still, and then she heard a sound from the study. Then more muffled, choked sounds. A man crying.

She went into the study, the knife in her hand, and she saw him, his head dropped in his hands, sitting at his desk, crying. He looked up when he saw her and said, "Oh my God, what did I do!" The animal was gone from his eyes.

The hallucinatory sense was still with her. It seemed to her as if she were watching this on a stage someplace, a spectator.

"Lee," she said, "you go upstairs and pack some things and you leave right now."

He sat still. "I'm sorry. Oh God, what did I do?"

"You leave right now." She was astonished that her voice was steady; she felt absolutely calm. "Do you understand?"

He nodded, got up and went upstairs. When he came back he had his suitcase in his hand. She was still holding the knife.

"Oh God!" he moaned.

"Go quickly, please."

"I didn't, I—oh God!"

"Go now or I will call the police."

He walked out the door and closed it behind him. She stood in the hallway, clutching the knife. She had no idea how long she stood that way. Five minutes. An hour? It was a dream. She would blink her eyes and it would disappear. She blinked. Her face and her stomach still hurt.

She went into the kitchen. Eleven-thirty. Not late. It should be late. Why? No idea. She felt a tentative grip on reality, as if the room around her might just shatter into fragments, a broken mirror, and disappear. She walked to the phone and dialed.

"Peg?" Her voice sounded odd to her. Tinny.

"Con? Is anything wrong?"

"Lee just beat me up."

"What!"

"Strange, isn't it?"

"Where is he now?"

"Gone. Packed his suitcase and left."

"Oh my God, I'll be over as fast as I can."

Con went into the study and sat on a chair. She tried to decide what she was feeling. She was aware of pain, all over. But no feelings. She put her hand to her cheek and it was warm and sticky. Blood. A thought wandered into her mind. The boys. She fell, got mugged. Yes, at the paper, in the parking lot, someone had hit her and taken her purse. Why is Daddy gone? Trip? San Diego. No, he was here when they went to bed. Why wouldn't her brain work right? The boys couldn't know. But why couldn't she *think?*

Then she heard a knock on the door and when she opened it, Peg rushed in, out of breath. Con saw the horror in her face when she looked at her. She had forgotten, she must look a sight.

"Oh *Con!*" Peggy said.

Peg took Con's hand, led her to the kitchen and sat her down in a chair. She began to wash her face, gently, with a cloth.

"Did he hit you anyplace else?"

"Ribs, he kicked me."

"Does it hurt?"

"Yes."

"Tomorrow, you get X-rays. Oh Con, how did it happen?"

"He was drinking. Accused me of sleeping around. And then he hit me. If I hadn't stopped him, he'd have beat me up real bad."

"How did you stop him?"

"The carving knife. I said I'd kill him. I would have, too. Funny thing. I said something weird."

"What?"

"'I'll kill you, even if you are my father.'"

"Oh, Con!"

"Yeah. There is a certain irony to this, Peg. I used to do this for my mother. Now I'm *her*. How's that for a neat trick? The one person in the world I didn't want to be."

"You're not her."

"What do I look like? Am I a mess?"

"Not too bad."

Con laughed; the laugh had an edge of hysteria to it. "That's exactly what I used to say to her! Whoops, here I am, Mrs. Frank Wepplener. Oh, this is funny!"

"Con, you fought back, you didn't let him do it to you. She never fought."

"That's right, isn't it."

"Yes."

"The one thing I knew would never happen when I married Lee, was this. I knew he would never be like my father. I married him because he *wasn't* like my father. Was it me, Peg? Did I make him do this?"

"No. No blaming the victim."

"You're right. It wasn't me. I never saw him like that. Crazy. Mean. I won't be like her, Peg. I will not be like her."

"Do you want a drink?"

"Yeah, if ever I needed one, it's now."

Peg fixed Con a drink. Then gave her a painkiller. "Where did he go?"

"I don't know. Out. He was crying. But I saw his eyes when he was doing it. My father's eyes."

Con took a swallow of the drink. "I don't want the boys to know. I won't have them pulled apart like I was. I was so wretched when it would happen. So helpless."

"We'll figure out a story, Con."

"He does love the boys, I know that."

"Maybe he'll get help."

"Lee, get help? The original macho man. Peg, he did the one thing I can't forgive him for. I could forgive running around with women, if he stole, if he was a spy. But *this!* I will never, ever be made to feel this way again. Never, Peg!"

"You're shaking. Come on, you should be in bed. I'll stay here tonight."

"We have to have a story, I got mugged—"

"I'll think of something."

Con crawled into bed and Peg pulled the covers over her and rubbed her forehead, gently.

"Do you still hurt?"

"Yes. but I'm getting kind of numb. The medicine is working. Or the Scotch."

"I'll be here, Con."

"Good," she said, and she was asleep in a minute.

THIRTEEN

Sean drove past the sign on the Baltimore-Washington Parkway that said Greenbelt. Peg, sitting beside him, was poring over a map.

"I called Con this morning," he said. "She sounded pretty cheerful. But you know Con. She puts on that tough lady act. I asked if I could help. Tell her that I mean it. It's not just talk."

"I will. She has a crack in her rib, but otherwise she's okay. She and Lee are separated. I think that marriage is blown sky-high. With Con's history, he did the worst thing possible. I still have trouble believing that Lee really did that. But Lee is seeing a lot of the boys, so it's not as bad as it could be."

"Sounds pretty awful to me."

"Yeah. Sean, do you know where North Avenue is? I don't know Baltimore very well."

"Yeah, I can find it. Peg, you're sure you want to do this?"

"It's a good story. If Elmore Brown has something to say, I want to hear it."

"So does the FBI. Peg, I did a lot of soul-searching on this. If it's possible that he's innocent, then it's my obligation to help. He's in my parish. I can't just say go away!"

"I think that's right." She stretched, folded the map. "The Panthers are an interesting group. A real mix of revolution-aries, street-smart dudes, college kids, some real street scum, too. They've done some good things, like the breakfast pro-grams. But let's face it, any group that comes out of the ghetto isn't going to be Harvard boys."

"They terrify white people."

"Of course, that's the point. A lot of the militant stuff is guerrilla theater. Mau-mauing the whites is a kick. But it can backfire. The black man on a rampage is a real nightmare to whites."

"Who take it seriously."

"Yes. A lot of whites are scared enough to want the Panthers wiped out. Any way at all. Legal or not."

"So what exactly did happen with Elly Brown?"

"When a black family moved into a white neighborhood in Moore County, some white kids firebombed the house. So the Panthers moved in to protect them. It seems the county cops got a report that arms were being stockpiled in the house. The cops say that when they moved in, shots were fired from the house. They say that a Panther gun killed a neighbor who was standing on his front porch."

"But Mrs. Brown says that there were no guns in the house. All the shooting was done by the police."

"One thing does sound strange. The man who was killed was on a porch on the same side of the street as the house. Police say a bullet fired from the house ricocheted and hit him."

"And three Panthers were killed?"

"Yes. Elly Brown and two others went out the back window and got away down the alley."

"Peg, do you think the cops are lying?"

"Well, suppose Mrs. Brown is right. There weren't any guns in the house. But the cops went in expecting some kind of arsenal. They'd be pretty keyed up."

"And the Moore County cops aren't the best in the world."

"No. They haven't had any training for this kind of thing. So it's possible that somebody hears a noise, and everybody opens fire."

"Where was the family?"

"Staying with friends in Baltimore. Because of death threats."

"And the cops knew that?"

"Apparently. So they rush in and find three dead men and no arms. What's the natural instinct?"

"Cover it up."

"Sure. You wouldn't expect them to come out and say,

'Sorry, folks, we just shot three unarmed men in cold blood and popped off a neighbor by mistake.'"

They drove to North Avenue, a street in Baltimore's black ghetto. Sean pulled up in front of a brick row house. They got out, went up the cement steps, and Sean knocked. A voice from behind the closed door said, "Who's there?"

"Father McCaffrey."

The door opened a crack. Then it opened halfway and a young black man wearing jeans, with a red bandanna around his head, ushered them in. He spoke not a word, but motioned for them to follow him upstairs. In a small bedroom, furnished only with a table and three chairs, Elmore Brown was waiting. Sean would not have recognized him. He had grown a full beard and was dressed in jeans and a shabby shirt. It was easy to see how he could disappear into the streets of the ghetto.

"Elly?" Sean said.

Elmore Brown nodded to Sean and Peg, indicating that they should sit down. When they did, he said, "They're lying."

Peg took out her notebook. "Your mother says you told her there were no guns in the house. Is that true?"

"Yes. We knew that if we had weapons, that would just give the cops an invitation to move in. We weren't stupid enough to have guns."

"Any weapons at all?"

"Nunchucks. Clubs. Just to protect ourselves. But no guns."

"The police claim a shot was fired from an upstairs window."

Elly Brown shook his head. "Those turkeys. I heard something. It might have been a car backfire. Or a door slamming. Then they just started shootng. Go *look* at the place. I mean, man, it was like World War Three, the bullets were all over."

"At the press conference the next day, the cops held up rifles they said they took out of the house."

"Sure they took them out. After they brought them in. There wasn't one goddamn gun in that house, and I *know* that."

"What about the neighbor? They claim he was shot from inside the house."

"Yeah a whole platoon of cops coming at us, and we're taking target practice on neighbors. Come on! I'll tell you what we hear. That there's an autopsy report that shows it was a police bullet that killed that sucker. But nobody ain't ever going to see it. No way."

"Are you sure there is one?"

"That's what we hear. Are you going to write our side? Nobody wants to listen to us. We're just a bunch of black punks; whitey is happy if we're dead. What are you going to write, lady?"

"I'm going to tell your version of the story. I'm going to try to get my hands on that autopsy report, if I can."

Elly Brown laughed. "Man, that report is buried so deep, it's halfway to China by now."

Despite his bravado, Peg could see that his hands were shaking. He was a very frightened young man, with good reason.

"Elly," Sean said, "your mother wonders if you shouldn't just turn yourself in and try for a fair trial."

Elly Brown snorted. "A fair trial? For me? Tell me another one."

Peg got Elly Brown to give her every detail he could remember on the shooting. When they got up to leave she asked, "How can I reach you if I have to?"

He wrote down a phone number. "Ask for Mr. Hawkins. That'll get to me."

Back on the expressway, Sean and Peg rode in silence for a while. Then Peg said, "I got to figure some way to get that autopsy report."

"Well, I don't know if I ought to suggest this—"

"What?"

"There's a group out in Moore County. Catholics for Peace and Justice. They're a pretty radical group."

"Are they part of the group that dumped blood on draft records in Baltimore?"

"Right. They're pretty good at—getting stuff."

"You mean stealing it?"

"Did I say that?"

She grinned. "Of course not, *Father* McCaffrey. You didn't say that."

"Oh my God, what am I getting involved in?"

"Just give me a name, Sean. Other than that, you're out of it."

"Father Jim Brannigan. Peg, what's the—journalistic ethics—of taking stolen property. I mean, if someone could make a Xerox of the report?"

"*I* wouldn't break in and steal it, but if I got something that could prove a man is innocent of murder, I'd use it. I sure as hell would."

Sean dropped her off at the paper and drove back toward St. Nasty's. The scent of her perfume lingered, still, in the seat beside him. When she had asked him to dinner he had suggested a restaurant instead. He was not too sure, these days, of his strength, and it had been one of his proudest accomplishments, once. To be a priest was to be able to do things ordinary men could not do. He rather enjoyed, in the old days, putting that strength to the test.

One day in seminary Father Peter had warned them against excessive fasting; a seminarian in Rhode Island had died after a four-day fast. Sean, who had been uninterested in fasting, promptly began a secret fast. It was his week to serve in the dining hall, so it was easy to do. On the sixth day of the fast he fainted, and Dennis, his roommate, found him lying senseless and carried him to the bed; woke him.

"Sean, have you been fasting?"

"Of course not, Dennis. Get me some orange juice, please. I think I'm coming down with a cold."

"Okay, Sean. I'm glad you haven't been fasting. Father Peter would have been angry."

Dennis left and Sean mumbled, "Right, Dennis, I was in a stupor on the floor because of a head cold. Lord, forgive my uncharity, but sometimes that kid is not exactly swift."

Father Peter would have been furious, of course, but Sean felt strong and proud. There was nothing he could not do. With God's help, of course.

It had been galling for him to discover he could not banish lust by sheer force of will. But he had never truly violated his vow of celibacy and now, while he could not keep his old lover from the realm of his fantasies, he could keep himself under rigid control around her. The only alternative was to cut himself off completely from seeing her, and the thought of that sent a spiraling gray mist through his brain. He hadn't realized how important their time together had become, a bright oasis in the stark landscape of his life. The thought of not seeing her sent a shiver of desolation along his spine. No, he could keep in control. He was stronger than other men. If that was pride, so be it. Macho priest was alive and well and living in Takoma Park.

He went into the rectory, and as he walked through the dark front hall, a shadowy figure stepped out of the dining room and seized him by the arm.

"Ahhh!" Sean yelped. Then he smelled the Scotch and he relaxed. Father Barry.

"Do you know what they are doing? You must *stop* them, Father!"

"Who? Doing what?"

"Stealing. They are stealing from the beano. The old ones, the senior citizens. They are smuggling in cards they don't pay for. The old lady, the Spanish one. With the gold tooth."

"Mrs. Ramirez?"

"Yes, and the colored man. Mr. Carver. You must stop them. This crime must be stopped! We will search everyone when they come in."

"Frisk them? Father, I don't think—"

"Perhaps we can set a trap. Special marks on the card that leave a stain on the hands of the culprit. I saw that on 'Naked City.'"

"But Father—"

"You are in charge, Father. Throw the moneylenders out of the temple! Like Christ did."

"I don't think the moneylenders were playing beano, Father."

"You are responsible!" Father Barry ordered, spun on his heel and walked away.

Sean sighed, a martyred sigh. Perhaps Father Barry was God's reminder to Sean McCaffrey that he was not such a big shot. *Beano Patrol.* Maybe a few German shepherds and storm troopers could do it, in a lightning raid on Loyola Hall.

The doors swung open. They had arrived. Their very name struck terror into the hearts of men. The St. Ignatius Loyola Beano Patrol! A hush fell on the room as the voice of the caller froze in his throat. "Under the b—"

The Oberführer Priest strode in, dogs at his heel, his cold green eyes surveying the room. He walked slowly up to Mrs. Ramirez and stopped. Her hands were trembling.

"Mrs. Ramirez, you are cheating at the beano." His men

grabbed her purse, emptied it on the table. The damning evidence was there. Two illegal beano cards.

"You lied to me, Mrs. Ramirez!"

"Have mercy, please!"

His men dragged the old woman to her feet. He slapped her across the face.

"Mrs. Ramirez, did you think you could escape the Beano Patrol!"

She fell to her knees, but his men dragged her off to the truck, screaming. Mr. Carver tried to make a break for it, to the men's room. The Oberführer Priest got the bullhorn.

"Come out, Mr. Carver. There is no point in resisting."

"You'll never get me!" Mr. Carver screamed through the door.

"Come out, or you will die like a dog!"

"Never!"

The Oberführer Priest nodded. The troopers riddled the men's room with machine guns, putting small holes in urinals two and three and Mr. Carver.

The Beano Patrol took its leave. "Proceed with your game, ladies and gentlemen," said the Oberführer Priest. "It's twenty-five cents a card and remember, all proceeds go to buy new altar linens."

Dan Amundsen took a sip of scotch on the rocks and shook his head. He and Kitty were having a cocktail in the living room.

"I don't know," he sighed. "The polls are like smoke. Lots of confusion."

He had been back in the state for a week and a half, campaigning. He was well received, but the polls were worrying him.

"Adam and his polls. If the polls said you should expose yourself in Lafayette Park, Adam would have his hand on your fly."

"You don't like him, do you."

"I think he's the most amoral man I've ever met. There's no—center to him, Dan. He's like a hurricane, all wind at the edges and dead still at the core. I don't know who he is. I don't think he does either." She sighed. "Dan, do we have to put in an appearance at the congressional reception tonight?"

"Yes, bad form if we don't."

"I know. I just hope the Nixons don't have some has-been movie stars again."

"The Democrats have all the good stars. *We* have Paul Newman and Marlon Brando."

"But Bonita Granville? Surely they could get someone who isn't in reruns of 'Lassie.'"

"Pat and Dick *like* 'Lassie,' Kit. This is not the New Frontier."

"It certainly is not. With Jackie we got Pablo Casals. Tonight it'll probably be Herbie Hampton and his Harmonocats."

"What have you got against harmonicas? I used to play one."

"You didn't."

"Yes, at the 4-H Fair. I did a solo. 'Lady of Spain.' I was very good."

"Dan, darling, do me a favor."

"What?"

"Don't mention that to Len Fineberg. He just gave two million to the Pittsburgh Symphony."

"So he would appreciate musicianship."

"Dan, Jews do not play the harmonica. The violin, yes. The grand piano, yes. Lennie Bernstein would *die* before he'd touch a harmonica."

"If you ask me, the score for *West Side Story* could have used 'Lady of Spain.'"

"You are an impossible man."

He leaned over and kissed her. "Time to get undressed, dark lady."

"Don't you mean dressed?"

He put his hand on her backside. "I am starving for your body, woman."

"I missed yours a little bit too."

"Did you, now?"

"Just a little."

"I bet a lot." He nibbled on her ear. "Let's try something new." He whispered in her ear.

She sighed. "I was a respectable widow lady before I met you. Now I am a slut."

"Come on, Kit, don't be shy."

"Oh all right. But there is one thing you must never, never ask me to do in bed, Dan."

He frowned. "What's that, Kit?"

"Play the harmonica."

"Oh Kit, my funny, funny lady. How did I ever get so lucky as to find you?"

Peg hung up the phone, leaned her elbows on her desk and frowned. Con had called to tell her that Kitty wanted to confer with Sean on the details of the Action fundraiser she was throwing. The glint in Kitty's beautiful hazel eyes when she looked at Sean had not escaped her notice. Peg was not a jealous sort. It was only Sean who brought out the green-eyed monster in her. She had watched Kitty ogling Sean the other day and had thought, idly, about tearing her eyes out. It would make a nice column for Con:

PULITZER PRIZE WINNER

TEARS EYES FROM HOSTESS

IN LOVE DUEL OVER PRIEST

What was Kitty's notion of *confer*? She saw Kitty, unbuttoning Sean's shirt and taking off his collar. She would be saying, as she ran her tongue up his bare chest and licked his nipple, "Oh Father, you must tell me more about the great Hillel!"

And Sean, the rat fink, was unhooking Kitty's bra and slipping his hand down inside her fifty-dollar-a-pair satin panties from Givenchy while he quoted some piece of wisdom from the learned rabbi. Peg saw them lying on the Kerman rug and Kitty was digging her nails into Sean's back and Sean was moaning away. He had always been a big moaner, Sean had. Nothing quiet about him when it came to sex.

"*Shit!*" Peg said, snapping her pencil in half. How could she concentrate on Vietnam Vets Against the War when she was so goddamn horny? Maybe Con was right, maybe she should just go out and get herself laid and be done with it.

No, it wasn't any good. There was only one person she wanted to get laid by. By whom she wanted to get laid. Never end a sentence with a preposition.

157

She looked up and saw Tom Friedman going into his office. She went over, rapped on his door and entered.

"Possible new development in the Brown story."

"What's that?"

"There's a Catholic group that's going to try to get hold of the autopsy report for me. I did not ask how."

"Meaning they're going to steal it?"

"Probably. But they didn't say and I didn't ask."

"Don't. I want us to be able to say we didn't know it was stolen." He leaned back in his chair. "I want to let you know that I think we're going to come out editorially for scrapping Interstate 80. You were very persuasive."

"Not to John Barret Putman the Third," she said. Putnam, the national editor, was Harvard, ex-*Washington Post*, and arrogant.

"You let me worry about him. Just keep after that autopsy report."

Peg left Tom's office and dialed Con.

"How about lunch?"

"Sorry, keed, I'm booked. Tell you about it later."

Lunch, for Con, was at the Watergate apartment of Senator George Billington. They had salmon mousse served by the cook, and after lunch she found herself stretched out, naked, on his bed, as the senator nibbled, languidly, on her left breast.

"God, you have such a beautiful body!" he said.

"Ummmm, that's nice," Con murmured. "Don't stop." She gave a little sigh of contentment. He was not the first man to tell her she had a beautiful body, but she was always a little surprised to hear it. Women who were chubby as teenagers always carry their fat persona with them through life, a little pull toy clacking quietly along behind. Con was certain that her old hips were lurking around someplace, just waiting to leap out at her—aha!—and reattach themselves. A fat soul lived in the body of the slender Constance.

She and the senator had started off talking about Cambodia and ended up nibbling on each other's private parts. How it had happened she wasn't sure. It probably had a lot to do with her battered ego. George Billington was bright, witty, rich and he didn't want to use her as a punching bag. He was very good in bed, careful in his attentions not to hurt her rib.

All in all, it was a pleasant interlude, and afterward, he didn't just roll over and go to sleep. He brought them both brandy, and he touched her side gently.

"I'm sorry they hurt you," he said.

"I should have just let them have the damn purse."

She hadn't told anybody except Peg and Kitty about what had happened—just as in high school she had never told anyone but Peg about her parents. Nobody was ever going to feel sorry for Constance Marie Wepplener Masters.

Kitty had been very solicitous, making Con wonder if she had ever had the same problem.

"Did a man ever hit you, Kitty?"

"Once, in my pre-Morris days. He was a Jewish prince, in med school. He slapped me. I hit him in the head with a bookend. Constance, one simply must not accept that sort of behavior."

"I know. I won't."

"Many women do, my dear. It would surprise you how many wives of high-ranking men don't come to parties some nights because of a headache that's really a black eye. But they're trapped by money and prestige. By the way, how did you find George Billington in bed?"

Con laughed. "Shit, Kitty, do you have bugs in everybody's bedroom?"

"George had a very satisfied look on his face this morning. And he was singing your praises. It's not hard to put two and two together."

"He's very good in bed. I suppose you've heard that report before."

"Not too often. George likes women, but he is not compulsive about it. He knows your publisher very well, by the way."

"I don't want to use him that way, Kitty."

"My dear, I do not mean that you should shriek out while he is in the middle of cunnilingus, 'Get me the Hill!' You can be subtle, Constance."

"Do you have *files*, Kitty? How on earth do you remember who likes what?"

"It is somewhat difficult. You would be amazed, my dear, at the wide variety of sexual practices in our stuffy little town. There is a subcabinet official who likes to wear a black dress and pearls. He went out like that when he was in Geneva for the SALT talks."

"Oh my God! And he has a security clearance?"

"Yes, but he's been dropped from the social register. His pearls were paste."

"This is wonderful. Tell me more."

"There is a congressman from a very conservative state who likes to be walked on in six-inch heels."

"Does he have a committee?"

"No dear, put away your spikes. He's not well-connected."

"Too bad. I'd walk on his tail for a real hot exclusive."

"It's not his tush he wants walked on, Constance."

"You're kidding."

"No, dear. And he *volunteered* for committees on the postal service and inland waterways, so you know he really is into pain. And there's a presidential hopeful who adores black lace crotchless panties."

"What's wrong with that?"

"He *wears* them, Constance."

"Oh."

"He'll never make it past New Hampshire. One trip to the urinal at the Sheraton Wayfarer and Jack Anderson would have those black panties spread across page one."

"Your depth of knowledge never ceases to amaze me."

"People have to talk about something at parties, Constance. Disarmament gets to be a bore."

Con helped Kitty with the arrangements for the Action fundraiser. Kitty did confer with Sean, but it was just white wine and mild flirting, no nipple-licking. She rounded up a good array of monied types: some ADA sorts who liked giving to liberal causes; social climbers who wanted to be the first in on a chic new cause; rich women bored with their husbands and looking for ways to spend money, along with a few of Morris' old business friends. At first, things were a little stiff, but Alex Hernandez, the young, charismatic leader of La Raza, sang stirring songs and played the guitar, the liquor flowed, and the members of Action became a little less awed by the surroundings and began to chat with Kitty's guests. Peg floated around, trying to get a sense of how things were going. In one corner, a well-dressed older man was making small talk with Alex.

"Where are you from, Mr. Hernandez?"

"Arecibo, originally."

"In Mexico?"

"No, Puerto Rico."

"Oh, I thought that was the place where the boys dive off the cliffs."

"No, that's Acapulco."

"Acapulco, right. These Spanish names sound a lot alike. Did you have any trouble getting a visa?"

"I beg your pardon."

"A visa. To get into the country."

"From where?"

"Puerto Rico."

"Puerto Rico is part of the United States."

"It is?"

"Yes."

"I didn't know that. So there aren't any Puerto Rican wet-backs?"

"No. We all come by Pan Am."

Peg drifted to another corner, where Chuck Washington was being admired by a woman wearing a Halston jersey and pearls the size of ball bearings. She was fingering the sleeve of Chuck's dashiki.

"Mr. Washington, do you wear this to show your pride in your African heritage?"

"Yeah, I do."

"Oh, it must be wonderful to be attached to your roots, to come up from oppression and slavery! Were your ancestors slaves, Mr. Washington?"

"No, they lived in Pittsburgh. Ran a bakery."

"Oh," she said, disappointed. "But maybe they came North by the underground railway? Followed the drinking gourd?"

"Near's I can figure out, they always lived in Pittsburgh."

"Did your dashiki come from Africa?"

"Could be."

"Did you get it at an African boutique?"

"Sears Roebuck in Wheaton. They got lots of them in men's sportswear."

Peg saw Sean across the room and she walked over to him. "How are we doing?" he asked.

"I just heard Estella telling the assistant secretary of state for

Latin American affairs that our foreign policy is anti-Hispanic."

"Oh God, Estella wouldn't open her mouth three months ago. Now she's making foreign policy. How about Chuck?"

"A while ago he was telling some lady about Sing-Sing."

"Sing-Sing? Chuck's never been in prison."

"He didn't say he'd *been* there, exactly."

"Oh God!" Sean groaned.

Then Kitty came up, grabbed Sean's arm and whisked him off to meet someone. Dan was out in the state, and Kitty, Peg noticed, always liked to have a man on her arm. A handsome one.

Peg saw Con and went over to get her assessment of how things were going.

"Sean is making a big hit with Kitty's rich ladies. And Donna Du Bently is feeling up Alex's guitar. She's big on Latins. Had a fling with the Brazilian chargé last year."

"Isn't she the heir to the cold cream fortune? She alone could keep Action going forever."

"She alone could kill Alex. I hear she's insatiable."

"Alex is tough. All that lettuce picking."

"Where did Alex ever pick lettuce?"

"Out of his salad at MIT. So he's not a bracero. He can hot-wire a Titan."

They were quiet for a minute and then Peg said, "Have you talked to Lee?"

"We're meeting for lunch tomorrow. It's the first time I'll see him—except when he's picked up the boys—since—" She shrugged. "He wants us to get back together."

"What about you?"

"No. I don't think we'll ever get back, Peg."

Bill Forbes, from the State Department, came up and greeted Peg warmly. "It's great to see you again."

"Bill! I didn't know you'd be here." She had been out to dinner with him three times and found him witty and charming. But that was all.

"Kitty told me about this shindig and I thought I'd drop over."

They chatted for a bit and he asked her out for a drink after the party.

"I'd love to, but I promised Sean—Father McCaffrey—that we'd get together afterwards."

"He's an interesting man, Father McCaffrey. Getting to be quite well-known."

Peg looked over at Sean, still in Kitty's clutches, and saw him frowning. She turned to Bill and gave him her most dazzling smile, thinking, as she did so, Peg, this is really stupid. You are acting like you are sixteen years old, back at the teen canteen, trying to make your boyfriend jealous.

As she and Bill chatted, she looked around and saw Con, talking to Senator George Billington. Con was leaning forward, and the senator had his hand on Con's shoulder, and Peg knew right away that something was going on there.

It was all very strange. Lee wanted Con, who looked very much like she wanted George Billington; Kitty was looking at Sean like a cat at catnip and Sean was frowning like he was just a bit jealous of Bill Forbes, who wanted Peg but Peg didn't want him, she wanted Sean, whom she shouldn't want. Oh Christ, tune in tomorrow, folks. Can a woman over thirty find happiness with a man who has taken vows of poverty, chastity, and obedience? And is she an idiot if she tries?

When the last guests had drained the last of the liquor, Sean, Peg, Con, and Kitty sat together on the couch and counted up the pledges.

"Thirty-eight thousand dollars," announced Kitty.

"My God, that's wonderful!" Sean said. "With that money we can get started on a community center. Kitty, you are a saint!"

Kitty smiled. "The archbishop would be surprised at a saint named Cohen."

Peggy and Sean walked together to the driveway, where both their cars were parked. Peggy had been waiting for this time. She and Sean could sit together, sharing a glass of wine at her apartment, celebrating the successful conclusion of the party.

"Peg, this was your doing. I owe it all to you. I don't know how to thank you, best friend."

He leaned over and kissed her chastely, on the cheek. He was wearing the same aftershave he used to wear years ago. The scent brought back a visceral memory; his body, naked, next to hers. She trembled, and he pulled away, quickly. His body tightened as he moved a respectable distance away from her.

"Come on over, we'll break out some champagne, and we'll toast a big day for Action."

He frowned. "Peg, I'm awful beat."

"We'll make it a quickie."

"I really can't."

In a minute she was going to make a real fool of herself, like the fat girl asking the captain of the football team to the prom: "I'll give you my priceless collection of Captain Marvel comics, my fathers car, my body, the dog, two hundred shares of Bell Labs from my grandmother's will."

"Well, Sean," she said lightly, "I will just sit and drink alone." She hoped her disappointment didn't show on her face. She had been battling memories, assaulting her like mosquitoes, all day. It was exactly two years ago, today, that Jeff had died in the flaming hulk of the chopper in the Mekong. She wanted to say to Sean, "I don't want to be alone tonight. I need you, Sean. I don't want to imagine the things I am going to imagine, alone. Oh God, I hope it was fast. I hope he never knew. Please God."

But she looked at him and saw the lines of exhaustion on his face, the bags starting to form again under his eyes.

"Peg—"

"Go get your beauty sleep. You look bushed."

"Are you okay?"

"Me? Sure, I'm fine. Never better."

"Well, goodnight, Peg."

"Goodnight, Sean. Congratulations."

He left her then, and walked to his car. She saw the line of his shoulders, the back of his neck, the retreating shadow of his form as he walked away from her. She put the key in the ignition.

"Story of my life," she sighed.

FOURTEEN

S ean walked into Dan's office with a manila folder under his arm.

"I did a little research on the just war," he said. "I also tried out a few graphs for you to work into your talks in blue-collar neighborhoods. Might be helpful."

"Sean, you're a better speechwriter than the ones I pay."

Sean grinned. "Don't mention this to the archbishop. How's it going?"

"The polls change all the time. I can't tell." He shrugged. "But I took my stand, I'm going to have to live with it."

"I think you're right."

"I know I'm *right*. Whether I'm going to get elected is another story."

As Sean went down the steps of the Rayburn Building, he thought again about the degree to which he had stepped over some invisible line. Helping a political candidate write speeches was a long way from a Sunday sermon. Still, he remembered the face of Richie Dano's mother. "Did Richie die for nothing, Father?" None of the words he had said to her were of any help at all. If the words he wrote for Dan could help save other Richies, then his conscience was at ease.

He climbed into his car. He was scheduled to do another national show on PBS, and the *Washingtonian* was slated to do a feature on him next month. He was becoming a celebrity, and that was what bothered his conscience. He remembered his father, wallowing in the glory of all the little bibelots the church gave him, Catholic Layman of the Year. God's Rotary

Club, that was what the church was to his father, and Sean had hated that so. God's work should be hard and dirty, and it should be done for those with little hope, not for suburbanites who drove Ford Galaxys and donated warm-up jackets to the baseball team.

Would Damien the Leper do TV? "Father Damien, just hold up that thumb there for our studio audience to see. It's turning *yellow!* Let's all give a hand, folks, to this brave man."

But, at the same time, he had an idea that his celebrity status—minor as it was—was helping to protect him from the dead hand of authority. Archbishop O'Toole might just have killed Action if it hadn't had such good national press. So turning down the interviews and the panels could hurt the neighborhood, in the long run.

He drove back to St. Nasty's, and as he went in the back door of the rectory, Brian grabbed him and pulled him into the kitchen.

"Sean, there's a guy from the FBI here to see you. You want to scram, so I can say you're gone for the day?"

"No, I'll see him."

Sean walked into the parlor, trying not to let his nervousness show. *Relax, just be perfectly calm.*

A tall, well-built man in his thirties stood up and greeted him courteously.

"Hello, Father, I'm agent McMahon, Federal Bureau of Investigation."

"Fordham?" Sean asked.

A small grin edged onto the agent's face. "Does it show?"

Sean grinned, in what he hoped was an ingratiating way. "J. Edgar Hoover ought to donate a wing at Fordham. How can I help you, Mr. McMahon?"

"We understand that you have met a few times with Mrs. Claudia Brown. Her son is a fugitive. He's on our most wanted list."

Claudia Brown had been right. They were following her, maybe even bugging the phones. They had been smart to be careful.

"I know Mrs. Brown is a parishioner of mine. You can understand that she needs emotional support."

"Yes, I understand that. But Elmore Brown was involved in

a murder. Did Mrs. Brown tell you the whereabouts of her son?"

"No, she didn't." Sean felt the dampness forming under his armpits. He had to keep the FBI man off the scent of Elly Brown, without actually lying.

"You don't know where Elmore Brown is now?"

"No. I don't know where he is."

"You understand, Father, that if Mrs. Brown gives you any information about her son's whereabouts, it is your duty as a citizen to inform law enforcement officials."

"Yes. I do understand that, Mr. McMahon."

"It's possible, Father, that she might try to enlist your aid in some way to help her son evade the law."

Sean exhaled; imperceptibly, he hoped. They didn't know about the trip to Baltimore.

"I doubt that she would want to get me involved." It was not a lie. A mental reservation, perhaps—a Catholic way of evading part of the truth for a just and good cause. Claudia Brown had not *wanted* to get him involved. She just felt she had no other choice.

"She has never told you anything about where he is?"

"No. She's never said a word to me about that." It had been Chuck Washington who gave him the address on North Avenue. Sean felt a quivering in the pit of his stomach. What could he say if the FBI man asked if he had seen Elly Brown? He hoped he seemed straightforward to the FBI man, not evasive. *Dear God, don't let him ask me any more questions.*

The FBI man sighed. "The kid is probably out of the region by now. Sorry I had to ask you these questions, but there are some priests and nuns, well, they break the law. Daniel Berrigan." He shook his head. "Priests and nuns, imagine that!"

"Some people are—misguided," Sean said.

"A strange time. Sorry to have bothered you, Father, but you understand, I have a job to do."

Sean felt so weak in the knees when the FBI man left that he had to sit down. Brian came in and said, "Did it go okay?"

Sean had not told Brian that he had seen Elly Brown, so Brian wouldn't have to lie, but Brian could guess something was going on.

"Yes. It's okay."

"Sean, be careful. This is dangerous stuff."

"I know. But Brian, an innocent man may be charged with murder. Somebody has to help."

Brian smiled, a little ruefully. "Sean, you may find yourself a cross after all."

"I'm not trying for it, Bri, believe me."

"If I can help, let me know."

"I will."

Sean glanced at his watch. He was due out at Transition House; he fairly ran out to his car. If only there were five extra hours in every day!

He picked up Bill, and helped his brother carry his bags into his apartment. Bill looked around in surprise.

"Hey, this place looks so clean! And flowers, yet."

"Peg helped me clean up. The flowers were her idea. Sort of a welcome home. The fridge is full of stuff. In the pot there's a beef Stroganoff that Peg made. It's great."

"Somehow, I never think of Peg as being able to cook. I remember her as a grubby-faced little girl always climbing trees. This is *quite* a homecoming."

"I'm real glad you're home, Bill."

"So am I. Dad tell you about my plan?"

"Real estate? Sounds good."

"The Gerber Agency is taking me on. I can work at my own pace. The law wasn't for me, Sean. Ed and Glenn were my drinking buddies, that's why they took me into the firm. I was always the weak link."

"Is your money still tied up in the firm?"

"Yeah. My old buddies are being hard-nosed about it. I put a lot of money back in that firm. Legally it's theirs, but morally it's mine. With that money, I could make a new start. Maybe set up my own real estate agency." He shook his head. "It's scary, little brother. My confidence is really blotto. Even little things scare me. I have to steel myself to make a phone call. It's really—scary."

"You were always good with people, Bill."

"Yeah, but a lot of it was an act. So maybe now I can do a little acting to pretend I'm not scared shitless."

"Take it slow. You don't have to burn up the track. Anything I can do, let me know."

"Know anybody who wants to buy half a million bucks worth of real estate?"

"Let me give you the name of a guy at the chancery to go see. The church does have a lot of property. I've been lobbying one of the archbishop's guys on Action, and he's an okay guy. Let me call him."

"I think I underestimated you, little brother," Bill said. "You are one hell of a guy."

Sean looked at his brother, surprised. He felt a sudden rush of gratitude toward Bill. "That means a lot, coming from you."

"Does it?"

"I always thought you were something special, you know. I wanted to be just like you."

"Well, I guess that's changed."

"No, I think you have a lot of guts. A lot of people would have just folded up after getting hit with all the stuff you got hit with. Not you."

Bill looked at him. "That helps, Sean, it really does." Impulsively, he stepped close to Sean, put his arms around him and hugged him, something he hadn't done since they were children. Sean was startled at first, but then he gave Bill a hard squeeze in return. The two brothers stood like that for a minute, holding each other.

Bill stepped back. His eyes were bright. "Pop's boys may make it after all."

Sean looked at Bill, the words hovering on his lips. Then he said them. "I love you, Bill. Not priest talk."

"I love you too, Sean."

Sean left the Westminster and climbed back into the Toyota for the drive back to the rectory. Bill was back on track, Action was going well with the money from Kitty's party, the FBI hadn't thrown him in the slammer, and he had his relationship with Peg firmly under control. He had wanted to go to her apartment the other night; wanted it so badly he made it a test of his strength. He had said no, even when he saw the cloud in her eyes when he said it. Macho priest.

He felt a flush of exultation, now, thinking of his victory over his desires. He was strong. He could be *in* the world but not *of* it, resisting its temptations. He felt, suddenly, wonderful, free and soaring; an eagle gliding toward the sun, its wings glinting with gold in the upper air. To be a priest was to be a breed apart—finer, stronger than other men. There was nothing, he thought, that he could not do. With God's help, of course.

When he arrived at the rectory, he went inside. Peg was coming over in a half hour to give him some material from the environmental impact study. Her ability to skim through material and pull out the salient parts was proving invaluable to him. Was he taking advantage of her? No, she had volunteered, it wasn't as if he had asked. He thought, idly, that Peg never asked for anything. He was always the one taking, she the giver.

He picked up a sheaf of papers he had been working on from the table in the hall, and as he went into the dining room to finish, he saw three kids from the neighborhood standing by the table. One was Kiki, from the drug counseling program. Standing behind him was Torch, a hulking six-footer, and Torch's friend, Eddie.

"Hi guys. What can I do for you?"

"Jes' came to see you, Father," Kiki said. His words were frayed around the edges. Sean looked at him closely, and shook his head. Kiki's pupils were dilated. He had been doing so well, too, drug-free for six months.

"Kiki, this is really dumb. You expect me to lie to your probation officer?"

"I'm clean, Father."

"Like hell you are! You go home and sleep it off."

Torch stepped forward. He said, in a voice that had more than a hint of menace, "There was a fuckin' FBI man sniffin' around here. You finkin' on Elly Brown?"

"Of course not. I don't know anything about Elly Brown."

"You're lyin', man," accused Eddie.

"I don't lie, Eddie," Sean snapped. "You guys ought to know that by now."

"Whitey always lies," Torch said. The big kid was bad news. Sean knew he had been on the fringes of the Panther group Elly had been involved in, but Torch was no revolutionary. He was just a young hood with a long juvenile record, who would probably wind up in Lorton Reformatory one day. Torch was mean, but not too smart. He was probably lost already. Kiki was another story.

Sean ignored Torch and said, "Kiki, I could call the police on you tonight, but I won't. If you go home."

Kiki giggled. Sean grabbed him by the shoulders and said, "All right, I'll *take* you home." He started to turn Kiki around to march him toward the door, when out of the corner of his eye, he saw a blurred motion. Torch. And then he found himself on the floor, his senses registering a confused jumble of images. What had happened? There was a throbbing ache in the side of his head, his sight was fogged.

His vision cleared and he saw Torch standing over him, holding the large brass candlestick from the table.

"Shit, he's bleedin' all over the place," Eddie said.

"Honky fink," Torch spat. "Talked to the motherfucking FBI."

"Get the bread, man," Eddie urged. "They got money stuck away, lots of it."

"No, no money." Sean's own voice sounded far away; everything seemed to be happening at the far end of a tunnel.

Torch kicked him, hard, in the side. "Lousy fink." Kiki giggled, his voice high and tinny.

"The money," Eddie said. "All the motherfucker priests got money."

"No," Sean protested. "No, we're poor—"

"Motherfucker." Torch kicked him again, in the head. The room blurred, darkened. When it swam into focus again, he realized that Kiki was kneeling beside him, and the boy had opened his jacket and now was unbuttoning his shirt. Sean thought they were looking for money and he said, "No, nothing."

Torch lit a cigarette and handed it to Kiki. It was all very odd, Sean thought. What were they doing?

And then Kiki pressed the lighted cigarette into Sean's bare stomach. For an instant there was no sensation, and then it came, a searing bolt of pain. He heard himself cry out, "No!"

Kiki took the cigarette away. "Money. You got to have money."

"No, we don't—"

"Burn the honky. The lousy fink," Torch said, and Kiki bent over him again. He could see the boy's eyes, glazed like a honey doughnut. There was no comprehension in them.

Kiki moved the cigarette close to Sean's body again and

Sean tried to twist away, but Eddie was holding his shoulders. "FBI fink," Torch sneered.

"For God's sake!" And then the pain came again, a white-hot sheet that sent the colors spinning in front of Sean's retina. There was a terrible smell. He realized, with horror, that it was the stench of his own flesh burning.

"The money," Eddie said. "Make him tell."

"Kiki, you don't want to do this! You don't!" Kiki bent down again, still grinning. "Dear God, don't!" Sean cried out, and Kiki, with that blind and shining face, touched the glowing edge of the cigarette to Sean's nipple. Sean thought, *Father, forgive them, for they know not what they do,* and then the white sheet of pain spread across his eyes and he knew no more.

"Oh shit." Eddie was panicked. "He's dead. You killed him."

"Torch!" Kiki called, disoriented, but the big teenager was already running for the door. Kiki scrambled off his knees and ran after him. "The fucker's dead," Torch said. "Come on."

They ran out the door and melted into the darkness of the alley beside the rectory. Peg was pulling her car to the edge of the curb, and she saw them only as three forms sliding across her peripheral vision.

She was surprised to find the rectory door ajar, and she frowned and walked into the front hall. Everything was quiet inside.

"Sean?" she called out. There was no answer. She walked into the parlor. The light was on but she saw no one. She walked into the dining room, and she saw the still form on the floor.

She walked quickly to it and as she did, instinct—honed from years of being in situations where an instant's reflex could mean life or death—took over. She felt a detached calm, as if her emotions had been peeled away like a piece of Scotch tape.

She knelt next to him, thinking—quite calmly—He's dead, exactly what she had thought when Stan Pavlick walked into the bureau in Tel Aviv. But she put her hand on his throat and saw that he was breathing, shallowly. There was a lot of blood on the carpet but his head wound had stopped bleeding and the blood had clotted. She saw the marks on his chest and with a sudden, sickening rush of disbelief, she knew what had been done to him.

Sean's eyelids fluttered and he gave a low moan.

"Don't move. Lie still."

His eyes battled for focus. "Peg?"

"Don't try to talk. I'll get help."

"Kids," he mumbled. "Dusted. FBI, they thought—"

She heard the door opening and her whole body tensed. She saw the blood-stained candlestick and she grabbed it, gripping it lightly around the base. She waited.

"Sean?" Brian's voice.

"Brian, in here!"

Brian walked into the room and his eyes widened in surprise.

"Brian, call an ambulance," Peg commanded.

"What happened, what—"

"Hurry, please."

He ran to the phone and dialed. "This is Father Byrne at St. Ignatius. We need an ambulance, fast." When he hung up, Peg said to him, "Brian, get me some ice."

"Ice?"

"They burned him."

"Oh my God!"

Sean gave another moan. She touched his face gently.

"Sean, the ambulance is on the way. Stay still. Are you in a lot of pain?"

"Okay," he said. "I'm okay." But his face was contorted with the pain.

Brian came in with the ice and they held it against the angry red circles on his body. Sean drew in his breath sharply but did not cry out.

"Who did this to you, Sean?" Brian asked.

"Kiki. Torch."

"Dear God, why?"

"Dusted. Said I talked. FBI. Then wanted money. Dusted. Ohhhh."

"Shhh, Sean, don't talk." Peg put her fingers against his lips. The ambulance crew arrived, and the paramedic looked at Sean and said, "What happened to him?"

"Kids on drugs. They burned him."

"A priest? They did this to a priest? What is the world coming to?"

They brought out a backboard and eased Sean onto it. As they lifted him, he grunted with pain.

"Easy," Brian urged. "Easy with him."

It was not until they were sitting in the ambulance that Peg's calm deserted her. Her hands began to shake, violently.

"Peg," Sean said.

"I'm here." She took his hand and held it.

"Don't go."

"I won't."

He was gritting his teeth with the pain of the burns, and one of the paramedics gave him a shot of Demerol. His body relaxed and he closed his eyes.

"Animals!" she said to Brian. "I'd like to kill them. Animals!"

"Sean worked with one of those kids, spent hours with him."

Sean stirred and, without opening his eyes, said her name. She bent close and touched his face. "I'm here, Sean. It's okay." The Demerol was easing the pain, but making him disoriented.

"No money. We don't have any."

She stroked his forehead. "Sean, it's all right. No one is going to hurt you anymore."

"Don't, for God's sake, don't!"

"It's all right. You're going to be all right, love." That last word just slipped out. She hoped Brian hadn't noticed it.

He slept then, and didn't wake when they took him to the emergency room. As Peg and Brian waited, anxiously, Peg asked, "Brian, who knew that the FBI had been to see Sean?"

"Nobody, I thought. But news gets around fast in this neighborhood."

Finally the doctor came out and told them Sean's head wound had required eight stitches. "He's going to be okay, but the burns are third-degree. He's going to have scars."

In a little while they brought Sean upstairs to a private room, heavily sedated. Peg asked the doctor if she could stay and he nodded but said, "He'll probably just sleep for a long time."

Brian left and Peg walked to the bed to look at Sean. His head was bandaged, and she could see the square line of his jaw against the whiteness of the sheet. She suddenly remembered, with stunning clarity, the night they had walked home from midnight mass together on Christmas Eve of senior year. She wore the silver bracelet he had given her, with the words "Sean and Peg" inscribed inside a tiny heart. His face was awash in silver moonlight and she remembered the feeling that had come on her abruptly—that she wasn't in that time and place but somewhere off in the future, looking back at the two of them, trying to reach back through time to touch the cool silver of Sean's cheek. But she couldn't reach him, couldn't touch him. She had called his name but he couldn't hear her, he just kept walking in the moonlight, beyond her reach. It was the first time she had really understood that he was lost to her, that it was the silver light of God's love that washed over him, and it was God's love that he would choose.

She had indeed been prescient that Christmas Eve. She felt the very same sense of loss flooding her that she had known under that long-lost Christmas sky. He was as near to her now as the length of her arm, and as far as the rings of Saturn. She had seen them in a trip to the Naval Observatory that year; hanging in space, silent, luminous, breathtaking, inaccesible.

She pulled over a chair and sat by the bed. There was no small irony in the fact that by helping him to become a celebrity she was cementing the bond between Sean and the priesthood. *Father Seanito* was in *Time* this week. If he had stayed just a parish priest, looking ahead only to an endless chain of days filled with junkies and beano he just might have given up in disgust. But now, his star was in the ascendant; the church knew the value of a young man who was the darling of the talk shows. Even O'Toole had backed off.

She sighed. Smart, Peg. Make him a cardinal. Make him the bleeping Pope. How big a sin could it be to have the hots for the Pope?

She reached over and curled a lock of his hair around her finger. She said out loud, "I love you, Sean. I always have." She sighed again. "This is one hell of an eternal triangle. You, me, and God. And that sucker always wins. If I ever got ahead on points, he could just turn me into a pillar of salt. 'I Am Who I Am and you are *salt*. Zap.'"

She shook her head. "And here I am talking to myself. Babbling. Because I can't stand the idea that anyone could hurt you. My beautiful Sean, who would want to hurt you? You've never wanted anything but good for anyone."

All the years they had spent growing up together, Sean had tried so hard to make things right. He had wrapped acres of bandages around mice and squirrels—so ineptly that the word had spread through the animal kingdom the way the news of man had passed from bunny to chipmunk in *Bambi:* Stay the hell away from the little kid with the green eyes and the iodine bottle.

She touched his face. "Oh Sean, still trying to bandage the world!"

The rest of the members of the class of '56 had launched their careers, invested in *making it*, bought their suburban houses and their gas-guzzling cars, and Sean was still plodding along, trying to make a difference. Under the fast mouth and the political savvy was the little boy with the green eyes and the loving heart who thought it was his job to set the world to rights. And he was lost to her. She had known it that Christmas morn, as surely as she knew it now. Time to stop pretending, time to let him walk into the future that God had chosen him for—or his father had.

She suddenly felt very tired, and leaned her head on the bed and fell asleep. When she woke, he was still asleep, so she got in her car, drove home, climbed into bed, and did not dream.

He was groggy every time she went to visit during the next two days, but on the third day she got a surprise when she walked into his room. He was sitting up, with the telphone in his lap.

"Oh yeah?" he was saying. "Is this in public records? Should we use it, or will it blow up in our face? Okay, do it, then. Get me the stuff."

"Sean, what are you doing?"

He grinned. "Guess what I just found out? Congressman Rylander got a ton of money from the highway lobby for his last campaign. No wonder he's pushing the interstate so hard. How about a story in the *Trib?*"

"I came over here to perform a corporal work of mercy and I get hustled for eight column inches?"

"You don't want it? I'll call *The Washington Post*."

"Blackmail! This is a man of God?"

"Thou shalt not blackmail is not in the Big Ten, as I recall."

She laughed and kissed him on the cheek. "How do you feel?"

"A lot better since they took me out of needle park." He shook his head. "They want to put Kiki in a juvenile institution, but I'm going to ask the judge for probation again."

"Sean, what he did to you was vicious!"

"But I know him, Peg. He's not really a vicious kid. It was Torch's idea to use me as a marshmallow, and Kiki just did what he said. And he was blasted. He's a smart kid, he's only fifteen. He's got a chance of not going down the toilet."

"You never give up, do you?" She said it with a smile.

The phone rang and Sean answered. "Chuck, you were *great* on WETA. You are a star, ole buddy. Listen, would you swing by Tom Halloran's office and pick up some stuff for me? Thanks."

Peg took the telephone off the bed and put it on the nightstand. "You are supposed to be resting, Sean McCaffrey!"

"I'm just dialing."

"I have something for you." She handed him several sheets of paper. "Tom's editorial in this afternoon's *Trib*."

He took the papers and began to read. "'The federal bulldozer must not be allowed to pave over the hopes and dreams of the people of the Takoma corridor.' Oh God, that's great. Much stronger than I thought it would be. Peg, you're a miracle worker!"

The phone rang again and Sean put it back on his lap. It was Alex. She watched Sean's face, enthused, animated, as he told Alex about the editorial, and about Rylander. He was in his element, that was for sure. He didn't need her. He had God and politics, and Peg Morrison ran a distant third. If she was in the running at all.

"Alex, listen to what we got on Rylander!"

He had called out her name in the ambulance, but it was nothing more than an echo of an old need. There had been a time, on those warm summer nights, when he *had* needed her—desperately, urgently. She remembered his body, the thick-matted hair on his chest damp with sweat, how he had nearly howled with pleasure the first time she had—

daringly—probed every part of him with her lips. It had never felt dirty with Sean, only good, right. She had never believed he could be celibate. All she had to do was wait.

"I say we neutralize Rylander. He'll be pissed, but we never had a prayer of getting him anyway."

Peggy Ann Morrison, '56, class idiot. She thought he would come to her. But the kiss in the bedroom was only a chink in the armor—and the breech had been sealed up, stronger than ever. Give it up, Peg. You spend too much of your life grieving for a man who loved death and another man who is dazzled by God. Who will never come to you. Not until hell freezes over. Give it up, Peg.

"Tydings is solid, we've got him nailed down," he said into the telephone.

She smiled and she blew him a kiss and he blew one back to her, not missing a beat in his conversation with Alex. She turned and walked out of the room and then went down to her car and drove away.

FIFTEEN

Adam Crabtree moved his considerable bulk across the floor at the Sans Souci to where Dan Amundsen was sitting, waiting for him. Adam put a page torn from the Omaha *Sun* in front of Dan. "You'd better read this."

On the society page was a large picture of Dan and Kitty, both holding drinks, standing with Leonard Fineberg. The article spoke of "Congressman Amundsen's great and good friend, Mrs. Kitty Cohen."

"What's this great and good friend shit?"

"You know what that means," Adam Crabtree said, sliding into a chair.

"So? I'm a single man, Adam. Nobody expects me to be a hermit. Look at Henry Kissinger."

"Kissinger doesn't play well on the banks of the Platte River. Neither does Kitty Cohen."

"Are you saying anti-Semitism?"

"In a word."

"It's 1970. Father Coughlin has been dead for a while."

"If Kitty was the daughter of some nice Jewish druggist from Omaha, fine. But she's Eastern liberal Jewish money. Right out of the elders of Zion, and that played very big out there."

"Come on, Adam, you're not serious."

"The story was a plant, Dan."

"What?"

"The *Sun* columnist is in bed with Rolvag. Journalistically speaking. She's going to help him go after you and Kitty. You were pushing it with the antiwar stuff. Put that together with Kitty, and it looks like you've sold out to the Eastern liberal city slickers."

"How do you know about this?"

"I have someone inside Rolvag's campaign."

"How did you manage that?"

"I have my resources."

"They're going to make Kitty a campaign issue?"

"If it gets rough—and it will—they are. They'll picture you as the Playboy Congressman. Lots of pictures of you and Kitty with the head of the UJA. The Israeli ambassador. They're not going to *say* you're in bed with a rich Jewess. One picture is worth a thousand words."

"That sucks."

"Sure. But it could work."

"So what do you advise?"

"Break it off with Kitty. Be seen around a lot with that little blonde you drag around for local consumption."

"Kitty's helped me raise most of the money for the campaign. I wouldn't be in the damn race if it wasn't for her."

"That was yesterday. Today, she could cost you the race."

"Adam, we're—very close."

"If you mean you screw her, hell, everybody knows that."

"I don't mean just that."

"Oh Christ, Dan, have I got Romeo on my hands?"

"We have a good relationship, okay," Dan said, testily.

"You want to marry her?"

"I was thinking, after the election, yeah I think so."

Adam shrugged. "The talk is already starting. The jokes. About you being in bed with Jewish ass and Jewish money."

"You think it could really make a difference?"

"Why take the chance?"

"I don't want to lose her. I want this seat, but I—hell, Adam, I love her."

"Look, you asked for my opinion. I'm your campaign manager, not Ann Landers."

"If I lose, I'm nowhere. An ex-one-term congressman. What's lower on the scale than that?"

"Amoebas. Three-toed tree sloths." Adam sighed. "Rockefeller could have been president, if he hadn't had hot pants for Happy. But after he lost, he was still *Rockefeller*." He took a sip of his drink. "Look, Dan, you win this Senate seat and all the doors will open for you. Maybe even the big one, someday."

Dan laughed. "Why not whistle 'Hail to the Chief' while you're at it."

"I know political horseflesh. I've peddled enough nags. You're a fresh face, from the heartland, the right liberal credentials, but you're not a space cadet like Jerry Brown, and you haven't got an excess of scruples, like McGovern. Right now you're pretty raw, but you could go a long way."

"Adam Crabtree's wind-up presidential candidate?"

Adam laughed. "I'm not that Machiavellian."

"Aren't you?"

"I smell the hunger in you, if we're into honesty. You want it. And you got to want it *bad*, to get it. You got to *like* rubber chicken and airplanes and the 'Today' show. When I look at a candidate, I look for four things. Smarts, charisma, a quick study, and hunger. Without hunger, the rest is just chicken pee."

"You're so sure I've got it?"

"Oh, you do. If ever there's a driven man, it's you, Danny. You kill your father every day."

Dan stiffened. "What do you mean by that crack?"

"I do my homework. I know you're the one who had to haul your father out of the loony bin all the time." He chuckled. "Another good sign in a candidate. A rotten relationship with his father. If Joe Kennedy hadn't been such a bastard, Jack and Bobby would be a couple of rich lawyers today. No, Jack might be editor of the Boston *Globe*. He didn't have the patience for the law."

"You're right. I do want it, Adam."

"You can have it. Just don't blow it."

"But *I* run my personal life, not you, not politics. I'm my own man."

"Whoever said you weren't?"

While Adam and Dan were talking, Constance Masters came into the restaurant and approached the maitre'd. "Commander Masters' table," she said to him. Lee was already seated at the table. He rose when they approached; he wasn't wearing his uniform, but a dark gray suit. He seemed like a stranger to her. A handsome blond man in a dark suit, getting up. Odd, that she'd lived with him for fourteen years and knew the exact shape of the mole on the inside of his thigh and yet he seemed a stranger.

"Constance."

"How are you, Lee?"

"Good. I'm good. How about you?"

"Good."

"The boys and I had a good time at the movies last night."

"Yes, they told me."

The waiter came up to ask about cocktails. She ordered a sherry; Lee asked for a Perrier and lime.

"No more drinking," he said. "I've quit cold."

"That's good."

"I want to find out about myself. About that night. Why."

"Did you really believe I was cheating on you?"

He frowned. "No." He paused. "Yes, I guess I was afraid that you were. But I had no right—I don't know—I'm trying to sort it out, Con. I hate myself for what I did that night."

She listened to him, but oddly, felt nothing. She had been reading a novel by a young woman who had died a suicide, Sylvia Plath, and she thought, suddenly, of the words that seemed to describe herself, as well. A bell jar had come down on part of her heart, and under it there was nothing. It was black and stopped as a dead baby.

"I want to save our marriage, Con."

"What's left to save?"

"It was *once*. It only happened once."

She laughed, mirthlessly. "You can only kill someone once, Lee. And you killed something in me that night."

"I didn't want to hurt you—"

"Yes, you did."

He nodded. "Yes, I did. I was in a rage, but when it was gone I didn't understand it. I never did anything like that before."

"Lee, you held my hair and punched me in the stomach. The same place I carried your babies. That's what you did to me, Lee."

She saw the misery creep across his face; the strong, chiseled face she still thought was the most handsome she had ever seen. But she saw it, now, as a stranger.

"Con, it wasn't you I was angry at. It was my boss, it was the whole goddamn world."

"That's what my father used to say. After he beat up my mother. You made me *her*, Lee. Can you understand—even for just a *minute*—what that did to me?"

He nodded.

"I won't ever forget your eyes. They were the eyes of some—animal. You would have killed me."

"No."

"Yes. And I was ready to kill you. Do you think people come back from that edge?"

"I don't know. But I hope so. It's what's keeping me sane. I'm in a group. With other men who've done this."

"You are?" She was astonished. Was this Lee, who handled everything alone?

"What I did scared the shit out of me. I know I need help. I'm just asking you not to shut the door on me."

"Lee, I'll be honest with you. I wasn't cheating on you. But after that night—there is a man, now. Because I felt like nothing the night you beat me up. He's helped me."

His face darkened, but he nodded. "I understand. I'll try to. Do you love him?"

"I don't think so."

"All I ask is that you don't divorce me right away. Leave the door open, a crack."

"I haven't any plans for divorce."

"We'll let the boys know we care about them. And each other."

"I never told them."

"I did."

"What?"

"Leezy was bad-mouthing you, so I told them. I told them I did something a man must never, never do. I hurt you. And that I had to learn why I did it."

"Do you think that was a good idea?"

"Yes. They'd know, eventually. It's better this way. Honest." He paused. "I love you, Con."

"Do you? Or are you just used to having me around?"

"Fourteen years. Good times and bad. Let's not just throw them away."

"Lee, right now I can't feel anything about you. Not love. Not hate. I'm just numb. I *do* know no one will ever hit me again. Not ever."

"I wouldn't ask anything of you, until I understand. Until I could make the promise I will never do it again. Because the thought of what I did that night is killing me, Con. It's killing me."

Con walked out of the restaurant feeling as if a large weight had been lifted from her chest. The boys knew. They had faced it, and they hadn't fallen apart. Her sweet, lovely boys. Lee was right. It was better this way. She told Peg about their meeting.

"I'm glad, Con. You don't have to pretend anymore."

"I even told him about George. Not by name, of course. He even seemed to accept that. If the boys don't get destroyed by this—well, that's what's important. I can accept the fact that my marriage is down the tubes—but not my kids. Not my kids!"

"They're great kids. I envy you that." She sighed. "I'm going to take your advice and start looking over the male crop."

"You're giving up on the Kissing Priest?"

"Yeah, the clock is ticking for me, Con. I've finally started to hear it. I was like some kind of Peter Pan, hopping from place to place while everyone else was putting down roots, starting families. You have two kids who are nearly teenagers and here I am, still—unsettled."

"A lot of people would envy your life. You have a glamorous job, no strings."

"Oh, I love my job. But if Jeff hadn't died, I know I'd be making a baby right now. I thought I was pregnant, once. I wish I had been. He wouldn't have gone to Vietnam."

"You want kids, Peg?"

"Yeah, I really do. I never used to think about it much. But now—you hit thirty and you know you have to do it fairly soon or forget about it."

"I'm thinking of having my tubes tied."

"You are?"

"Yes. I adore my boys, but I don't want the chance of having another baby. For such a long time I've been taking care of everybody else. Doing things for everybody but me. And now it's my turn. And dammit, why should I feel guilty about feeling that way? Men don't."

"No. They don't."

"Want me to set you up with my twenty-six-year-old Georgian? He's still available."

"Why not? I have to stop kidding myself. Sean didn't choose me ten years ago, and he won't now. I don't know that he could, even if he wanted to."

Sean walked into the kitchen, where Brian was having a cup of coffee.

"I think we're getting a building for the center. I can run over to get a look at it after the drug group. And I'm seeing Halloran at four, but maybe I can get back by five-thirty—"

"Sean, if you don't take it easy you're going to wind up flat on your back again. You're just out of the hospital."

"Yeah, but the construction guys are making their big push on the interstate. We could lose it all, Brian."

"You've got good people in the group. Just let them take some of the load off. You don't have to do it all yourself."

"You're right, maybe I'll get Chuck to look at the building. But I have some stuff to give Dan for his next swing through the state—"

"Sean!"

"Okay, Brian, I'll slow down."

"I'll believe that when I see it."

Just then Father Barry walked in, clutching a magazine in his hand. "Father!" he said to Sean. "Father, you must do something!"

Brian finished his coffee and ducked out the back door, with a sympathetic glance at Sean. Father Barry, in full morning glower, bad breath steaming, could drive away invading armies.

"Filth!" Father Barry ranted. "Vile odious filth! Sent to a house of God!"

He handed the magazine to Sean, who took it from the outstretched, bony hand. The cover was all black, and it said in white letters, *Summer Fun with Big John and Vivecca.*

"Big John and Vivecca?"

"Filth! Filth!"

Sean opened the magazine to a page of black-and-white

grainy pictures under a headline: Big John and Vivecca Do It with Dogs.

The headline did not lie. In the pictures, Big John and Vivecca—who must have been double-jointed—were indeed performing various sexual acts on two bored-looking German shepherds. He flipped a page to see Vivecca, a lissome brunette, with all available orifices occupied by the private parts of three gentlemen.

"That's amazing." Sean flipped to another page where a headline announced, Big John Does It with Fruit. Big John—and he certainly deserved his name—was humping a watermelon. The sight struck Sean as so ridiculous that he burst out laughing.

"It is *not* funny!" said Father Barry, scandalized.

"No, Father." Sean was still grinning. Father Barry glared at him. "It was the watermelon," Sean explained apologetically. "It's sort of funny."

"Father McCaffrey, this is foul. This is sick. This is *anti-Catholic!*"

"Anti-Catholic?"

"Yes! Don't you see?"

Sean looked at Father Barry blankly. He could not for the life of him see anti-Catholicism in Big John and Vivecca doing it with members of the animal and vegetable kingdoms. They were not wearing miraculous medals, flaunting their Catholicism along with their amazing muscle control. Sean looked at the table of contents: Snakes, Chains, Water Sports.

"Father, it's smut, but I don't see—"

"They are trying to destroy the moral fiber of priests by sending us this filthy trash. See, it's our address!"

"But it just says occupant. It's just a mistake."

"They are clever, Father. They *want* us to think it was unintentional."

"They?"

"Yes. The people who hate the church. They want to sink us in filth, to lure priests from their holy vows through fleshly weakness."

Sean had a sudden vision of Big John and Vivecca, sitting in the bedroom with the shades drawn. They would be poring over an addressograph list purloined from the Holy See, trying to match up clergy with the list of available perversions:

"Father Kevin in Queens has a weakness for water sports, Viv."

"And Brother Benedict in Kansas City will be converted to the *Playboy* philosophy by these blurred photographs of ritual bondage practices in Guam."

"Isn't it fun, Viv, destroying the Catholic Church with smut?"

Father Barry waved the magazine. "We are going to find the people that sent this."

"We, Father?"

"You! You are going to hunt them down. It is a crime to send this filth through the mail!"

Wonderful, Sean thought. Beano Patrol could now go after Big John and Vivecca, hunting them through the flesh-pots of major urban centers. But how could you make them confess to their nefarious anti-Catholic schemes? If you whipped Big John and Vivecca, they'd only scream, "More, more!"

Sean decided that he would just let this one ride and hope Father Barry would forget about it. Which he did, until two days later, when *Water Sports Illustrated* arrived. So Sean had to make an appointment with the postal inspectors. The young inspector tried not to grin the whole time Sean was in the office. There was something fairly comic, Sean realized, about a Catholic priest arriving at your office with the latest issue of *Water Sports Illustrated* under his arm.

He complained to Brian about his latest errand. "Brian, he is driving me *nuts*! I had to go downtown with all that stuff."

"No more fun reading?"

"I hope not. Father Barry has a fit."

"Yeah. He thought *Water Sports Illustrated* was about boats. He figured there would be nice pictures of a forty-foot Chris-Craft."

Sean sighed. "They did not tell me in seminary that among my priestly duties would be swearing out a criminal complaint against people who pee on each other."

Brian grinned. "At least you didn't have to hear their confessions."

"Yes, my son," Sean said in his priestly voice. "And what sins do you wish to confess? I see. With a watermelon. Ten times. And a pomegranate. A tomato. For your penance say ten Hail Mary's and make a firm resolve to stay away from the A&P."

Brian cackled and leaned back in his chair. "Oh Sean, we have to laugh, don't we? Thank God you're here. I sometimes think I'll never get out of St. Nasty's."

"You will, Bri."

Brian shook his head. "Maybe. But it's more than that. I've really been questioning my vocation. What good am I doing, Sean? I say mass and nobody comes. I spend half my time trying to keep the damn church from falling down. Well, maybe it should."

"Come on."

"No, I mean it. I'd be doing a lot more good for people if I were a social worker. You're really getting something accomplished with the antiwar stuff, with Action. But me—this isn't why I went into the priesthood, Sean, to cover up for the incompetence of a drunken pastor."

"You don't mean you're thinking of leaving?"

"Yes, I'm thinking about it. Seriously. I'm so fed up with the bureaucracy I could scream. Having Father Barry yell at me every time I want to try something new."

"You're just down, Brian."

"Maybe. I can't stand the sense that I'm wasting my life. God never meant for us to throw our lives away, Sean. That's what I feel I'm doing here. I really do."

The housekeeper called up the stairs that there was a call for Sean, and he went down and picked up the phone. It was Alex, saying that he had just heard that one of the key men on the governor's staff had fallen off the fence—and come down against scrapping Interstate 80. Sean put down the phone, frowning. He had a good idea what was going on. The election wasn't far away, and the Montgomery County suburbanites—the ones with cars, who cursed through the rush-hour traffic jams—were voters. The construction guys were using their muscle, and the blacks and Hispanics couldn't pull out that much of a vote. Half of La Raza's members were across the district line, no help to a Maryland governor.

He rubbed his head, which was beginning to ache. He had been plagued by headaches since the blow on the head. They would go away in time, the doctor said, but he had to rest. Rest! He couldn't rest now. To get so close, and to be stopped now, to see defeat snatched from the jaws of victory— He slammed his fist down on the table. Damn! Damn!

A wave of weariness washed over him. He was healing well from his injuries, but he still didn't have his strength back. He had always had a boundless store of energy; it had carried him across the shoals of life at St. Nasty's—Father Barry, beano, the endless chores. All the petty annoyances had been mice, nibbling at the legs of his trousers. Now, with his energy sapped, the mice had grown to eye level. Keep going, Sean. Just keep going.

What if Action failed?

O'Toole was keeping hands off because Action was riding high. He'd be there with the rest of the vultures if it faltered. And Sean McCaffrey? Exiled to God knows where, probably to the sand dunes on the Eastern Shore, never to be heard from again. No more TV shows, no more antiwar marches, no more hobnobbing with congressmen.

"Not my will, but Thine be done," he prayed, trying to mean it.

He got up, picked up a batch of new studies he was supposed to read from the table, and went back upstairs to his room. He sat on the bed, and he shivered. It wasn't from cold, but fatigue. And loneliness. The loneliness was getting worse, a permanent chill that had settled in his bones. He remembered, with a shudder, the white flash of pain that had seared through his brain when Kiki had put the cigarette up against his skin. He tried to block out the memory, but couldn't, and he heard himself give an audible moan of remembered agony. A few days earlier he had thought of himself as an eagle, gliding toward the sun. He thought, now, what a fatuous image that was. Now he was only a man, hurting, afraid and lonely. There was nothing heroic about Sean McCaffrey right now.

He picked up a study and tried to read. *Keep going!* He was always running, he thought. From what? His feelings, his pain, all the things that made him human? The Perfect Priest, in track shoes.

He looked around the room, at the yellow curtains, the peeling wallpaper, the bureau drawer that wouldn't close, and he thought he would go mad if he had to stay in this room another instant. He went downstairs, picked up the phone and dialed the number he knew by heart.

She answered and he said, "How would you like to give one pooped priest a cup of coffee? Loaded with booze."

The coffee was on when he got there and he sat at the kitchen table and drank it, gratefully. He told her about the call from Alex.

"We can't lose it, Peg, not now! Not after we've come so close! Dear God!"

"Sean, you're not going to lose. You've got two people on the governor's staff, solid, and good support in the delegation. You're just down because you're exhausted."

"I guess so. I'm not holding things together very well. And Brian's thinking of leaving the priesthood. I don't think I could survive St. Nasty's without him."

"Brian? Oh, you do need some cheering up. Here, have more of this stuff." And she poured another shot of brandy into his coffee.

"Peg, if it hadn't been for you, Action would never have come as far as it has. You don't know what you've done for me."

"I'm glad, Sean."

They were quiet for a minute and he said, "You know I've kept my vows. I had to be the Perfect Priest. I didn't just keep them, I made them a test of strength. A real macho thing."

"You were always harder on yourself than anyone."

"I had to do it by the book. I saw other guys, they'd take their collars off on weekends. Forget they were priests for a while. I had such contempt for them."

She was silent, staring into her coffee. He looked at her hands, curled around the cup. Her fingers were long and slim, strong but graceful. The nails were clean, but ragged. She still bit her nails. The base of her throat was very white, and in the middle of that hollow, he knew, you could feel her pulse, a tiny drum.

"I think, Peg, that I was more the sinner than they." He didn't quite know what he was going to say, but he had the sense of being on the surface of a moving body of water, rushing toward a precipice. "I thought I could be perfect. The Hero Priest of Takoma Park."

"Do you want to be a hero?"

"No," he said. "No, I don't. What I want is for you to touch me. Please touch me."

She looked at him. "Sean, are you sure?"

"For ten years, Peg, you've been in every little room with me. You didn't know it, but you were there. When I got so lonely I couldn't stand it anymore, I'd imagine I was holding you and then it would be better, somehow. I've tried not to want you, but my God, Peg, I do. Touch me. Please touch me."

She walked over to him, stood behind his chair and put her lips to the back of his neck. He shivered at her touch, inhaled the warm, sweet smell of flowers in the park, of her. He was wearing a V-necked sweater and she slid her hand under it, across his chest, and her touch sent a current through him. He got up, knocking over the chair and pulled her to him, feeling himself come erect against her body. He kissed her, needily, and whispered to her, "I want you. I want you so much!"

She took his hand and they went into the bedroom. His hands shook as he unbuttoned his shirt. She undressed quickly, not sensuously, but with that little-kid awkwardness of hers that was more erotic, somehow, than a striptease. Her body was the same, but different. She was still slender, but there was a new fullness to her breasts and hips. Womanly, he thought.

There was a moment of shyness between them, and then she stepped close to him, so that her body fit close to his, as smoothly as the pieces of a child's puzzle. He knotted his fingers in her hair and put his lips to hers.

"I'm glad. I'm so glad!" she whispered. Then they lay on the bed together, and he let his hands explore the geography of her body, slowly, with a delicious wantonness. He caressed her breasts and said, "Beautiful. So beautiful."

She smiled, then. "Not as perky as they used to be."

"Better. Sexier. Much better."

"Remember what you used to like to do?"

"I remember. Do you still like it?" He put his lips to her nipple.

"Yes. Oh God, Sean, do anything to me. I want you. I didn't think you'd come to me."

"Like this?"

"Yes. That's wonderful. Oh."

He had forgotten the marvel of real flesh under his lips, his fingers; had forgotten how a woman's body was like a spring, with its own silent language of consent.

When she said to him, "I want to do something to you," he knew what she wanted. Her mouth, her lips and tongue were soft, searching, primal. He heard himself cry out, ripped out of time and space, out of control, and he felt the same sensation he had known so many years ago on a hot summer night in the Greystone. He felt loved, accepted, in a way that no one else could love him. Not even God.

"I want you. Please, I need you," he said, and she said, "Yes," and he entered her, sure and strong. He felt a surge of joy in his own male power—the power to give pleasure—that had been so absent from his lonely fumblings over the years. As his own explosion seemed to blur the room he heard her voice, in tune with his own body's rocking: "My love. My love. My love. *Sean!*"

Afterward, he held her tightly against him, as if she might turn to vapor and simply float away if he didn't hold her, and she nestled her head against his shoulder and gave a small sigh of contentment. He touched her hair, her face, her lips, trying to inhale the textures with his fingers. He had forgotten how lovely it all was.

"Was I too fast?" he asked.

"Oh no. You were wonderful. Just right."

"I wanted it to be good for you, Peg. I didn't want to just take."

"Sean, you were lovely. Don't you know how good you were?"

"No," he said, honestly.

"Would you like me to compose a sonnet?"

"Ummm."

"It's called, 'Big Sean.'"

He cackled and bit her ear, playfully. That was another thing he had forgotten, how they had laughed afterward, how they were goofy and silly and funny.

"I knew I never should have told you about that."

"You promised to show me and you didn't. He really did it to a watermelon?"

"Yeah, that was easy. The big challenge is to do it to a radish. Especially for Big John."

She tickled him and he twitched and begged for mercy and then he tickled her and they laughed some more and then he pulled her to him and said, "Peg, I love you. I do love you so."

"I love you, Sean. Now. Always."

"Peg, what have I got to give you? I love you, but all I have to give you is—"

She put her finger to his lips. "You're here. We're together. That's all that matters."

"I can come two nights a week. It isn't much."

"Do you want to?"

"Yes. If you want me to, Peg, wild horses couldn't keep me away."

"I want you, Sean." She bent her head to gently kiss the scars on his chest and stomach. "I can't bear to think of them hurting you."

He smiled. "Kiss it and make it better."

"I used to do that all the time. You were the most accident-prone kid I ever saw."

"Yeah, I had more Band-Aids on me than my patients." He laughed. "When you were my zort, I even made you kiss my patients. You did it too, dummy."

"Kissing a mouse in a cast is disgusting. It's a wonder I didn't get rabies from those horrible germy rodents." She sighed. "The things I did for you, Sean McCaffrey."

"The things you do for me now, Peggy Morrison, are even better."

She curled up and went to sleep in his arms, and he held her, his lips pressed against her hair. He felt a deep sense of peace descend on him, a peace that had long eluded him. Her flesh against his was a benediction, warm and healing. How very odd, he thought, that flesh should give such comfort, when he should be thinking of this as forbidden, wrong. But he felt not wrong but nourished, the desperate hunger to be touched at last quiet. Could a man starve to death for lack of a touch? His heart, perhaps. And if any heart was starving, it was his. She stirred in his arms and he kissed the top of her head and she was still.

He knew there were things he should think about. Was it Sean McCaffrey she needed, who came and went in her life like some capricious wind? He tried to think of fairness and morality but all that filled him was the touch of her body against his. Don't think, Sean, Feel. Tonight is real. He cupped her breasts with his hands, loving the weight of them. Feel, Sean. Be a man, not a priest.

Tomorrow morning, for the first time in ten years, he would not wake up alone. A wave of possessiveness gripped him. He had no right to it, but there it was. *My woman. Mine.* The body was as sublime, in its own way, as the spirit. And did you move into the realm of pure spirit with celibacy, or just beyond the wonder of the body? What was the price you paid? Did you become light as air, transcendent, or did you simply shrivel like a leaf cut off from the juices of the trunk?

Questions, he had. No answers. He was too tired and too peaceful for either. Accept, Sean, accept. *Dominus vobiscum.* The Lord be with you.

And then he slept.

SIXTEEN

Kitty heard a noise—thump-thump-thump from the back of the house, so she went to the back door and peered out. She saw Peg, wearing her good coat and heels, dribbling a basketball as she ran full-tilt toward the basketball hoop Morris had put up for Jason at the far end of the back driveway. Kitty was astonished as Peg stopped a few feet from the net, jumped into the air in a decidedly unfeminine way, and released the ball at the top of her jump. The ball swished cleanly through the netting.

Kitty leaned out the door. "My dear, if your skin were just a shade darker, I would think I had invited Wilt Chamberlain for lunch."

Peg grinned, tucked the basketball under her arm and trotted to the door. She handed the ball to Kitty.

"I couldn't resist. I saw it and I just had to see if the old jump shot worked."

"You used to play basketball, I take it."

"Play? I was the all-star forward in the CYO. I was *fantastic*." She slipped out of her coat. "Did you ever play, Kitty?"

"Jewish princesses did not play basketball, dear. We might break our nails."

"Catholic girls wore black hi-top sneakers and we liked to sweat."

"In Great Neck we would have worn little yellow stars on our sleeves before we would wear high-top sneakers."

"Yeah, but *we* couldn't wear diaphragms. Hi-tops and sweat were the nuns' idea of birth control."

Kitty laughed, and looked at her guest. Peg was rather more put-together than usual. Her nails were ragged and her shoes were scuffed, of course, but her blouse matched her skirt and her nylons had no runs. Peg, Kitty had noticed, was able to come up with the most amazing combinations of prints, stripes, and plaids, apparently unaware of the fact that one might not exactly blend with the other. Her hair, often, was stuck on top of her head—with strands of it escaping to drift down one side of her neck. But today her hair was long and carefully styled, just turning upward before it reached her shoulders. The color had risen in her cheeks; her skin seemed actually to glow with a light that had to come from within. She was, Kitty thought, the very portrait of a woman in love.

Kitty handed her a glass of wine, and motioned for her to come to the glassed-in porch, where lunch was to be served. They sat down at the table and Kitty said, "We do come from different backgrounds, don't we? But we have one thing in common."

"What's that?"

"Falling in love with totally inappropriate men."

Peg looked at her. "How did you know?"

"Con, of course. But it is written in neon lights on your forehead, my dear. You're very much in love with him, aren't you?"

"Oh yeah. It's wonderful. And awful. The usual thing."

"I know." Antonio brought the chicken salad divan with avocado wedges. "Peg, I don't want to intrude on your private life, but is this—wise?"

"Wise? Oh no, of course it isn't. It's one of the dumber things I've done. And I've done some *dumb* things."

"I'd hate to see you get hurt again. You've already had your share."

"Right now I'm just taking each day as it comes."

"I hope that that young man appreciates you."

"He does. Oh Kitty, he's warm and he's funny and he's gentle and he's—"

"Very good in bed."

"Umm. Oh yes, he is that."

Kitty sighed. "I can tell. I just *look* at a man, and I know. I wonder if it's a marketable talent?"

"Kitty, why did you say we *both* fell for inappropriate men? Dan's single, and he certainly hasn't taken any vow of chastity, and he's nuts about you. Anybody can see that."

"Yes I think he is, but—"

"But?"

"Dan's a bit of a mystery to me. Sometimes, there are things that don't—add up. Parts that don't come together. Do you know what I mean?"

"I know that sometimes he's just not there. Off inside his head someplace."

"He had a terrible childhood. His father was a schizophrenic, and his mother wasn't able to cope, so Dan ended up taking care of things. I think Dan's afraid a lot of the time. That his life is just going to fall apart and he won't be able to stop it."

"That must be an awful feeling."

"Yes. And I can't—I can't make it *all right* for him. I wish I could."

"And I can't make it *all right* for Sean to love me. I wish I could."

"We are in the same boat, aren't we? The Bobbsey Twins. And we both loved men who died too soon."

"At least Morris didn't want to die, Kitty. I've never really been able to convince myself it wasn't my fault, somehow, that Jeff went off to Vietnam."

"Oh Peg, no, don't blame yourself." She sighed again. "We women do get to clean up the messes that men make, don't we? And if we're not perfect at it, we blame ourselves."

They ate in silence for a moment, and then Peg said, "Kitty, Sean says there's trouble in Dan's campaign."

"Yes, I guess it's why I've been so anxious lately." She told Peg about how Rolvag's people were trying to exploit her relationship with Dan.

"That's really rotten."

"Yes, he was starting to pull ahead in the polls, and then *this*. It's a new sensation for me, and I don't like it at all. I'm used to being behind the scenes. I feel so—exposed."

"You're sure this is a deliberate attempt to get at Dan?"

"No question about it. Adam Crabtree has a plant inside Rolvag's campaign. My dear, it seems I am *infamous* in Omaha."

"That's a sleazy trick."

"It's a sleazy business, so I shouldn't be surprised. But what can I do? And of course, they're very careful. The word Jew is never used."

"How is Dan reacting to all this?"

"Oh, he tries to brush it off, at least in front of me. But I know he's worried. He *is* slipping in the polls."

"Adam Crabtree is smart. What's his idea?"

"A firing squad at dawn. For me. Adam and I do not get along. He looks at me and all he sees is three points on the Harris Poll down the toilet."

"Would a story help? Call attention to what Rolvag is doing?"

"Adam thinks it would make things worse. Oh Peg, is it possible that *I* could cost Dan the election? Could I live with that? Knowing that every time he looked at me, he'd see his lost chances?"

"Kitty, I think when people pull that lever they have more on their minds than who Dan—"

"Sleeps with?"

"Yeah."

"You know, for the first time in my life, well, I'm just glad Israel's *there*. Hell, my family spent a fortune on that place, but I never thought—well, it's nice to have someplace to go."

"You think all the crap is gone, and you find it isn't."

"Yes. Living in Washington, you forget. Our little world is a bit like Paris; people from all over who are very cosmopolitan. People here can work together and like each other even when their governments are at swords' points. It made me forget the rest of the world isn't like that."

"Oh Kitty, what can I do? I hate to see them get away with this!"

"Yes, so do I. I'm a doer, the thing I hate about this is feeling so helpless. If Dan and I were married, it would be different. We could meet this head on." She shrugged.

"Maybe you two just ought to get married."

Kitty shook her head. "We've been talking about it. But I don't want Dan to marry me just to win an election." She shook her head. "Oh, why am I so unsure of him? I know he loves me, but everything seems so uncertain."

"We *are* in the same boat, aren't we, Kitty?"

Kitty reached over and put her hand on Peg's. "And likely to stay that way. But it helps to talk about it, doesn't it."

After lunch with Kitty, Peg spent the rest of the day writing a piece on campus protests she was putting together. She left early because it was Thursday and she had a special reason to get home.

When she walked into her apartment, she saw Sean's jacket on a chair. She heard the water running in the shower, so she slipped quickly out of her clothes and stepped into the shower with him.

"Oh my God!" he said. "You scared me."

"Who did you think it was?"

"The killer from *Psycho*."

She picked up a bar of soap and started to rub lather across his chest. "How was your day?"

"Rotten. The governor is still sitting on his duff. How was yours?"

"Aggravating. I had a call from Jim Brannigan. They're having trouble getting their hands on the autopsy report. It may take time. Here, stand under the spray to get the soap off. Oh, good. Running water is so sexy. Why didn't we ever do this before?"

"In the Greystone, if we wanted running water, we'd have to stand in the toilet and flush."

"Ugh." She picked up the washcloth and swatted him with it.

"Ohhh! Ohh! It hurts so good."

"Nothing like a little flagellation to get an Irish Catholic in the mood. Let me put some soap here, too."

"You play with that and you know what happens."

"You turn into a frog."

"Yes."

"So that's why you say ribbet! ribbet! ribbet! when we make love."

"Yes. And frogs just love zorts. I will kiss your green and warty toes."

"That's disgusting."

"Okay. I'll kiss these, then. They're not green."

"Or warty!"

"These little things could be warts. Umm. Umm. Tasty." '

"Oh that's nice. Oh don't stop. Oh yes. Oh, I'd like to do something to you."

"Yes. Oh yes, please."

"I love you. I love doing this to you."

She pressed her lips to his belly, his thighs, teased him until he could barely stand it anymore, then pleased him until he hardly noticed that he was inhaling so much water he was in danger of drowning. Coughing, he pulled her to her feet and pressed her against him, moving his body against hers.

"Sean. Ohh. Ohh. Sean, Here?"

"Ribbet! Ribbet! Ribbet!"

Afterward, he toweled her off, gently, and said, "All that time I had you fetch my Mallomars, and I didn't know my zort's real talent."

"Zorts have three talents," she answered, in a throaty, snuffly zort voice. "We fetch Mallomars. We eat bugs. We give great head."

He put his arms around her. "I love you, Peg. Oh God, I love you so."

Later on, they sat close together on the couch and he said to her, "You made those noises in your sleep last night. Was it the dream?"

She nodded. "I wonder if I'll ever get rid of it. The awful thing is that it's in slow motion, we're moving across the sand, and I know what's going to happen. And then I see the head. I want to run, but I can't. I wonder if I'll ever get that image out of my head."

"I have something that might help. Somebody for you to sleep with when I'm not here."

He got up and went to a bag that was sitting on a chair and pulled out a teddy bear. Its grin was one quarter missing, its once golden hair had faded to a dingy yellow, and one of its eyes drooped.

"Fuzzy! Oh, it's Fuzzy!"

He tucked the bear in her arms, and she hugged it as she would a long-lost friend. "Oh Fuzzy, you look so disreputable. What have you been up to these last twenty-five years?"

"He's totally dissolute. After the sights he saw in his youth."

"That's right. He was in the tent the day we played doctor. Fuzz, you old pervert, it's good to see you." She laughed. "I thought at first you were going to bring in Big John."

"No, he's busy over in the grocery aisle."

"Oh I love him!" She planted a kiss on Fuzzy's begrimed nose. "I will keep him forever."

Sean flopped down on the couch and put Fuzzy between them. "What's the movie tonight?"

"*Casablanca.*"

"Round up the usual suspects."

"We'll always have Paris."

"Peg, do you mind not going out? I mean, just hanging around watching old movies?"

"I love old movies."

"I know. But you shouldn't spend all your time with me. You ought to have more friends. Go out to parties."

"I'm not a party person. I don't do well in groups."

"Peg, it's just— Oh damn, I love you, and I don't ever want to hurt you. But it seems I always do. Sooner or later."

"Sean, you never made me any promises. I know what you are. What you'll always be."

"But you have to think about the future."

"When I was in Sinai, I learned a lot about living for today. Who the hell knows if there is going to be a future. Let tomorrow take care of itself."

"I do love you, Peg."

She nestled close to him. "I think we are like these little birds I read about. They hatch together in the sand, and each chick gets imprinted on one special chick very early. They always try to find that other chick, and they can tell it from five thousand other chicks who look exactly alike. They just know."

"I'll always love you, Peg. Even if, even—"

She pressed her fingers to his lips. "Tomorrow doesn't exist, Sean."

"We'll always have Paris."

"Yes," she said, "we will."

But she had the dream again that night. The face on the head on the sand was that of the young Israeli soldier, and then it had Jeff's face and then Sean's, eyes blank and staring. She woke up crying, "No, oh no!" He put his arms around her and wiped the sweat from her forehead and the image dimmed. But it was a long time before she was able to sleep again. Why was she having the dream so often, lately? Was her subconscious trying to grapple with that basic fear of hers, the fear of being left? A fear that her love was a poisoned well? Everybody she had loved in her whole life had left her. There was another dream, not as bad as the half-track, but one that sent a shiver of desolation along her spine when she awoke from it. She was wandering in a fog, crying out people's names. She didn't know who the people were, but no one would answer. She called louder and louder, to be answered only by silence. There was no one there, just the night and the fog and the eerie wail of her own voice, calling unknown people's names.

She pressed closer against Sean's body, needing the comfort of it. She buried her face against his neck, and the warm, musky male scent of him reassured her. Until the thought came. It always did.

I am going to lose him.

She shivered and he said, "Peg, are you okay?"

"I'm okay."

She had him now, but God was there, in the wings, patient. He would win. He always did.

It would hurt when he left, even more than before. She was older and less resilient, now. She had the sudden thought that each time someone left her they took part of her soul with them, and that perhaps in the end there wouldn't be anything left of her at all. She would only be a wraith wandering in the fog, calling the names of people who had long since gone away.

She shivered again, a tremor that shook her whole body. He touched her hair and said, "Peg, what is it? Tell me."

She wanted to say, "Sean, don't leave me! Don't you leave me too!" But she said. "It's the dream. It makes me cold."

"I'm here. I'll keep you warm. It can't hurt you, Peg."

"Hold me close. Hold me."

"I will," he said. "I will."

"Faggots!" James Barret Putnam said, his voice a high, patrician twang. Tom was out of town, so Putnam was editing her copy. JBP (as he liked to be called) had little sympathy for anyone who didn't want to trot off to Vietnam to get his head blown off.

"Little fairies," he muttered, at a line about antiwar demonstrators. The closest James Barret Putnam had come to combat was getting mugged in Harvard Square. Men who had never been in a real war, she observed, were the ones who always talked about it with nostalgia.

"You are not *objective*, Morrison." It was his old refrain. If you weren't a robot, pretending your emotions were in permanent cold storage, you were not objective.

"If you mean I have feelings about Saigon, you bet your ass I do. I've seen the body bags piled up like garbage."

"I know you have a personal—problem with Vietnam, and I'm sorry. But you are letting emotions get in the way of this story."

"Emotions *are* the story! What do you think this is, some nice little exercise you can debate in *Foreign Affairs Quarterly?* It's about kids who don't want to come back as garbage from a war that doesn't make any sense!"

JPB gave a martyred sigh that said, "Deliver me from this overwrought broad."

"Have you ever seen a kid put in a body bag, JPB? I have. He was eighteen. He had such smooth skin, like a baby's. He didn't have a mark on him. Bled to death, internally. His head fell to the side, almost like he was asleep, and then they closed up the bag and tossed it on the pile. They had more garbage to package. When you've seen that, JPB, then you can tell *me* what the story is. Because I damn well know it. I can hear it, I can smell it. I can *feel* it!"

She was still fuming when she met Con for lunch at the Washington Roof. But Con was grinning from ear to ear, and Peg knew what it was.

"You got the Hill!"

"I got it. Constance W. Masters, congressional corespondent, that's me."

"Champagne. On the *Tribune*, what the hell."

Con took a sip of the champagne and said, "Dammit, Peg, you *know* they're going to say I got this because I'm sleeping with George. But I *earned* this."

"They always say it. Every time I had an interview with some general they said I was screwing him."

"Were you ever?"

"No. I had a firm rule, no sleeping with sources. But I heard people say it about me in Sinai. A hundred and ten and we were getting shot at and I was *screwing?* Crazy."

"I want people to know I didn't get this on my back. I work hard, and so do most of the women reporters in this town. Okay, there are a few who peddle their asses, but no more than the men do. Some of these guys would suck anybody's cock. Metaphorically speaking."

"If you want to count whores, the men outnumber the women two to one. It's funny, Con, all my life I wanted to join the male club. Play on the turf with the big boys. But I was always—out of step. Feeling things they didn't feel. I'm just now starting to realize that I don't have to apologize for beig a woman. It makes me a good journalist. It's like I grew up in a whole different culture than they did. I see things they don't."

"But you're supposed to keep your mouth shut."

"For the first time I'm starting to see that the things I feel are legitimate. I'm right about this story and Putnam is wrong. He's off base. And that's a surprise."

"Why?"

"Because I bought the whole package. I thought *their* world was the right one. It was a package deal, all or nothing."

"It still is. Don't kid yourself."

"But if I was part of their world, then I was *better* than other women. I was proud of that. At parties, I used to avoid reporters' wives, because I didn't want people to think I was one of *them.* Boring. Unimportant. I had such contempt for women."

"Self-hate, Peg. We were bright little girls. We looked around and saw who had the power and who got to do the fun stuff. So we wanted to be like men."

"Like blacks who want to be white?"

"Sure. Jews who want to be Episcopalians."

"I bought such *shit.* I bought a world invented *for* men, *by* men. Where we didn't count."

"You have just described the navy."

"If you don't have the power to define *yourself,* Con, you don't exist. If you let other people tell you what you are, you've given up the most important power there is."

"You know, that's what we did back at Immaculate Heart. *We* defined our little world. Not the nuns, not the church. Us. We decided what was important. With our little two-bit newspaper."

"Well, if I'm going to define the world, dammit, I'm not going to do it as a pseudo-man anymore. But it's risky when you challenge their rules. They get you by ridicule. Putnam just gives me this big sigh like his wife has just asked him for money to buy the drapes, and he has to put up with this silly broad."

"I like your idea, Peg. The real power is to say we *will* look at this and we *won't* look at that. Everything else flows from that one decision. And who gets to make it."

"Us, that's who." Peg lifted her glass. "Cheers on your new job. Sean will be really glad when I tell him."

"How are things going?"

"We laugh a lot. I think we can get through anything if we just keep our sense of humor."

"Peg, I am getting vibes. I think you are planning to be Sean's mistress for the long haul."

"Well, why not? He has the church and I have my work. We don't have to be together all the time."

"You were talking about kids."

"I'm thinking about adopting a child. From overseas, maybe. I have lots of connections."

"Don't go building castles in the air. This thing is going to end one of these days, then where will you be?"

"Who knows. Right now, it's great."

"Oh Peg, are you setting yourself up for another big smashup?"

"No, Con, I'm not really kidding myself. I know there's no real future for Sean and me."

"Would he leave the priesthood?"

"No. I fantasize, sometimes, that the Vatican will let priests marry, but it'll come too late for Sean and me."

"Oh God, Peg, it didn't turn out like we expected, did it? I've left my husband, I'm sleeping with a married man."

"And I'm screwing a priest. We are not exactly candidates for the Catholic Woman of the Year award, Constance Marie."

"Why not? Why should it go to those dull broads who iron

altar cloths?" She raised her glass. "To us, Peg. Catholic women of the year."

Peg touched Con's glass. "To us. Girls Forever Brave and True. Who define the world."

"I have something for you, Constance," George said, walking into the bedroom. "But you have to be completely naked."

"George, you are not into strange things, are you? You're not the guy with the crotchless panties?"

"No, he's twelve points ahead of me in the Harris Poll. Come on, darling, undress."

She took off her clothes and he took her by the hand and led her to the mirror. Then he opened a little box and took out an exquisite emerald-and-pearl pendant. He fastened it around her neck. The jewels hung in the cleft between her breasts.

"Oh George, it's lovely. But I can't accept this! It's too expensive."

"In college, I read this very silly book by Ayn Rand. The hero gave the heroine a necklace, but he said she could only wear it naked, because her body was so perfect. I always wanted to do that. Now I have."

"So I can only wear it starkers?"

"Yes. Now can you accept it?"

"Yes, but I'll find a way to show it off."

"You will?"

"Yes, I'll wear it to a nudist camp. I'll have three things bouncing around in the volleyball game."

He laughed and put his arms around her. "Oh Constance, you're wonderful. You make me feel young."

They made love, unhurriedly, and he was, as always, careful to please her. She enjoyed his lovemaking; it did not have the passion she had shared with Lee, when things were good. Lee didn't have skill, but he had a force that battered at her, carried her along, a hunger that was so contagious it made her as ravenous as he. Lee was beer and skittles, and sweat. George was a gourmet who played her like some fine instrument. It was sweet, and lovely. Why did she miss the sweat?

After they made love he lay on the bed beside her and ran his finger along the necklace.

"I love giving you presents. You're not jaded or greedy. You appreciate things so."

"That's because I was poor."

"Were you?"

"Yes. Not welfare poor. But our things were tacky. My mother used to buy clothes secondhand from the St. Vincent de Paul Thrift Shop. Once I went to a party and a girl recognized a dress her mother gave away. I was humiliated."

"Oh my darling Con. How very sad. Don't worry, your days with St. Vincent de Paul are over."

Later, at the house on Foxhall Road, Con found Kitty drawing up the guest list for a gala she was giving for the Kennedy Center.

"Kitty, I talked to George about campaigning for Dan. He says he would be happy to do it."

"Oh that's lovely. George is so—solid. So *Protestant*. I think it would help."

"Is Dan still dropping in the polls?"

"Not as bad as it was. I hope it's turning around. Oh I do hope." She chewed on the end of her pencil. "George Stevens Junior. A definite yes. Handsome men do spice up a party. I'm keeping busy. Get my mind off things."

"Kitty, is there anyone you could never get over here?"

"Yes. J. Edgar Hoover. Oh, if I had his *files!*"

"Does he know everything about everybody?"

"Yes. Knew about Jack Kennedy's girlfriends. Rubbed Bobby's nose in it. Edgar sent an agent to see me once, about a young congressman I was quite fond of. He was a bachelor. Hoover distrusts bachelors. Except himself. Thinks they are all gay."

"Was he? The congressman?"

"Of course. But very discreet. Didn't pinch ass in the cloakroom. Hoover's man asked if my friend had any habits that might make him a security risk."

"What did you say?"

"I said he smoked, but I didn't think the Kremlin was big on lung carcinomas. Then he asked me—these were his exact words—if my friend was a sodomite. I said, no, I thought he was a Methodist."

Con laughed. "Kitty, you're great."

"I dislike fascists. Hoover puts anybody who doesn't stick with strict missionary position right into his files."

"You think you're in there?"

"Yes, for being Jewish. He thinks that's a perversion too. Probably a notch below transvestite."

"You could use what *you* know."

"No, I collect chips by being quiet. Bipartisan ones."

"How are Republicans and Democrats different in their hijinks?"

Kitty sat back, her lips curving into that feline smile. It was a favorite subject of hers.

"Republicans come to Washington in the same spirit as being sent to the foreign missions. Back home they're bankers and businessmen, and they can't wait to get back home where they're comfortable with people as dull as they are. But when they go off the deep end, it's *very* bad."

"Like how?"

"Like the assistant secretary at HEW who had himself beaten every Tuesday night by black hookers dressed as nuns. Very kinky, dear."

"And Democrats?"

"From small towns? Cheap women, wild parties, cheap booze. Southerners go for cute young things right off the bus from Knoxville. A little fellatio between roll calls. You can tell by the newsletters. The secretaries are not getting fifteen thousand for typing, but they are not untalented."

"Northerners?"

"Liberals like smart career women. Associate producers, AA's—"

"Reporters?"

"Reporters. And white wine and exotic sex. Not kinky, exotic."

"What's the difference?"

"Kinky means people think it's very dirty when they're doing it. Exotic means you're proud at having mastered a new skill. Like learning to hang-glide."

"Fellatio is exotic and a blow-job is kinky."

"Exactly. Velvet whips are exotic and a belt from K-Mart is kinky."

"Vibrators?"

"Exotic. Unless you use your Mickey Mouse toothbrush."

"Anything from Fredericks of Hollywood is kinky."

"Yes. If it's black lace from Yves St. Laurent, it's exotic. Even if you're a guy."

"Gay sex?"

"Exotic. Unless it's at the YMCA men's room. Then it's kinky."

"Back to liberals. Are they all good in bed?"

"Liberals read *everything* in the sex manuals, like they read all 1,500 pages of the GAO report on Food for Peace in Ghana. They feel guilty, Constance, if you don't have an orgasm. It's like getting a low rating from the ADA. In fact, lately they feel guilty if you don't have *multiple* orgasms."

"Conservatives?"

"They don't know women are supposed to have orgasms. If they did, they'd file a bill outlawing them. Party hacks go for B-girls. They don't know a lot about orgasms because they pass out from booze before they have them. But they think maybe they did."

"Congresswomen?"

"Vestal virgins. Have to be. If a woman so much as dared to put her hand on the knee of a well-hung AA, they'd stone her in the cloakroom. And the man throwing the first stone wouldn't have his fly zipped from his session with Daisy Mae."

"That bad?"

"Oh, a discreet affair is tolerated, but there's no way a woman can raunch around like a man. The double standard is alive and well on the banks of the Potomac."

"What about a reporter who sleeps with a senator?"

"Newspaperwomen are expected to be a little round in the heels. No one is scandalized. Until she gets promoted, then they say she's sleeping her way up. So be a little discreet, Constance. Don't go back to the district with him. They like seeing mistresses even less than they like seeing how he voted on welfare. Wear a high collar. Tits in the East Room are okay for wives, but mistresses should stick to ruffles. Don't call attention to yourself, and you'll be all right. Flash does not sit well in Washington, dear, the men distrust it. What plays in Manhattan is *death* in Foggy Bottom."

"I'll remember that."

"You had better," Kitty said.

SEVENTEEN

Peg drove up and down the street twice, looking carefully at the row house on the modest street, lined with other houses very much like it.

"Nobody around," she said to Con. Peg was wearing jeans and a pea jacket. Con also had on jeans, and a red car coat buttoned against the cold December air.

"What about the family?" Con asked.

"Still staying in Baltimore."

"It looks boarded up, Peg."

"Yeah, maybe we can get in through the back. Thanks for coming with me. I didn't want to ask Sean. He's already had an FBI guy on his back."

"So just ask your old friend, Constance Marie. She won't mind going to the slammer."

"We'll flash our press cards if we get caught."

"What if they recognize me from my picture on 'Cocktail Capers'? What am I supposed to say? 'Oh, you mean this *isn't* Blair House?'"

Peg parked the car on a street around the corner from the row house. She and Con walked to the house and tried the front door. It was locked. They walked around to the back, went up on the back porch and tried the door. It was locked as well.

"Tight as a drum." Peg walked over to one of the back windows, which was covered over by nailed-on boards. She pulled at one of the boards. It came away slightly.

"One tug and the whole thing's off," she said.

"I think this is what they call breaking and entering."

Peg gave a yank and the whole board came loose in her hand. There was no glass in the window the boards covered. "No sweat. Come on, Slim. Let's go."

"This is true friendship, Peg."

"There's nobody here who will put his hand on your ass, like the last place you took *me*."

They climbed in through the window to find themselves standing in a furnished dining room. It looked undisturbed. There were even dishes on the table. They walked to the front of the house and into what had been the parlor. Peg gave a low whistle.

"Look at that wall. Jeez, it looks like D Day in here."

"Is this the room where the three guys were killed?"

"Yeah, it's a wonder anything got out alive." She stuck her finger into one of the many bullet holes on the back wall. "No wonder the cops never let the press in here. How's the light?"

She took a 35-millimeter camera out of her handbag and began to shoot pictures of the bullet-pocked wall. "Keep an eye out, Con."

Con moved to the window and looked up and down the street. "All quiet."

"Okay, just let me get a few more. These might come in handy."

"Oh shit, Peg."

"What?"

"Black and white just turned into the street."

"Let's go."

They ran to the back of the house and climbed through the window. As they hurried down the back steps Con looked at the end of the yard—which she hadn't noticed before—and said, "Oh no, there's a *fence* back there!"

"Hurry up, we can't go out the front!" Peg said, and she scrambled up and over the chain-link fence. Con, right behind her, was struggling, trying to get her body over the top. "Shit, shit, shit!"

Peg grabbed her arms and half-pulled, half-dragged her over the fence. "Jesus, Con, you'd think you'd learn to do this!"

"I'll kill you, Peg, I swear I will," she said as the two of them sprinted down the alley in back of the house. As they ran, the back door of one house opened and a middle-aged man leaned out and yelled at them, "Hey, you girls, what the hell were you doing in there?"

They broke into a dead run, darting across a street, then into another alley halfway up the block. They were both breathing hard as they passed an open garage door a few feet up the alley. Peg grabbed Con's arm and pulled her into it. They both stood still for a minute, out of breath. Con peered out into the alley and saw another black-and-white squad car going up the street.

"We are up shit's creek, Peg."

Peg looked out, and she saw the car had stopped, and the man who had yelled at them was standing on the corner, talking to two cops.

"We've got to get to the car."

"That guy saw us. He can ID us. They even know what we're wearing. How far would we get?"

"They're looking for a couple of teenagers, in jeans. I've got a whole load of clothes in my car, I was going to take them to the laundry."

"Where the hell is your car, anyway? My direction's all screwed up."

"At the far end of this alley, I think. Wait here."

Peg looked out, then scampered up the alley to the far end. She peered out into the street. Her car was parked almost directly opposite where she stood. There was no one on the street. She ran to the car, started it, and pulled it slowly down the alley and into the garage where Con was waiting. She jumped out and pulled the laundry bag out of the backseat.

"You made it. Thank God!" Con said.

Peg reached into the bag and tossed a blue jersey dress at Con. "This will fit."

Con wrinkled her nose. "Peg, this *smells*."

"Would you rather be fresh as a daisy in the Moore County lockup?" Peg asked, as she wiggled out of her jeans and into a wrinkled sweater and skirt.

Con slithered out of her jacket, jeans, and shirt. "My God, the dead of winter, I'm going to die of pneumonia."

As she was about to step into the blue dress, a male voice drifted through the open garage door.

"Goddamn kids. Probably wanted someplace to smoke dope."

"Yeah, let's check up here," said another voice.

Con looked at Peg, panicked, and Peg hissed, "Car! On the floor!"

Con, wearing only her bra and panties and clutching the dress, made a dive for the floor of the backseat. She just got there as the two cops rounded the corner. Peg, standing by the open front door of the car, said, "Oh my! Officers. Oh my! Is anything wrong?" She opened her blue eyes wide, the picture of innocence.

"Ma'am, is this your car?"

"Oh yes. Yes it is. I just got home."

"Did you drive down this alley?"

"Yes, I did."

"Did you see a couple of teenage girls, wearing jeans, one had a red jacket?"

"No. Oh no, officer, I didn't."

"Ma'am," one of the officers said suspiciously, "why is it that you aren't wearing a coat?"

"A coat? Oh." Peg giggled. "Well, I left my keys in the car so I just dashed out here to get them. I just forget everything." She giggled again. "My husband says I'd forget my head, except it's screwed on." Another giggle.

"Well, if you see those kids, will you please call us?"

"Oh yes, officer, I will. I have to go out again, but if I see them on the street or anything, I'll call you, right away."

"Thank you, ma'am."

She heard one of the policemen say, sotto voce, as they left the garage, "That one was a dip, wasn't she?"

Peg scrambled into the front seat and peered over it. Con was huddled on the floor, shivering, the goose bumps standing in rows on her skin.

"They're gone. You can come out now."

"Where's the goddamn dress? Oh my God, I've got pneumonia, I know it!" Con said, her teeth chattering. Peg helped her slide into the dress, and get into her jacket. Con stood, shivering, as Peg buttoned it up. "Peg, I was never so cold in my *life*. Thirty degrees and I am in my bra and panties, on the *floor*."

"Come on, let's get out of here."

She pulled the car out of the garage into the alley, and slowly drove it out to the street. The two patrolmen were standing on the sidewalk. Peg waved to them and smiled, as Con ducked her head. Con stayed down until they were three blocks away from the house.

"Heat. Oh God, turn on the heat."

"Here. It'll be warm in a minute."

"That was fast thinking, Peg, about forgetting the keys. I thought we were goners, for sure."

"That was my dippy broad act. Saved my life in Rhodesia. Some nutty colonel wanted to shoot me."

"What do you think those cops would have done if they'd found me on the floor in my bra and panties?"

"They would have said, 'Constance Masters! Aren't you supposed to be at Blair House?'"

Con sighed. "Why do I hang out with you, Peg? Whenever I do, it's trouble."

"Does seem that way."

Lee walked up the front walkway, his arm thrown casually around Leezy's shoulder. He was looking at Terry, laughing. Leezy had Con's dark hair, but Terry was the picture of Lee. Watching them through the window, Con thought, as she often did, seeing them together, My men.

And then she remembered.

The door slammed, and they came in, noisy as always. They were such noisy boys.

"We went swimming, at the Officers' Club," Leezy said. "It was fun."

Lee came into the kitchen behind the boys. "Terry almost beat me in the hundred meters. He is getting fast."

"I'm going to my room," Terry announced. She noticed that Terry always tried to get his mother and father alone together. A clever young man, her son.

"You got my stereo," Leezy whined.

"You can listen with me if you want to."

"Can I? That's neat. Neat."

"Oh, don't have an orgasm."

"Terry!" said his father.

"Aw, Dad."

Lee laughed. "All right. I guess that's not a swear."

Con looked at Lee and thought, suddenly, of the night Terry was born. Lee had brought her a huge bouquet of flowers and a stuffed elephant for Terry, and he had said, "We're a family now, Con. A real family. Navy all the way!"

He stood at the door to the kitchen, watching her marinate the steaks she was going to give the boys for dinner.

"Con, I found out something. It was in my group."

She looked at him, curiously. He hadn't said anything about the group since he had first mentioned it to her.

"It was my turn to talk. And the leader, Don, asked me if I had ever been abused as a child. And I said no. And he asked me, 'Not ever?'"

Lee's face was intent, earnest, as he told the story. Under Don's prodding he had said, "But I did have a dream, once. It was so vivid."

"Tell me about it."

"It was a nightmare. I was little, maybe five or six, I guess. And we had this cellar—it was a farmhouse—where my dad stored stuff he needed for the livestock. I was always scared of it because it was dark and it smelled."

"What happened in your dream?"

"My father took me downstairs. He was dragging me by the hand and I was crying, 'No, dad!'"

"What happened then?"

"It was cold and dark. I guess I must have done something bad, because in my dream my father made me take off my pants and lie across his workbench. It had a stain on it, in the shape of a pumpkin. Funny, that I would dream that. And he kept hitting me and hitting me with his belt. And I was screaming and begging him to stop."

"And did he?"

"There was blood, I remember. And he stopped hitting me, but he called me a coward and said he'd shut my mouth. And he took a hammer and jammed the handle of it down my throat. It hurt so much. And then he took it out and raised it up and said he was going to kill me."

"Then what."

"Nothing. I just woke up, I guess."

"Lee, that doesn't sound like a dream," said Curt, another member of the group.

"Oh, it's a dream. Things are all—floaty, disconnected, like they are in dreams."

"What words come to mind when you think of your father, Lee?" Don asked.

"Big. Very big."

"Is he a big man?"

"He's dead. Funny I should say that. He wasn't very big. Five-seven. But strong, he could lift hundred-pound sacks easy."

"What other things do you remember about the dream?"

"Not much. Blood. The belt buckle. Something about the belt buckle. He was scared. When he stopped hitting me, he— Oh my God!"

"What?"

"I have a scar. Now it's just a white line. On the back of my thigh. My wife asked me how I got it, and I said I didn't know."

"It wasn't a dream," Curt said.

"There was a lot of blood."

"You didn't dream it," Curt repeated.

"Not a dream?" Lee asked, blinking.

"It happened, Lee," Don said.

"The hammer. I was choking. It hurt so much."

"Lee, no child dreams details like that. The hammer, the pumpkin stain on the bench. Monsters, demons, yes. Not that."

"He did it to me? It was real?"

"Yes. *You* made it a dream."

"Why?"

"You were a child. How could you fight your father? You made it a dream so you could live with it."

"Why? Why did he do it to me? I was so little."

"You were a target. For his anger."

"But what did I do to deserve that?"

"Nothing," Curt answered. "We've all made people targets, haven't we? Isn't that what we talk about?"

"Oh God!"

"It's a bummer, isn't it?" said Bill, who had also been abused by his father. "The guy who's supposed to love you, and he hurts you."

"I still remember the feel of the hammer in my throat. It

hurt. God, it hurt! And I was gagging, and I—" Without warning, he began to sob, the memory washing over him in a torrent. He could feel the hard wood of the hammer against the pink, soft part of his throat. He couldn't stop sobbing. Bill and Curt walked over to him and put their hands on his shoulders until it finally halted.

"It's okay, Lee. It's okay."

"Lee," Don asked, "how do you feel about your father?"

"I hate him! I wish he wasn't dead so I could kill him! Jam the goddamn hammer down his throat. I hate him!"

Con listened, amazed, as Lee told the story. It was so different from the picture of his childhood he had presented her with—a childhood straight out of *Boy's Life*, the close-knit farm family, the sunny, story-book Midwestern life. His parents had died in a car crash when he was a plebe at the Academy. He had often said to her, "Con, my parents would have loved you so." She saw them all sitting around the table in the farmhouse having Thanksgiving dinner, Lee's father carving the turkey with his big, sturdy farmer's hands, in his eyes a glint of laughter as he made a homespun joke. Later, the boys would sit on his knee as he read to them. And it was a lie. All of it.

"It's out now. It's real," Lee told Con.

"That's good."

"You said I made you *her*, remember? And I made myself *him*. Oh Con, are we all trapped in some crazy cycle where we do things over and over, like in Dante? Do we live our parents' lives all over again?"

"No, we don't. I wasn't like my mother. I fought back. So it doesn't have to go on."

"Can I stop it? I'm so filled with hate for him. Was it *him* I was hitting when I hit you? Can I stop it?"

"I can't answer that. I just know it's possible not to be like your parent."

"Do you hate me like I hate him?"

"No. If I hadn't fought back, I think I would. In a funny way I know something about myself that I didn't know before. I won't ever be a victim."

"I was always so good. Well-behaved. Top of my class at the Academy. Because I was scared shitless that if I wasn't good something awful would happen to me."

"But it had already happened."

"Yes. Under Dr. Jekyll, was Mr. Hyde always there? Wanting vengeance? I don't know myself anymore, Con."

"Or maybe you're just starting to."

"Is there a monster in me? One I can't control? I don't think it could ever happen again, but I don't know. And if it did, I'd kill myself. I won't live as that kind of person."

"But the monster has a face now."

"My father."

"Yes. Maybe that's the first step to getting rid of it."

"Jesus Christ, life is hard enough without having our parents fuck us up."

She nodded. "Isn't that the truth."

He was quiet. "I miss you. Con. God, I miss being with you." He reached out to touch her shoulder. Involuntarily, she flinched. He took his hand away, as if it had been burned.

"I'm sorry." She regretted her reaction, unintended as it was. She reached out to touch his shoulder.

"Lee, I'm not ready, yet. There are scars you don't see. I'm not ready to know if we have anything. But I do remember the good things. Like the night Terry was born, that stupid elephant. Bigger than he was. But I can't—"

"I know. I'm trying to learn to be patient."

After he left, she wondered why she had blanched at his touch. Was it that night? Or was it because she was sleeping with George?

It was so easy with George. He made things easy. He was handsome, he was rich, he was witty. Life with George would be like the big slide she used to love at Glen Echo Park when she was a kid, a long, easy carefree glide with no big bump at the end. There were no monsters gnawing at George. He was ambitious, but not driven. Intelligent, but he didn't have to show it off. He had that lovely sureness that only old money stamps on the genes. It was so easy with George.

Sean was walking the four blocks from the Rayburn Building to the spot where he had parked his Toyota, and he was worrying, something he was very good at. The governor was dallying with the interstate, and while he did, the opposition was rolling up its big guns. Dan was barely holding his own in the polls, and Kitty was shaky because of the rotten stuff they were pulling on her. The prosecutors were putting pressure on him not to testify for Kiki, and the man from the FBI had been by again. A nice, polite visit, but a reminder they had their eye on him. He was starting to get paranoid. If the FBI found out what he was doing for Dan, could they leak that to the press? A leftist priest with ties to the Panthers would really help Dan's campaign. He shook his head, told himself it was just paranoia. The FBI didn't give a damn about him. And then there was Bill; As a real estate salesman, he was no P. T. Barnum.

"I thought it would be a snap, little brother. Show people around a bathroom and then pick up your commission. But you bust your butt showing a house to people, and it turns out they're just amusing themslves on a dull Sunday."

"A lot of wasted effort, huh?"

"Yeah. And Rene doesn't want me back. She's got some new guy, a lawyer. And my partners, the bastards, are giving me a real hard time about the money. If I don't get the money— Sean, I'm not making a living at this."

"It'll get better. As people get to know you."

"I hope so. But it's so hard, Sean. Every day I get up and say, 'Shit, can I get through today?' It's so goddamn hard."

Sean walked on, worrying. He had plenty of things on his mind, but mostly he was worrying about Peg. "Live for today," she said, but it wasn't in his nature. As he walked, he slipped into the fatuous romantic reverie he had been entertaining of late. He saw Monsignor Sean McCaffrey—a few touches of gray at the temples—walking along the Seine with internationally known journalist Peg Morrison—who also had a few wisps of gray, but otherwise hadn't aged at all. He was in his civvies, of course, and they strolled to a small café where they had medallions of veal and a good red wine before they went back to her apartment overlooking Sacre Coeur for an energetic night of lovemaking. After this charming interlude, he would go back to his churchly duties and she to her byline, having pledged to meet in two weeks in Rome.

"Adolescent twaddle!" he said aloud. He was thirty-one years old, and this was the fantasy of a seventeen-year-old mind. What Peg needed was not a man who dropped in and out of her life the way Sean McCaffrey did. She had lost too much—her parents, her fiancé in a terrible accident. And she was a very private person, not one who had lots of friends around. She needed a man who would be there every night when the dream attacked her with grotesque images. She needed a man who would give her children. She would be a wonderful mother, with all the warmth and laughter she had to give, and she wouldn't smother them, because she had her own work to sustain her. He thought of her, married, with another man's child, and it felt like barbed wire being drawn slowly through his gut.

There was something else as well—his conscience, tender as the underbelly of a snail. Why was he cursed with it? He had decided to deal with the whole situation by dividing himself into two watertight compartments. One of them was the man who loved Peg Morrison, loved her in every way a man can love a woman. The sensuality they fired in each other was astonishing, and it was he who led the way. When he stood, naked and erect before her, he had wondered if this was how Adam felt in the dawn of time, vulnerable, powerful, exactly as God intended his creation to be. But there was the other compartment as well, the man sworn to chastity, who tried to follow in the footsteps of the Living Christ, who had heard a call on a morning in spring when the world had turned golden around him and the presence of God was an amber liquid in his veins. He had known, suddenly, that his life's outline had been stamped by a force other than his own.

Like matter and antimatter, the two parts could not touch—without blowing each other to bits. So he tried to keep them tightly sealed. But sometimes the priest was a man, the man a priest. A thought of the little drumbeat in the hollow of her neck, of the sloping line of her breasts in the darkness, would come into his mind and the need for her would be so great he would actually feel faint. And other times, at night, in bed with her, the priest would chill the heart of the man, and he would hear a cold, quiet voice saying, "Lord, have mercy on me, a sinner."

He walked on and a thought crossed over the barricades he had erected in his mind against it. *I could be like other men.*

It was what lay behind a door in his mind, one he had never opened. He had taken vows, and he had meant every word he had uttered as he knelt under the dome of the cathedral and said the words that forever separated him from the broad river of other men. His whole life hung on them, and if he ever let that door swing open—no, it couldn't be opened. Without the priesthood, who was Sean McCaffrey? He had the odd notion that if you took away the collar, it would be like Dorothy throwing water on the Wicked Witch in *The Wizard of Oz*. He would just disappear, call out in a cackling voice, "I'm melting! I'm melting!", and all that would be left was a pile of black vestments in a crumpled heap on the floor.

He was restless and irritable all day. Peg sensed that as soon as he walked into the apartment. She had a way of picking up his moods without his having to say a word. She walked over to him, kissed him and said, "Let's go out to a movie tonight. Getting out will do us both good."

"I don't think that's a good idea."

"We could go over to Alexandria. Nobody would see us."

"Peg, there's a whole lot of people who would like to discredit Action. I can't risk it."

"People know we're friends. We used to go out a lot together."

"That was before we were—sleeping together."

"What difference does that make?"

"Because, if the archbishop called me in, before I could just say to him, 'No, I'm not having an affair.'"

"Why is that his business?"

"He's my boss."

"My boss doesn't get to know who I sleep with."

"If he asked me, what am I supposed to do? Lie? add *that* to—"

"To what, Sean?"

"Nothing."

"To what?"

"Let's just drop it!" he snapped.

"No, we aren't going to drop it."

"Dammit, Peg, you never let anything go, do you?"

"Fornication? Is that what you mean, Sean? Do you confess to *fornication*? Jesus!"

She walked to the window, looking out at the street. He saw the misery in the line of her neck, her shoulders. Suddenly contrite, he went and put his arms around her, and said, "I'm sorry, Peg. Please, let's not fight. Please."

He held her and kissed the back of her neck. "I love you. You know I do."

She turned to face him, and rested her head against his chest.

"Oh yes, Sean. We shouldn't fight. Life is too short. We don't have time to fight each other."

"We'll go out. We can go out, if you'd like."

"No, it's crummy out. Who wants to drive to Alexandria? Let's just stay in and relax. We need it, our nerves are on edge."

"What's wrong, Peg?"

"I got the autopsy report. And there's going to be a big fight over the story. It seems like I'm always fighting them, Sean. I just want to do my job, I get so tired of fighting. It's like gnats, always there. I get so tired."

"Peg, I'm sorry. I always dump my troubles on you. Do the same to me, let me help. Don't always be so tough."

"You help, just by being here. You don't know how much you help."

"Tell you what. Let's order something really fattening and expensive from that catering service around the corner. And a bottle of champagne."

"Oh, that's a wonderful idea."

They ordered the beef Wellington, and when the order came, Peg started to open the champagne, but Sean shook his head and said, "Let's have the white wine. Save the champagne for later."

After dinner, he took the champagne bottle from the bucket and said, "Get undressed, we're going to drink this in bed."

They sat together naked in bed and Peg said, "Oh Herb, we've come a long way from the Greystone. Champagne." Herb and Thelma were the names they had used when they called each other about Elmore Brown—in case any phones were bugged. He struggled with the cork, and they laughed as it shot across the room. He poured two glasses of the champagne.

"This is elegant. I am out of my league."

"You should be used to glamour, a big-time foreign correspondent."

"Hah! Usually it was Spam in a Jeep. Or some guy trying to

pinch my ass over a warm beer in a bar at the edge of the known world."

He smiled and drew the covers back from her body.

"You have something in mind, Herb."

"I do, Thelma."

He took his glass and gently dipped her breast into the champagne. Then he leaned over and tenderly sucked it off her nipple.

"Ummm. Oh, that's good." He dipped again, and tasted. "The year is 1939."

"The champagne isn't that old."

"I am not talking about the champagne."

"Ummm, yes, I do like this. Oh, this is nice."

She closed her eyes and let the sensation sweep over her, and then she opened them again and said, "My turn, Herb," and she pulled the sheet away from him. She looked at his body, thinking what a wonderful invention it was, the muscles taut across the belly, the mat of hair like a thicket on his chest and thighs, and between his legs, the part of him that had thrilled her so when she first saw it when she was six years old. The passage of time had only added luster to its endearing young charms.

"Thelma," he said, "do you mean—"

"Come on Herb, let's try it. Don't be a chicken."

"It's always trouble when you say that. Ahhhhhhhh!"

"What's the matter?"

"Peg, it's *cold!*"

"Just wait. I'll warm you up."

"Oh yes. Ummm. Peg this is very nice. Oh."

Then she dripped the champagne up his body and started licking it from his chest.

"You are a sexy wench, aren't you?"

"I just can't help myself when I'm with you."

"Good."

He pushed her down on her back and lay on top of her, pinning her wrists to the bed. Then he moved slowly up and down, teasing her with his body. "I am never going to let you up. I'm going to keep you like this until you beg for it."

"I won't."

He moved on her, teasingly. "Won't you?"

"No I won't."

"We'll just see."

"I never will. I won't. I won't. Oh. Oh. Oh yes I will. Oh Sean, don't stop. Don't stop. Please don't stop that. Oh, please."

"I love to make you crazy. Come. Just let it come, come on me, oh yes, that's right. Oh God, I love to do this to you."

She sank her teeth into the warm skin of his shoulder and left marks there, though she did not break the skin. Then she thrust her hips up to him so he could enter her. When he came into her she felt herself spinning away again, out of control, her own voice a strange cry to her ears. When he exploded inside of her she felt as if he had broken through into some secret chamber, pierced it, flooded it. She was gripped, suddenly, urgently, by the desire to be filled in another way, to keep inside of her a part of him that would grow and live and swell inside of her. She had never experienced such a visceral need to be pregnant. She wanted to reach up and rip away the diaphragm that blocked the rush of his sperm to her womb. It wouldn't be hard. One good tug would do it. And sperm lived for hours; hardy little buggers.

He touched her face, gently, and said, "Peg?"

She smiled at him. "Just too overwhelmed to speak."

She wondered what he would say if he knew what she was thinking. A mistress with an illegitimate child just might be a stumbling block on his move up the hierarchical ladder:

"Archbishop McCaffrey, we are considering you for cardinal."

"Oh good, Your Holiness, I'm ready."

"There is a problem, however. You have a mistress."

"She doesn't get in the way much. A couple of nights a week. Most guys spend more time on the golf course."

"Archbishop, you have a bastard!"

"No, he's a sweet kid most of the time. He only gets mean when his Little League team loses. He plays third base."

"Archbishop McCaffrey, that is a scandal to the faithful!"

"I could switch him to short. Would that be better?"

"Princes of the church are not supposed to be Little League dad-dies!"

"Well, I considered Pop Warner, but it's too damn rough. Lots of knee injuries."

He traced the outline of her lips with his fingers and said, "Peg, my beautiful Peg. Are you happy?"

"Yes, I am, Sean."

"So am I. I've never been so happy in my life. I wish—"

"Don't wish. Just hold me." She shivered in his arms.

"What is it, Peg?"

"I don't know, it's just—"

"Just what?"

"I don't know. I just had an awful feeling all of a sudden. Like things are going wrong. Like the world is tipping upside down."

"I'm here, Peg. I won't let it. I won't."

And he held her, until the shivering stopped, and she felt warm and safe, in his arms. But outside the winds were blowing, the same ones, she thought, that had blown everything away in her life before, and nothing could stop them. No one. Not even God.

"Hold me," she said. "Just hold me."

EIGHTEEN

"Just how did we get this?" James Barret Putnam barked. He, Tom Friedman, Buck Stollmeyer, and the metro editor, Ed Kraft, were meeting with Peg in Tom's office. Putnam had the autopsy report, and a copy of Peg's story, in his hand.

"I told you," Peg said. "It comes from Catholics for Peace and Justice in Moore County. In the story, they're the 'reliable sources' that furnished a copy of the document."

"And how did they get it?"

Peg looked at Tom, then back at Putnam. "I don't know. I didn't ask."

"They stole it," Buck Stollmeyer snorted. "That's how the hell they got it."

"Probably," Tom said.

"I don't care how they got it," Peg snapped. "The report shows that the bullet that killed the neighbor in the Panther case came from the same kind of rifle issued to the Moore County cops."

"No wonder they didn't want the report out." Ed Kraft was salivating; the story would run in his section, and *The Washington Post* didn't have it.

"This may prove a man charged with murder is innocent," Tom Friedman said.

"It doesn't prove anything," Putnam argued. "At the press conference, the rifle the police said they found in the house was the same kind of rifle."

"You believe *that*, and you believe Chicken Little." Ed Kraft laughed. "The sky is falling."

Peg continued to push. "Elmore Brown says there were no guns in the house."

"You believe *him*, a nigger street scum?" Buck Stollmeyer asked.

"It does seem like a bit of a coincidence," Tom Friedman said, "for the Panthers to have *exactly* the same kind of rifle the police used. And fired a shot with it that killed a man on the *same* side of the street."

"I can guess what happened." Ed Kraft smiled wryly. "The cops panicked, covered up. There's a lot of real jerks on the Moore County force. The Untouchables, they ain't."

Tom reached into his drawer, passed around blow-ups of the pictures Peg had taken of the wall in the Panther house. Ed Kraft looked at one and shook his head. "Holy shit!"

"Where did we get these?" Buck Stollmeyer asked, suspiciously.

"I took them."

"You? When were you there?"

"Last week."

"How did you get in?"

"Back window."

"Jesus, breaking and entering."

"No, simple trespass. I didn't take anything, I had no intent to rob."

"You see what we're looking at here," Putnam said. "Receiving stolen property, trespassing, consorting with a known felon. Are we a newspaper, or are we an accomplice of crazy radicals and black hoods?"

"So maybe we should give the story to the *Post?*" Peg suggested.

"Oh Jesus!" Buck Stollmeyer was torn between his desire to stomp all over the *Post*, and his fear of this story.

"This is one hell of a story." Ed Kraft whistled low.

"This story doesn't prove anything," protested Putnam. "It's still the word of a bunch of hoods against the police."

Kraft looked disgusted. "Come on, JPB. This report blows the police story all to hell. Anybody can see that. Why the hell didn't they release it? It smells. We can't sit on this story!"

"It's a bitch, but we got to go with it," agreed Stollmeyer.

"If it goes page one, it jumps to metro," said Kraft.

"We've got to lawyer this one. We can't just rush this one into print. For God's sake, this is dangerous stuff. I think we ought not to use it at all. We are a responsible newspaper, not a rag."

"Christ, JPB, you'd sit on the goddamn second coming."

"Just because I am *responsible*, Kraft, and you'd jump the gun and land us in a libel suit—"

"We're a *newspaper*, not a damn Harvard journal."

"All right, let's not take potshots at each other," Tom said. "I just wanted to hear what you all had to say. If I ask go or no go, what do you say? Buck?"

Stollmeyer nodded his head reluctantly. "Go."

"Ed?"

"Go. We have to go."

"JPB?"

"No. I don't like it."

"Thank you, gentlemen. I am going to run this by our lawyer. I'll listen to him, but the decision about what we use will be mine."

The three men filed out and Peg said to Tom, "What if they'd all said no?"

He grinned. "Nobody said this is a democracy." Then his smile faded. "This could be a rough one."

"I know."

"I want you to know exactly what you're getting into. If we have trouble, it's going to be from Justice. They've been coming down hard on reporters lately."

"Tell me something I don't know."

Relations between the press and the Nixon administration, never good, were becoming increasingly strained as the antiwar protests increased. The Nixon men seemed to regard any dissenters as their personal enemies.

Tom sighed. "There are people over there who think it's their sacred duty to stomp out dissent. To use all the powers of the federal government to do it."

"That's why this story is so important, Tom. We could be heading for another McCarthy era. People too scared to speak up."

"What if they ask for your notes on Elmore Brown? Your source in Moore County?"

"I don't give them up."

"They can subpoena you. If you don't cooperate, a judge could cite you for contempt. Throw you in the can."

"I know."

"Does that scare you?"

"Sure. Scares the hell out of me."

"We've got good lawyers, Peg. I'd be behind you all the way. But there are people here who wouldn't be. You'd be out in front. It could be pretty lonely."

"Tom, we have to go with it. We haven't got any choice. You know that."

"You're right. But I wanted you to know all the risks."

"I do."

"You've got guts, Peg."

"Yeah. Those I got. Smarts, that's another story."

"Okay, let's call the lawyer. We'll probably have to fight with him on every goddamn line."

Dan rolled away from Kitty and threw his forearm across his eyes. He was silent.

"It's all right, Dan," she said.

"That hasn't happened to me—for a long time."

"You're exhausted. It happens. Forget it."

"I *can't* forget it. Don't you know how it makes a man feel, not to be able to—perform?"

"You haven't slept, you've had a long plane ride."

"Stop making excuses for me!"

"You're not Superman, leaping tall buildings at a single bound."

"Oh Christ, I hate it when you're so goddamn understanding. You're mad, why the hell don't you say so?"

"I'm not mad. I don't expect you to be some kind of super-stud who can turn on any hour of the night or day."

He looked at her. "You're really not angry?"

"No, I'm not, darling."

He sighed. "Kit, I'm so beat, running between here and the state. There's so many votes I can't afford to miss, but Rolvag is spending a fortune, so I have to keep pressing the flesh. I'm better one-on-one than he is."

"Any more of those wonderful ads?"

"Oh yeah, a new 'Playboy Congressman' number. Lots of pictures of you and me, me with a drink in my hand, all the time. Christ, it makes me look like I don't do anything but guzzle booze."

"It's so unfair. You work so hard."

"I think we ought to hit hard at Rolvag, at his defense record, at his sucking up to the moneymen while the farmers go hang. When he was in office, his record was lousy."

"So why don't you?"

"Adam says people like Rolvag. He has this grandfather image. So we try to build *me* up as the vigorous young leader. Take the high road. He's probably right."

"What about going after him on the war? Isn't that where he's really vulnerable?"

"No, Adam says we accentuate the positive. We talk about my leadership on bringing the boys home, but we don't hit Rolvag. But he hits me, of course."

"Maybe you ought to have somebody besides Adam."

"He's the best there is. And the polls are still dicey on the war stuff."

"I think your instincts are better than Adam's polls."

"I can't take any chances. I've bet my life on this race. My future. I can't even allow myself to think about losing."

"It wouldn't be the end of the world if you lost. The Senate isn't everything."

"For me it is, Kit. It's what I've aimed for since I was in law school. I planned every move to get to where I am right now."

"You're good, Dan. Smart. There would be a place for you in government."

"Stuck in some lousy bureaucracy, shuffling papers? You think that's what I've worked for all my life?"

"Dan, you're young. You have your whole life ahead of you. If you don't make it this time, there's always next time."

"I have to give up my House seat, so I have no power base. In six years, Kit, they'll have forgotten my name."

"Dan, my love, life isn't always a straight line. Sometimes setbacks can really be blessings in disguise."

"What bilge!"

"No, it's true. If you were fifty, I'd say, yes, maybe it's your last shot. You're only thirty-four."

"I feel like this is it. That I have to make it now. I feel it in my bones."

"Dan, your color is awful. You're so tense. Let's go down to Aruba for a few days. You'll see things in a new light."

"I can't. My schedule is jam-packed all month."

"The election is months away. You can't keep up this pace."

"I can't get so far behind that I can't catch up. Rolvag is going to have a big media blitz in the fall. I have to build up my support, slow and steady."

After Dan left, Kitty went downstairs, had breakfast, and, as usual, looked at the mail. There was a letter with a Nebraska postmark, and she opened it first. Inside was a picture of her clipped from the Omaha *Sun,* and scrawled in the margin was, "Go back where you came from, Jew bitch."

The letter sent a tremor through her. She had seen anti-Semitic filth scrawled on walls, in toilets, but this was directed at her. It was sprawled across her face. *Jew bitch.*

She went upstairs to Morris, and as always, the small smile on his face calmed her. She read the letter out loud to him; did the smile dim, just a shade?

"If you were here, Morris, you'd never let them get away with calling me *Jew bitch.* You'd send someone to break their legs. Oh, I know you had some interesting friends. Jews can break legs, when pressed. That Mr. Bloomfield who used to come around sometimes was not with the UJA.

"I'm in terrible shape, Morris. I drink too much coffee, I have trouble sleeping. My hands shake, sometimes. I'm just so afraid that Dan is going to lose the election because of me. Because of *Jew bitch.* They don't *know* me, those people. Why should they hate me? And Dan isn't like you, you were so strong, you could handle whatever came along. Dan seems so—fragile. I'm such a fixer, I could always get the right people together and make things happen, but I can't do anything about this. It's just out there, like—like *air,* and I can't touch it. I can't make it go away."

Con was coming for lunch, and Kitty was looking forward to seeing her. Con's breeziness could blow away the cobwebs of her anxiety. She seemed to have such energy, she was never still. She could do just about anything she put her mind to, Kitty thought.

In the middle of the trout almandine, Con suddenly asked, "Kitty, how much money does George have?"

"In the family? Twenty million or so. He is a good catch, Constance, as we used to say."

"Oh, I know."

"One does not live well on a navy pension. A tacky retirement village in Ft. Lauderdale."

"Kitty, I am not that old!"

"It is never too early to think about your financial future. Is George dropping hints?"

"His wife is divorcing him. All nice and polite."

"Now that *is* news."

"She's being paid quite handsomely. And George keeps saying what a wonderful team we'd make. I think he's shopping for a potential First Lady."

"He could do worse, my dear. We haven't had anybody with taste since Jackie."

"I don't have taste, Kitty. I'd call in the St. Vincent De Paul Society to do the drapes in the East Room. Hell, they'd be clean and cheap. Who cares if they once hung in the Shoreham?"

Kitty laughed. "But you're clever, Constance. You can buy good taste. No one will know."

Con looked around at the elegant furnishings. "Did you?"

"God, yes. My mother kept plastic sheets over the living room couch and had wax fruit in bowls. Her idea of art was photographs of the children touched up to look like paintings. In pastels. We all looked Swedish."

"You learned all this?"

"It's not hard. I hired the best people, and I watched them. Now I can toss an antique quilt next to a hard-edged modern sculpture, and people think I'm a genius. You must be a bit quirky. If you're too perfect, everybody knows it's hired."

"*You* do the East Room for me, then."

"Delighted. But who will dress you? Somebody elegant. You have large breasts, Constance, and they can be tacky if they're not done right."

"They've been called a lot of things, but *tacky* is a first."

"Now, don't take offense. I'm sure men love them, but it's women who give the First Lady the once-over."

"They are attached, Kitty."

"Yes, but you need the right kind of bra. No jiggling."

"Sometimes I *like* to jiggle."

"Constance, remember, ask not what your country can do for you, ask what you can do for your country. Do you want Nixon in *forever?* No cleavage before the election, and no stretch bras. A nipple poking against the fabric could cost George five states."

"This is very complicated."

"Jackie almost had it down: elegant, flat-chested, never mixed in politics, and photographed like a dream. But she was too Frenchy and spent way too much on clothes. Probably to try to punish Jack for flitting. A First Lady's wardrobe shouldn't be Sears catalogue, but not Givenchy either."

"I never could get all this down."

"A few days with Bill Blass would do wonders."

"He'd probably turn me down because of my tacky breasts."

"Dear, if you were going to be First Lady, he'd dress you if you had three breasts. The publicity would be worth a million in sales."

"Three boobs, Bill, count 'em, three. Make 'em look elegant or we lose the Solid South."

Kitty chuckled. "One thing you would never be as First Lady, Constance, is boring."

"I just reworked this a little bit." Sean handed a copy of a speech to Dan. "More casualties. The death toll keeps rising."

Dan glanced at Sean's changes. "Oh yeah, this is good. Very good. Just the right tone. Where did you learn to write like this?"

Sean laughed. "Every time I had a dangling participle, Brother Edward smacked my knuckles with the metal edge of the ruler. Great motivation."

"I think I'll try it with my staff."

"You look worn out, Dan. How is it going?"

"Slow. I do think I'm getting through to people on the war,

Sean. I can feel it when I talk to them. But the polls don't show it. It's an uphill road."

After stopping in to see Dan, Sean made the rounds of the Maryland delegation, lobbying, as usual, on the interstate. Then he paid a quick call on his father, who as always was fretting about Bill.

"That bitch, his wife, is sleeping with some bum."

"Pop, don't butt in. This is between Bill and Rene."

"What kind of a woman is she? A tramp."

"Rene put up with a lot. She's not a saint."

"Oh, if I only had some money to give Bill, to help him out. I invested it all in the condominium. But he can go back to the law one day. When he gets on his feet."

"Pop, don't push him on that. He didn't like it. He wasn't good at it."

"Bill was good at everything."

"Pop, just let him be. Okay?"

Sometimes Sean wondered why he bothered. Talking to his father was like talking to a wall. He looked at his watch. Just enough time to get back for the housekeeper's meat loaf—didn't that damn women know how to cook anything else?—and hear confessions. This was his night to go to Peg's, but she had a Press Club dinner she had to go to and wouldn't be back until eleven. After confessions, he and Brian had a beer in Brian's room.

"Sean," Brian said, "I've been doing a lot of thinking. I'm going to hang on. I do have a vocation. A real one, and I don't want to throw it all away just because things are rough right now."

"I'm glad, Brian. You're the best we have. I'm glad to see you stay."

"Have you ever considered leaving, Sean?"

"I've thought about it. Not seriously. Why?"

There was a silence, and Sean saw Brian studying him.

"Why do you ask?"

"Just wondering."

"No, there's more to it than that."

"Some areas of the life are a lot harder for you, Sean."

Sean looked at him. "You know, don't you."

"Know?"

"Come on, Brian."

"Yes, I know that you and Peg are lovers. That story about staying at the Paulist Center two nights a week for a late course was pretty thin."

Sean looked away. "I guess it was."

"I'm not judging you, Sean."

"You have a right to. You keep your vows. I don't."

"You're in love with her, aren't you?"

"Yes. God yes, Bri. It's not something quick and dirty with us."

"I know. I know it never could be with you."

"Would you do it, Brian? If there was a woman you loved?"

Brian hesitated. "I don't know."

"The truth."

"No."

"You're stronger than I am. I was so lonely, so damn lonely, and I'd loved her for so long."

"You're a man, Sean, not a saint. I know it's hard for you."

"But I'm a priest, Bri. What you're saying is that if I'm going to wear this collar I have to live up to what it stands for."

"I didn't say that."

"You're thinking it."

Brian looked away."

"Who invented the goddamn celibacy rule, anyhow? In every other religion, clergymen have wives, children, lead normal lives. Why do we have to live this crazy way?"

"It's a hard life, but maybe it brings us closer to God. Having no rival for His love."

"But by loving other people I *do* love Him, Bri. By loving a woman I'm a better person. More open. Less selfish. The rule was made centuries ago. Why can't it be changed?"

"Maybe it will be, someday."

"But in the meantime, we have to live by it?"

Brian was silent.

"Bri?"

"Yes."

"Brian, I love her! She's part of me! Part of every breath I take, she's in my soul. I can't give her up. Dear God, I can't!"

"Can you give up the priesthood?"

"No! It's what I *am*. It's what I've wanted since I was fourteen years old!"

"Sean, this is ripping you up, isn't it?"

He nodded. "Yes. God, yes!"

"I didn't mean to add to your pain. Forgive me."

"You haven't said anything to me that I haven't said to myself, a hundred times. A thousand times!" He got up and walked to the window. "I thought I could be *perfect*. That's a laugh, isn't it?" When he turned to face Brian, there was a mist of tears in his eyes. "You shame me, Brian. You're what a priest ought to be. Me, I'm so full of myself, of my own ego, and I can't keep my vows—"

"Sean, don't do this to yourself. Don't!"

"I can't leave her, Brian. I can't."

"Oh Sean, I wish there were an easy way out of this. I wish there was!"

"There isn't, Bri."

"I'll pray for you, Sean. And for Peg. You'll be in my prayers. I promise, Sean."

Sean went downstairs to pick up some papers he had forgotten and as he walked into the hall he found Father Barry blocking the way. That was a surprise. The pastor was usually blotto by now. The old man's eyes were glittering, but not from drink. Something else. Anger. He held a letter in his hand.

"I know about you!"

"I beg your pardon?"

"Fornicator!" the old priest said. "Fornicator!"

Sean felt the color drain from his face. "What?"

Father Barry handed him the letter. It was on an old piece of notebook paper and was handwritten in ink: "Your assistant pastor is fucking some woman's brains out."

"That's garbage," Sean said. "Some kind of nut." But his hands trembled as he held the letter. He tried to step past Father Barry but the priest moved to bar the way.

"Is it, Father? I've had my suspicions about you for a long time."

"I have work to do, Father." Sean's voice was cold.

Father Barry grabbed his arm. "I know that you laugh at me, both of you. Call me a drunk. You think you are better than me."

"No, Father."

"Yes, I drink. But I don't break my vows. I am a priest, I am fit to wear this collar."

"I never said you weren't."

"I see how you look at me. With contempt. You reserve your charity, Father, for those who wear no collar."

Sean felt a flush of shame at the old priest's words. He was right. He had never spared the pastor an instant's pity, never tried to understand his pain. Never thought that he, too, was flesh and blood.

"Oh, I was like you, Father, young and full of arrogance. And I was tempted, believe me. But I never did what you do. You shame the collar, Father McCaffrey!"

"Father, my personal life is my business."

"No!" Father Barry snatched the letter and shook it in Sean's face. "It is *my* business when I get a letter telling me one of my priests is a lecher. A man who cannot keep his hands off women. You *disgust* me!"

"Father, I have always behaved with decorum while I was in the parish."

"You think this a job you can quit at five o'clock when the whistle blows, Father? Tell me, are you a fornicator?"

Sean was silent. Father Barry's eyes blazed, accusing.

"Are you?"

"I don't have to answer that."

"Is that what you will say to the archbishop when I make a formal complaint?"

"No!" Sean said. "You can't do that!"

"And why not?"

"You know why. It would destroy everything I've tried to do! Destroy Action."

"You should have thought of that when you decided not to keep your vows."

"Father, in the name of God, don't destroy this parish to get vengeance on me. Innocent people must not suffer for my"— he swallowed—"my sins."

"You are a sinner, Father. Do you think I didn't hear you in the bathroom at nights? The sounds you made when you touched yourself, the animal sounds. Oh God! You can't keep your hands off your own body, and you can't keep your hands off some filthy woman."

"Don't say that!"

"Some whore! What kind of a woman would lie with a priest?"

It was warm and airless in the hall. Sean began to feel nausea churning in the pit of his stomach.

"Is that what women are to you, Father? Pieces of dirt? Can't you imagine that a man could love a woman? Even a priest?"

"What kind of love is it that defies the holy vow made to God. I loved a woman once, Father, oh yes, a withered old prune, like me, I felt love. But I kept my vows, and you did not. Did you? Did you?"

The nausea was climbing into Sean's throat. "No, Father."

"Fornicator!" The old priest slapped Sean in the face. The old man's blow stung, but it didn't hurt. It had little force behind it.

"Fornicator!" Father Barry slapped Sean again. Sean stood still, feeling sick and dizzy. What was he doing, standing in this dark hall with a crazy old man hitting him? What did this have to do with God's love?

"Fornicator!" Father Barry raised his hand to hit Sean again, but instead he turned and leaned against the wall, his shoulders sagging and his eyes closed.

"My God, my God, why hast thou forsaken me!" he cried out, in a voice so bereft of hope that it sent a chill through Sean. And then the old man began to weep, his whole body trembling.

Sean stepped up to Father Barry and put his hands on the old man's shoulders. He was amazed at how little flesh there was; the bones were so near the surface. He realized with a mixture of shame and pity how frail the old man was. He rubbed Father Barry's shoulders as the priest wept.

"Forgive me, Father. I have sinned with my lack of charity. Forgive me, please."

The old man's body grew still. He moved away from Sean's arms, his pale eyes red with tears.

"I will tear up this letter, Father. Forget I ever saw it. As for your conscience, I leave that to God. I will pray for you, Father." And he turned and walked quickly up the stairs.

Sean turned and walked out of the rectory. The cold night air blew away the nausea, but his hands were still shaking, badly, as he started the car. He drove to Peg's apartment and let himself in. She walked into the living room from the bedroom, smiling, and started to chatter about the dinner. Her good spirits offended him. Why couldn't she sense the churning inside him? Why did she have that stupid smile on her face?

"Bad day, hon? You look beat."

The endearment annoyed him. Why did she call him that? He glared at her.

"I feel like a thief, sneaking in here!"

"What? You have a key, nobody sees you."

"I see myself. I see what I do. What I am."

"Sean, what is this? What's the matter?"

"I break my vows for you."

"For me? Sean, what are you talking about?"

"I could be a good priest, if it wasn't for you."

"That's not fair. It was *you* who came to me. I didn't seduce you, Sean."

"No, it was my weakness. You're right. I'm some priest, I am." He laughed, but there was no mirth in it.

"Sean, what's happened?"

"Nothing."

"I know something has happened."

"I said it's nothing!" He was angry.

"Is this it, Sean? The night you leave me and go back to the rectory for good?"

"Maybe it should be."

"Do you really think you could do that? Be celibate?"

"Yes. I did it for ten years."

"And it made you an emotional time bomb. I could hear you. Tick, tick, tick. Celibacy is—unnatural."

"No, it's more than that. It's an offering."

"It's medieval tommyrot."

"I wouldn't expect you to understand."

"Why? Because I'm not some pompous cardinal who sits on his ass and makes pronouncements?"

"It's more complicated than you think."

"For some men, yes, a life of celibacy could be a way to live. But not for you, Sean. I know you. You were made to touch and be touched."

She moved to put her hand against his face, but he took her hand and held it. "Don't touch me!"

She yanked her hand away angrily. "What do you see, Sean? The whore of Babylon? Is that what I am to you?"

He was silent, misery etching his face.

"If I'm a whore, why not pay me?" She pulled his wallet out of his trousers while he stood unnaturally still. "Five bucks for last night, a real bargain. And you know I'm *clean*."

She turned away, to hide the spurt of tears that came to her eyes. "Oh God, I feel like I ought to take a bath. I feel dirty, Sean. No one has ever made me feel like that before!"

"Peg, don't!" he said, still standing rigid. "Please, don't. I didn't mean that!"

She turned to face him. "You—*recoiled* from me. Like I was filthy. And that's what I have to be, isn't it? That's what your rules make me."

"They're not *my* rules. Do you think I made them?"

"But you bow to them. Sometimes. Last night you were a man and you wanted me. Tonight you're a priest and you won't touch me! Look at your hands. Frozen, so you won't have to touch me! Do you have any idea how that makes me feel?"

He reached out his hand to touch her face.

"I'm sorry. Peg, I'm sorry."

She stepped close to him and slid her hand under his shirt. "Tell me, Sean, that you don't want to be touched."

His whole body trembled when she touched him. "Tell me that you want to spend your whole life with nobody touching you like this!"

She leaned over to kiss the side of his neck, and her hand caressed his bare chest, flitting lightly across the nipples. She thought, as she touched him, that it wasn't fair, his passion was so easily fired.

He gave a small cry, and she knew it was surrender. She drew him down on the floor, and his mouth sought hers. And they made love there, on the floor, with a savagery that was more combat than it was love. Her fingernails dug into his back and his body battered at hers, a weapon, and when he came inside of her his cry was filled with as much pain as release. Afterward, they lay side by side, panting like exhausted animals. He was staring up at the ceiling, his mouth a tight line, and she wondered how much he hated her at that moment. She had punctured his illusions, brought him back to earth, to sweating, panting flesh. Men of God distrusted women because they reminded them that they couldn't be archangels. She thought, perfectly calm, *I have lost him.*

"I'm sorry," she said. "I had no right to do that to you."

He was silent.

"What was it? What happened tonight?"

"Father Barry knows. Called me a fornicator. Threatened to complain to the archbishop."

"Will he?"

"No. He tore up the letter."

She gathered up his clothes and handed them to him. They both dressed, wordlessly. When he stood up she saw the sagging line of his shoulders. He looked haggard. That was what her love had done to him. *A poisoned well.*

"I'm sorry you had to go through that, Sean."

"It's not your fault."

"You were right about one thing. You can be a good priest except for me."

"I didn't mean that."

"It's true.

He was silent.

"I was kidding myself. I have no right to you. I never had."

She thought, *The winds are blowing, blowing my life away. Stop them, Sean.*

But he was silent.

"I guess the answer,"she continued, "is just for me to keep the hell away from you."

"Is that what you'll do?"

"I would have been happy to be your twice-a-week woman. But it's tearing you apart, isn't it, Sean?"

"I thought I could cut myself in half. Half a priest and half the man who loves you."

"But you couldn't."

"I love you. I do love you. Dear God, please believe that. I tried, Peg!"

"I know you did."*I will call your name, in the fog, but you'll be gone. Like the others. Don't leave me. Don't!*

"You'll be in my heart. Until the day I die."

She nodded.

"You've thrown away too much of your life on me. Too much love. On a man who can't give you enough in return."

"So it seems."

They stared at each other, for a long minute. She thought she heard his heart beating. Or was it hers? She was the one who moved first, toward the door.

"Where are you going?"

"Out. Let's do it fast and clean."

"God, Peg, you're strong. Stronger than me."

"Yeah, I eat nails."

"I'll take my things."

"The print is yours. The Vlaminck."

"I know."

"Peg. Can we be—friends?"

"Sure. We'll see each other from time to time. You tell me about the Pope. I'll tell you about Nixon. It'll be—swell."

"Oh God, *Peg!*" he said. She couldn't bear to see his eyes so she walked out the door.

She drove, she had no idea where. Wheaton? Alexandria? Bowie? There were only roads and headlights.

He was gone when she got back; he had been methodical, he had even wiped the hairs from his razor out of the medicine cabinet. She walked through the rooms. It was as if he had surgically excised himself from her life.

And then she saw Fuzzy, sitting in the chair, smiling his half-crooked smile at her. She scooped him up.

"You drink, Fuzz? Good. We are going to get schnockered, you and me."

She poured two glasses of scotch, and every time she took a sip she dipped Fuzzy's nose in the Cutty Sark until the end of his nose was quite bedraggled. The room was spinning when the phone rang. It was Con, asking about lunch tomorrow.

"Peg? You sound weird. Are you okay?"

"Just drunk. Fuzzy and me are getting plastered. He's drunker than me."

"Who is *Fuzzy?* And where's Sean?"

"Gone. Back to God. Old bastard always wins." She giggled. "Is it a sin to call God a bastard?"

"What the hell are you drinking?"

"Scotch rocks. So is Fuzzy."

"You are not making any sense. I am coming over."

Peg hung up and then picked up the bear and looked it in

the eye. "You and me, now, Fuzz. Do you screw? Oh, that is a problem. But you don't need them. All they are is trouble."

When the doorbell rang, Peg stumbled across the room to answer it. Con took one look at her and said, "Peg, you are *blotto.*"

"Yeah, we are. This is Fuzzy. He hasn't got any balls. That's why he drinks."

"And you?"

"I don't have any either. They're back in the rectory, where they are no damn good at all."

"How do you feel?"

"Feel? Oh, I think I am going to puke."

Con helped Peg into the bathroom and rubbed her shoulders as she vomited up the Scotch. Then Con wiped her face with a washcloth and helped her into the bedroom.

"Ohhh. I am a terrible drunk."

"Feel any better?"

"No. Just sober. I really do love him. Jesus, I do love him."

"I know, Peg."

"I have this dream. I'm walking around in the goddamn fog calling people's names. But I don't know them. Who the hell are these people?"

"Did you ask him to stay?"

"Hell, no."

"Always the strong one."

"People keep saying that."

"Want to cry?"

"Not my thing."

Con helped Peg climb into her nightgown, and pulled the covers over her.

"Want me to stay, Peg?"

"No. Sleep. That's all I need. Sleep."

Towards dawn, when the light had yet to streak the sky, the dream came again. This time the face was Sean's.

She woke up screaming his name. Her hands clawed at the sheet on his side of the bed, but there was nothing there.

"Sean! Where are you! I'm afraid!"

She felt her heart thumping as a surge of panic swept through her. She had to control it before it claimed her, sent her shrieking out into the hall.

She took three deep breaths and said the words, the ones she had said so often before: in Sinai, where the shells were deafening; in East Africa, heading into the bush.

I am a cowgirl, brave and strong.

In her fifth year she had become obsessed with cowboys, trooping about the house in oversized boots, a large metal gun stuck in the waistband of her trousers. For her birthday, her father gave her a white leather holster, ordered from Texas. It was the most beautiful object in the universe, with glass emeralds and rubies embedded in the leather. They shone like stars.

She buckled it on and ran out to display her treasure. Ronald Harrington, who was eight, scoffed at her, cloaking his envy behind squinting eyes.

"You can't be a cowboy. You're only a girl."

Faced with incontrovertible fact, she trooped in to her father, boots scuffling on the rug. "I can't be a cowboy!" she said, her blue eyes wide with despair.

"But you can be a cowgirl," he said. "That's every bit as good. Cowgirls are brave and strong."

So she trooped out to the backyard, planted her feet and announced to Ronald, "I am a cowgirl, brave and strong."

The steely glint in her eyes caused Ronald to retreat in silence. The gun in her new holster was big and ugly and she had been known, on occasion, to smack people across the nose with it when they incurred her wrath.

She sat still, breathing deeply. She thought of Sean's face, misery lacing his lips into a tight line, as he tried to love her and ripped himself apart.

Oh Sean. Sean, my dearest love. I'd die before I would hurt you. I would.

She never thought it odd that in their relationship she hovered about him like a guardian angel, seeing his vulnerability so clearly and blind to her own. When they were children, he had taken his hurts to her and she had soothed them, but she crawled off, alone, like some feral creature, to lick her own wounds.

How will I live without you? I don't want to be alive without you!

She had said it once before, only once; the night Jeff had burned to death in the helicopter in the Mekong. She thought she would die that night, the pain was so terrible. The pain, she thought, would stop her heart from beating, choke the air from her throat, jam the machinery in her body until it ground to a halt. But, of course, it didn't.

She pulled up her knees and held her pillow against her chest. She sat, watching the dawn creep into the sky. It was like the dawn in the Paris sky the day she had buried Jeff; blazing, beautiful. She had asked herself, "How will I get through this day?" and she had answered, "I will. I just will."

She pulled the pillow closer against her, and watched the light spreading across the sky, staining it at first golden and then a reddish pink, and then the hues flattened out into the vivid tones of day. She sat watching, not moving, as the bedroom flooded with light. "I will, I just will," she said.

I am a cowgirl, brave and strong.

NINETEEN

"What's Dan hearing about Cambodia?" Con asked Kitty. They were riding together in Kitty's limousine along MacArthur Boulevard on a dreary Washington winter morning, freezing rain icing the streets.

"Just what you'd expect. Reports about the bombing, though the administration keeps denying it."

The Nixon administration had been trying to put pressure on the North Vietnamese with a series of secret bombing raids on Vietcong "sanctuaries" in neighboring Cambodia. But the secret was ill-kept; reports were flowing out of Southeast Asia, circulating around Capitol Hill and showing up in the press.

"I'm putting together a piece about sentiment on the Hill. Stories are leaking all over the place."

"Yes, the damn war just seems to keep growing, all the time. This could help Dan, though.

"I saw him the other day. He looked exhausted."

"He spends half his life on airplanes these days. And as hard as he works, he can never quite seem to catch Rolvag."

"You look worn out yourself."

"Yes, the whole thing just seems to drag on. Every time I think it's finally faded away, there's some new picture of me in the Omaha paper. But there's nothing I can do but ride it out." She shook her head, wearily. "Peg was over for lunch yesterday. Putting up a good front, but you can see she's hurting. She didn't want to talk about Sean, and I didn't press her."

"It's been more than a month, but I don't know that it's getting much better. She hides it, of course. And the damn FBI has been harassing her."

"She told me about her little visits. Oh, that Hoover is such a wretched man. Lyndon did such a stupid thing, appointing him director for life. And Nixon! He said he was winding down the war, and now this. Male menopause, that's what Cambodia is all about, my dear. Have you ever looked at the shape of bombs, Constance?"

"Phallic symbols?"

"Of course. Military men may go on about aerodynamics and such, but it's all very Freudian. Can you imagine a woman inventing a bomb?"

"You mean a woman wouldn't kill?"

"Of course she would, but not so *randomly*. A woman might kill someone she really hated. She'd put ground glass in his meat loaf to rip his intestines to bloody shreds. But she wouldn't be at all interested in knocking off the servants as well."

"Why menopause?"

"Waning powers, and all that. Bombing the bejesus out of some small country feels like getting it up three times a day."

"Why not bomb great big countries. More bang for a buck."

"*They* bomb you back, Constance. No, I think we have to give them some small country they can bomb to their heart's content. Some small island in the Caribbean. One with terrible beaches."

"The natives might object."

"We could give every resident a bomb shelter, and *tons* of money, so that when the smoke clears they could tootle about in Cadillacs with color TV's in them."

"They ought to make you Secretary of State."

"Yes. And if *I* want to be taller, all I have to do is slip on my Capezios, not send in the B-52's."

The chauffeur pulled the car up in front of Garfinkle's, and Kitty and Con took the elevator to the designer salon.

"De la Renta might be nice," Kitty said. "Is this little soirée for the governors?"

"Yes. George is having a reception for some governors from key states. I am to be unveiled, I guess, now that the divorce is public news."

247

"You're going to be the hostess?"

"Nothing as formal as that. Just his guest."

"You look well in white, Constance. But that might be a bit too virginal."

"No one will believe me as a virgin. Not with these tacky breasts."

"I *did* hurt your feelings, didn't I, dear? But you're right, white is out. Elegant doesn't play well with the Sun Belt types. They like tacky breasts, actually."

"So how about I let it all hang out?"

"That would not go for New England. They like good bones, character in the face."

"God knows I have't got those."

"The cheekbones are just right. The mouth is too full. Sensual. Try pressing your lips in a thin line, like Pat Nixon. Oh God, no, you look like you've got gas. With your dark hair and olive skin, you have a bit of a Mediterranean look. Maybe we should go with that."

"Eh, paisan, want to fuck? Eight hundred lire. For *you*, GI, six hundred."

Kitty groaned. "Constance, I do not mean Naples hooker Mediterranean. Something more classic. Greek, perhaps."

"Eh, Thucydides, want to fuck? Six hundred drachmas."

Kitty sighed. "You are hopeless, Constance. You are going to *wisecrack* your way out of twenty million dollars."

"Oh all right, I'll behave."

"Good. Now let's see the De la Rentas."

Peg opened the door. "We are going to have to stop meeting like this." Agent McMahon and Agent Spiers walked into the apartment.

"All we ask is your cooperation, Miss Morrison," Agent McMahon said.

"*Ms*. Morrison."

"You have been consorting with a known felon."

"We did not go disco dancing, I interviewed him."

"This man is on the most wanted list of the Federal Bureau of Investigation."

Peg sighed. "Do you guys all take speech class from the same person? You're like a record, all of you. Why are we going over this again?"

"We need information which we think you can give us."

"You read my story. You have all the information."

"Where did you meet Elmore Brown?"

"At the counter in Schwab's drugstore."

"Miss Morrison, this is not a joke. This is serious federal government business. A capital crime has been committed. This is not to be taken lightly," Agent Speirs chided.

"I agree. And I have told you the entire substance of my conversation with Elmore Brown."

"Who gave you the autopsy report?"

"A confidential source."

"Did you know it was stolen?"

"I have no comment on that. Speak to my attorneys."

"What does Father McCaffrey have to do with Elmore Brown?"

"I've told you that, too. He has no connection. Elmore Brown saw an article I wrote about Father McCaffrey's group. That story prompted him to contact me."

"Was Father McCaffrey the go-between?"

"We've been over all this before. Look, I am trying to be helpful to you people. I am not trying to give you the runaround. But you know there are certain sources I am not going to reveal. So I have to construe this visit as harassment, plain and simple."

"Why are you helping these people, Miss Morrison? People who have said that they want to overthrow the government of the United States."

"Oh God, *that?*"

"There is evidence that the Black Panthers have associations with known subversives," Agent Spiers said.

"Yeah, and your boss is on record as saying Martin Luther King was a commie. Anybody who doesn't agree with his Walt Disney idea of a nice little white Protestant world is a subversive. Tell me, do you think Dr. King was a communist?"

Agent McMahon, looking uncomfortable, said, "That has no relevance to the matter at hand."

"Right, you're just doing your job, not making policy. Well, you're welcome to look under the bed. If you find any Reds, you can have them. And now, if you'll excuse me, I have to go to work."

As she walked into the city room at the *Tribune*, a man in a dark suit, his hair cropped short, stepped up to her.

"Margaret Morrison?

"Margaret?"

"Are you Margaret Morrison?"

"Yes."

The man handed her an envelope. She took it, and saw Tom Friedman standing by his office, watching. He waved to her.

"It's a subpoena, right?" she asked.

"Yes. He's been here all morning."

"Oh, Jesus."

"Take it easy, Peg. We've been expecting this."

"I know. What do I do now?"

"For the moment, nothing. Our first step is to move to quash the subpoenas. It's not just you they're going after. They're hitting on a *Times* reporter and a guy from Time-Life as well. We're not going to take this sitting down."

"I hope not. I don't really want to go to the Big House, Tom."

"We got a lot of high-priced legal talent working, Peg. So just take it easy. This is going to be a long process."

Peg tried to keep her mind on the story she was working on, about an environmental group, but with little luck. Finally she gave up altogether, and spent an hour shopping at Woodies before she met Con for lunch at the Washington Roof. She hadn't seen Con since her friend had jetted off to Martinique with George Billington for the weekend.

"You should see this place, Peg. It's bigger than my whole block. George calls it a *cottage*. His family owns it."

"Just you and George?"

"Yes, Lee took the boys for the weekend."

"Have the boys met George?"

"Yes. They were hostile at first, but one ride in the Lear jet did it. I really brought them up with great values. As the wheels touched down they were saying 'Daddy who?'"

"Your tan looks great."

"Yeah, and they have a houseful of servants there. I asked George where I should put my dirty clothes, and he said just drop them on the floor, the maids will pick them up."

"You are in the fast lane."

"I *couldn't* do it. I put a dress on the floor, Peg, but I couldn't do it. At home, *I'm* the maid. I spend more time bent over than a migrant laborer. It is a *sin* for grown-ups to leave their clothes on the floor."

"You'd better get used to being rich."

"George does seem to be counting on the fact that I'm going to marry him. He's pushing me to file divorce papers on Lee."

"Do you love him, Con?"

"I like him a lot. We're very compatible."

"Is that enough?"

"I loved Lee. Look where *that* got me. I'm not sure where love gets any of us, Peg."

"Amen to that. Oh I got a nice little present today. My subpoena from the Justice Department."

"Oh Christ."

"Yeah. The idea that I might have to go to jail terrifies me. I'd rather go to a war anyday. I just think about getting cooped up in a small place, and I want to scream."

"You won't go to jail."

"They're playing hardball these days, Con. I think the Justice Department would love somebody to make an example of. They could cite me for contempt, and put me away indefinitely."

"Does Sean know about all this?"

"No. I haven't talked to Sean since—since the night he moved out."

"He got you into this damn thing. Why should you take the heat alone?"

"He didn't get me into it. I'm a big girl, Con. I knew what I was getting into. I'm keeping his name out of this."

"You're always protecting him, Peg."

"I have high-priced lawyers. I've got at least a chance of a legal defense. If they linked Sean to this, it could destroy him. The archbishop would like to nail him, anyway."

"God, look at you, carrying a torch a mile high."

"No, I'm— Oh, I don't know what I'm doing. Keeping too busy to think about things, I guess."

"Did you see Bill Forbes got married? Some socialite."

"Oh, I didn't know that."

"You could have snapped him up. George has some nice

rich friends. A little dull, but when the conversation gets slow, they just rustle hundred-dollar bills."

"No thanks. If I go to jail, Con, will you bring me a cake with a file in it?"

"Come on, Peg, you're not going to jail.

"Just keep saying that."

She went back to the paper to finish up her story. She tried not to think about the subpoena, about what was going to happen. She had been telling Con the truth; she was afraid of few things, but the thought of being confined in some tiny room, for months on end, made her blood run cold. She wondered if she could survive that, without going mad. She felt herself shiver, involuntarily.

The phone at her elbow rang, and she picked it up. "City Room. Morrison."

"Peg?"

The voice on the other end of the line had a visceral impact; she felt her heart pumping. She tried to keep her voice steady.

"Sean?"

"We just got the word, Peg. The governor did it! He scrapped Interstate 80."

"Sean! You did it! Oh God, that's great! You did it!"

"Not just me. A lot of us. You were a big part of it. Listen, Estella's having a little party in the neighborhood, to celebrate. I'd really like you to come."

"Oh, Sean, I—"

"Peg, you're so much a part of this. We— I mean, it doesn't make sense for us not to—talk to each other, does it? Please come, best friend."

"If you put it that way, how can I say no?"

She walked up the steps to Estella's house later that evening, feeling like a reformed drunk going to her first cocktail party. She couldn't spend the rest of her life avoiding him. Maybe she'd be lucky. Maybe she would be able to look at him, and not feel anything at all. Yes, that was the ticket. Control.

Numb, Peg. You will feel nothing.

She walked into the living room and saw him standing in the corner, wearing a blue sweater and chinos, singing a chorus of a song in Spanish with Alex, who was strumming the guitar. Her knees nearly buckled when she saw him. She thought of standing naked in the shower with him, as he kissed her breasts; she thought of kneeling before him, pleasing herself as she pleased him, adoring him, loving him more than life itself. She thought of his eyes, the night she left the apartment, to drive to nowhere. *The winds are blowing my life away. Stop them, Sean.*

She wanted to turn and run away, but she never ran, from anything. *Control.* Paste a smile on your face, Peg, and just pretend it's all fine.

He saw her, and came over, his face flushed with excitement and victory. The color had risen in his cheeks, making him seem more like the little boy who lived next door than a grown man. He kissed her lightly on the cheek and said, "Can you believe it? We won! We actually won!"

His enthusiasm was contagious, and she impulsively reached out and took his hands in hers.

"This is your night to howl, Sean!"

"We couldn't have done it without all your help."

"But it was you who put the pieces together. You made the damn system work. You kicked it, you bullied it, you charmed it. You are quite a pol, Father McCaffrey."

He laughed. "I feel so goddamn good about this. I really do feel like I've done something solid. Something *real.*"

"You have. Enjoy it, Sean. You're entitled."

He frowned, then, as if he had just remembered something. "Peg, Con called me. She said you've been subpoenaed."

"Oh yeah, I have."

"She said maybe you could go to jail."

"No, it's a big game. The Justice Department lawyers will talk to our lawyers. Sound and fury. Nothing will come of it."

"What can I do, Peg? This whole thing happened because of me."

"You can just stay away from it, I mean that. The paper pays our lawyers a zillion dollars to take care of it."

"You're not worried?"

"Of course not. Do I look worried? Sean, steer clear of this. The FBI is suspicious of you already. Just stay clear, this thing is going to work out."

"I will. Peg, I—ah, I had a call the other day. From Chicago."

"Chicago?"

"The Catholic Institute for Social Justice. They want me to be their number-two man. I told them I couldn't consider it until this thing was resolved."

"I've heard of them."

"Yes. They want me to set up some new programs. My kind of Catholic action, Peg."

His eyes were shining, the way they used to when he was a child and something excited him.

"Chicago. A nice city." *I will call your name in the fog and you'll be gone, like the others.*

"Yes. And so much that needs to be done."

"You're the man to do it. You'll knock 'em dead."

"Maybe I can push that big elephant, the church, a couple of steps in the right direction."

"Feeling your oats, Father?"

He grinned, sheepishly. "I guess I am."

There was a moment of silence between them and he said, "Peg, how are you?"

"Fine, Sean."

"I mean really."

"I'm fine. Don't worry about me. When are you going?"

"I have a flight a week from Thursday. Chuck and Estella are going to take over Action. They'll do a great job."

"Want a ride to the airport? You'll probably have a lot of stuff to take."

"Would you mind?"

"Of course not. What are friends for?"

Then Estella came over and dragged Sean off to talk to somebody. Chicago. It might as well be the far side of the moon. Well, it would probably be a good idea. That would make it clean, final. That was what she wanted, wasn't it? Better than having him here, because here, he was too solid, too real. Chicago. The moon. No more stupid fantasies. No more hoping against hope that the phone would ring, and he would be on the other end of the line: "Hi. It's me. I don't wanna be a priest anymore. Let's neck."

Sean zipped up his battered leather suitcase and he said to Brian, "That's it. All of it."

"Not much."

"Keep an eye on Chuck and Estella for me, will you?"

"I'm already talking about plans for the new community center. Don't worry, Sean. I'm going to be a member of the board of Action."

Sean shook his head. "I can't believe I'm leaving, Bri. I feel like I've been here forever."

"Ten minutes here feels like forever."

"I'd never have been able to take it if it wasn't for you. Will you come and see me. Please?"

"I will. I—you're a good friend, Sean."

"You've been patient with me, Brian. I laid a lot of stuff on you. God, I'm going to miss you!"

"I'm going to miss you too. I've never had a friend like you."

"Bri—" Sean said, and then he threw his arms around Brian and the two men held each other. There was a special intensity between them, like men who had shared combat together. It was not a bad analogy, Sean thought.

"God bless you, Brian. Keep me in your prayers."

"I will. May the wind be at your back, Sean. May God hold you in the palm of His hand."

Sean picked up his bags and walked downstairs. *The priest in track shoes.* He had never run faster than in these past two months; from memories, from regrets, from pain. He had picked up the phone a dozen times to call her. But if he heard her voice he would have to see her, and if he saw her, how could he not want her? So he put the phone down. Was he running now, to Chicago, because he could not be a priest and live in the same city with her? Would he always be running?

He walked to her car and tossed the suitcases in the trunk.

"That's all of it?"

"Vow of poverty, remember?"

"What about your car?"

"I gave it to Brian. It would never make it to Chicago."

They drove in silence for a minute, and he studied her, out of the corner of his eye. Her hair had grown longer, it touched her shoulders, now. He knew exactly what it felt like, knotted in his hands. He knew the feel of the pulsebeat in the hollow of her neck against his lips. Why were they pretending that none of this had happened at all?

"I'll take the beltway. It's quicker."

"Ok."

Her fingers, on the wheel, were slim and white and soft, but the nails were chipped and ragged, as usual. She was probably wearing, under her skirt, underwear that was tearing and ratty. Women were supposed to love lacy, seductive underwear, but she always bought practical, inexpensive panties; Catholic girl underwear, he thought. She stripped them off, for passion, like she was undressing for gym. Why did they touch his heart and make him suddenly want to cry, the ragged nails and the ratty undies?

"How's work?" he asked.

"Okay. Meetings with the damn lawyers, all the time."

"Peg, I'm letting you take the heat on this. Running out."

"Don't be silly. It's just a pain in the ass, that's all."

They chatted, of unimportant things, on the way to the airport. She walked with him inside the terminal. Anyone seeing them would have assumed they were old friends, but certainly not lovers. Their bodies did not touch as they walked. When they got to the gate he turned to face her, and he saw, for an instant, a flicker of the expression he saw in her eyes the nights she woke from the dream. It came and went so fast he thought he had imagined it.

"Well," she said.

"Well." He looked at her, and he thought he heard his heart crack, heard it distinctly, like the sound of a pencil snapped in half.

"You're always seeing me off, Peg."

"Seems that way."

He thought, suddenly *You never ask me to stay* but he said, "Write me. No, better, pick up the phone and call me."

"I will."

"Will you be staying in D.C.? Not jetting off someplace?"

"Yeah. Time for me to settle in. Find a place."

He felt cold, then, and he shivered. "Now it's me who's knocking around."

"You have a home, Sean. The church."

"The Big Tit."

"You've accomplished a lot. Stop putting yourself down."

The announcement of the Chicago flight came over the PA, covering their voices.

"That's you."

His tongue felt thick in his throat, and he had to clear it before he said, "I love you," and the tremor caught at the edge of his voice and made it ragged. But hers was clear and firm as she replied, "I love you too, Sean. Be happy."

He walked to the edge of the ramp that connected the terminal to the plane, and he turned and looked back. She smiled and waved at him. He remembered the day she had smiled and waved from the train platform fourteen years ago. But then he was going off to a golden dream at the end of the train ride. *I will make you fishers of men.* Was there anything at the end of this journey that could sustain that dream? Had to be. *Had* to.

He walked into the plane, took his seat, and buckled up. He tried not to think of her face, but it defied his will and floated in the space of the cabin in front of him, the one he had loved so well—and so unwisely.

Brian was right. You wore the collar, and you had to accept the life it symbolized. He would have to take the compartment inside of him that held his love for her and seal it forever, the feelings bricked up like the man behind the wall in "The Cask of Amontillado." And what of the part of him that would be entombed there? Would it shrivel, a brittle skeleton? He closed his eyes as the jetliner surged upward, trying not to think, only to pray.

"I will bless Thy holy name, I will serve Thee all the days of my life. Let all that is within me praise Thy name, Lord. Amen."

As the jetliner lifted its huge body and began the leap into space, inside the terminal few people paid any attention to a young woman walking slowly away from the gate, through the crowded concourse, to the door. She was utterly silent, her hands sunk in the pockets of her coat. Only one man, who looked because her graceful form caught his eye, noticed that as she walked the tears were silently washing down her cheeks.

TWENTY

"This does not make our publisher exactly gleeful," said R. Randall Jefferson. "He plays golf with a lot of Nixon appointees. Makes things a bit of a sticky wicket on the nineteenth hole."

"So he'll earn his title this month," Tom Friedman snapped. They were meeting in his office—the editor, the paper's chief lawyer, and Peg.

"Oh, he'll keep a strict First Amendment profile in public," Jefferson went on. "If not, Kay Graham and the Sulzbergers would sneer. But privately, he's fuming."

"Wonderful," Peg said. "I take it I am not on his dance card."

"He's rather ambivalent, where you're concerned. Likes strong women, like his mama. Has noticed you have great legs. On the other hand, this could cost the paper a great deal of money."

"So where are we at?" Peg asked.

"We've been negotiating with the boys at Justice. We have a new subpoena."

"The scope of this one is more limited, right?" Tom said.

"Yes. They won't ask to look at notes or unpublished material. They want your testimony before the grand jury."

"The grand jury can ask me about my sources, can't it?"

"Yes."

"And if I refuse to answer?"

"That's up to the judge."

"He can cite me for contempt and throw me in the slammer."

"Yes, he can."

"What the hell good is that?"

"Well, they've pulled in their horns a bit."

"So do I go to court?"

"Oh no, my dear, the idea is to keep you *out* of court. We're going to move to quash this subpoena as well. We're going to argue that if the Justice Department can compel reporters to reveal their sources, their methods of gathering information, then we simply become an arm of the government. Which the First Amendment was designed to prevent."

"What are our chances?" Tom asked.

Jefferson shrugged. "There has been a federal court ruling on a subpoena very much like ours. The move to quash was denied. But it was in a different district. We'll just have to see how the cards fall. The federal bench is pretty good. If we can stay away from Hanging Harry."

"Hanging Harry?" Peg said.

"Judge Benton. Johnson appointee. Always talks about how they used to hang rustlers in Texas."

"God, what does he do to reporters? Disembowel them?"

"Even John Mitchell isn't asking for that, my dear. Be of good cheer."

Jefferson left, and Peg perched on the edge of Tom's desk. "I'm going to have to appear before a grand jury, right?"

"Maybe not. Jefferson is pretty shrewd. He still has a fistful of legal maneuverings."

She sighed. "I'm going to jail. Dammit, I knew it."

"You have the choice, Peg. You can reveal your source."

"No way. Randall Jefferson is right. If we let them get their paws all over our notes, our sources, we might as well be on the payroll of the Justice Department. I've been in so many damn countries where the press has no freedom at all. I won't be a part of taking an ax to the First Amendment. It matters, Tom. This isn't just silly shit we're doing here."

"You're right, Peg. It matters." He looked at her. "You ought to take some time off, Peg. You look pale."

"Great. I'll fit in with the rest of the inmates. I'll have prison pallor *before* I go."

"Peg, I promise, we'll do everything we can."

"I'm okay, Tom. I'll hang tough."

"That much I know."

Peg tried to be cheerful when she met Con for lunch, but Con could see the news had unsettled her.

"There's a nice federal prison where they send all the embezzlers, Peg. It has a golf course and a library and art classes. Club Med without the beach."

"My luck I'd get D.C. jail. Gang rape in the showers."

"They do that at Club Med. But it costs you five hundred a week. That's right, Peg, laugh. Come on, your friends will stick by you. A lot of people really appreciate what you're doing. You have more support than you know about."

"Thanks. That helps. How are things with you?"

"I'm filing my divorce papers."

"How's Lee?"

"He's doing good. Has a girlfriend. A couple, I guess. The boys talk about 'Daddy's girlfriends.' They say they're not as pretty as I am. Loyal kids, but they need to get their eyes checked."

"So you *are* going to marry George?"

"Oh Peg, it would be so easy with George. Money makes things so easy. And I've never had it easy. With George I'd have three houses. I'd learn to throw my clothes on the floor. I'd never have to worry about ending up as a bag lady at Garfinckel's. That's my big fear, you know. I've got my spot all picked out."

"Yeah, me too. At the door of the Press Club. If the bastards won't admit women, let them support me in my old age with change from the bar."

"Kitty says George has a real shot at going all the way. If not this time, then next time. What if I didn't marry George and some other broad got to be First Lady and I had to interview her? I'd kill myself."

"Being First Lady would be a pain. You'd have to pick some dumb project and spend your life planting flowers in the middle of expressways."

"Yeah, women do get the important stuff, don't they? I'd want the space program. Fondle a few astronauts."

"First Ladies do not get to fondle. Presidents can keep

whores in the closet, but a First Lady who felt up moon men would get sent up in a rocket. The part that falls off."

"But Peg, George's world is so nice. So *easy.* I never used to be greedy, but I never knew what it was like to have money. God, it's so different."

The next day, a Saturday, was Lee's day to take the boys to a movie, or bowling. She was working, in the kitchen, on a story when the three of them came home, laughing and talking as they came through the door. One thing the separation had done, she thought, with a touch of irony, was bring Lee and the boys closer together. He was really working hard at being a good father.

Lee came into the kitchen, kissed her lightly on the cheek, and suggested that the four of them go out for an early dinner. The boys prodded her to say yes, and so she did, and they all piled into the station wagon and drove to their favorite pizza haven in Wheaton. As she buckled her seat belt, she realized how familiar it felt, the four of them together, Lee kidding with the boys. Family times. But they weren't a family anymore. A broken home. The words had never meant anything to her, before. Now they sounded unbearably sad, carrying a burden of failure and mangled promise. *Broken.*

After dinner they dropped the boys off at a friend's house where they were spending the night at a sleep-over party, and Con asked Lee to come in for a cup of coffee. It was odd, she thought, inviting him into his own house. They sat on the sofa and drank the coffee and she asked him, "How's work going?"

"Not too bad. I'm learning not to let things get to me the way they used to. At least I'm trying not to. How's the Hill?"

"Hectic. But I really do love it. It's nice not to have to go to all those damn parties."

They were quiet for a minute and then she said, "Are you still with the group?"

"Yes." He shook his head. "Funny, if anybody had told me a year ago that I'd be in therapy I'd have said they were crazy. But it helps."

"I'm glad, Lee."

"Don helps me understand what makes me tick. I know a lot of things about myself I never knew before."

"Like what?"

"I never believed all the good things that happened to me. I always had this sense, deep down, that I was bad. Thanks to my father. I thought the Good Lee was just a cover-up for the real me, the Bad Lee. But I couldn't ever let Bad Lee out. Because he was so awful."

"And he came out that night?"

"Yes. I had what I'd always wanted, a wife and a family. You and the boys. But somehow I couldn't accept all that because Bad Lee didn't deserve that. So he had to find a way to fuck it up. Prove that he was really bad."

"But Lee, you aren't bad."

"No. I'm starting to figure it out. I'm a good person who's done some bad things. And that's better than being a bad person who has to be good all the time. If you follow."

"I do." She touched his arm. "You never did anything to the boys like your father did to you. They adore you."

"I hope so. That's so important to me, Con. I don't want to mess that up. They're great kids. Due to you, mostly."

"Not just me, Lee."

"You gave up a lot, all those years. When you started doing your own thing, I didn't give you much support."

"You were all wrapped up in your own problems."

"Yeah, all of us, all the guys in the group, we were like that. Seeing only *us*. I'm learning to get out of that. It's hard, though. Nobody ever teaches men how to understand other people. We just stumble around, in the dark, bumping into things. I don't want the boys to have to learn about themselves the way I did. It hurts too much."

He looked so earnest—and so young—sitting there. He always did have something of a Boy Scout poster look about him, with that square jaw and the cleft in his chin, the light hair, getting darker now. She had always been a sucker for his serious look, because it made him seem like he was eight years old, wanting help with his homework. A sudden wave of tenderness for him surged through her. He saw her looking at him, and he put his arm on hers and said, "Oh, Con!"

And the next thing she knew she was in his arms, part of her thinking, This is really stupid, Constance Marie, the other part hardly thinking at all.

He was tearing at her clothes, as if they were aflame and

burning her flesh; he was like some great, blind bull, all passion and need. A farm boy, she thought, used to rutting.

She drew him down on the rug and they fairly tore at each
other; teeth, nails, fingertips. He drew back, for an instant,
and said, "I don't want to hurt you!" and she said, "No,
you're not hurting me, don't stop!" She loved his roughness,
the sheer bulk of him; what they were doing to each other had
nothing to do with *hurting*. She pulled him on top of her,
wanting to feel the weight of him all along her body; he was
such a big man. She loved to lie under him as he plunged into
her, a crude, relentless piece of machinery. He was covered
with sweat and desperate with need; she whispered a filthy
word into his ear. She loved to be as crude as he, it excited
her. *Rutting* could be an acquired taste.

And then he carried her beyond the veneer of civilization,
to some dim animal past where all that existed was the
pounding of blood and the rush of secretions, He screamed,
"Oh God!" at the height of his passion, and then they lay
together on the rug, and she was panting and covered with
sweat as well.

He reached over to touch her face with his large hand with
an infinite tenderness, and said, "Let's be in bed together, just
for a while."

He took her hand, and she followed him to the bedroom,
and they crawled into the king-sized bed, and she lay with
her head resting on his chest, listening to his heart beat. She
thought, suddenly, that she knew the surface of his chest as
well as she knew the topography of her own hand.

"It was good, wasn't it, Con?"

"Yes. Yes it was. But it doesn't solve anything, Lee."

"I know. But it's still there. I thought you'd never want me
again. It's still there." He laughed. "Remember the first time?"

"How could I forget? I bled like a stuck pig. I was *mortified!*
Ending up in the emergency room."

"I was panicked. I'd found the girl of my dreams, and I'd
killed her. What a bummer."

"I was sure you'd never call me again. I was going to be a
nun."

"I was sure you'd never forgive me."

"I never would have, if I'd become a goddamn nun."

"Oh, those were such good days, Con. Back at the Academy. I was so happy there. Really happy, for the first time in my life. If only we could live those days over again."

"But we can't."

"No. Con?"

"Ummm?"

"I know you're seriously involved with that senator. But we had a lot of good things. Two great kids." She was silent. "If there's any chance, I want us to be a family again."

"I know."

"Could you forget that night?"

"No," she said.

"Oh. I thought, maybe—"

"But maybe we could get past it. I just don't know."

"All I ask is that you give it time. Give *us* time."

"Lee, do we really have anything anymore? Were we just going on habit? I care about my work. I'm ambitious. Could you live with that?"

"Yes, I think so. Con, I was always proud of you. But I guess I was afraid of letting you get too far away. You were like—mercury. I was certain that I could never hold you. That I'd wake up and you'd be gone."

"You felt that way? Why didn't you ever let me see it? You were so distant. I thought you didn't care."

"See, I knew you loved me because I was strong. I could handle things. And if you knew how I felt I thought you'd have such contempt for me. I didn't want to be weak."

"Oh Lee, loving somebody that much isn't being weak. Any woman would want to know that."

"But if I let you know, then I wouldn't be in control. And if I was out of control—I *couldn't* be, because then something terrible would happen. But I am different, Con. I don't have to be in control all the time now. I can let go. It's scary, but I can do it. I can even admit I'm wrong, apologize to the boys. I can even tell you that I'm scared. And I am. So damn much of the time."

She pulled his head against her breasts and she held him, loving the familiar feel of him against her. The past had such a pull—such a terrible, wonderful pull. She knew she was going to call the lawyer tomorrow and she'd say, "Mel, on those papers, hold up a few days, would you?" But it was stupid. There was a man who wanted her, who would make it all so easy. Who would never hurt her.

Be smart, Constance Marie. Be smart. You could mess it all up. With George, you will never, never be a bag lady.

Thinking that, she fell asleep in the big bed beside him.

The plane circled, out over the lake, then swung back and headed again toward Chicago. Dan Amundsen could see it all laid out before him: the Loop, the Sears Tower, the whole magnificent sweep of the city as it stood staring out into the lake. City of the Big Shoulders.

It made him think of Adam Crabtree. *All the doors could open for you, Dan.*

Was it possible? Was it really possible? He hardly dared to think of it. The son of a schizophrenic and a depressive from nowhere, Nebraska, going All the Way? No, it was just Adam's talk. Just talk. And yet.

Who were they, the men who sought that office? Sons of small-town, middle-class men, not always a Kennedy or a Rockefeller. Richard Nixon came from Nowhere, too. Hubert Humphrey had been a druggist. George McGovern, Birch Bayh, Ed Muskie—men who went into politics, did well, were in the right place at the right time. Was he so different?

Chicago, at his feet now, fueled his fantasies. He had no reason *not* to dream. Adam was shrewd, ambitious. He would not waste his time on a man who had no future. Adam was a kingmaker. What man would not wish to be a king? If Adam's words were only a siren song, it was pleasant music to the ears. It did him no harm to listen.

The plane landed, and he walked into the terminal. He had a four-hour layover, because a flight had been canceled. He went to the phone and dialed the number of the Catholic Institute for Social Justice.

Sean, surprised to hear from him, said, yes, he'd be happy to meet him at one of the hotels in town for dinner. As he hung up the phone, he had to admit that he felt a throb of self-importance, getting a personal call from a congressman. The people at the Institute were suitably impressed.

"Dinner with Dan Amundsen?" said Father Jurevich, the director. "You move in fast company, Sean."

"I knew him pretty well in D.C. Wrote some speeches for him, actually."

Sean blushed slightly, at his own words. *Name dropper.*

But Father J. only nodded. "Those contacts can come in handy, Sean."

Sean grabbed a cab, hurried to meet Dan at the Hilton. Dan was already at a table when he arrived, having a Scotch.

"How do you like Chicago?" the Congressman asked, as he sat down.

"I like it a lot. I'm still in the settling-in stage, of course, but I like it. A lot to be done. How's the campaign going?"

"Did you know you are drinking with the Playboy Congressman?"

"They're still playing that tune?"

"I guess it works. The latest is just a series of pictures of me with various drinks in my hand. No words. In the background you hear, 'The Party's Over.'"

"Nasty. But clever. Do people buy that stuff?"

"Some do. Rolvag's got Ray Cramm, from Manhattan, doing his ads. No cornpone."

"Don't people see what he's doing?"

"He's so likeable, Sean. He looks like everybody's nice granddad. Nothing sticks to him. It's so frustrating. Adam says I'll just look like a snot-nosed kid if we knock him. But *God*, it's frustrating."

When Sean's drink came, Dan ordered another one as well. He looked exhausted, Sean thought. He had circles under his eyes and new lines around his mouth. He downed the Scotch quickly, ordered another.

"You've got plenty of time, Dan. Things can change pretty quickly. Especially this year. Cambodia should help you."

"Yeah, I think so. I hope so." His voice, Sean noticed, had a slight ragged edge to it. The Scotch was starting to take effect.

They talked politics for a while, and Dan had another drink. His voice got a touch louder. He stared for a moment into his drink, and then he said, quietly, "It's coming apart, Sean. It's coming apart."

"The campaign?"

"Everything. My life. Everything." He took a drink of the Scotch. "Did I ever tell you about my father?"

Sean shook his head.

"He was a schizo. He'd be a different person Tuesday than he was Monday. Hell, he'd be different after *lunch.* He used to think he was me, that's the strange part. He'd sit on the floor and draw stick figures and play with my soldiers and call me Daddy. He was so crazy."

"You survived pretty well, going through that, Dan."

"Did I? I've done some things—I've done some pretty crazy things myself. I used to think I was just going to end up crazy, so I'd do any damn thing at all. What the hell. I guess I wanted to experience everything before it happened to me. But then I saw maybe I had a shot at being somebody. But I have to keep going, keep moving ahead."

"Nobody goes in fast forward all the time."

"Me, I got to. Remember Satchel Paige?"

"Sure. I even saw him pitch."

"Great man. Wise man. He said, 'Don't look back, somethin' might be gaining on you.'"

Sean laughed. "It took a long time to catch him. He was fifty when I saw him pitch."

Dan didn't smile. "It's back there, Sean. It's gaining on me. Do you believe in demons?"

"No."

"Some kind of Catholic *you* are. I believe in them. They're here, sometimes." He pointed at his chest. Then he looked at the Scotch. "I think I've had too damn much to drink." He took another swallow. "Kitty. She's some woman. God, I never thought I'd have a woman like that. All that class. So beautiful. I love her body, I—jeez, I shouldn't be saying this to a priest."

"I'm a man, too, Dan. Kitty loves you. She really does."

"Yeah, great woman, nobody like her. They're using her against me, the fuckers. Oh, they never say *Jew*, the fuckers, they never say it."

"That won't work. It's going to backfire."

"I love her, God, do I love her. I never loved anybody in my life the way I love her. Kitty, she's the only one I can—rest with. The only time I don't have to run. With Kitty."

"You're a lucky man, Dan."

"Lucky. Oh yes. Lucky. God, I think I'm drunk."

"You look exhausted."

"I've been trying to get back to the state as much as I can, but there's so much important stuff in committee. God, it's a hell of a way to run a railroad."

"Dan, after dinner, why don't you just check in and stay here. I'll get you on a flight out in the morning."

"I've got a committee meeting at noon."

"I'll get you an early flight. You need some sack time."

Sean helped Dan get settled after dinner—the congressman was less tipsy after he had something to eat, but still worn out. Sean arranged a morning flight, and had the ticket sent over to the hotel. Dan would be back in Washington for a day, then out to the state again the next. He was right, Sean thought. A hell of a way to run a railroad.

When he got into his office the next morning, Sean found a note on his desk from Father Jurevich, clipped to the memo Sean had sent to the director two days before: "Sean, good idea, but let's hold off on this one."

Sean walked into the office next to his and tossed the note on the desk of Ben Hanafee, head of the Institute's family counseling service. Hanafee's unit had been so successful it had been widely copied across the country.

"Godammit, Ben, why?" Sean said, scowling.

Ben Hanafee, a man in his late thirties with a receding hairline and alert blue eyes, picked up the note and read it.

"He backed off, huh?"

Sean shook his head, angrily. "Ben, it's a lot like what I did at St. Ignatius. The neighborhood doesn't want a thruway interchange, for good reasons. We could win, and it's right under our nose."

"Did Father J. say why not?"

"I can guess. Some key aldermen are for it."

"And some prominent Catholic construction types."

"Ben, Father J. hasn't approved one of my ideas yet. And he's asked me to stay away from doing any antiwar stuff so the Institute won't get hurt. Why in the hell did he bring me here? All I do is push papers."

"Politics, Sean. And the *board* brought you here. Father J. wants to move more carefully than they do."

Sean raised his hands in a gesture of futility. The web of political interests in this city was a tangled one. The militant Blacks distrusted the church and hated the Daley-organization Blacks; the Hispanics didn't trust anybody; the working-class whites despised the Blacks and were bitter about the church. Everybody had their own little bit of turf, and Sean McCaffrey wasn't getting a piece of the action.

"I guess I was lucky at St. Ignatius. I saw an issue, and I ran with it."

"We're tied into the church bureaucracy here, Sean, that's the problem. I'm always trying ways to get around the rules. Sometimes they close their eyes."

"Like when you tell teenagers there's such a thing as a condom?"

"Yeah."

"But I can't start anything until Father J. approves it."

"He's pretty savvy, Sean. He's survived three decades of political wars out here."

"But he seems more interested in the soup kitchen approach. And if we don't try to change the system we'll just keep doling out soup."

"He fought hard, Sean, to get the counseling service set up—back when the idea of the church paying *shrinks* was heresy. But he's getting tired. I'll try to work on him. You're right, the times call for a more aggressive approach. We should be in front of the pack, not behind it. Listen, Sean, Lisa asked me to ask you for dinner."

"Are you sure? The baby is due any day."

"Don't worry, we'll all pitch in. She's the one who asked."

Sean didn't protest again. He loved spending time with Ben and Lisa. The warmth of their friendship, offered so generously, helped to temper his growing frustration at the lack of progress he was making in the job. Ben, he thought, was the perfect example of a layman living a good life "in the world" as they used to say in seminary. With his credentials, Ben could have made a comfortable living in private psychiatric practice. But he worked at a modest salary to keep the service going, and he put in long hours. No priest worked harder, Sean thought.

After dinner with the Hanafees, Sean went back to his room, or, to be precise, his suite. He had three lovely rooms on the third floor of the gracious mansion that housed the Institute. It had a study with an Oriental rug on the floor, and the walls were solid oak. There was no drunken pastor, no sound of retching to seep through paper-thin walls. But strangely enough, the unaccustomed luxury only made his loneliness more intense. Loneliness had seemed appropriate at St. Nasty's—where everything was crumbling. Here, the ache that crept into his bones at night seemed even harder to bear.

On an impulse he picked up the phone. He waited until he heard her voice.

"Hello," he said. "It's Herb."

"Herb, I have a complaint to register. Remember that fellow you brought to live with me? One Fuzzy D. Bear?"

"Sure."

"He's a lush. Drinks my booze, sings at all hours of the night. Debauched bear."

"He was sober when I brought him to you, Thelma."

"My fault. I gave him booze. Since he's only one foot tall, he doesn't hold it great. Will you still speak to me, Herb, when I'm in the slammer?"

"What's happened?"

She told him about the new subpoena and Hanging Harry.

"Oh Peg, what can I do? I got you into this."

"It's just good to have somebody to talk to. I try to keep a stiff upper lip around the paper, but I am scared. You know me and small, confined places. Oh Sean, I do have some hot news for you. Guess who got married?"

"Who?"

"Estella and Chuck. They just went out and did it."

"No kidding!"

"Her family is ripshit. Her mother calls Chuck *negrito*. Chuck's dad keeps saying, 'your wife, the spic.'"

"I did start something, didn't I?"

"Yes, probably a race war. The wedding was like the Paris peace talks. I thought Brian was going to have to frisk the guests."

"Poor Brian."

"Yes. And I am getting ever more popular at the *Trib*. I am the house lezzie-peacenik-save-the-seals freak. We get nice letters that say 'Kill the dyke! Send her back to Russia.' Come to think of it, jail might be safer."

"I'd go to jail for you if I could."

"I know, Sean. Oh best friend, it's so good to hear your voice. I just get—tired of it all, sometimes."

"Peg, call me anytime. Any time, day or night. I'm here, Peg. Call me."

When he hung up, he lay on the bed and let her image float in the air in front of him, as it often did. Her voice had a strange power; it kept the loneliness at bay. He stood up, hesitated—then walked to the closet. He opened the closet door and slipped a red woman's silk blouse off the hanger. It had gotten mixed in with his things the night he had moved out of her apartment. He had meant to mail it back to her, but it had been lying on his bed one night, and he had pressed it to his cheek and the smell of her curled up into his nostrils—her perfume, her body scent. It had lulled him quickly to sleep.

Now, at night, when the loneliness was a sluggish liquid inside him, he would put it on the pillow and press his nose against it, and her presence would fill the room, a benign spirit. Better than belting gin. He hoped he wouldn't die in his sleep, though. The housekeeper would find him some morning, stiff as a board, with a woman's blouse draped across his face. That would really freak the poor woman out.

The next morning, Ben walked into the office, beaming. Lisa had given birth to an eight-pound baby girl the night before. Amanda. Sean was both pleased and surprised when they asked him to be the godfather. At the christening, he thought he would be afraid to hold her, but when Ben nestled Mandy in his arms it felt so very natural.

"I baptize thee," the priest said, "in the name of the Father, the Son, and the Holy Ghost."

As Sean held the infant, he felt a stirring that he could only dimly recognize as paternal instinct. She was so tiny, so vulnerable. He wanted to hold her, protect her, put iodine on her. Standing inside the great old stone church, holding Mandy, he understood for the first time how great was his hunger to be needed. His boyhood collection of squirrels and mice—all injured and all held against their will—was a testament to that need. He would go off to sleep with a warm glow in his heart, knowing they were safe in their boxes filled with cotton, wearing their splints.

Ben took the baby out of his arms, and he felt a sense of loss that seemed to reach the marrow of his bones.

I will always be holding other people's children. Never my own.

In the seminary, when Father Peter spoke of giving up natural fatherhood to be a father to all, it had seemed a fine idea. But why did his arms feel so empty, deprived of their tiny burden?

Little Mandy, all eight pounds of her, imprinted herself in a mysterious fashion on his brain cells. For days after the baptism, he found himself thinking of her at all sorts of unexpected times. Had the tiny infant radioed a message directly to his genes, triggering a subterranean impulse to carry on his line, one that could override the vow of celibacy? He began to have *very* strange fantasies, even for him. When he looked at women, he made them pregnant.

It was most embarrassing. Old women, young women— even a nun—he saw them blooming with life, bellies swelling and ripening, even as he watched. As he walked along the Loop, he was impregnating females faster than a prize bull set loose in herd of eager cows.

A blond young woman moved into his range of vision. She had clean, shining long hair that moved gently as she walked and she was wearing a blue silk dress under her raincoat. She passed him, and he did it. She swelled up like a balloon. This was getting crazy, it was totally nuts. Still, she kept getting bigger, the stomach under the blue silk firmer and rounder, an icon of fecundity.

He stuck his hands in his coat pockets and tried to walk faster, looking at the sidewalk, trying to avoid passing women. He sighed, deeply.

The Flasher Priest had picked up another talent.

TWENTY-ONE

Peg sighed as she looked at Con, whose skin was a glowing, golden tan. She glanced ruefully at her own arms, skin the shade of dead fish bellies.

"Martinique, again?" They were meeting at the Washington Roof on a Tuesday afternoon in March.

"You could use a little sun, Peg. You look pale."

"I don't have a lover with a Lear jet."

"I was terrified at first. I thought God was going to zap me, right over the Bermuda Triangle. I wouldn't *touch* George until we got to the house."

"God couldn't get you in a beach house?"

"Maybe. But if He sees every sparrow, He'd be sure to notice a Lear jet. Seriously, you ought to come. There's plenty of room in the jet."

"What would I do while you two made love on the beach?"

"Dally with the houseboy. He's cute, for sixteen."

"The *Trib* would really get letters about me if I was arrested for statutory rape."

"They'd stop calling you a dyke."

"What was his name again?" They both laughed, then Peg asked, "Have you filed divorce papers yet?"

"Not yet."

"Are you dragging your feet for a reason?"

"No. Yes. I don't know."

"There's a woman who knows her mind."

"I'm going to do it. George and I do get on. It's so nice with George."

"God, that's romantic."

"Come on, Peg, I'm not seventeen."

"Constance Marie, people are more enthusiastic than that about George when the Harris Poll comes around. Even if they're voting for Muskie. Nice is not enough to build a life on."

"My mother and father did it on contempt. *Nice* is a step up."

"You know, when you married Lee, I was pissed at you. For not going to New York with me. But then I figured it was nice that one of us got the fairy tale ending. I knew it wasn't going to be me when I read 'Cinderella,' and they kept going on about her cute little feet. Glass slippers do not come in 10B. But I thought you two really loved each other."

"We did. But it wasn't enough."

"Shit."

"Peg, I think that deep down, you still believe in fairy tales. Seven little men and a girl living in the woods with no weird sex rites going on. You are a romantic, God help you."

"And you?"

"A realist. Happy endings are a fantasy. Listen, what was this important thing you had to tell me?"

"Con, guess what I am."

"I hate guessing games. You're not Cinderella and you're not a dyke. Okay, you're pregnant."

"Right."

"What!"

"Preggers. It is what I am."

"I was kidding!"

"I know."

"How the hell did that happen?"

"I wore the damn diaphragm every time but the last. But my period had just ended, so I thought I was safe."

"How far along?"

"Three months. I get real irregular when I'm under stress, so I didn't think anything about it when I missed a couple of periods."

"Oh Peg, what a dummy."

"Yeah, not smart."

"What are you going to do?"

"Good question. Oh Con, what a mess I've made. I am going to jail, and I'm knocked up."

"You could have an abortion."

"No, Con, I *want* this baby."

"Have you thought about this?"

"Come on, I'm not some poor teenager who got herself knocked up and has to go on welfare. I can support a child. I was thinking of adopting one, anyway."

"Peg, this is not a decision you make lightly."

"I've thought a lot, Con, since I found out. I've always liked the idea of seeing a child grow. I want to know what that's like. Why should I miss out on it just because the goddamn glass slipper doesn't fit?"

"It's a lot of work, a lot of heartache, raising a child. And a baby is no substitute for a man. If you want someone to love you, this is not the way."

"No, it's the other way around, really. I've always thought I have a lot to give. I have my own life, I don't need something to make me—complete. But I really do think I could be a good mother."

"I know you could, Peg."

"But what I have to figure out, is how do I do this? I'm not some movie star who can just announce I'm having a love child."

"There's the obvious solution of course. Marry the father."

"Sean made his choice, Con. I have no intention of trapping him this way. I thought what I might do is just start wearing a wedding ring and just let it out that I've been married for a while. I'm a bit of a hermit, nobody at the paper knows about my private life."

"That's true. It could work."

"But who am I married to? Somebody that no one would know, maybe in another city. A commuter marriage."

"A navy man."

"What?"

"Of course. He's on a nuclear sub. Twenty thousand leagues under the sea. A perfect cover."

"Constance Marie, that's brilliant."

"I could even get a guy in a white uniform you could drag around once in a while."

"Yes, and then later on, I could just get a quiet divorce. Or his sub could hit a rock."

"Peg, that is not a great idea. People would know if we lost a nuclear sub."

"Okay. Quiet divorce." Peg dug in her handbag and took out a small box. She opened the top and let Con peer in. A little gold band lay nestled in the cotton. "See, I come prepared. Help me get the little sucker on."

Con helped Peg slide the ring on. "Somehow, this is not how I envisioned your wedding."

"Me neither." Peg looked at the ring for a minute, then blinked several times.

"Oh, Peg!"

"I am not going to blubber, Constance Marie. I will just *not*. Besides the Washington Roof is a classy place to get married."

"How do you feel? You do look so pale. Any morning sickness?"

"No. The funny thing is, I feel wonderful. I have lots of energy. I feel like an earth mother. Fruitful. Ripe."

"You are going to make me barf, Peg."

"I always thought I'd hate being pregnant, but I think I love it. I must come from peasant stock. You know, milk the cow, drop the baby in the field, and go home and make supper."

"Not me. I am strictly the aristocracy. I threw up for three months. I asked them if they could give me the anesthesia the day I got my first maternity dress. Just feed me through a tube and wake me when it's over, I said."

"Oh, I want to see *everything*. It's such an important experience. I'd even like to have movies. Wouldn't you like a movie of yourself being born?"

"Oh sure, Peg. My mother would run it every week, complete with a sound track of her screaming. It was her big line when I was a kid. 'I endured the pains of childbirth for you.' She still says it, actually."

"In those days, Con, they gave everybody twilight sleep. They didn't feel a thing."

"Are you kidding? Thirty-one years of guilt, and she was *asleep* the whole time? I'll kill her!"

"How were your deliveries?"

"I remember screaming, 'Is it over!' And that was when the nurse was typing out the admission form."

Peg laughed. "You are not a big stoic, Constance Marie."

"Damn right. I made them zonk me with so much stuff I thought I was in Disneyland. When I saw Terry I said, 'Dumbo!'"

"I wonder if I want a boy or a girl."

"Peg, you have to tell Sean."

"Why? I got myself into this."

"Oh, a virgin birth? Be sure to tell the Pope."

"This light flooded the room, and I heard the voice of God. 'You are going to have my baby.' I said, 'But sir, don't you need a virgin?' He said, 'I looked but I couldn't find one over twelve years old. You'll have to do.'"

"Jeez, Peg, I guess if we can laugh, we can get through most anything. The nuns didn't tell us, did they?"

"They didn't know."

"You're going to need your friends, you know. It's tough enough having a baby when you have a husband; there's so many changes, so many new feelings. Don't try to be heroic. I'm here, and I know Lee will want to help, he's always liked you, and Kitty. We'll all be here for you."

"Thanks, Con. That really helps. It does. Makes me feel I really did make the right decision."

"Sean ought to know, Peg. You can tell him that you absolutely won't marry him if you want to, but it's his child. Not just yours."

"Sean has such a conscience. Of course he'll want to do the right thing and marry me."

"Peggy, he can't force you to marry him. But it's not fair not to tell him. I mean that."

"I do have to get to Chicago to do some interviews."

"So you'll tell him."

"I'll think about it."

"Think *hard*, Peg. That is an order."

"Aye aye, *sir*."

Kitty looked at her calendar for the day, and noticed that she had written, at the top of it, "Call Peg Morrison. Re: veggies."

She picked up the phone and dialed. When Peg answered, Kitty said, "Now Peg, you be sure to eat some greens every day. And take the vitamins I sent over. It's very important, the first six months, for you to take care of yourself. And eat breakfast. You must eat breakfast."

"Kitty, I am going to be so *healthy*."

"Dear, have you told the people at the paper about your— marriage?"

"Yes, I've been letting it get around, quietly. Nobody seemed too surprised. They think I'm a bit odd, anyhow. But nobody seemed at all suspicious."

"Yes, and in this day and age nobody counts back on their fingers. If you walk down the aisle sometime before you go into labor, that's considered good form these days. Peg, when you start to show, I have some maternity clothes I saved from when I was pregnant with Jason."

"That would be a big help. I'll need things for work."

"I have some nice tailored things. You're welcome to them. And Peg, make sure you get enough rest. Put your feet up when you can."

After her talk with Peg, Kitty went downstairs, where Antonio was waiting with a petit breakfast served on the sun porch. It was the usual routine she followed when Dan was out of town: the *Post* with breakfast, a skim through the *Times*, and then an hour or so on correspondence. As she was reading Maxine Cheshire, the phone rang. It was Con.

"Kitty, have you seen the *Times?*"

"No, I haven't gotten to it yet. I was a bit lazy this morning."

"Then you don't know."

"Know what?"

"Oh shit."

"Constance, what is it? Is anything wrong?"

"It's Dan."

Kitty felt her breath catch; the same sensation she had felt when she got the call from her husband's partner: "Kitty, it's Morris." She didn't breathe. She could feel her heart beating. "Con, what about him?"

"He's— Oh Kitty, why do I have to be the one to tell you this?"

"He's dead. Dan's dead."

"Dead? Oh God, no, he's not dead."

"Constance, what is it? For heaven's sake, tell me!"

"He's married."

"Married? Constance, if this is some sort of a joke, it is not amusing."

"Kitty, it's no joke. The *Times* says he was married yesterday in Omaha. To someone named Joyce."

"Joyce?"

"Yes, just a minute, here it is. Says she works for the Omaha Chamber of Commerce. You want any details?"

"Yes, please, Constance."

"Married in the chambers of Judge Samuel McIntosh, a small ceremony, Adam Crabtree was best man. Bride and groom will honeymoon in Bermuda, briefly. He will be back on the campaign trail next week."

There was a silence on the line. Con said, "Kitty?"

"I'm here."

"Who is Joyce?"

"A photo op."

"What?"

"She's nobody, Constance."

"Did you know about her?"

"Yes. I knew."

"What in the hell does Dan Amundsen think he is doing?"

"Becoming the junior senator from Nebraska, I suppose."

"You had no idea? He didn't tell you anything?"

"No. He said we were going to be married after the election. At least, that's what I think he said."

"The lying, rat-faced son of a bitch."

"Yes. Rather my sentiments."

"Oh Kitty, how could he? How the hell could he?"

"I don't know. I really don't know."

"Kitty, want me to come over?"

"Constance, I think I really want to be alone for a while."

"You're all right?"

"Yes. I am."

"Oh Kitty. Oh damn! I'm so goddamn sorry."

"So am I, Constance."

She went back to the sun porch, picked up the *Times* and turned to the society page. The story was brief, four paragraphs. The bride wore a dress of blue *peau de soie*. The matron of honor wore mauve. At the bride's request, the judge read a stanza from Kahlil Gibran.

"Kahlil Gibran!" Kitty said. "Even Rod McKuen would be better."

She went upstairs to the bedroom, and she got out a pair of scissors, and she took Dan's three suits from the closet and began, methodically, to cut them to pieces.

"I hate you!" she said, as she hacked up six hundred-dollar worsted. "You stinking *goniff*, I hate you! I hate you!" When it was done she looked at the mess and sank to the floor, scissors in hand.

"Dan! Oh, Dan!" She took the scissors and began to stab at pieces of the suit, sobbing uncontrollably as she did so. Then she threw the scissors down on the floor and she rocked back and forth, the grief flowing through her like a current. She rocked, and wept, until something crumpled inside her. Then she just sat still for a very long time. When she looked up at Morris, over the bed, she could tell he was frowning.

"I know. I know. I look like a crazy woman, don't I? Sitting here with eighteen hundred dollars' worth of suit scraps all over the place. Shapiro the tailor would *plotz*. He worked so hard on the inseam."

She got up slowly, and sat on the bed. "Oh Morris, it's my own damn fault, isn't it? My mother always told me, stay with your own. She told me that non-Jews beat their wives. Like it said so in the Torah. Well, Dan didn't lay a hand on me. He just ripped my guts out. One quick tug. And I thought he loved me, isn't that a laugh? It's the classic story, older woman makes a fool of herself over a younger man. But to tell you the truth, Morris, I don't think of myself as *older*. Do you think I look older? Right. I damn well do not.

"Oh damn, it *hurts*, Morris. So much. So much. I feel so— used. *Violated.* Not a word to me, Morris, not a phone call. Not a Candygram. Not a little sprig of flowers by wire with a little ceramic cup and the message, Sorry, wedding off. Harris Poll eight points down.

"The worst thing, the very worst thing is that if he walked in here right now I'd still want him. I loved his body, Morris. It was so beautiful. I loved the way he could make me feel. I would have lived with him, been his wife, I would have held him when he was feeling like his world was falling apart. I might even have had a baby with him. Oh yes, I was thinking about that. If he'd wanted it, I would have tried for a little half-Jewish, half-Norwegian prince or princess. Oh, I was so stupid, Morris. Once, when Dan said he'd like to have kids someday, I got out my old Dr. Spock and got all teary. Remember when Jason swallowed a button and I was frantically thumbing through the B's? Oh, I was an idiot! I was thinking of making a baby, and he's off marrying one. She's got a big butt, too. In five years she'll look like Kate Smith."

She cried again for a few minutes, and then she said, "I gave him money. I used my connections for him. I taught him how to dress, I took him to Shapiro the tailor, who should only have stabbed him in the heart with the pinking shears. Without me, Morris, what would he be? A little nebbish from Nebraska. He's going to the Senate on Jewish money, Morris, isn't that a laugh?"

She stood up and began to pick up the suit scraps and toss them in the wastebasket. "One thing, Morris, he's not going to get away with it. *Turn the other cheek* is not in the *Old* Testament. Oh yes, he'll pay. Maybe not today. Or tomorrow. But someday. One thing I have learned, Morris my dear, and that's patience."

At six o'clock Peg and Con showed up on the doorstep, carrying two bottles of Scotch whiskey, bagels, and a cold pasta salad.

"We are here to cheer you up, so no back talk," Con announced.

"Yeah, we're going to have a hen party. We are going to let our hair down and cry and beat up on men, the rats."

They sat in the kitchen, toasting bagels and drinking Scotch, and Kitty said, "Oh, it's good to have friends like you. I was supposed to go to the gala for the National Endowment, but I couldn't face it. They'd all be whispering, 'Poor Kitty. She's been dumped, you know.'"

"Men are like streetcars." Peg shrugged. "Besides, gossip gets stale in this town faster than you can say pocket veto. Next week it'll be old news."

"Why was I so stupid? I didn't see it coming. Why didn't I?"

"You were in love with him," Con said.

"Why? You're right, I was in love with him. Why?"

"He was charming."

"He was handsome."

"He was good in bed."

"The only problem," Con concluded, "was that he was a lying snake."

"Did you see it, all along?" Kitty asked Con.

She shook her head. "No. I really didn't. Not *this*."

"Peg?"

"It's funny, I've seen a lot of ambitious men, and some of them burn hot and others burn cold. Those are the ones you have to watch."

"He was so afraid. Afraid that he would be nobody."

"There are two different kinds of people in Washington, I think," Peg began. "They're all ambitious, but some of them have a dream, a sense of history. They can do a lot of harm if their dreams are paranoid, or evil. But if they are good ones, true ones, that's how history moves ahead. It's the other ones that scare me. The empty ones. *The hollow men*."

"Is that Dan? A hollow man?"

"I think so. Yes, Kitty, I think he is."

"Then I was such a fool."

"Where men are concerned, we are all fools," Con said.

"*We* ought to run things." Kitty sat up. "We're not hollow. We're fools, but we're not hollow."

"You're right," Peg agreed. "Let women have a turn."

"Do you want to have power, Constance?" Kitty asked.

"For a long time I was scared even to think about it. I'd find myself sitting next to the Chief Justice, and I'd think, 'My God, it's the *Chief Justice*, and I am only the mother of two from Crystal Springs. I don't belong here!'"

"But you do," Peg said.

"Yes. They're not gods, are they? The world belonged to them for so long we thought they were all giants. But they're not. No smarter than us. Yes, I'd like to swing some weight. Why not?"

"When we were kids, remember the TV show, 'The Pall Mall Big Story'? Reporters were always getting people out of jail. They were Robin Hoods, doing good. That's what I wanted to do."

"Rob from the rich, give to the poor? My dear, you are a Democrat."

Peg laughed. "I have this feeling that when things are unfair I have to walk around pointing my finger and saying, 'Do something!' I don't want to feel this way, because it makes you a pain in the ass. But I do. Power is for fixing things."

"You feel that way because you're a woman," Kitty said. "Big Mommy. Most men don't feel that way. We're the ones who are supposed to *take care*. But who takes care of us?"

"Good question."

"Look at us," Kitty said. "They told us not to worry our little heads because some man would take care of us. Look at *me*. One man died on me and the other dumped me."

"And my husband punched me out."

"And Sean got me pregnant and went back to the church."

They were swilling down Scotch at a rapid rate as they talked. To a woman, they were feeling rather light-headed.

"Maybe," Kitty said, "we should all be lesbians."

Peg giggled. "Yeah, if I'd been screwing a nun, I wouldn't be pregnant."

"No foam, no pills, no diaphragms," Con said. "Free at last!"

"That settles it." Kitty was also giggling. "We'll be lesbians."

"What do lesbians *do*, actually?" Peg asked.

Con thought for a minute. "Grope each other, I suppose."

They all stared at each other, and then they broke out laughing. They laughed until their sides ached, just laughed and laughed.

"I don't think this is going to work," Peg hiccuped.

"Yeah, Kitty," Con said, "I don't think I could get turned on by somebody who's wearing a bra."

"Or perfume," Peg added. "Con, you reek, you know that?"

"This is expensive stuff. Four-ninety eight at Discount Drugs."

"Well, I don't want to grope anybody who smells like a dead flower."

"And *I* will never touch anybody whose feet look like the USS *Missouri*."

Peg pulled her feet back close to the chair, and Con and Kitty cracked up.

"She *hates* her feet," Con said. "Want to reduce her to a quivering mass of jelly? Stare at her feet."

They stared and Peg started to giggle and said, "Stop that! Just *stop* it!"

"I think," Kitty sighed, "that we would be *terrible* lesbians."

"What we need," Peg said, "is a third sex."

"That sounds like a good idea. What would they be like?"

"Just like us. Only with penises."

"I'll drink to that," Con said.

They all raised their glasses.

TWENTY-TWO

S ean was struggling with the annual report when Lisa came in, carrying Amanda.

"Want to say hello to your godchild?"

"Oh I sure do. Can I hold her?"

Lisa gave the baby to Sean, and she nestled in his arms. He tickled her stomach, something she liked very much. "Hi there, Mandy."

He rocked her gently, as she gave a contented gurgle.

"Sean, you must come from a big family. You're so good with babies."

"No, just an older brother."

"How did you learn about babies?"

He grinned. "Practiced on squirrels. But they bite."

"Squirrels?"

"I had my own veterinary ward. Before I wanted to be a priest I wanted to be a vet. I had a big practice."

"You must have been good."

"Terrible, actually. The survival rate in my ward was only slightly better than Andersonville Prison."

"Well, Mandy has confidence in you."

"If she breaks a wing, don't let her near me."

Mandy cooed again and Sean tickled her tummy with his nose. "Sweet as sugar candy," he singsonged.

"I hate to take her away, Sean. You two seem made for each other."

He smiled. "I think we are." He reluctantly handed the baby to Lisa. He went back to the annual report, but the figures blurred before his eyes. They weren't making any sense. Like his life. He was driving himself nuts, thinking.

He walked into Ben's office and said, "Got a few minutes?"

"Sure, Sean."

"I think I'm here as a client."

"That's okay."

Sean dropped into a chair across from Ben. "I've spent so much of my time as a priest trying to whip myself into shape. Fighting *me*. But lately, I wonder if what I'm fighting isn't the best part of me."

"How do you mean?"

"Obedience. Is it a virtue for a grown man? Or is it for little boys and buck privates? Does it infantalize you?"

"You *are* in a crisis, aren't you."

"Yes. I had such a romantic image of the church. Damien the Leper. It was so—glorious, that for a long time I didn't want to see what was around me."

"Which was?"

"Incompetence. Men playing politics to climb the ladder. Trimmers, saying what the boss wants to hear. Timid men. Narrow men. I know, even churchmen are *men*. But must I obey them? Do I betray what is best in me to take the voice of fools as the word of God?"

"That's pretty harsh."

"I know. But do I have a duty to grow up, Ben? To do what I know is right? And can I do it, wearing this collar?"

"Some men do, others don't. The church is a big place. It has all kinds."

"But I don't play the game very well. I'm too impatient. And I—Oh, maybe I ought to be honest and say it's not just that. All sorts of things are sort of churning inside. Mandy has had this strange effect on me."

"Mandy?"

"Yes. This is going to sound very weird. But ever since I held her at the baptism, I—I, ah, get people pregnant."

Ben raised an eyebrow.

"I just see a woman, and zap!, she's pregnant. I think I've knocked up half the North Side. So you can see why I need a shrink."

Ben laughed. "That's not uncommon, Sean. It's a pretty basic drive."

"But I'm a priest."

"You're also a man. And one who's at the age when most men marry and start families."

"Ben, what's it like, having a wife and child? I mean, does it make you feel like you have—a purpose? That life is worth living?"

"That's a big question."

"I know."

"When Mandy was born, I felt like I had really contributed something wonderful to this earth. Lisa and I, we're part of the cycle of life, now."

"Yes, that's what I meant. I feel—sometimes I feel like a shadow. Like something is missing. Amputated."

"An interesting choice of words."

"I guess so."

"We all need roots, connections, Sean."

"That's what I don't have. I go someplace and then I get yanked away. Here, I thought this could be a place for me. But all I do is push papers. Ben, have you talked to priests much about—"

"Sex?"

Sean nodded.

"Yes, but I'll admit, I'm not the best person to talk about celibacy. I think it's too hard, we lose too many good people because of it. I was in seminary for a year myself, but I realized that I wanted a wife, kids." He paused. "Can I ask you a question, Sean? You don't have to answer if you don't want to."

"Go ahead."

"Have you always been celibate?"

"No. I wasn't a virgin when I went in. I was celibate for ten years. But then I had a—relationship."

"Was it serious?"

"Serious?" He laughed. "I've loved her since I was five years old. She says we're like little birds. We got imprinted on each other so early there's no one else for either of us."

"You haven't seen her in a while?"

"No. We broke it off—she did, actually. It was tearing me up, trying to be a good priest, and—" He shrugged.

"You're missing her. A lot."

"Want to hear something pathetic? I sleep with a blouse of

hers sometimes. It smells like her. I'm getting so I can't sleep without it. Does that shock you, coming from a priest?"

"You're a man, Sean."

"I—I have a lot of trouble with celibacy."

"You're not alone."

"It's not just sex I want. I can jerk off and get relief. I—this is going to sound corny."

"I don't think so."

"When I made love to her, when I was inside her, I felt as close to God as I've ever been in my life. Or maybe just close to some primal force. I want, I need—" he paused.

"Go on, Sean."

"I need her to touch me. I don't think I can live anymore the way I do, not having anybody touch me." He leaned back in the chair and closed his eyes. Then he opened them again. "But I took vows. Sacred vows."

"How old were you when you went in the seminary?"

"Eighteen."

"Just a kid. Did you really understand what those vows entailed? Did you understand what it would mean never to have children?"

"I guess not. I just figured I'd offer it up."

"Which may make your vows invalid. You can't make a true promise when you don't understand—emotionally—the full extent of what you're promising."

"All my life I've wanted to be a priest. To fail, now—"

"I don't think you ought to look at it in those terms. People grow and change. The point is, what do you want to do with your life so it will be meaningful? You're not feeling that way now, I gather."

"No. I'm not."

"So either you work out a way to make the priesthood a meaningful place for you, or you leave and find out where you do belong. Either way, it's not a question of failure, Sean."

"I think it would kill my father if I left."

"It's amazing how parents can adapt. You'd be surprised."

"I think I'm afraid. Who would I be without the collar? It's a security blanket."

"You'd be the same man Sean McCaffrey is now. All the talents, all the faults."

"But I think it's like a rope, and I'm holding on, and if I let go—I'll just fall and keep on falling."

"Not deciding *is* deciding, Sean."

Sean was quiet for a minute. In his mind he saw the door, clearly; it was arched and had a metal handle. It was the one he had always been afraid to open.

"And if I don't choose, I live my life by default."

"Yes."

"I don't want to do that."

"Maybe you ought to ask yourself what does Sean McCaffrey want? Not what the church wants or what your family wants or what you're *supposed* to want. What does Sean McCaffrey want?"

He got up and walked to the window and looked out on the quiet street. He had his hand on the latch of the door, now, and he trembled. It was the one question that was taboo, the one he had never let himself ask: What does Sean McCaffrey want?

He took a deep breath, and opened the door.

"I want to love her. I want her to be there every morning when I wake up. I want to make babies with her. I want to be like other men. Do I have a right to be?"

"If you want to be, yes."

He turned around to look at Ben.

"I never let myself say that before. It's so easy to say."

"Not so easy to do."

"I'm not a terrible person because I said it, am I?"

"No, Sean, you're not."

"I'm no different."

"What did you expect?"

"Oh, flashes of lightning, I guess. It's crazy, but I thought, without the priesthood, I—there wouldn't be any *me*. Do you know what I mean?"

"The collar isn't you, Sean. You're not the collar."

"I'm not, am I? Did I ever choose it? Or did my father choose it for me, and I let him do it? I wonder if I've ever known the answer to that."

When he left Ben's office he walked up the stairs, and into his room. He looked at the clock. Five-thirty. She wouldn't be home yet. What did he say to her? "Ms. Peg Morrison, *Mr.*

Sean McCaffrey requests your hand in marriage?" "Hey babe, let's get hitched?" "Peg, if you're not booked up Saturday—"

Come live with me and be my love.

To live with her; he would have the things that were missing from his life. Her pantyhose, hanging in the shower stall like some peculiar fungus; the smelly green junk she dabbed on her face at night. The hairs in his razor when she was out of blades and shaved her legs with his Schick. The little mole on the inside of her thigh that looked like a tiny brown apple. The sweetness of her breasts against his skin when she slept with him. The way she thrust herself up to him in the act of love, impaling herself on him, her eyes wide and blue, making him feel stronger than God.

Come live with me and be my love.

He would be like other men. He would live with her and hold her and laugh with her and fight with her. He would lie, no more, in a narrow little bed, and shiver at night from loneliness. He would fill her belly with a child. He could give her that. He could give her a miracle.

Five-thirty-five.

He started to pace around the room, his head a whirl. What would he *do*? Talk about a man with an interesting resume! And what do you do, sir? "I say mass, I organize Blacks and Hispanics to stop highways, and I run a mean beano game."

He could always run a beano van and peddle soft drinks on the side. Beano Van could clear a hundred bucks a week, easy.

That was ingenuous, of course. He had found the arena where his talents could be used. Politics. He had learned where the gears and levers were. There was a new kind of politics being born of the turmoil of the time. Martin Luther King had done it, Ralph Nader practiced it. If you could mobilize the media, and get enough savvy, active workers, you could get to the good people who held office, and you could make the system work for people who had never found their way to the controls before. The hard, glorious work was not to be found only in leper colonies and heathen jungles. The halls of the Rayburn Building could be a place to do God's work.

Six o'clock. He dialed. There was no answer. He kept calling, and then he called the paper. The operator said that Ms. Morrison was out of town for two days. Expected back late tomorrow. He kept trying her home phone, just in case, until midnight. He kept pacing between calls. He wished he had mental telepathy so he could project it into her mind.

Come live with me and be my love.

While Sean was pacing, in his room, Peg was doing the same thing in a small room in the Palmer House, only two miles away. Then she walked into the bathroom, stripped off her clothes and surveyed herself in the mirror. Four months, and she wasn't even showing. Was there a new roundness to her belly? Or was it simply her imagination? She poked out her stomach as far as she could, to see what she would look like.

Sometimes, it didn't seem real at all. The months would just go on, nothing would happen. At other times, she was absolutely terrified. She was going to bloat up like a dirigible, her belly was going to flop over the typewriter keys so she wouldn't be able to make a living. She was going to be terribly ugly. People would look at her on the streets and *know*. Shoppers in Woodies would pick things off the counters and hurl them at her, screaming "Harlot!"

An illegitimate child, good God, only movie stars and black teenagers had *those*. Peg, you fool, what have you done?

Other times she felt like a madonna, full, ripe, and pure. She felt smug, walking by other women with empty bellies. She wanted to poke out in front. *See what I can do!* Sometimes she burst out laughing, for no reason at all. Or sobbed. Sometimes she wanted her mother. Through it all, she kept turning out copy at a prodigious rate. Fecundity had given her enormous energies. Even the endless meetings with lawyers couldn't drain them. Sometimes, in her fantasies, she was in a federal courtroom being sentenced for contempt when labor began and Hanging Harry Benton began screaming, "Boil water! Boil water!" Her baby was born in the jury dock. Hanging Harry cut the cord and reduced her sentence to probation and a fifty-dollar fine.

She dreamed, all the time now. Often they were vivid sexual dreams about Sean, in color and full of sound. Sometimes she awoke, sweaty and groaning, certain that he had been there beside her; she even dreamed the way he smelled. Her body was doing peculiar things to her mind.

She put on her nightgown and went back to pacing. Her

interviews were done. She would go to see Sean in the morning. Con said he had a right to know, but she still wasn't sure. How in the hell could she tell him?

Coy? "That's right, Sean, I'm knitting little booties. Cute, aren't they? But we're not getting married."

Aggressive? "Okay, so I'm knocked up, but I'm going it alone. Buzz off, Father."

Poetic? "God rest ye merry gentlemen, let nothing you dismay/the girl that you knocked up one night is here with you today."

Rock and Roll? "Do-wah-do-wah Do-wah ditty/your teen angel's in pregnant city."

She climbed into bed and tried to go to sleep. Sean would never go for her plan. Knowing he was the father of her child, he'd feel duty-bound to marry her; he'd be chained to her for the rest of his life. She'd hear the clanking of the chains when he came down for his morning coffee. It would be like living with Marley's ghost.

After a wretched night's sleep, she presented herself at the front door of the Catholic Institute for Social Justice. She was led into his office by a pleasant young woman who said, "You have a visitor, Father McCaffrey."

He looked up as she entered, and her heart gave a thump when she saw those green eyes flash with unalloyed pleasure. He jumped up, ran over and gave her a big hug.

"Peg! I tried to get you, all last night. Peg, we have to talk!"

They both noticed the young woman looking at them, oddly, and they stepped back.

"Sean, you're looking wonderful! Hey, this is quite a place you have here."

"Isn't it? It used to be the mansion of a wheat baron. They don't build 'em like this anymore. Peg, let's find a place where we can talk."

"Sean, would you show me around first? I love old houses."

"Sure. Then we'll talk. Come on, let me show you what used to be the living room. Can you imagine how many servants it must have taken to run this place?"

She watched him as he spoke. Gone were the tired lines around his eyes. He looked five years younger than he did the day she took him to the airport. There was a bounce to his walk as he ushered her through the mansion, showing off the

Tiffany lamps, the stone fireplace, the inlay made of real elephant tusk.

As they toured the kitchen, a young woman entered and Sean introduced her. "This is Molly Scanlan. She's head of our day-to-day operations."

"We're delighted with Father McCaffrey," the young woman gushed. "I hope we can keep him when they make him a cardinal."

A cardinal! Great, I've been knocked up by a cardinal. Wait till he gets to be Pope, his kid will really be proud. "Wave to daddy, dear, he's the one in the big gold hat."

"Listen," Sean was saying, "You have to see the solarium. The millionaire who built this place had it put in on the top floor."

"This sure beats St. Nasty's."

"I miss the old place. I brought a tape of Father Barry puking so I can get to sleep."

"You are terrible, Sean McCaffrey."

He grinned. It was a long time since she had seen him in such high spirits. The color in his cheeks had come back; he had been pale and haggard so often. He seemed like the old Sean McCaffrey, the boy who lived next door, whose highs had been as contagious as the flu.

As they walked upstairs, they encountered a handsome, white-haired man in a well-tailored black suit, wearing a Roman collar.

"Father J.," Sean said, "I'd like you to meet Peg Morrison from the Washington *Tribune*."

"Sean has shown me a number of your articles, Miss Morrison. They are superb."

He asked them to have coffee in the library. Sean seemed to hesitate for an instant, and then he accepted, graciously.

They sat in a book-lined study that looked out on the quiet street; a maid served coffee in elegant Limoges cups. Peg asked Father J. about the Institute, and he smiled and told her of the battles of the early days. He was a handsome man; articulate, obviously a scholar. Such a contrast, she thought, to poor drunken Father Barry. Indeed to the whole suburban church she had known—mundane, too often silly, parochial. This was the church she had read of only in books, where learned men debated great issues in marble halls. It was the

world Sean had entered. No longer would he say mass at six
A.M. for bag ladies and winos. He was on his way. It was,
indeed, not out of the question that he might one day be a
cardinal. She saw him, striding through the halls of the Vatican, a scarlet cape sweeping out behind him like Batman. She
thought, inexplicably, of a scene in *The Caine Mutiny* where a
little band of navy men left their small ship to complain about
their demented captain. But once aboard the mighty carrier
with its glistening white uniforms, the aroma of rank steaming from its decks, they lost their nerve. "This is the real
navy," one said. And this was the *real* church.

"How do you get on with the mayor?" she asked Father
Jurevich. He laughed and told her a witty anecdote about
Daley. Seeing her laugh, he told another.

She stole a look at Sean while the older priest was speaking.
There was something new about him. What was it? Serenity.
Contentment. Definitely new. He had the look of a man who
had made a choice. He looked—happy. She had done the
right thing the night she had sent him off with his Vlaminck
print and his Miles Davis albums. Whatever it had cost her, it
had been the right decision for Sean. She remembered what
she had wished for him the day she had sent him off to the
seminary at the train station so many years ago. Whatever
you do, wherever you go, be happy, my love. And he was. At
last.

After they left Father J. they walked down the curving staircase together; she was acutely aware of his body beside hers.
What was love all about, anyhow? It was not about making
people miserable, not in her book. *There* was an idea for a
Hallmark card. "I am not going to rip your guts out. A
friend."

*Sean, Sean, my dearest love. I'd die before I would hurt you. I
would.*

At the base of the stairs she faced him and said, "Sean, I
have something I want to tell you."

"I have something to tell *you*," he said with a smile.

"I'm married, Sean."

She saw the color drain from his face; he rocked slightly
back on his heels. He looked as if she had just slapped him in
the face. He just stood there, staring at her in amazement.

"I meant to tell you, but it happened—very quickly. Sort of a whirlwind courtship, I guess."

He looked at her, not moving, standing utterly still.

"Who—?"

"A navy man. Funny isn't it, me and Con. He's attached to a nuclear sub. You'd like him, I think."

He was still staring at her, as if he hadn't understood. Then he said, his voice a croak, "When did you get—married?"

"Last weekend. We'd been dating for a couple months, so we figured why wait."

"Are you—happy?"

"Yes, I am, Sean. Just like you. I'm really glad to see you so happy. I guess we both have found our niche, huh? Took us a while."

"Peggy, I—" He seemed to be having a hard time getting his thoughts together. She was surprised at his reaction; to be honest, a little pleased. One wanted at least a twinge from an old love. But he looked so wretched she wanted to blurt it all out, put his hands on her stomach and say it was his child inside her. Fortunately, she had outgrown such adolescent behavior.

"I'm going to settle in, Sean. Have a child or two. I'm not going to be a tumbleweed anymore."

"You love him?"

"Oh sure. I mean, I wouldn't go marry somebody just for kicks."

"What's his name?"

"Tony. Anthony J. Harriman." (She had picked the name from Averell Harriman; she thought it had class.)

"You're Mrs. Harriman."

"But I'm keeping my own name. I like the old byline. Besides, I'm the last of the Morrisons."

"I hope—I hope you'll be very happy, Peg."

"You too, Sean. Oh best friend, I do want you to be happy."

They stood facing each other awkwardly. He still seemed to be trying to digest her news. Odd, how many times in their lives they had seemed to do this.

"Well, I have to catch a plane."

"I wish you the best. Peg. Every happiness."

Then she kissed him on the cheek, and she was gone. He

stood watching the place where she had been for a long time. He did not even notice that Ben had moved beside him.

"She's lovely. Is that her?"

Sean nodded.

"Let's break this gently to Father J. These things upset him."

Sean shook his head. "She's married."

"Married?"

"Got married last weekend."

Ben looked at him. "I'm sorry, Sean."

"So am I."

"Want to talk?"

Sean just shook his head. "No."

He went back to his office and started to work again on the annual report. He tried to fill his mind with numbers, only numbers. He worked all day at his desk, cramming the numbers into his mind, as if numbers could murder thought. He had the housekeeper make him a sandwich, so he could work through dinner. But finally, all the numbers were gone, there was no more work he could do.

He got up from his desk, climbed the curving staircase and went into his suite. He went into his study and took out first one book then another, trying to read, but the words jumbled before his eyes, made no sense. He walked into his bedroom and a line from Saint Augustine fluttered across his mind. *Late, have I loved thee.*

Then he knelt down by the bed, his nightly habit, but he did not pray. For the first time since he had grown to manhood, he cried—for the loss of love, for the end of youth, for the end of dreams. Finally he got up, lay down on the bed and tried to will sleep to come. When it did, when he closed his eyes, the tears were still wet upon his face.

TWENTY-THREE

The trees had turned green again on Foxhall Road, and Kitty was in the study, working on bills, when Antonio came in and announced that she had a visitor.

"Who?"

"Congressman Amundsen. Shall I let him in?"

"Yes. Please do."

She stood up, waiting for him to enter, and he walked into the room. At least he wasn't wearing one of the suits she had bought for him. That would add insult to injury. He was tanned, but there were deep lines around his eyes. She had expected her heart to give a lurch when she saw him, but it didn't.

"Hello, Dan." Her voice was cool and steady. "I suppose congratulations are in order."

"Kit—"

"Sorry I missed the ceremony. I'm sending a little something from Garfinckel's. Thirty pieces of silver might be appropriate."

"Kit, nothing has to change."

She looked at him, wondering if she had heard him right. "What?"

"With us."

"Us?"

"Kit, we're good together. We've always been good together. It can be like it was."

"It seems to have slipped your mind that you were married a month ago. Nice tan, by the way."

"Kit, I was going to lose it. The way they were using you against me, it was working. I had to do what I did. You see that, don't you?"

"You married her to get the Senate seat? That's all?"

"Yes."

"How do I love thee. Let me count the ways."

"Kit, we're adults, you and I. This town is full of—marriages of convenience."

"That's certainly true."

He smiled his winning smile. "We'll just have to be a little circumspect, that's all. Things won't have to change."

"You're serious, aren't you?"

"Of course I'm serious. I've been eating myself up about the way I did what I did. I was too much of a coward to face you. But I need you, Kit."

"Have you informed your bride of this little arrangement you have in mind?"

"She has what she wants. She's Mrs. Senator Amundsen, she can lord it over all her friends in Omaha. She doesn't like Washington. She'll probably spend most of her time back home."

"My God, you are a cold-hearted bastard."

"Nobody loses. Joyce gets what she wants, I get the Senate and we keep our relationship. It may work out for the best."

"It certainly is tidy."

He smiled again, the boyish, naughty smile. "I was nervous about coming here, Kit, had to screw my courage to the sticking point. But it's okay, isn't it?"

"There is just one slight problem?"

"What?"

"I have a moral scruple. I don't sleep with married men."

"You're a sophisticated woman, Kit. Maybe it'll even add a little spice, huh?" He moved forward to touch her, but she stepped away.

"Do you know what chutzpah is, Dan?"

"Of course."

"The word was invented for you."

"Kit, you're a funny lady."

"Yes, I'm going to be chuckling the whole time I throw you out of here."

"Kit, Kit, you have to understand—"

"I understand that you said you loved me, that you wanted me to be your wife. You are not only a coward, you are a disgusting cad."

The trace of the smile vanished from his lips. He was quiet, for a minute, and then he said, "Would you have wanted me if I was the ex-congressman from Nebraska? You liked it that I was the bright young man on the way up. I would have lost you anyway, Kit. I didn't kid myself about that."

She turned away from him, took a deep breath, then turned to face him again.

"Yes, I liked your success. Of course I did. But you're wrong about me. So wrong I don't think you ever knew me at all. The answer to your question is yes. Yes, I would have wanted you. Christ, you think the Senate seat is what I cared about? I'd have wanted you if you were the goddamn busboy in the Senate dining room. It was *you* I wanted, Dan."

"I couldn't lose it, Kit. I'd be nobody, and I couldn't stand to be nobody. You don't understand that, because you've always had it, the money, the prestige. You don't know what it's like to be nobody."

"I'm the daughter of a junk dealer from Long Island. Who the hell do you think you are talking to, Queen Elizabeth?"

"You're the only person I've ever needed, Kit. Everything else in my life moved, like a merry-go-round, you were the only thing that stood still. Everything moves, but you're there in the middle, still. Give me a chance to prove it can be all right again. Please!"

"I won't be your whore, Dan. Your lover, never your whore."

"I'll divorce her in a while. I promise, I will!"

"Go home to your wife. You're a married man."

"I'll do anything, Kit. I will."

"How could you do it to me, Dan? Nothing in the world could have made me do to you what you did to me. They could have ripped my fingernails off, one by one, and I never would have done it."

"Kit, you need me. As much as I need you. You know you do!"

She looked at him, and she thought she might as well be talking to a wall. He didn't even understand. She had loved him, but never really known him; and he had never been worth it. Pearls before swine.

"I made you come alive, Kit. No man ever had you in bed like I did, made you feel like I did."

"Do you think you're the only prick in town, Dan?" She laughed. "In this town, there are thousands of them."

"You'll come to me. You'll get the itch, and you'll come. You never had anybody better than me."

"The man I had, you're not good enough to lick his boots."

"You'll come to me, Kit. I'll be waiting."

"Do me a favor, Dan."

"What?"

"Hold your breath until the phone rings."

And she turned on her heel and walked from the room, leaving him standing there, staring into the air.

Con rapped on Peggy's door, but she was somewhat taken aback at the apparition that appeared when the door opened. Peg was wearing a black raincoat, a big cartwheel hat with her hair tucked up under it, and outsized dark glasses.

"Peg, what on earth—"

"I'm not here," Peg announced.

"If you're not here, where *are* you?"

"San Diego, the naval base."

"What are you doing there?"

Peg looked at her watch. "In San Diego it's nine A.M. Tony and I are probably screwing."

"Is Tony good in bed?"

"Yes, except he has this annoying habit of screaming, 'Dive! Dive!' at the crucial moment."

"Peg, this is getting absurd."

"I took four days off for this trip, plus the weekend. I told *everybody*. So I can't blow my cover story."

Con shook her head as Peg peered furtively up and down the street and then ran for the car. As they drove along, Peg said, "Tell me about San Diego, in case somebody asks."

"They have a great zoo."

"Good. Tony likes zoos."

"What else does Tony like?"

"Fireplaces. Glenn Miller. Whips and chains."

"Nice, Peg."

300

"He especially likes it when I chain him to the fireplace and whip him to 'In the mood.'"

"Why do I try to talk sense to you? Peg, don't you think it's about time you told Sean?"

Peg sighed and leaned back in her seat. "Con, he seemed so happy. He was where he belonged."

"I think he belongs here, with you."

"He could have come to me if he wanted to. Scads of people leave the priesthood these days. Hell, they leave just because black doesn't go with their complexion. But he didn't."

"He'd come, if you asked."

"Because I'm knocked up? No thanks. Sean told me once the thing he loved most about being a priest was saying mass early in the morning, when the sun was coming up, holding the Host up and feeling one with the universe."

"That sounds like Sean. Irish mystical mumbo jumbo."

"What can I give him to compare with the whole fucking universe?"

"His child, Peg."

She shook her head. "No, I'd always be watching him, Con. Watching for the day I'd see it in his eyes, the resentment. I'm too proud for that. I'll never be a millstone around any man's neck."

"You were always stubborn. For the record, I think you're wrong."

"Commander Harriman does not agree."

"No wonder. You're whipping him, and he's loving every minute of it."

"No, now we're at the zoo."

"That was fast."

"Had to be. He bruises easy."

When Con and Peg marched into Kitty's house, she took one look at Peg and said, "My God, it's Greta Garbo. What a coup!"

"She's supposed to be in San Diego with Tony."

"Peg, you do lead a mad life. Come in, I have the dresses on the couch."

"Kitty, how are you doing?"

"I'm bruised, my dear, but feeling lucky. I think I got off the *Lusitania* before it went down."

Peg took off her hat and her hair tumbled around her shoulders.

"I love your hair long, Peg," Kitty said. "You have beautiful hair. But what is that *shmata* you're wearing?"

"I haven't had time to shop."

"You are showing, aren't you? Come, try these on."

Peg picked up a few of the dresses and said, "Oh Kitty, they're all desgner labels! I will be so chic!"

Peg went to try on a dress and Kitty said to Con, "She is blooming, isn't she? I've never seen her look so beautiful. Oh Constance, I can't bear to think of her having that baby all alone."

"She plans to work right up to the day and then pop over to the hospital and drop the kid."

"I'm sure she can do it. She's a very competent lady, our Peg. But terribly lonely, I think."

"It's very bizarre, Kitty. She and Sean chat on the phone all the time, like high school kids."

"He knows she's pregnant?"

"Oh yes. Thinks she's married. It's nuts."

"Love is a very strange thing, Constance."

Peg came back in a cowl-collared blue mohair-and-silk dress. "I can ask the meanest questions when I'm pregnant. 'Is it true, General, that you are grinding up babies for gunpowder?' And he can't snarl at a *mommy*."

"You're not working too hard, are you, Peg?"

"This week I'm taking a swing through some campuses. Oh, and I'm reading Doctor Spock. I wonder if he's kept up, though. He spends so much time getting arrested."

"No, Peg, he tells you to put leeches on the kids when they have a cough," Con said.

"I'm buying toys, too, but only creative ones, made in Sweden. None of this disgusting American junk that breeds materialism and violence."

"Peg, that's what kids *like*, materialism and violence."

"My child, Constance Marie, will be raised scientifically."

"I think I am going to avoid you for the next twenty years. You are going to be a goddamn pain in the ass."

On the first of May 1970, Richard Nixon announced that U.S. troops had moved into Cambodia, widening a war that was already convulsing the nation at home. Protests broke out like brush fires on campuses all across the country. Peg's timing for her trip to write an "Other Voices" feature for the *Tribune* was perfect. She was doing interviews at Ohio State when the news flashed over the UPI wires: Violence had broken out at Kent State. The governor had ordered the National Guard onto the campus. She phoned Tom to say she was going to rent a car and get over there.

"Peg, you be careful. We can get the action stuff from the wires. Stay away from trouble."

"I will."

"I mean it. No heroics. I want you and that baby back here in one piece."

She was standing, now, on a Monday morning in the first week of May, on the Kent State campus, watching the mini-drama unfold in front of her. It was a warm spring day, a skein of clouds streaking the blue sky, and what was happening in front of her eyes seemed a bizarre playlet. A group of national guardsmen were gathered on a knoll near Taylor Hall, a pillared, neoclassical building of the sort state officials commission to create an aura of genteel learning, instead of an academic assembly line. A group of students had been ringing the victory bell, which usually chimed when the football team won, all morning. The noise only heightened the oddness of the scene. Just below where the guardsmen were encamped, a group of students were taunting the young soldiers, shouting insults at them. The size of the student group seemed to ebb and flow as the morning wore on. But the largest contingent of students was gathered at the edges, watching. It reminded Peg of a pageant; actors recreating the battle of Bunker Hill, for on the fringes of the crowd there was almost a carnival atmosphere. The tennis courts were in use, and a pickup basketball game was in progress at a nearby hoop.

Now and then the guardsmen would kneel in firing position and aim their rifles at the students. At other times when the students would advance, the guardsmen would lob tear gas cannisters at the kids. The bolder of the students would pick them up and hurl them back. In the midst of it all, not far from Peg, a boy and girl were necking passionately, oblivious to the scene.

The events of the night before had been more reminiscent

of actual combat. Bands of students had roamed the streets, tossing rocks and chunks of concrete at guardsmen. The whole area had taken on an eerie glow, from trees doused with gasoline and set afire. But the worst thing, Peg thought, were the firecrackers. Students were setting them off and tossing them at the guardsmen. The sound was so much like gunfire, and the guardsmen were so inexperienced, that she worried that one of them would crack. And the rumors only fanned the flames: the students had guns; Weathermen were going to blow up buildings on the campus; they were coordinating more violence.

Today the violence seemed contained, almost symbolic. Guerrilla theater. Several times guard officers had driven around the commons in a jeep, announcing, "Evacuate the commons! You have no right to be here!"

The faint scent of tear gas drifted into Peg's nostrils, and she moved back a few feet. It was good she was nearly in her sixth month; the baby's limbs and nervous system were already formed. And the gas was dissipating in this open area almost as soon as it was released.

"Ma'am, I'd keep away from this area if I were you," a young man advised her. "There could be trouble."

"I'm a reporter."

"Oh." He nodded his head and walked away.

Peg turned to watch as the little battle dragged on. She felt a sudden sense of foreboding. The guardsmen really didn't know what they were doing. They seemed more like little boys playing with guns than soldiers. Her years of covering battles had taught her that if you wanted to survive, you found people who knew what they were doing and stayed at their heels; people who knew that in war the unexpected was the rule and who could handle it without panic. It was why she felt comfortable with the Israelis, whose officers were well-trained and seasoned. It was the green recruits who could get you killed.

Across the commons, a small group of guards—twenty or so—had marched down the knoll to toss tear gas at the students. There was no plan, no strategy to it. They were playing it by ear. No good.

"Pigs!" shouted a student. Another hollered, "Off the pigs!"

A boy stepped next to her to watch the proceedings.

"If those damn guys would just get out of here, everything would be okay," he said.

She nodded and looked back at the commons. The guardsmen, now out of tear gas, had turned and were retreating back up the knoll. The students, ragging at them like a small dog snapping at the trousers of a mailman, followed, shouting insults and taunts. All of a sudden, a number of the guards, perhaps a dozen, whirled and raised their rifles.

"Get down!" she yelled at the boy beside her. She knew instinctively that it was no longer a game. The body language of the men with the guns told her that. Their movements were swift, ragged, the movement of action, not bluff. The sounds came cracking out through the spring air.

Panic enveloped the scene. Students began to run, in all directions, screaming. Some dropped to the ground or ducked behind any available cover.

"It's blanks!" someone screamed. "Just blanks!"

"No, not blanks!" Peg yelled. "Get down!"

She curled up in fetal position to make herself as small as possible. The ground was the best place to avoid being hit; most rifle fire went high.

As often happened, a dead calm came over her. She stayed utterly still until the sound of the volley faded away. She raised her head, to see the guardsmen standing at parade rest. It was absurd. What the hell did they think this was, weekend drill?

The boy who had been standing next to her was sitting on the ground, dazed, holding his head. The blood was running down his face and onto his shirt. He was crying.

"They shot me. Oh God, I'm shot!"

She walked over to him, knelt down and said, "It's all right, kid. You're okay." The wound was only superficial, and she took out a handkerchief and pressed it against his head and held it firmly.

"They shot us!" he said, unbelieving.

"This will stop the bleeding. You're okay."

She looked around to see if anybody else had been hurt. On her right, perhaps fifty feet from where she stood, a girl with long dark hair lay face down, near the edge of the parking lot. Two girls knelt by her, sobbing. Peg walked over and knelt down. She knew immediately that the girl was dead. She had seen enough bodies to know death in all of its guises.

On the battlefield, death was grotesque, but expected. But this was not a soldier, just a girl walking across her campus on a warm day in spring. The out-of-placeness of it gave the scene a nightmare quality, as if from *Alice in Wonderland*. Peg almost expected the guardsmen to turn into playing cards and drift away on the wind.

A powerful wave of nausea hit her, and she staggered to her feet and leaned on the side of a building, doubled over. She inhaled several times and then her head cleared and she straightened up. Another girl was sobbing hysterically, bleeding from an arm wound. Peggy calmed her as a girl wrapped a long scarf around her arm, following Peg's instructions. Ambulances and paramedics began to flood onto the scene. Students were being carried out on stretchers, others were led away, dazed, by friends. All over the area students stood in small groups, staring in disbelief at what was happening. The girl with the dark hair was being lifted onto a stretcher by a team of medics. Four students were dead, Peg would learn later from the police.

She looked at her watch. She'd have to file soon to make the deadline. They'd want to rip up page one for this story. She ran to a nearby dorm, grabbed the pay phone and got right through to Tom Friedman.

"I was right there, Tom. I'll do an eyewitness."

"Are you all right?"

"Yeah, I'm fine. A girl was killed right near me, Tom. This is a stinking crime!"

"We're hearing somebody fired on the guards."

"No, I saw it. They panicked. Somebody might have thrown something, but there was no shot. None!"

"Let it run, Peg. Keep the phone line open and give it by takes, if you have to. No time for Western Union."

She saw a boy coming by and she grabbed his arm, and thrust a twenty-dollar bill in his hand. "Hold this phone for me," she instructed. "Don't let anybody have it!" She ran out to her car, grabbed her Olivetti and ran back to the phone. She sat on the floor, the phone dangling over her shoulder, and took a deep breath. An image, totally unexpected, flashed into her mind. An attractive woman with gray hair was moving around a kitchen, making dinner. She was humming as she worked. She didn't know that in a moment the phone would ring.

Dear God, no! Don't let the phone ring!

Not realizing what she was doing, Peg moved one hand to her stomach. Her baby was there, inside her, safe. But she had just seen another woman's child shot to death on a sunny afternoon in a place where she should have been safe.

There is no way I can keep my child safe. No way at all.

Death had touched her before. She had looked at a corpse face-down in the mud and felt the coils of her own mortality tremble. But she had never thought, That person has a mother. Some very profound change in her emotional gyroscope had taken place. She was seeing death as the mother of a child. You could have a child, love it, nurture it, and in an instant, that child's life could be snuffed out like a cigarette.

She trembled, her back against the cinderblock wall, more afraid than she had ever been in her life. Had *her* mother ever felt that way? Had everyone's?

She put both hands on her stomach. She had seen her child often, in her mind's eye: Megan, a mop of curly hair and freckles across the bridge of her nose, sturdy little legs; or Sean, green eyes and brown curly hair, serious, a miniature of his father.

She knew, then, what she was going to write about: the woman in the kitchen, the dead girl, her own fears. It was the real story. After the millions of words, the acres of newsprint, accusing, charging, defending, there was only one truth. A dead girl and a woman's grief that would still be raw when all the newspapers had turned yellow. "Not people die, but worlds die with them," Yevtushenko had written. She had seen a world smashed that day, obliterated. And for what?

She was suddenly irrationally angry, at the whole stupid goddamn male world. All that shit they wrote about Mother's Day, and they sent people's children off to be slaughtered. To hell with them. To hell with Clausewitz! "War is an instrument of national policy." *Damn it, you butchers, you won't get my baby!*

That would really play swell in the city room. Raging female hormones, they'd say. But what she felt was real, more real than the cold columns of print she had written, over the years, about strategy and tactics. If it was her hormones talk-ing, let the shitheads listen. Her hormones were making bet-ter sense than all of them.

She started to type and a boy, large and surly-looking, came by and stared at her. "I got to use the phone."

"Sorry, I'm on deadline."

"I got to use that phone, lady," he said, making a grab for the receiver. She put her hand on it and looked up at him.

"Touch that phone, kid, and you're dogmeat!" she snarled.

The boy backed away, startled. She had worked on that snarl, honed it to pit-bull meanness. Coming from a pregnant lady with a typewriter on her knees, it had the added element of surprise.

She finished the story, dictated it, and then went back to the scene and began to talk to people. It would be a long time before events were sorted out, blame affixed, if ever. One eye-witness saw a guard commander give a signal to fire. Another said there was none at all. Someone claimed a guardsman had fainted.

Finally, tired and unable to absorb any more facts, she went back to her hotel room. She sat on the bed and had a Scotch. She wondered what they were saying on the desk about her story; she could see Buck Stollmeyer's face as he read it. She felt vulnerable, naked. There was no mask of objectivity there, no "reliable sources" to hide behind. It was all out there—her anger, her fears. She was—exposed. She shivered. It was so easy for journalists to be chameleons, never showing their col-ors. Never taking risks. Firing at people from behind trees.

Oh, what the hell.

The phone rang and she picked it up. It was Tom Friedman.

"That is one hell of a story, Peg."

"It wasn't too—emotional, Tom?"

"It's real. Honest. It's a fine story."

"It all hangs out there."

"You don't play it safe, Peg. Makes you a rare bird in this business. Listen, can you fly home tomorrow?"

"I'd like to stay and do some follow-up."

"I know. But we have to go to the grand jury Wednesday."

"Can't we stall?"

"I guess not. Looks like we're about out of stalling tactics."

When she hung up the phone, she leaned back on the bed

and thought again of the dead girl in the parking lot and her hand went to her stomach again. She propped her pillow behind her back and addressed her stomach, as she did often these days.

"Am I doing the right thing? Am I? Megan Emily Morrison or Sean Joseph Morrison, whichever one of you is in there, am I doing right by you?"

She sighed. "Oh yeah, it's going to be Morrison. I'm certainly not going to give you Tony's name. Not after he callously deserts us, or runs his sub into a rock. And you see, I can't name you after your real father. Somebody else has a prior claim; somebody who has a lot more clout than we do, kiddo."

She had been tossing that one around in her mind a lot, recently. Her child would have no father. How would the lack be felt? As a dim sense of something lost, a gray December sky without the sun? An ache, like a bone bruise, that wouldn't go away? She had been thinking of herself, before, and of Sean, but now she thought of her child. She could give the baby a father, all she had to do was pick up the phone.

Oh yes, she could give her child a father, but one who would come out of guilt, and of shame. Could love grow from such a beginning?

But she remembered that when she spoke of children, Sean would look away, uncomfortable. She had never heard him talk about children, never said he regretted *not* having them. He was so filled with God that, in the end, two nights a week with Peg Morrison were more than he could give.

A child couldn't compete with God, even with the memory of Him. Changing diapers, could you feel *one* with the universe? Sean had told her once that when God called him, the world had turned golden all around. With your hands in shit, *gold* was not the color of the day. Mysticism and dirty diapers did not mix. No, Sean needed to be special, and only God could give him that. Any man could be a father.

Children had antennae; they *knew*. Oh, he would try to pretend. Sean had such a conscience, he'd work hard at it. He'd only slip sometimes. But of course, his child would know. Was a father who didn't want to be your father worse than none at all?

She patted her stomach. "I am going to try to be a good

mother, but stick with me, because it's going to be real on-the-job training. Okay, I'll admit it, I'm scared. Scared shitless, to tell you the truth. I talk big, but I don't know if I can pull this off. But I do want you, I really do. When you kick it's so funny, you make me laugh, and I know there's really somebody there. *In* me. That is just goddamn fucking miraculous, if you'll pardon the language. I have a foul mouth, you'll just have to get used to it, I guess. I am not going to be like the mommy in the stupid house you'll read about with Dick and Jane and Spot. But I'll take you lots of places. You can even meet the President. The one we've got now, forget it, but maybe the next one will be presentable."

She took another sip of Scotch. "The world, what's it like, you ask? Sometimes it can be wonderful, and sometimes—well, it was really stupid out there today. Ugly. And I'm scared for you, I really am. You'll depend on me, and there are so many things that can hurt you, never mind bullets. There's cars and electrical outlets and stuff you could stick in your mouth and choke on. I think about it, and I get terrified. But I'll try not to let it show. You can't live your life afraid. You have to be brave.

"There's not a lot I can do about the world, kiddo. Not a whole lot. You'll just have to take it as it comes."

TWENTY-FOUR

"Lee, where are we going? Why are we on the parkway?"

"Take your clothes off, Con."

"What?"

"It's something I've always wanted to do. Drive at night with a beautiful naked woman beside me."

"Lee, that's crazy!"

"Is it?"

"Yes."

He chuckled. "So how come you are taking your clothes off?"

"Because I've never done it before. Oh, this damn bra. This is totally, totally crazy."

"My God, what a body you have. Does this excite you, Con?"

"Yes. Oh yes, it does. Oh dear, I think I'm an exhibitionist!" She giggled. "This is crazy, but I'm so turned on!"

"Maybe I'll get a little gas."

"Don't you dare!"

"I'll just feel for a while. Oh, that's nice. I've always wanted to do this."

"Oh God, I hope nobody sees us."

"Want me to stop?"

"No. Oh no, don't stop. Ohhhh! *Lee!* Keep your eye on the road!"

"Unzip me, Con. Oh yes, that's right. Oh God. Oh my *God!*"

"Look out! Oh Jesus, Lee, that was a semi!"

"I better pull over."

"This is crazy, Lee. Grown-ups don't make love in the car," she said as he bounced the car along the shoulder road and pulled to a stop.

"I am going to have my way with you."

They climbed into the backseat, and they had sex that was fast and sweaty and thoroughly satisfying. She was thinking about that the next day, after making love with George, lying in his bed while he caressed her backside, languidly.

"A penny for your thoughts," he said.

"Oh, nothing. You look tired. Need some time in the sun."

"Wouldn't I love it? I'm so booked up I haven't time to breathe."

"George, '72 is two years away."

"I know, but the grass roots are where it's at now. You just can't woo a bunch of party bosses in September and get the nod in July. They're out there, my rivals, beating the bushes, sucking up to party chairmen in Oshkosh and Pawtucket. Hell, there may be somebody out there we've never *heard* of who'll get the damn thing."

"I think the old way was a lot easier. Smoke-filled rooms. I'd see a lot more of you."

"Have I been neglecting you, Constance?"

"No, we've both been busy. George, have you ever wanted anything so bad you'd die if you didn't get it?"

He looked thoughtful. "No, I can't say that I have. I want the nomination, I'll bust my butt for it, but if I don't get it, I won't die."

"You are a civilized man."

"Do I hear a note of disapproval?"

She smiled. "No, we need civilized men. Too many barbarians at the gates."

"We could have a nice life together, Con. A lovely life. But you're hungry, aren't you? And not for what money can buy."

"I have nothing against money, George. God knows."

"You have ambition."

"Is that bad?"

"No." He laughed. "Oh, sometimes you let the raw edges of it show. But it's all right."

"You don't know what it is, do you George, to be nobody from nowhere? A kid from Crystal Springs who wears secondhand clothes."

"No, I don't."

"Makes one a little raw around the edges."

"I want to make things easy for you, Con. I don't want you to have to struggle anymore."

"When I was young, I wanted to be a writer for *The New Yorker*. I wanted to be famous and dazzling. But I didn't have the guts to try."

"I think you're dazzling."

"You are a nice man, George." She laughed. "Would you kill for me? With your bare hands?"

He chuckled. "No."

"And honest."

"Con, we can be a wonderful team. I trust your instincts. You're ambitious? Well, come with me. I just might go all the way to the top. Beats working your tail off, running up and down Capitol Hill."

"I like what I do."

"I know. But you don't want to be a reporter forever. It's a job for—"

"Nobodies from nowhere?"

"I didn't say that."

"It may be a *little* job to you, George, but it's mine. It's something I've done on my own. Nobody handed it to me."

"I know that too. But look around, Con. How many women are bureau chiefs? How many are managing editors? The higher up the ladder you go, the harder it's going to get."

"That's true. God knows, that is so true."

"Are you hungry?"

"Clawing my way to the top."

"I mean for dinner."

"Sure."

"Let's go somewhere very French and very expensive. I had to eat tacos last week. Nearly vomited."

"You had better learn. Barf on a taco, there goes the Latinos."

The following day, a Monday, she told Peg about her weekend as they were having lunch.

"One man Saturday night and another on Sunday. Peg, am I a whore?"

"I hate hate hate *hate* you, Constance Marie. I am as horny as a goat and I can't see my toes. And you are screwing two guys, happy as a pig in swill."

"I am not happy. I am guilty. Christ, I'm a Catholic, remember. Oh, I have some news, not to be noised around. I've had a feeler from the L.A. *Times*. Rosewald's going back to be ME, so a spot is opening up."

"Are you going to take it?"

"If they offer, I am. George doesn't want me to. He wants to hire me full time to do his press. He's used to having his way, George is. Comes from having twenty million dollars. Kitty wants me to grab George, now."

"He's ripe."

"Yeah. But Peg, a big part of me wants to do it, and that scares me. I loved Lee when I married him, but I also knew marrying him meant I wouldn't have to put myself on the line. I was relieved, despite all my big talk."

"You're on the line now, Con. And you're making it."

"But I'm this little bird who's just hopped out of the nest. I went into somebody else's world once, and it swallowed me up. And George Billington's world is so formidable. Money. Politics. George wants me to have work of my own, but it would never be as important as his. I just see myself getting smaller and smaller in that world, Peg. But oh God, never to have to worry about money again. To be safe for the rest of my life!"

"What's the alternative?"

"Do it on my own. Keep flying by myself, not hitching onto George's star. But I might wind up sitting in front of Garfinkel's with my bag."

"What about Lee?"

"Oh, it's great in the sack. And with the kids, they love to see us together. But we're such different people. And there's still—I mean, he's still in his group, but could it happen again? That scares me, Peg. Oh Jesus, I am just so confused about my life."

"Well, that makes two of us."

"Oh Peg, here I am babbling on about me. How did the grand jury go?"

"They only kept me for an hour. I didn't reveal my source. The big question is Judge Benton. He's been out with a disc problem, but he's the one who has to say if my testimony is good enough."

"I think you just may be off the hook. Even Hanging Harry wouldn't send you to jail now, you're such a blimp."

"I don't know. Of all the guys on the federal bench, we had to get him. Jefferson thinks he's getting a little senile. He gave a speech before the Illinois bar that sounded like goddamn Agnew."

"Beating on the press?"

"Yes. Says we're arrogant."

"Nattering nabobs of negativism. Agnew hit a nerve, Peg."

"Yeah, I just might go to jail because of fucking Spiro T. Agnew. That's a hell of a thing."

Antonio walked into the study and said to Kitty, "A gentleman is here to see you. He says you don't know him, but that it is extremely important."

"Who is he?"

"A Mr. Gordon Truebland."

"Show him in please, Antonio."

Antonio ushered the guest into the room, and the moment she saw him, Kitty knew the face was familiar. The name as well. *Truebland.* How did she know him?

"Mrs. Cohen, it's good of you to see me."

He was a tall man, in his fifties, Kitty guessed. Handsome in a slim, elegant way that reminded her of a British actor, what was his name? Michael Rennie. He had a finely chiseled face, long-jointed, elegant hands, which he moved nervously at his sides. His clothes were cheap but well cut. A man, she thought, who once had expensive tastes and knew how to do the rack at J. C. Penney's to find a reasonable facsimile.

"I'm very sorry to disturb you at this hour."

"Have we met before, Mr. Truebland?"

"No, we have not. I work at the National Historic Trust. Assistant historian. We—ah—do not exactly move in the same circles."

And suddenly, she knew. Gordon Truebland, winner of the Wilson prize in American history for a brilliant biography of William Jennings Bryan. Dr. Bevlinger, her professor at

Barnard, had a mad crush on Gordon Truebland's mind. The class had been marched off to Low Library to hear him speak. He had a whole page in *Time*.

"William Jennings Bryan."

He smiled, and his whole face lit up with genuine delight. "You know of it?"

"Of course. It was a tour de force."

"It's very nice to find someone who remembers the book."

"You were out in the Midwest someplace. But weren't you going to Harvard?" As she said it, another piece of memory slipped into place. Some sort of scandal, a sex thing. She had heard nothing of him in twenty years.

"I—ah—did not go to Harvard." There was a pause, as he rubbed his hands nervously against his trousers. He shook his head. "Perhaps it was a mistake for me to come here."

"Why did you come, Mr. Truebland?"

"To offer you—things. I—ah—have some things that might be of interest to you."

"Of interest?" she said, searching for the details of the incident she remembered dimly from the news coverage. It had been an affair with a male student, and it had caused a furor at the time; yes, that was it. The student had left campus and Gordon Truebland had been summarily fired, despite his tenure. He did not go to Harvard.

"I have come upon hard times of late, Mrs. Cohen. I have some debts."

"Debts?"

"I approached a person for money. I should have been smarter, but I was desperate, and now—"

"A loan shark? You owe a loan shark money?"

"Yes, unfortunately."

His mouth worked, silently, and his hands twisted. His skin was pale and looked clammy. Was he on some sort of drugs? But perhaps the thought of the crude but efficient collection methods of the local *goniffs* would be sufficient to induce more than pallor. "I have material which might be—of some value to you."

"To me? You want to sell me something?"

He paused, then nodded.

"What on earth is it?"

He withdrew from the briefcase he was holding a photograph, browning with age and curled at the edges. She peered at it. A much younger Gordon Truebland stood in front of a car with his arm thrown in a gesture of camaraderie over the shoulder of a very young Dan Amundsen.

"Dan? You were a friend of Dan's?"

He nodded. She looked at the picture, baffled, for an instant. Then she understood.

"You and Dan?"

He nodded.

"But Dan isn't, I mean, is he—"

"Dan is a sensualist. An adventurer. He was quite young. But I think there are no limits for Dan. No—"

"Rules?"

"Yes."

"And you and Dan were lovers?"

"For a time, yes."

"And you have things to sell me."

"I have letters. They leave no room for ambiguity."

Kitty walked to the bar and poured herself a glass of sherry. "Would you care for a drink, Mr. Truebland?"

"No thank you."

"You know that I was—involved with Dan."

"Yes. I have watched his career with some interest."

"And why do you think I want this material?"

"I just think you do."

"Well, let's get down to brass tacks. What kind of money are we talking?"

"With interest, my loan comes to fifty thousand dollars."

"You certainly aim high, Mr. Truebland, for a government employee."

"It was a business arrangement. I—misjudged someone."

"Apparently so. And you wish to elude your creditors by peddling this stuff to me."

"Yes."

"You know what this would do to Dan, if it leaked to the press."

"It would destroy him."

"Is that what you want to happen?"

He walked to the window, looked out, and was silent for a moment. Then he said without turning to face her, "Yes."

She felt a sudden surge of pity for him. Hatred must have been eating at him for such a long time.

"He was more than just a casual affair, I would imagine."

"Yes, he was." He was still looking out the window, not at her.

"Well, if we're going to deal, I had best see the merchandise."

He turned, reached into his briefcase, brought out a manila folder and handed it to her. She reached in, pulled out a sheaf of letters and began to read one. It was from Gordon Truebland to Dan Amundsen. By the time she had read three paragraphs, she had the terrible sense that she had violated a space that was meant to be sealed forever, like the tomb of some Egyptian king. The words on the page revealed such pain, the unraveling of one soul desperately trying to touch another, that her eyes blurred with tears. She had expected smut, but had come upon a love letter so fierce in its intensity, its joy and pain, that she could hardly bear to read it. He had returned to the window, and was standing very still.

"You loved him, very much."

"Yes, I did."

"Funny, so did I."

He turned to look at her, and the desolation in his eyes touched her so that she could almost feel its chill.

"He takes, Dan does. You think he's giving, when he's only taking. There is a piece of him missing. A moral sense. He uses. And then he goes on."

"I know."

"He was a kid going nowhere when I met him. He was bright, like quicksilver, but he had no direction. No discipline. I suppose I saw myself as Pygmalion."

She laughed. "That makes two of us."

"I got him into law school, with my influence. Dan tested well, but his grades were indifferent. I got him interested in politics. My friends became his friends. And he learned so very, very fast."

"He is a quick study."

"One day he just—moved on. He was not cruel. He was just finished. I was no longer of interest."

"It was a long time ago."

"Yes."

"Would you like me to write you a check?"

"Yes, that would be fine."

Kitty went to the desk, took out her checkbook and wrote a check for fifty thousand dollars. "They will probably call me, with this amount. I will give the authorization."

"Thank you."

"If this material were to be used, you would be involved. You might even lose your job."

"Yes."

She put the check in an envelope and handed it to him. "Have you written anything," she asked, "since Bryan?"

"I have been working on a biography of James Gordon Blaine."

"Blaine, Blaine, from the state of Maine."

"A fascinating man. And a wonderful period in history. I work in my spare time, but—" He shrugged. "For a long time, no publisher would touch me."

"Mr. Truebland?"

"Yes?"

"He isn't worth it."

"When Dan left, I was—I suppose, for a time, I was a little bit mad. I had carefully ordered my life. I was discreet, because I was also ambitious. And then suddenly, nothing mattered. I did all sorts of things. I was very careless. The incident that led to my dismissal took place shortly after Dan left me. He has cast his shadow across my whole life."

"You still love him, don't you."

"God pity me," he said. "I do."

And he turned and walked from the room.

TWENTY-FIVE

"Just come into the Green Room," said the pert young woman with the curly hair. "We have doughnuts and coffee."

Peg walked in and poured herself a cup of coffee. A thin, bespectacled man was sitting on one of the green vinyl couches. Two other men, dressed in what Peg thought of as campus casual—corduroy trousers, tweed jackets, and turtlenecks—were seated on another couch.

"Hello." She addressed the man with the glasses.

"Are you the makeup lady? I'm yellow."

"What?"

"I photograph yellow, unless I have powder with beigy tones. I don't want to be yellow on 'Wake Up, USA.'"

"I'm not the makeup lady. I'm a guest."

"This is my book, *The Skin Trade. Cosmo* called it *terrif!* Squeeze half a lemon on your stomach every day. Helps prevent stretch marks. Remember that."

"Uh, I will."

"Hello," said the man in the lime-green turtleneck. "What are you here for?"

"To discuss campus disorders."

"Oh. I thought you might be the lady who wrote *Zen Childbirth.*"

"No, that's not me."

"I suppose not. She wears orange robes and meditates. We were supposed to be on with her in Seattle, but we got the Happy Hooker instead. This is our book."

He held it up. It said, in silver letters on a blue background, *You and Your Penis.*

"Catches the eye."

"Our publisher wanted to have a drawing of a penis on the cover—very artsy, not porn. But I said no one would walk out of a bookstore flashing a blue-and-silver penis."

"Not many people have them, anyway."

Just then the young woman came in. "Chet wants you on the set." She led them out onto a brightly lit set with two large sofas on it. Chet, a man with a broad smile and a lot of hair, smiled and said, "Nice to see you."

As the red light on the camera blinked on, Chet began, "We have a wonderful segment coming up. We're going to talk about a subject I know will fascinate you: your penis. And proper care for your skin. And oh yes, campus riots."

Chet held up *You and Your Penis.* "You did a fascinating study, gentlemen. Tell us about it."

"Well," said the man in the baby-blue turtleneck, "we made composite pictures of the same man with a small penis and a large penis."

Lime-green added, "We showed the pictures to people and asked them to rank several of his characteristics."

"His intelligence, his personality, and his generosity."

"What happened?"

"Well, Chet, would you believe it, people rated the man with the large penis as generous, intelligent, and personable."

"But with a small penis," chimed in lime-green, "he was called miserly, wimpy, and dumb."

"Well, that's incredible." Chet turned to Peg. "Ms. Morrison, what do you think of penis size?"

"I—ah—er—"

"Did you know," said baby-blue, "that the penis of a camel is ground up for a virility potion by certain nomadic tribes?"

The skin doctor, seeing his chance, jumped in. "It says in my book, *The Skin Trade,* that the skin of the penis is the softest on the human body."

"Men in the Moog tribe of the Kalahari decorate their penis with pictures of animals," lime-green persisted. A picture flashed on the monitor of a lizard etched on human skin. "In our culture, tradition prevents men from drawing on their penises. A pity, really."

"Egg whites are good for the penis skin. I say so in *The Skin Trade*."

"What would you do, Ms. Morrison, if your husband came home with a picture of a lizard on his penis?"

"Have him committed."

"Heh-heh," laughed Chet, gritting his teeth.

"Egg whites are good for any kind of skin. I say that in *The Skin Trade*."

"But penis size doesn't have anything to do with performance, right?" Chet asked, a tad anxiously. Peg looked at his feet. Tiny.

Baby-blue chuckled. "No, that's a myth. Any man who isn't actually deformed should be able to perform perfectly well."

"Oh, that's good. Now, Ms. Morrison, what is the mood of the campus these days?"

"There's a lot of anger and bitterness about the war. A lot of suspicion of our aims in Vietnam. We—"

"Oh dear, I'm sorry, but it looks like we're all out of time on this segment. Stay tuned everybody. The author of *Broccoli Through the Ages* is coming right up. Don't turn that dial!"

Kitty had taped the show for Peg, and of course was disappointed that Peg only got to say nineteen words. But they were going to run it anyhow, just for kicks. Con and Kitty had the tape set up in Kitty's study.

"You sure she's coming?" Kitty asked, when Peg was twenty minutes late.

"Yes, she had to stop off at her OB's. Monthly checkup."

"She's not slowing down at all, is she?"

"No. If she does, she has to think about the fact that she's going to have the baby at the end of the summer and it's not going to have a father, and there's a good chance she could go to jail. So she keeps moving."

Just then Peg came hurrying in. "Sorry I'm late. Hannibal moved faster across the Alps than I do these days." She walked across the room and dropped into a chair with a sigh.

"Are you okay?" Con asked. "What did the doctor say?"

"Something *very* interesting."

"What?"

"He said he heard two little heartbeats in there."

"Twins!"

Peg nodded.

"Oh my God!" Kitty said.

"Oh Peg, that's some news!"

"Yeah, I called my baby nurse, and she doubled the price. Why do I have to be an overachiever!"

"What does Commander Harriman think of this?"

"Who cares? I'm divorcing him."

"Why?"

"He is miserly, wimpy, and dumb."

"Small penis, eh?"

"No, his penis is enormous. He's just miserly, wimpy, and dumb. Come on, let's see this thing."

They watched the tape and Peg said, "Chet wasn't interested in riots. He was fixated on penises."

"Let men worry about their penises," Kitty said. "Serves them right. We've spent enough time worrying about our boobs."

"I had boobs in the fifth grade," Con said. "When the class read 'Trees,' everybody stared at me."

Peg laughed. "Against the earth's sweet-flowing *breast*."

"Elsie Feldstein told me that after you got your period, you could get pregnant if any man touched your breasts. Even by accident," Kitty said. "I used to panic on the IRT. What if the blind clarinet player knocked me up? And he was *black*."

"The *Playboy* centerfolds used to make me feel so inferior," Peg said. "Those women were *cows*."

"We are hitting a sensitive subject, here."

"Constance, you do not know what it was like not having boobs."

"At least you two didn't have guys saying cute things like, 'Shake 'em but don't break 'em, wrap 'em up and I'll take 'em.'"

"How would you like to be known as No Tits Titlebaum?"

"Oh no, that was you?" Con giggled.

"Yes. And it was bad enough being stuck with Titlebaum. American men are so hung up on boobs. Not European men. They like the kind you can cover with Band-Aids."

"I'm in trouble," Con said. "I'd need surgical dressing."

"Yards of it," Peg laughed.

"Certain people among us should not make fun of other people's *size!*"

"You know, my stomach is so pushed out, I can see the inside of my belly button."

"Peg, don't be gross."

"It's fascinating. Something you don't usually see, like the dark side of the moon."

"I am *not* looking at the inside of your belly button."

"Some friend you turned out to be."

When Peg went back to the office, Tom Friedman waved her to his cubicle. "First the good news, Peg. I want you to start a column, after the baby's born, and you get back into the swing of things."

"A column?"

"Yes. You have something to say, an interesting point of view. And it's high time we had a woman doing a serious column for Op Ed. What do you say?"

"A column. Well. I wasn't expecting this."

"You've earned it. What do you say."

"Yes. Tom, yes. I'd love it!"

"Now the not-so good news. We have a command performance with Judge Benton. Thursday."

"His back's all better."

"So it seems."

"Can we go stomp on it?"

"I'd like to, I tell you that."

Randall Jefferson sent his limo on Thursday to pick up Tom and Peg for the drive to the courthouse. Jefferson was not happy about the way things were going.

"Benton's a maverick, a showboat," he groaned. "He runs his court like a little empire."

"The word around is that he's getting a bit senile," Tom said.

"More than a bit."

"Jesus, Randy, can't we do anything about him?"

"He's a federal judge. Hard to lay a glove on him. Of all the guys on the federal bench, we get Hanging Harry."

"Do I get to say anything?"

"You just keep quiet and look very pregnant," Tom advised.

"You don't think it looks good, do you?" Peg asked Jefferson.

"Benton's had a burr up his ass since the *Times* went after him on a couple of decisions."

"We're not the *Times*."

"Yeah, but the *Times* isn't in his jurisdiction. We are. This whole setup looks like a grandstand play to me. Benton plays fast and loose with procedure."

Outside the courtroom, camera crews from Channel 4, ABC and CBS Evening News were waiting. Jefferson hustled Peg past the reporters, saying, "We'll talk later, people."

Inside the courtroom, the press gallery was filled. Hanging Harry, his hair slicked down and his robes freshly pressed, called Randall Jefferson up to the bench. Peg watched as they talked, and saw Jefferson shake his head several times angrily. He was scowling when he walked back from the bench. Judge Benton pulled himself up to his full height.

"The judicial process," he intoned, in a voice that carried to the press gallery, "is under attack, from forces in many areas of our society. From those who would reshape this republic in their own image, by those who would use violence to redress grievances, instead of due process."

"It's a speech," Tom Friedman said, under his breath.

"And most distressing, it is under attack from an institution that should be one of the bulwarks of a free society, the Fourth Estate. The First Amendment is not to be used as a facade to cover activities that display nothing but contempt for the majesty of the law."

"Oh, shit!" Peg groaned, sotto voce.

"The Washington *Tribune*, and its reporter, have displayed untrammeled arrogance, this court finds, in its pursuit of sensationalism. Its reporter was involved in illegal trespass, in not only receiving, but it appears soliciting, stolen property, and in refusing to reveal the whereabouts of a man charged with a capital crime. A man who is a menace to his fellow citizens."

"That's such bullshit!" Peg whispered to Tom.

"Whether that man is guilty of that crime is a matter for the courts to decide, not the Washington *Tribune*. I hereby find the *Tribune*, and its employee, Margaret Morrison, in contempt of court. I am fining the *Tribune* three thousand dollars a day until such time as this court's subpoena is complied with. Margaret Morrison will be confined until such time as she complies with the order of this court."

A buzz broke out in the courtroom. Hanging Harry gaveled the room into silence.

"However, in recognition of the—delicate—condition of Margaret Morrison, this court, in its compassion, delays imposition of sentence until such time as her delivery of child has been accomplished."

Peg sat on the bed, exhausted, her hands resting on her stomach. The apartment had been full, earlier, of people offering their support. Both Con and Kitty had offered to stay with her, but she thanked them and said she needed some time alone to unwind. She spoke to her stomach, which had become a habit these days.

"Well, gang, that's it. Your mother is going to be a jailbird." Someone inside gave a kick, and she said, "Right, I agree. It was a rotten decision. A judge has a screw loose and a hair across his ass, so we get sent to the slammer. *Shit.*"

There was another kick. "Do I detect a lack of confidence? What's that? No, the Foreign Legion does not take infants. Stick with me. Look, life won't be dull, right? Besides, maybe Doctor Spock will be in the cell next to ours, and we'll get personal service. Jails are very enlightened these days. Nursing mothers get to take their babies along. Some kids go to preschool and play with dumb little blocks. In the Big House, you can learn to kite checks and tailgate trucks before you're two. Eat your heart out, Maria Montessori."

She cried a little bit, then, from weariness, and tension, and then she climbed into bed and tried to sleep. She had trouble, lately, finding a comfortable position. There was just too much stomach to contend with. And there was the heartburn. Everything gave her heartburn.

She heated up some milk in a saucepan, drank it, got back into bed and finally drifted off to sleep. Then it came again. The dream.

She watched, frozen with horror, knowing what was going to happen. It did. The face on the head on the sand was Sean's, and then the young woman at Kent State; and then it dissolved again and it was little Megan, with the curly hair and freckles; and then little Sean, with the round cheeks.

She woke up screaming. The sound split the air around her. For an instant, she didn't know where she was. On the sand in Sinai, screaming inside her mind as she saw the severed head on the ground?

"Oh God! Oh God!" She was disoriented. Where was she? She looked around. In her bedroom. She began to tremble all over, violently. She tried to will the trembling away, but couldn't do it. Could a dream cross the placenta? Were her babies screaming, too, inside their little sacs? She looked at the clock. Midnight. That was all? The whole night was ahead, a darkness that could invent a thousand phantoms.

She got up to get a glass of milk, drank it, and then sat down on the bed, waiting for the shaking to stop. If only it was close to dawn; dreams died with the daylight.

On an impulse she picked up the phone and dialed. She waited until she heard his voice.

"Hello?" It was alert, not groggy with sleep. He was a night owl.

"Sean? I didn't wake you, did I?"

"Peg? No, I'm awake. Is anything the matter?"

"I'm going to jail, Sean."

"To jail? You were in court?"

"Yes, today. Contempt of court. And I just had the dream again. Christ, I hate to be such a crybaby, but it was so vivid. I'm shaking all over."

"Being at Kent State didn't help. Are you still shaking?"

"Yes."

"Your husband, he's still at sea?"

"Yes. At sea."

"Listen to me, Peg, remember when you used to have the dream and I'd hold you, and it would go away?"

"Yes."

"I'm there, Peg. Holding you. You're safe. It's only a dream. Dreams can't hurt you."

"Keep talking to me, Sean."

"Just relax. Let your muscles relax. Are you doing that?"

"Yes. Yes I am. It's working."

"It's your subconscious. You keep things inside. But they have to come out somehow, so you dream."

"I'm getting so I hate the nights. Hate to go to sleep. It's been worse since Kent State."

"You've seen so much death. So much violence. Men in combat have dreams like you do."

"This time it was worse. On the sand, I saw, I saw the babies."

"Babies?"

"I'm having twins. I just learned."

"Twins! Oh Peg, that's great. That's good news, huh?"

"I'll have the only cell with two potties."

"Oh Peg, what can I do to help? God, I feel so helpless. What can I do?"

"Just talking to me, it helps, Sean. Your voice, it makes me feel—calm."

"Close your eyes, and you'll feel me holding you. I'm there, Peg. Can you feel it?"

"Yes. Don't go away."

"I won't. Think of the good things. You're going to have two beautiful babies. You're going to have a happy life. You have a husband who loves you, friends who love you."

"I wish my parents had lived to see their grandchildren. I think about them. A lot. I wish they were here."

"I think they'll know. They loved you so. I think, somehow, they'll know. Peg, are you crying?"

"It's these damn hormones. I cry at everything, Sean. There was a tenor singing 'O Canada!' before a hockey match on TV, and I got all choked up. I've never even been to fucking Canada. I cry when the parrot says the man has ring around the collar. I cry at denture stains."

He laughed. She loved the sound of his laugh, a deep rumble that started in his chest and danced up to his eyes; she loved everything about the father of her babies, the way he talked, the scent of him, the safe, warm feel of his arms around her.

"Sean—"

"Uh-oh, what's that?"

"Sean, I'm so alone. I'm so scared. They're your babies, Sean. You're their father."

And then she realized that he was not on the other end of the line.

"Sean?"

Then he was back. "Sorry, the damn smoke alarm is on the fritz. I have to hit the damn thing to make it stop."

"Oh. Is it all right now?"

"Yeah. Have to get a new one. What were you saying?"

"Uh, I was going to ask you about the tenant project. How's it going?"

"Good. I've been working with Paul Siegel. Heard of him?"

"Oh yes."

"Dynamite guy. Working with him has really been an inspiration."

"You're doing the work you were meant to do, aren't you, Sean? I'm really glad for you."

"Peg, what can I do? Can I come out there, will that be any help?"

"No, I don't have to start serving my sentence until the babies are born. I'll be okay. I'm pretty tough. But I'm going to have to stop this crazy business of calling you at all hours of the night."

"Peg, I'm here. Call me anytime you need me. Call me, Peg."

When he hung up the phone, Sean leaned back against the pillow. He closed his eyes, but he knew it would be futile. Sleep just didn't seem to come these nights. The insomnia was getting worse. Some nights he'd just roam the mansion, letting his thoughts careen off each other like billiard balls. Often he would try to imagine what it had been like when the millionaire owned the mansion, when gas lamps lit the streets and the sound of carriage wheels clattered outside the windows. If nothing else, that occupied his mind when his eyes were too tired to read.

He got up and walked to the closet. The red blouse was there, on a hanger. He slipped it off the hanger and caressed it with his hands, loving the feel of the silk under his fingers. If he pressed it to his cheek, the scent of her would curl into his nostrils and the lovely ghost would float into the room, peaceful as a guardian angel.

But he shook his head. Time to grow up, Sean. She was a married woman, about to become a mother. She belonged to another man, now, another life. You couldn't hang onto the past. You had to let go and move on. To wherever it was you were going. Wherever the hell it was.

He took the blouse and crumpled it, gently, in his hands, and walked to the wastebasket. No, that was wrong, somehow. A sacrilege. He opened the window.

There was a stiff breeze blowing, and it whipped the lace

curtain back against his body. He leaned out the window and gave the blouse, tenderly, to the wind. It leapt eagerly from his hands and soared off like some huge red bird set free to play in the sky. He watched as it tumbled, twisted, flew, and then vanished into the night. He shut the window and went back to his bed. He closed his eyes, waiting for sleep to come, but he knew it would be a long time before it did.

TWENTY-SIX

"Peg, my dear, I saw your column on Op Ed. The first of many?"

"I'm just trying a few in July and August to break it in, Kitty. Before the babies are born. You know, I think jail will give me lots of material. I have decided to look on this whole thing as an interesting experience."

"Oh that beastly man, Judge Benton. How could he?"

"Who knows? But Jefferson is asking him to delay sentence until three months after the babies are born. Even Hanging Harry might not want to drag the mother of twins off to the slammer right from the delivery room."

"What if that young black man—Brown—were to turn himself in? Wouldn't that make this whole issue moot?"

"Yes. There'd be no reason to put me in jail. Sean got in touch with Elly Brown. I told him not to. It's too risky. But he did, anyway."

"What did Brown say?"

"He won't come in."

"Not even with the autopsy report?"

"The report makes the police version look fishy, all right. But when you come right down to it, that report doesn't *prove* that a Panther didn't fire the fatal bullet."

"So he thinks a jury could still find him guilty?"

"Yes. If they believed the police story about those rifles being in the house. And if the trial were held in Moore County—well, there's a lot of feeling about the Panthers out there."

"I can imagine."

"You know, if I were Elly Brown, I don't know if I'd take the chance either. He's afraid he might not get to trial."

"Some sort of accident in jail, you mean?"

"Yes. He told Sean they'd find him hanging by his belt. And the awful thing is, Kitty, that I can't say it wouldn't happen. It just might."

"But surely he will be caught?"

"I'm not so sure. There's an underground already. Radicals who have gone underground. They have networks. Safe houses. I think he can just drop off the face of the earth. For years, maybe."

"So you can't count on the police picking him up."

"No, I can't. I'm getting myself ready, psychologically. I can't afford to let myself be too optimistic. If I keep telling myself it's going to happen, get ready for it, I think I'll be okay."

"You won't reveal your source, I take it."

"No. My source is too vulnerable. At least I've got the paper, with its clout and its lawyers behind me. And I know I've got my friends. That's a big help. It won't be so bad."

"Are you being sure to keep your legs elevated at least a half hour a day? It's important in this hot weather. Remember, when you start feeling any labor pains, you call Con or me right away. Don't you dare try to go to the hospital alone."

"I won't."

"And, my dear, don't listen to these natural childbirth fanatics. If God wanted women to have babies like they do in rice paddies, he would not have invented anesthesiologists.

"My doctor suggests a spinal. And I'm going to nurse, Kitty. Several prisons have pilot programs where mothers have their babies with them."

"It's a lovely experience, Peg. Makes you feel so close to the baby. But wear a good bra. You don't want to sag."

"I wonder if I'll ever be perky again."

"I'm sure you can be, if that's what you want."

"I want *humongous*, but I haven't got a prayer."

"My dear, humongous is for topless dancers. A great many men like breasts with a bit of reticence."

"Mine aren't at all reserved right now, Kitty. They are all over the damn place."

Kitty smiled as she hung up the phone. Dear, brave Peg. She was keeping up a good front, but Kitty knew the idea of going to prison terrified her. There had to be some way of putting pressure on Hanging Harry Benton. He was a maverick, perhaps a bit crazed to boot, but some of the people in the Texas delegation ought to be able to help. Yes, she'd make a few calls this afternoon.

She went upstairs to the bedroom and saw the manila folder on the dresser, where it had been lying for a week. What to do about *those?* What, indeed.

She picked up the sheaf of letters and sat on the edge of the bed, looking at Morris.

"Well, Morris, I've got the bomb," she said, raising up the letters so they would be in his line of sight. "I wonder what's the best strategy. Jack Anderson? No, it's all a bit too tacky for Jack, not enough reason for him to run with it. If Dan were selling secrets to the Russians, or taking bribes, Jack would toss in the sex as a sidebar, but it would be too thin for a main event. Jack has more of a conscience than old Drew Pearson ever did.

"The *National Enquirer* would take it in a minute, of course, but who wants to read 'Two-headed Boy Rapes Mom' right next to it? Do I want to give it to Rolvag's people, the anti-Semites? You saw what they did with a nice Jewish widow lady. Imagine what they'd do with gay sex.

"This has to be done discreetly, of course. I don't want even the shadow of suspicion to fall on me. But I can pay enough to make sure of that. There are people in town who deal in that kind of information. You'd be surprised, Morris, at the responsible positions they hold. There's one man at USIA— well, you don't want to know the details.

"It will finish him, Morris. If Rolvag has this information, he'll kill Dan with it. He'll stick one on every cornstalk in the state. Farmers would find copies of it under cow flap and in the spokes of their John Deeres.

"It does seem curious, doesn't it, that people should care so much about who their elected representatives sleep with. But people do get upset over these things. Remember that aide to Lyndon who got caught in the YMCA men's room? I would have fired him too, not for being gay, but for being stupid. I mean, you just *know* the vice squad is there all the time. The stalls have better sound than Dolby stereo.

"I've never had *this* sort of power before, Morris. I suppose Hoover has drawers of stuff like this. Now there's a thought. Send it to J. Edgar. Other people having sex makes him froth at the mouth. Maybe I should drop Dan a sweet little note on my blue stationery. 'Darling Dan. You'll be so happy to know you're in J. Edgar's photo album—along with JFK's girlfriends and an assistant secretary of state in drag.'"

She sighed. "I wonder, Morris, if I am really going to do it. Dan was a shit, all right, but do I want to be like poor Gordon Truebland, eating my heart out over the man that got away? Gordon wrote a lot of his letters to 'Byron.' That was his nickname for Dan, after Lord Byron. That's what comes from getting involved with a highbrow. At least he doesn't call you 'cuddles' or 'honeybuns.'

"Do I hate Dan? Oh, there are times I want to see him smashed, torn apart. It's not fair that men like Dan move along unscathed, when they leave such carnage behind them. But it would be worse if he had been better. Know what I mean? I was a fool, but what did I lose, except a man who could never care for me, not really. Oh, I suppose in his way, Dan did care, as much as he ever could. He's amputated, Dan is. Part of his soul is missing.

"If I do this to him, do I forge a bond between us that I'll never be free of? The Chinese say that if you save a life, you are responsible for it ever after. And if you destroy one? Is an act of vengeance as powerful as an act of love? Does vengeance touch the ven*ger* as deeply as the vengee? Actions have consequences, Morris, you don't walk away scot-free.

"Another question, Morris, is Dan worth destroying? If Dan was Hitler, I'd do it in a minute, but how much of a menace is Dan? Except to those who have the bad luck to have their private parts entwined with his, one way or another. Miss Cornhusker is certainly going to get mangled, but that doesn't exactly qualify as a holocaust. Do I care enough about getting Dan to risk what getting him might do to *me?* Now that's the question I have to think about, Morris."

She shook her head and walked to the window. "But he can't just get away with it, free and clear. After all, fair is fair." She turned to face the picture again. "Maybe the best thing to do is just to let him know *I* know. And he's not sure of me, not anymore. He really did think I'd come to him. Hah! Before I'd have gone back to his bed, I'd have screwed a cucumber. Sorry if that shocks you, Morris, but some people do it with veggies when there's nothing else around. Oh, not *me*, Morris. I prefer more animation than you get from the vegetable bin.

"It would be lovely wouldn't it, to keep him in suspense? He'd *think* I wouldn't, but he'd never be quite sure. There he'd be, twisting slowly, slowly in the wind. Oh Morris, I think I like it."

Kitty was humming as she went into the bathroom and drew warm water for a long, hot soak. She examined the inside of her thighs—they were white and soft. That was one benefit of getting rid of Dan. The crotchless panties had given her a rash. They'd all gone out in the trash; in fact, she'd had the chauffeur drive her around until she found a dumpster, into which she'd dropped the trash bag with the panties in it. Mitzi the wolfhound had a habit of getting into the trash, and no way did she want purple lace crotchless panties strewn across the lawn. This *was* Foxhall Road.

Kitty settled back and let the warm water wash over her. Len Fineberg had the grace to be furious at Dan, had sworn not to give him another cent. But she had told Len that Israel needed his vote in the Senate, cad or not. After all the Israelis had dealt with South Africa and Samoza, so one more *goniff* couldn't hurt.

She thought of her packet of letters, and she smiled again. Dan was going to be one of the biggest supporters of Israel in the Senate, she'd make sure of that. If he didn't vote right on fighters or the PLO, off would go a little note to J. Edgar. Those letters were going to do more for the State of Israel than all the goddamn trees her mother planted. She was going to be a true heroine of Judea, forget Judith, forget Esther. Could Esther get even one lousy phantom jet? She would probably never get her story preserved for the ages, though, in those "Tales of Jewish Heroines" books little girls read in Sunday school. How would you explain about blackmailing a Norwegian to the little bubbelehs?

*　　*　　*

Sean bit into a kosher pickle, and Paul Siegel grinned.

"For an Irishman, Sean, you wolf down more Jewish food than anyone I know."

"This is a great discovery, Paul. Irish cuisine is not great. Boiled potatoes and a six-pack."

The two men had been working together all summer on a package of bills that would unify the crazy quilt of housing legislation and make the laws clear and enforceable. They were going to be introduced early in the fall, with much fanfare.

"We've got support from groups all across the state on this." Siegel was a small, wiry man, with a face that bore the lines of years of battles, more lost than won. He was, Sean thought, more a model of a holy public life that Christ set a pattern for than any Christian he could think of.

"Your testimony will be a big help, Sean. Seeing that collar will quiet some of the grumbles that it's a group of hippies and radicals who came up with this. Flash 'em that choir-boy smile. You come across as a straight arrow, not a pinko radical like me."

Sean laughed. "Don't tell the cardinal, but I'm really a bombthrower at heart."

"Ah, but you don't look like one, boyo. Me? Even if I was a cardinal, I'd look like I was about to torch the cathedral."

Sean was in a good mood after his meeting with Siegel. Finally, he was doing something real after spinning his wheels all these months. He was whistling as he walked up the steps to the Institute and through the door. Mrs. Baker, the receptionist, smiled at him.

"Aren't we in a good mood, Father."

"Unusual, huh?"

"Oh no. It's just that you work so hard, Father. It's nice to see you looking cheerful. Oh, Father J. said he wanted to see you when you got in."

Sean walked into Father Jurevich's office. The older priest looked up as he came in. "Sean, I'm afraid I have some bad news for you."

"Bad news?"

"Yes. Word from the chancery. You are not to testify on the housing legislation."

"What!"

"I'm sorry, Sean."

"What on earth is the reason? I've worked hard to pull this package together."

"Yes, it's good legislation. Sound."

"Why, then?"

"Officially? Paul Siegel is a Marxist."

"Good Lord, of course he's a Marxist. Been one for thirty years. Everybody knows that. But he's a respected community activist."

"The chancery thinks we might give scandal to the faithful by being publicly affiliated with a Marxist."

"What's really going on?"

Father J. sighed, and put his hands behind his head. "As I figure it, it's Ed O'Malley. He's the head of something called Holy Name Laymen. Big givers. I mean *big*. Buy and sell this whole place and not notice it."

"What's O'Malley got against Siegel?"

"Siegel organized a group of tenants in a rent strike a few years back. Called O'Malley a slumlord, and the name stuck. O'Malley had political ambitions, and he hates Siegel for spoiling it for him. The press played the story big."

"Does O'Malley have a lot of clout?"

"Yes. A lot of the men in Holy Name are in real estate. They don't want the new legislation. And a lot of them contribute to an alderman who is one of Siegel's special targets. Clout in more ways than one."

"So we get zapped."

"Put yourself in the cardinal's place. He puts your testimony on the scale against a new wing for a hospital. O'Malley's giving a whole *wing*. What would you do?"

"I feel like a rat in a maze. Every time I feel I'm getting someplace, it's just another blind alley."

"It's better than it used to be, Sean."

"Is it? God, what *was* it, Father? We're not fighting the bad guys, we're fighting our own church. We want to do what Christ did, and who's stopping us? Our own hierarchy! We spend most of the time fighting them."

"The church changes. But it changes slowly. You need patience."

"*I* need patience? What about the people who can't keep the rats out of their kids' cribs? What about the old ladies who make ketchup soup because all their money goes to rent?

Should *they* be patient? How many lives are going to be crippled while we spend our time being patient! Father, the church should be our instrument. But we're hamstrung! What's the point?"

"The point is that we care about the church. Care enough to be patient."

Sean slammed his fist on the desk. "I don't give a damn about the church. Not when it's just an obstacle."

"You don't mean that, Sean."

"Maybe I do. Maybe I do, Father."

"We're priests because we *do* care. Because we believe the institution *is* important. More important than our own ideas. We care enough about the church to try to change it."

"No, that's not why I'm a priest, to nudge some institution into the twentieth century."

"Why did you become a priest, Sean?"

"To do something good with my life. To be useful. Not just to throw it away."

"You could have been a social worker or a doctor. Wasn't there a special commitment to God?"

"I don't need some cardinal to tell me about God!"

"You're young, Sean. And angry. You'll see this thing in more perspective when you calm down."

"Can't we fight this?"

"No. This one we lose."

"I lose them all, Father. When do I get a win? When in the hell do I win?"

And Sean turned and stalked out of the office, and out the door of the Institute building. He walked quickly along the street, trying to let his anger dissipate, thinking murderous thoughts about the cardinal. Old men. Cautious old men. John the Twenty-Third had tried to hurl them into the present, to open the window and let the fresh winds blow in, but cautious old men were nailing the windows shut again.

He went back to his room, his mind still churning. He got out his prayerbook and knelt by the bed. "Lord, inflame my will so it will bend; let me always remember to be submissive to my superiors. Make me patient in my undertakings, docile in afflictions."

He closed the book, thinking, My words fly up, my thoughts stay down below. And what did the words mean?

What was God's will? Who decided what it was? Ed O'Malley, a slumlord?

"Dear God," he prayed, "how can I obey men who are foolish and cowardly? How do I serve Thee in this way?"

He thought of the words of Christ, as a twelve-year-old boy, when Joseph found him preaching in the temple. It was what he wanted to say to the cardinal: "Know you not that I must be about my father's business?"

Am I arrogant? he thought. Do I deceive myself that I know better? Am I filled with pride? The sin of Lucifer?

He stood up and paced around the room, and then he went over to the bed and slammed his fist, hard, into the bedpost. The pain surged through him, but it felt good, it was real. Nothing ambiguous about pain.

He sat on the bed, suddenly drained. *I don't give a damn about the church.*

The words were true. He had known it as soon as he said them. He had been trying, these past months, to outrun them, the priest in track shoes. It had been a boy's dream, shining like silver wire, but it had proved, in the end, too fragile. A boy's dream could not carry the weight of a man's life.

He felt, for the first time in his life, the cold breath of despair. It chilled the room. He imagined he could see it, freezing the legs of the chair, glazing over the spines of the books. He had lost both love and dreams. He had lost it all.

He shivered, a tremor that shook his whole body. They had told him, in seminary, that someday it would happen, that he would question God Himself, that a huge, gaping maw would open up at the center of the universe.

He never believed it, not for himself. He had God safe in his pocket, like a favorite marble or a penknife. Sean McCaffrey would never know the sin of despair. And now he knew, and he let out a cry. He imagined it sailing like a missile out beyond the sun, going on and on, to the edges of the universe, where there was nothing. Nothing at all. He remembered Father Barry, an old man weeping in a hallway: *My God, my God, why hast Thou forsaken me?*

He thought, inexplicably, of Peggy Morrison, the day they had hiked through the storm sewers together and she got the nail in her foot. He had carried her, and she had not made a sound, even when the doctor pulled the big ugly nail from her swollen foot. She was so reckless, and so brave; it had made him want to be brave, too, for her. He thought again of that small, determined face, streaked with sweat but not with tears, and the set of her little shoulders as the doctor reached for the nail. It made him brave.

He walked to the window and looked out at the sun, shining through the trees onto the sidewalk, and he thought, Glory be to God for dappled things. Odd, the places where you found God. Sidewalks. And perhaps the center of the universe was not empty at all. Perhaps God was like a planet hidden by the sun. Astronomers never saw it, they knew it was there only by other things that happened in the solar system which shouldn't happen if there was nothing there.

He turned away from the window and walked to the bed. The glaze of ice was gone from the chair, the books. He thought of what Ben Hanafee had said. You have to find some way to make the priesthood a meaningful place or you leave and find out where you do belong.

Could the priesthood be just a job—one in which he could do good, but not one in which he was special, a fisher of men? But then, why should he be different? Most people lived their lives devoid of golden dreams. What ever made him think he had a right to be different?

But one right he did have. He would grow up. He would be his own man, serve God his own way, no matter how much hot water it got him into.

"I am thirty-one years old. I know what I know. To obey orders that I know are wrong is betrayal. Of God. Of myself. I will testify at the hearing. And the cardinal can stuff it up his ass."

He remembered, suddenly, that he was supposed to have been at a meeting of the Catholic Interracial Council five minutes ago. He went to the closet, pulled on his black jacket, and was about to go out the door when the phone rang. He went to answer it.

"Sean?"

"Hi Bill." He let the impatience show in his voice, just a little. Bill could really bend your ear, once he got going.

"You sound like you're in a hurry."

"Late for a meeting. What's up?"

"I just wanted to talk."

"Things going okay?"

"I guess so. Well, no, I heard the final word on this thing with my partners. Judge threw it out of court."

"Bill, you expected that. Your lawyer told you it was a long shot."

"I guess in my heart I was hoping I could get them to settle."

"Do you need money?"

"I'm okay for now, I guess. Rene is going to marry that guy."

"But you'll still see the kids, Bill. She's been good about that."

"They're going to move to New York, though. To New York."

"That's a half hour on the shuttle. It's not that far, Bill."

"That's right. It really isn't. Sean—"

"Yeah, Bill?"

"No, you go on. I know you're in a hurry."

"I'll call you when I get back, Bill. About ten. Is that okay?"

"Sure, Sean."

He hung up the phone and hurried out to his car. The sun was warm, the shadows of the trees still dancing on the sidewalk, the sky overhead clear and blue. Sean stood still for a minute looking up at the sky, at the planet he couldn't see.

"I believe, Lord," he said. "Help Thou my unbelief."

TWENTY-SEVEN

Kitty saw Con coming out of the ladies' room at the Mayflower, and hurried over to her. They had both stopped in at the cocktail party given by the Democratic National Committee.

"Constance, where's Peg? I thought she was coming with you."

"She was on her feet all day, so she was tired. She's home watching TV with the boys."

"I'm so glad you convinced her to stay with you. I didn't like the idea of her being all alone in her ninth month."

"I practically had to bludgeon her to get her to come."

"I helped her set up the nursery the other day. She's taking the top floor for the baby nurse. It's a lovely space, actually, for a converted attic."

Con looked suspiciously across the floor to the spot where a tall, broad-shouldered blond young man was taking a glass of sherry from a waiter.

"Kitty, I have something to ask you."

"Yes, Constance?"

"Who *is* that man you are with?"

"His name is Todd. He's new at Covington-Burling. But on his way up, I am told by a reliable source."

"How *old* is he?"

"Older than he looks."

"How old?"

"Oh all right. He's thirty. But almost thirty-one."

"What a body! My God, Kitty, he looks like a California surfer."

"He is from California, originally. I wonder if he surfs. I forgot to ask."

"How did you meet him?"

"At a party a few weeks ago. I just chatted to be polite, I didn't think he'd be interested in *me*. But he was."

"Kitty, are you, ah——"

"Sleeping with him?" She sighed. "I'm afraid I am. Younger men seem to be like potato chips. Try one and you can't stop."

"Is he as delicious as he looks?"

"Yes, he really is. And bright. And gentle. Do you know, Constance, there's a gentleness about young men these days I really do like. And they're not such chauvinist pigs."

"Shoulders like that and he's *liberated*, too?"

"Yes, and he's not ever thinking about running for office. First thing I asked."

"Kitty, just be a little careful. Remember what you told me, it's better to be married. You get a *rep* so fast."

"Are you calling me a slut, dear?"

"Who, me? Ms. round-heels reporter? I just don't want you to get hurt."

"No, Constance, this is quite lovely. My heart isn't involved, I don't think. I rather like it."

"He hangs all over you, Kitty, I have been watching. What if he finds he can't live without you? Would you marry a California surfer?"

"I am hardly thinking of marriage, my dear. My mother would disembowel herself, right in front of the B'nai B'rith building. But you know, I do look well with a tan. My goodness, do look what's dragged in."

Con looked across the room and saw Dan Amundsen, walking in with his wife beside him; or nearly beside him. She was actually a few paces behind. He stopped to chat with another congressman, and she stood, listening to the conversation, shifting her weight from one foot to another. She glanced about, now and then, as if seeking a friendly face. Seeing none, she shifted her eyes back to her husband. He did not acknowledge her presence.

"Poor Miss Cornhusker. I do feel sorry for her."

"How long do you think that will last?"

"A long time, probably. What's she going to do, go back to Omaha and marry the boy next door? And being married certainly won't slow Dan down."

"He's been seen with Margaret Olive, the TV reporter, I hear."

"I wonder if she has a rash. Would you excuse me, Constance, dear. I have a small errand to run."

Dan Amundsen had walked over to the bar to get a Scotch and soda. Kitty walked up beside him.

"Hello, Dan."

He looked up, surprised. Something flickered in his eyes that looked a bit like pain. But then he smiled.

"Kit! It's wonderful to see you."

"You're looking well. I saw Adam Crabtree on 'Meet the Press' and he says you're ahead."

"So far, so good. You were right, Kit, the war is the thing that's helping us. Kent State shocked a lot of people."

"Yes, indeed it did."

He looked at her and said, "You're looking beautiful. How are you doing?"

"Wonderfully, Dan."

"Kit, I want us to be friends. At least that. We can be, can't we?" He flashed the familiar smile, the I-know-I'm-naughty-but-I'm-so cute smile.

She smiled back at him. "Of course, Dan. In fact, I have a little present for you."

"A present?"

"Yes, I was browsing in one of those antique bookstores in Georgetown, and I came across it. I knew you'd adore it."

She reached into her purse and drew out a small volume, bound in red leather, and put it into his hand.

"The binding is superb. It's quite old. Eighteen-nineties, I think."

"The poems of Lord Byron?"

"Yes. I just loved it when you used to read those to me."

"Kit, I didn't, I never read—" he looked at her, comprehension dawning in his eyes.

"Didn't you? I'd have *sworn* you did. But perhaps I was mistaken."

She saw what she wanted to see in those light blue eyes. He'd never be sure of her. Not ever.

She patted the volume in his hand. "Keep it in good health, Dan. Old Jewish saying." Then she smiled, letting her lips curl up just slightly at the edges, a feline smile, and she turned and walked back to Todd.

"It's awfully stuffy in here," she said to him. "Why don't we go back to the house and relax?"

He took her arm. "Oh Kitty," he smiled, "I was hoping you'd say that."

Brian Byrne was getting ready to go across the street to hear confessions when the phone rang. He answered it.

"Father Byrne? It's Bill McCaffrey. Sean's brother."

"How are you, Bill?"

"Well, I think, Brian, can I call you Brian?"

"Yes, please do."

"Tell Sean, tell him—"

There was a silence on the other end of the line.

"Bill? Are you there?"

"Yes. I'm here."

"Are you all right?"

"Yes."

"You want me to tell Sean something?"

"Yes. Yes."

"Why don't you give him a call? I know he likes to hear from you."

"No. You tell him, please."

"Tell him what."

"I did try."

"Bill, you're doing fine. Sean says you're doing great."

"It was so hard, Brian. Nobody knows how hard it was. Just to pick up the phone, a hell of a thing. But it was so hard."

"Bill, you sound funny. Are you all right?"

"I wanted to study marine biology, you know? I might have been good at it. I might."

"I'm sure you would have."

"Maybe not. Sean and I, we love each other, you know. We do."

"I know."

"I used to toss him on the bed, and tickle him. He used to laugh, and laugh. And I'd laugh too. I'm going to think about that."

"That's a nice memory, Bill."

"He'd be wearing these red pajamas, with feet, you know, and he'd laugh. I loved to hear him laugh. I love him, Brian. And I tried. But it was so hard. I hear him laughing. I like the sound, Brian. I really do like the sound."

"Bill? Bill, are you on the line? Bill?"

Brian held the phone in his hand for a minute. Then he picked up the phone book, found the number and dialed Dr. Liam McCaffrey. There was no answer. He dialed Peg Morrison's number, and then he flipped through the Montgomery County listings for another number.

The phone rang in Con's living room, and Con picked it up.

"Mrs. Masters, this is Brian Byrne from St. Ignatius. Is Peg there by any chance?"

"Yes, she's here, Brian."

"Can I talk to her?"

Peg picked up the phone and Brian said, "Peg, I just had a strange call from Bill McCaffrey."

"From Bill?"

"Yes. He sounded sort of like he'd been drinking."

"Oh no."

"He was saying—strange things. It just—I don't know, I'm worried. I called his father, and there was no answer. I'm probably overreacting, and I'd go over there myself if I didn't have to hear confessions—"

"He's only a couple of minutes from here. Con and I can run over."

"I hate to ask you, Peg. Especially now."

Peg laughed. "I'm just pregnant, Brian. Not crippled."

Con and Peg climbed into Con's car, heading for New Hampshire Avenue.

"You think he fell off the wagon?" Con asked.

"Maybe. Brian did sound worried."

"He doesn't get violent when he's drunk, does he?"

"You think I am in no condition to defend you?"

"Hardly."

"I don't know that he's ever been violent. If he's really blotto, we can call the police and get him to that place in Ellicott City."

"Maybe he'll just need to sleep it off."

"I hope so. He is a big guy. He could be hard to handle if he got mean."

They walked into the Westminster and pushed the elevator button for the ninth floor.

"I saw Bill in Wheaton Plaza last week. He looked good."

"He'd been sober for months. Until now, anyhow."

They got out of the elevator and walked along the corridor. Peg knocked on the door. There was no answer. She tried the door, and it opened. "Bill?" she said. "Bill?"

There was silence, and Peg and Con walked into the living room.

"Bill?" Con called out.

"Doesn't look like he's home, does it?"

"He could have been calling from a bar."

"Well, let's just take a quick look around."

Con walked into the bedroom. "Nobody here."

Peg walked to the bathroom. It was empty. Then she pushed open the door to the den—and she saw him. He was sitting in a chair, his torso slumped over the desk.

"He's passed out," she called to Con.

She walked into the room, and that was when she saw the gun, lying on the floor; and on the wall, little gobs of blood and gray matter sticking to the wallpaper. She steeled herself and walked close to him and touched the back of his neck. There was no pulse. She saw the blood clearly now, staining the surface of the desk.

She turned around, and saw Con standing behind her, mouth open with surprise and her face pale white. Con made a gagging noise and ran for the bathroom.

Peg went into the living room and sat down on the couch, fighting nausea. When Con came back in, still pale, but calm, she said to Peg, "On the wall, was that—"

"We better call the police."

"Sit still. I'll call."

Con called the Montgomery County police and said there had been a suicide, could they get over as soon as possible.

When she hung up she looked at Peg, and Peg said, "Oh damn. *Damn!*"

Con sat down beside Peg on the couch. "Was he drinking?"

"I guess. There was a bottle in there."

"The poor bastard."

"Somebody has to tell his father."

"Not you, Peg. Not your job."

"Sean is going to have to tell him. Oh God!"

"Do you want me to call?"

"No, I'll do it." She dialed Sean's number, but there was no answer. She hung up the phone, and Con and Peg sat in silence, waiting.

"Anything we should be doing?" Con asked.

"I don't think so. He must have died instantly."

Suddenly the phone rang, and Peg and Con looked at each other. They both had the same thought. *Who would call a dead man?* But of course, nobody knew he was dead.

Peg picked up the phone. The voice on the other end of the line was familiar."

"Hello, Sean."

"Peg? Oh Peg, I must have dialed the wrong number. I was trying to get Bill."

"You dialed the right number."

"What?"

"I'm at Bill's."

"At Bill's? Peg, what are you doing over there?"

"Sean, I'm so sorry to have to tell you this."

"What is it? What's happened?"

"Bill's dead, Sean."

"Dead? But I—Peg. He's dead?"

"Yes, Sean, he is."

"An accident, did he—"

"He shot himself."

"Oh dear God! Dear God!"

"Oh Sean, I'm so sorry."

"How did you—"

"Brian called a little while ago. He got a call from Bill and got worried. So he asked Con and me to come over. We found him."

"You found him? Where—"

"In the study. It was instantaneous. I'm sure he didn't suffer."

"Oh God, Peg, he called me earlier, he wanted to talk but I—I was late for a meeting—"

"Don't start blaming yourself."

"Oh my God! Bill!"

"Sean, your father doesn't know."

"My God, Peg. How will I tell him? This will kill him."

"Sean, he's stronger than you think. Doesn't he have a brother around?"

"Yes, Alexandria. John T."

"I'll call and get him over here."

"I'll call Rene. Maybe she could come over too. I'll call my dad as soon as I know someone is with him. I'll get the first plane out."

"Do you want me to call Collins? Didn't they bury your mother?"

"Yes."

"I'll call them. They'll come and get the—they'll come and get Bill. But there will have to be an autopsy."

"I can't believe this! I talked to him a few hours ago!"

"I know, Sean. I'll call Brian. He can help arrange things at St. Malachy's. You'll need death certificates. I'll tell Collins to get those."

"Paperwork. Oh God, you die and right away they start the paperwork!" She heard the break in his voice.

"Sean, are you okay?"

"Yes, I'm okay. Peg, I'm glad it was you who found him and not some stranger."

"I'm glad too, Sean."

"This isn't a nightmare, is it? It's real."

"It's real."

"Bill, my brother Bill!"

"Sean, he won't have any more pain. At least that."

"Peg, how could it have ended up this way? He was everything I wanted to be."

"I know."

"It's crazy, *I* should have ended up as the one—not Bill. It's so crazy."

"Sean, your father is going to need you, now."

"Poor pop. The wrong son killed himself."

"Sean—"

"It's all right, Peg. I'll call him. God, what will I say? How will I tell him. But I will."

"Oh Sean, I'm so, so sorry."

"I'll find a way."

TWENTY-EIGHT

"What's right for a funeral?" Lee asked Con. "The blue uniform?"

"Yes, that's fine, Lee. I think I have a black dress that's not too dressy."

Con, dressed in her bra and panties, went into the bathroom to put on her makeup. Lee waited for her to come out. And waited.

"For heaven's sakes, Con, what are you doing in there?"

"Putting on my makeup."

"We are going to a funeral, Constance, not to the prom."

"Well, Lee, I don't want them to mistake me for the deceased."

"We're going to be late."

"Just a minute. Oh, damn!"

"What's the matter?"

"Run in my stocking. Oh well, maybe nobody will notice."

"Con, I *have* to use the john."

"Just a minute."

He laughed. "This does seem like old times, us fighting over the bathroom."

She came out and looked at him. He did look very handsome in his uniform, she thought; every woman would be jealous. She had always loved showing him off. She slipped into her dress and ordered, "Zip me up." He zipped and she said, "Lee, you do look dashing in that thing. A real sea dog."

He smiled. "A carrier. The biggest and the best. My boss

350

said to me, when he gave me the news, that I had friends who could really pull strings."

"Never underestimate Kitty's connections."

"I won't. I'm very grateful to her. Oh Con, I'm going back to sea! I never thought I'd get there!"

"It's not your own command."

"No, but it's a step in the right direction. And Newport News is just a hop, skip, and a jump."

She smiled. "The boys are really bragging that their father is going to be on a carrier."

"I'll see them a lot, Con. Not as much as when I'm around all the time, but they won't forget they have a father. I promise."

He was quiet for a minute and then he said, "You're not going to marry him. The senator."

"No, I'm not."

"You could have."

"Yes."

"Am I part of the reason?"

"Yes. Not all of it. But yes, you are."

"You know what I want."

"Lee, we're such different people than we were fourteen years ago. We have such different lives. You'll be at sea, you'll come home and you'll want me to be there for you. But I can't always be there."

"I know. But I think we can live with it. I think *I* can, Con."

She sighed. "I always wanted the story-book marriage. The one my parents never had."

"We had that for a while. It wasn't enough for you. So maybe it won't work. Maybe we'll find we're just two strangers. But I don't want to quit before we find out. I remember the first night I saw you, sitting there in that orange dress, I just saw you, and I said to myself, 'That's someone I could love for the rest of my life.'"

"Did you think that? Did you really?"

"Yes. That was the *second* thing I thought."

"What was the first?"

"Oh God, what tits!"

They both laughed, and he said, "You still excite me, Con. I get a hard-on at my desk, just thinking about you."

"We are good in bed."

"That's not nothing. It isn't everything, but it's not *nothing*."
They were both quiet for a minute, and he said, "And the
boys are happy, when we're together."

"I know that. They love to do things as a family."

"But I'm sending them to the movies tonight. Alone."

"Horny already, and you haven't even been to sea, Commander?"

"Just wait. Thirty days from now I will be crazed with lust."

"Now that does sound interesting."

Sean went to the closet in his old room in his father's house,
and he put on a clean shirt, his collar, and his black suit. He
said a prayer for Bill: "The sun shall not burn thee by day, nor
the moon by night. May the Lord keep thy going in and thy
coming out. For He hath delivered his soul from death and his
eyes from tears. May my brother Bill dwell in the House of the
Lord forever."

He buttoned his jacket. "Bill, I pray you've found peace. I
don't know why life was so hard for you. I don't know why
you came to the point where you couldn't go on any longer.
But you did. May God keep you in the palm of His hand. I
did love you, more at the end, I think, than any time. If I
failed you, forgive me. I will always love you."

Earlier that morning he had found his father roaming
around the house, looking out of windows, as if he could see
the past in the backyard; in the basketball hoop, where the
nets had long since rotted away; in the sandbox, refilled with
sand for the grandchildren. What else did he see in that backyard?

"Pop, are you okay?"

"Why? Sean, tell me. He had everything, Holy Cross,
Georgetown Law School. We gave up so much, for you boys,
for your education. Every summer I taught both sessions.
And overload, to pay for your education. We didn't go on
cruises like our friends did. We put all our money into education. Where did I fail?"

"It's not your fault, Pop. It's hard to know where the fault
lines are. Where each of us will break under the pressure."

"But life has been hard for you, Sean, and you didn't break.

Living in those terrible places, and those boys hurt you. I never thought being a priest would be so hard for you."

Sean gave a small smile. "Neither did I."

"We were so happy. We'd all sit around after Bill's games, your mom would serve hot chocolate. We were happy, weren't we?"

He remembered sitting on the couch, invisible, thinking, I am Zabor from the planet Urf, look at me, Pop, I command you to look at me. But he said, "Yes, we were happy, Pop."

"I made Bill go to law school."

"What?"

"He wanted to go to the University of Miami and be a marine biologist. Whoever heard of that? Going to college to sit on the beach."

"I didn't know that."

"I told him I'd pay for law school but not for a Holy Cross graduate to sit on the beach."

"He could have gone and worked his way through."

"Bill never liked doing things that were hard."

"You knew that?"

"Maybe I made it too easy for him. Maybe I did."

"You're not God. We are what we are. For whatever reasons."

"Did I make you a priest, Sean? I picked it out for you, you know. I really wanted one of my sons to be a priest."

"I know, Pop."

"You're a good person, Sean. You helped Bill so much."

"Pop, don't make me out to be a saint."

"You helped him."

"Sometimes. Sometimes I rubbed it in. How good and noble I was. Sometimes the sight of me was enough to make him puke."

"Don't say that!"

"It's true. Oh Pop, see me as I *am* for once. I'm not a saint. All you see is the collar. I have faults. I'm not a holy priest."

"I know."

"Do you?"

"I know you were sleeping with Peggy."

"You know? How—"

"All I had to do was look at you. I'm not such an old fool."

"Then you know what kind of a priest I am."

"I just know you're not happy. One of my sons shot himself, and the other one, the strong one, is miserable. I don't care what kind of a priest you are. I did once. I was so proud of being the father of a priest. But—some things don't matter anymore, now. I'm old, Sean. All I want is for you to be happy. Maybe you ought to leave the priesthood and get married."

"Oh God!"

"Did I say something to offend you?"

"Why didn't you say that to me years ago? Don't you know how much I wanted to please you? I think I became a priest so that for the first time in my life you'd see me. You never saw me the way you saw Bill."

"I never meant to do that to you, Sean. I swear to God I didn't!"

"I know, but God help me, deep down inside I was glad when I found out Bill was a drunk. He called me a sanctimonious little shit and I was. I was!"

"Sean, don't do this to yourself!"

"He called me the other night, but I was in a big hurry. I put him off. If I hadn't, he might not be lying in that box at Collins' right now. I failed him, Pop. Like I failed Peg. And God too. I've fucked up my life, Pop, and I hate it when people think I'm some kind of a saint. Love me for what I am, Pop. If you love me at all!"

"Sean, I don't want you to be a saint! I just want you to be happy. You're all I have left, Sean. I love you whether you're a good priest or a bad priest or not a priest at all. My God, Sean, I do!"

Sean put his arms around his father, held him and stroked his back. "I love you, too, Pop. And we were happy, we really were. I'm going to be okay. You said I was the strong one. And I am. I'm going to be okay, Pop."

The sound of the doorbell brought him back to the present, and he went to answer it. Peggy was standing there, wearing a full blue dress and a lace mantilla. She smiled at him, a sad smile.

"How's your dad?"

"Holding up. He's going to Florida with Uncle John and

Aunt Rita day after tomorrow. That'll help. He needs to get away."

"Shall I take my car to the church?"

"No, you ride with me in the second car, I want Uncle John and Rita to go with Dad in the first car."

"I made sure there were stories in the *Trib* and the *Post*. The church will be full."

"Peg, you've been such a help, all the arranging you've done. I couldn't have done it without you."

He looked at her; they said pregnant women have a special kind of beauty, and they were right. He loved watching her, as she led him, quite efficiently, through the arrangements— the funeral, the flowers, the church. He thought often of the day he had carried her, piggyback, through the storm sewer, feeling quite manly with her arms around him and her soft cheek against the side of his neck. Why did the sight of her, pregnant, trigger that memory? *I carried her.* And if life had turned out differently, if his timing hadn't been so abysmal, maybe it would be part of him she carried now, and not some other man. They had played house, once, when they were six, and she had proudly stuffed a pillow in her underpants and strutted about, saying she was a mommy, while he, insanely jealous, sulked. But she had a kind heart, so she said he could put a pillow in his underpants too, and they sat together, two happy mommies, stuffing their faces with Mallomars.

Now, her roundness stirred a fierce desire in him. She seemed sultry, an earth mother. He wanted to lift her skirt and kiss her round belly and feel the softness of her white breasts against his face. That exact image surged into his mind as the salesman was showing them the coffins, saying, "This is the oak, our very best for the beloved, only six thousand dollars." He was going to say, "Oh yes," but practical Peg, the earth mother with the beautiful round belly, snapped, "The metal will do very nicely" and added that a blanket of roses would make everybody think it was the Preakness. Carnations would suffice.

Oh Peg, my beautiful Peg. Late have I loved thee.

Peg walked around the living room, touching the bookcase,

355

the backs of chairs. "It seems strange to be in this room again."

He smiled. "We spent a lot of time here. How's Fuzzy?"

"Terrible. He's born again. A Jesus bear. We watch Oral Roberts together. He was much more fun as a lush."

The cars arrived, and Sean took her arm and they walked together out to the car. Peg had been right, the church was packed. Brian said the requiem mass; no black vestments and mournful music like in the old days. Brian wore white and over Bill's coffin was draped a white cloth with the embroidered words: "Rejoice: He is Risen."

The choir sang the Georgetown hymn, and Brian gave a brief eulogy that was touching and heartfelt. "The measure of a life is not its ending," he said, "but its battles fought. Bill McCaffrey fought as hard as he was able. Let us honor him for that. God keep his spirit, forgive him as He forgives us all."

After the mass, they drove to the Gate of Heaven Cemetery to bury Bill in a cool green spot under a tree, next to his mother. It was not far from the spot where Joe and Emily Morrison were buried. As people began to gather at the grave site, waiting for all the cars to arrive, Peg saw Con and Kitty standing together. She walked over to them, and Kitty extended her hand.

"Peg, my dear, will you please tell Sean how sorry I am."

"I will. Your flowers were lovely."

"So sad. Such a young man."

Con sighed. "I had a mad crush on Bill McCaffrey when I was in seventh grade and he was captain of the Sacred Heart basketball team." She looked at the coffin. "To think he's in there. It seems so small."

"We're not immortal anymore," Peg said.

"That's right. When did it happen?"

They were quiet for a minute and then Kitty said, looking at the bronze metal box, "Makes you want to do something really important in this world before it's your turn. And my dears, unlike our mothers, we have a chance."

Peg nodded. "Yes, it's a good time to be a woman, isn't it? Maybe the best time in history. We're not going to stay on the sidelines anymore."

"It's not going to be easy," Con said. "A lot of people don't like pushy broads."

"Too bad for them. We'll roll right over them."

"Right now, Peg, you could roll over Belgium, without a tank."

"Very funny."

"The *Pushy Broads!* I like that!" Kitty decided. "We'll have meetings. And luncheons. And bake sales."

"Coffee mugs."

"T-shirts."

"A bowling team."

"Bite your tongue, Constance."

As the last of the cars arrived, Brian moved to the head of the coffin and took out his missal. Sean walked over to Peg, took her arm, and she went with him to stand beside his father, next to the coffin.

Brian began the prayers and Peg stood very still, listening. Sean spoke the responses, in English, to the prayers, and he looked at Peg, wondering if she was remembering the day fourteen years ago when he stood beside her as the bugler played taps over her father's grave. So much of their lives had been twined together for so long. He was her twin, her lover, her friend. How diminished his life would have been without her.

"I think Bill would have liked it," she said, as they walked to the car.

"Except I think he'd rather have had the Holy Cross fight song. He never did like Georgetown much."

"When they bury me, Sean, I want a party."

"I'll have *The Washington Post* march played on an accordion."

"Rat!"

They got into the car, and the three limousines headed slowly toward the front gate of the cemetery. Sean looked out the window as they drove.

"It's funny how fast you get used to things. He's gone. He's really gone. If only—"

"No second guesses. He's at peace, Sean."

It was a warm day, one of the perfect days Washington so often produces in the summer. There was barely a trace of a cloud in the fine blue sky, and the scent of new-mown grass drifted through the open window. Unexpectedly, Sean felt a surge of joy. He was alive. He was young. And the sun was shining. He felt guilty at this sudden freshet of joy, but there it was. He was alive.

He turned around to look at Peg, and he saw that her mouth was open in astonishment. She looked as if somebody had just goosed her.

"Oh no!"

"What's the matter?"

"My water broke."

"Your water?" He stared at her, uncomprehending.

"Yeah. It breaks when labor starts."

"*That* water!"

"Yeah."

He looked; indeed, the seat of the limousine was soaked and there was a huge, dark stain on the back of her dress.

"Oh good Lord, Peg! It's not time yet!"

"Oh dear," she said, looking at the seat. "I wonder if it stains."

"Peg, you're going to have the babies!"

"Not here I'm not. I'll be damned if I'll have my babies in a hearse."

"We've got to get you to the hospital."

"Listen, tell the driver to stop on Georgia Avenue, and I'll get a cab. I'll just zip over to GW Hospital."

"Are you kidding?" Sean leaned up to the driver and said "This woman is about to have a baby. Can you take us to GW Hospital?"

"Let me radio my boss." The driver pressed a button on his two-way radio. "Milt, we got a woman here who's going to have a baby. Can I take her to GW?"

"Tell him my water broke."

"Her water broke. No, *hers*, Milt. The radiator is fine." He turned to Sean. "He says I can, but it's three dollars a mile. It's not included in the price of the funeral."

"Three dollars a mile!" Peg sputtered. "That's highway robbery!"

"Lady, if it was me, I'd do it for free, but Milt's the boss."

"You just let me out. Cabs only charge a dollar for a whole zone!"

"Peg, shut up." Sean leaned toward the driver again. "Take us to the hospital. I'll pay whatever it costs."

Peg leaned up too. "Look, it's five miles back to the Mc-Caffrey house. That's part of the funeral. So knock off five miles."

"It's four and one-tenth miles."

"Okay, knock off four."

"Done."

"I don't believe this! You're about to give birth, and you're haggling like a camel driver in Damascus."

"One must be an intelligent consumer, Sean. At all times."

"Listen," Sean told the driver, "tell your dispatcher to tell the first car we're going to the hospital."

The driver gave the message, and then said, "Milt says he'll tell 'em, but it's three bucks for the message."

"Next time somebody dies we are going to use McIntyre, not *you* guys."

"Lady, don't blame me."

"Just get to the hospital, fast!" Sean commanded.

The driver obligingly pushed the pedal to the floor, and the limo pulled out of line and shot ahead of the other cars and roared out the cemetery gate.

"On our way!" the driver sang out, cheerily.

They careened down Georgia Avenue at breakneck speed, and Sean said to the driver, "Maybe you ought to go a little slower."

"Buddy, if she has that kid in the limo, Milt will kill me. The seats are real suede."

Sean gripped the handrails as the limousine sped along, closing his eyes every time the driver zipped through a stop sign or ran a red light. He looked at Peg. Her face was flushed and she was grinning like a kid on a sleigh ride.

"I love going fast!"

"Oh God!"

And then they all heard it; the wail of a siren.

"Oh *shit*," groaned the driver. "Where did he come from?"

The driver pulled over to the side of the road, and an enormous state trooper walked over to the car and leaned against the door.

"Where do you think you're going, buddy, to a funeral? Because the way you're driving, you may be right."

"There's a lady going to have a baby."

"In a hearse?"

"It is not a hearse," said the driver, offended. "It is a funeral *limousine!*"

Sean leaned up to talk to the officer. "It's true, officer, she is going to have a baby."

"Father? There really is a pregnant lady back there?"

"Me," Peg said. "You can see I'm real pregnant."

"What are you doing in a hearse, ma'am? Doing ninety?"

"Funeral *limousine!*" the driver corrected.

"We were coming from a funeral and my water broke."

"And *this* is the father?" The policeman looked at Sean.

"No, I am the brother of the deceased."

"Ah, I see. The deceased was the father of the baby. Sorry, ma'am."

"No, he's in a nuclear sub."

"The deceased?"

"No, the father."

"You people are not making any sense."

"Ohhhh!" exhaled Peg.

"Officer, we have to get to GW Hospital, fast!" Sean said.

"Okay. I'll give you an escort. If I don't, you people are going to kill somebody."

They sailed down 16th Street, across Military Road, and finally pulled up to GW Hospital with the siren wailing.

"We are going to panic them, pulling up in a limo with a siren," Peg said. "They're going to think somebody shot the President."

"Any more pains?"

"Ohhh. Yes, there's one."

"Come on, I'll get you inside, and then I'll pay the driver."

"Remember to knock off the four miles."

"Peg, come on!"

Inside the hospital the nurse took charge of Peg, helped her get into her hospital gown, prepped her, and then took her to a small waiting room with a bed in it in the maternity suite. A resident came in, examined her, and asked about her contractions.

"They were about eight minutes apart. But I think they've stopped."

"It's going to be a while. We've called your doctor. You can just relax in here for a while."

"Can my friend come up? He's the only person with me."

"Sure. He can't go into the delivery room, though."

Sean came into the room, looking anxious. "Are you okay, Peg?"

"Yes. He said it could be hours."

"My father says to wish you good luck. I just called him. I think he's pleased." He was silent for a minute. "Life does go on."

"It does. Sean, will you stay with me until it's time?"

"Of course." He put his hand on her stomach and smiled. "You know all about this, I guess."

"Not exactly."

"Didn't you take lessons?"

"Who had time? I had to read the whole goddamn HUD budget this week."

"Peg, for Chrissakes—"

"Sean, they know what to do here. It's not like I was dropping my babies in a rice paddy. Ohhh!"

"Oh my God! I'll get somebody."

She grabbed his hand. "It's only a contraction."

"How long since the last one?"

"I don't know. You time them."

"Okay." He sat down in the chair next to the bed.

"Sean, tell me about Daley's operation on the South Side."

"Peg, you are having a baby. Babies. How can you think of Mayor Daley at a time like this?"

"We have to talk about *something*." She yawned.

Sean put his hand on the mound of her stomach and smiled. "There's certainly a lot of this."

"Well, in a little while I'll be thin again. The doctor says I have a pelvis like the Holland Tunnel."

"That's good."

"Yeah, but I guess it will still take a while."

"No more contractions?"

"No. I wonder if they stopped?" She yawned again. "All of a sudden I feel sleepy."

"Go to sleep. I'll be here, I promise."

She closed her eyes and drifted off to sleep, and she

thought she dreamed, a confused jumble of images. She awoke suddenly, feeling that somebody was jumping on her stomach.

"Ohh. Ohh." She felt a hand, touching her face, gently.

"It's all right, Peg. I'm here."

"Sean? Was I asleep?"

"Out like a light. How do you feel?"

"I think that was a big one. It woke me up."

"I'll start timing them again."

They were silent for a minute and he said, "Peg, why didn't he come?"

"Who?"

"Who! Your husband, that's who."

"Oh, him. Ohhh. He's at sea."

"Don't they let them come home to have babies?"

"No, they just drop them in the conning tower." She chuckled.

"Very funny. Couldn't he get a leave?"

"Well, the truth is, we're separated."

"Separated! And you're going to have twins?"

"Ohhhh!"

"Four minutes."

"It was just one of those things, I guess. Didn't work out."

"Oh, Peg, how did you get yourself in such a mess?"

"I'm separated and I'm having twins and I'm going to jail. Oh Sean, I have really screwed up, haven't I? Ohhh."

"Three minutes. Should I call somebody?"

"I don't think so."

"Why did you marry him, anyhow?"

"He had nice teeth. That was his best feature, I recall."

"You don't marry someone for *teeth*, you idiot."

"I did."

"If it's nice teeth you wanted, why didn't you marry me? I got great teeth, see? Free Catholic dental clinic."

"If you remember, your employer frowns on that. Ohhhh."

"Three minutes."

They were quiet again, and then he said, softly, "I was going to ask you. The day you told me you were married."

"Ask me what?"

"To marry me."

"What!"

"I called you the night before to tell you I wanted to leave the priesthood and marry you. Then you showed up the next day. Married."

"Ohhh."

"Three minutes."

"Sean, you wanted to marry me? You really did?"

"Yes, I did. My timing was great, wasn't it."

"Oh Christ, what a fuck-up!"

"I know," he said, glumly.

"Not you, *me*. You looked so happy, Sean, so *right*. And the lady said you were going to be a goddamn cardinal. So I couldn't tell you. Ohh!"

"Three minutes. Tell me what?"

"That I was pregnant."

"That you were— Peg, you were pregnant *then*? You're not early?"

"Yes. No. Ohhhh!"

"It was *me*? I got you pregnant? That's what you were going to tell me?"

"Yes."

"What about the navy guy?"

"I made him up."

"You did *what*?"

"Made him up. Ohhhhh! That was a big one."

"You're not married?"

"No." She lifted her left hand to show him the ring. "Fake, turns my finger green. Ohhhh. Ohhhh. That one *hurt*."

He put his hand on her stomach in wonderment. "They're mine? Dear God, my babies? I'm having *twins*! Oh, Peg!"

"Nice of you to mention my name at the end there."

"I love you. Peg, oh Peg, I love you!" He leaned down to kiss her mouth, gently.

"I love you too, Sean. I've loved you all of my life. Ohhh. Ohhhhhh. Oh Sean, I think— Ohhhh. Oh damn, it hurts. Oh Sean, help, I think it's happening."

"Oh Jeez, I'll get the doctor!" He ran out of the room and came back with the resident in tow. The resident pulled the drape, examined her, and said, "We better get you to the delivery room."

Peg reached up and pulled the drape open and grabbed for Sean's hand. "Ohhhhh. Sean, come with me!"

Sean looked at the doctor.

"Sean, I need you. Ohhhh. Please, Sean, I need you!"

"I'm coming."

"Only the father is allowed in the delivery room, Father," the resident said.

"I am the father."

"No. I mean the baby's father."

"I *am* the baby's father!"

"You? But you're—"

"Ohhhhh! For heaven's sake, stop fighting!"

"He says he's the father."

"He is. Ohhhh Ohhhh! Damn!"

"See."

"This is very irregular."

"Doc, if I have my babies in this crummy room, I am going to sue your socks off!" Peg snarled in her best pit-bull style. "And I'm not going anyplace without *him!* Ohhhhh. Ohhhh, *Christ!*"

"Nurse!" A nurse walked in and the resident said, "Get this man a mask and gown. Hurry!"

"Him?"

"Yes."

"But he's—"

"Ohhhhhh!"

"Just do it, nurse."

They wheeled Peg down the corridor as Sean trotted alongside, struggling into the gown and mask.

"Sean? Ohhhh, I think the baby's coming, I can feel it. Oh God, hurry!"

"I'm here, Peg!" He grabbed her hand. "I'm here."

As soon as she was wheeled into the delivery room, a nurse pulled up the back of her hospital gown and ordered, "Arch your back."

"You've got to be kidding. Oww!"

Her obstetrician came running through the door of the delivery room, pulling on his white coat. "Peg, you are a speedy one, my dear."

"Peg," Sean asked, holding her hand, "are you all right?"

"Oh yes. But I can't feel anything anymore. The stuff works."

The OB looked at Sean. "Commander Harriman?"

"Uh, no."

"Who *are* you, then?"

"It's a long story."

Sean wiped Peg's face tenderly with a towel as the nurses secured her feet in the stirrups. The doctor examined her.

"Looking good. Very good. Peg, who is that gentleman?"

"He's the baby's father."

"What happened to the commander?"

"I made him up."

"You—made him up?"

"Yes."

"Peg, can you push a little? See if you can push."

"I'll try. Uhh. Uhh. Am I pushing?"

"Good. That's good. You made up a navy commander as the father of your child?"

"It's sort of complicated, doc."

"I would guess it is. You *do* know who this gentleman is, I assume."

"He's Zabor, from the planet Urf. And I am his zort." She giggled.

The nurse put her hand on Sean's arm, reassuringly. "Don't be alarmed. It's the medication, makes them say weird things."

"Oh, there we are. Push, Peg."

"I want the mirror. I want to see it!"

"Nurse, swing the mirror over."

Peg looked up as the mirror was swung into position. She saw a pinkish aperture swathed in white cloth; she didn't recognize it as anything remotely belonging to her. It was like watching a TV screen.

"More push, if you can, Peg."

"I'm trying, but I can't feel anything. Uhh! Uhh!"

Suddenly, in the mirror, something small and dark hove into view. It was a tiny head covered with white lather that looked like shampoo.

"Sean! Look! Oh look!"

"Peg, it's— Oh my God, I see it!"

"It's a baby, Sean! An actual *baby!*"

And then, so fast that it astonished her, a baby slid out of the opening; like a child coming head first down a sliding board, she thought.

"A girl," the doctor announced.

"Megan. Oh it's Megan! Oh my God!"

A nurse took the baby girl and began to wipe her off gently. Peg glanced at the doctor, the smile splitting her face, and she saw that he was frowning. Her smile died.

"Something's wrong."

"The second baby's breech, Peg. I want you to try to push hard."

"I'll try. Oh, I'll try."

Sean's face went as white as marble. A nurse put a hand on his arm. "Do you want to leave?"

"No. No!"

Under the lights, the sweat glistened on Peg's brow. "Am I pushing? I can't feel it! Am I pushing?"

"Dear God!" Sean whispered. Peg gripped his hand, hard.

"It's going to be okay. I'm here."

"Come on," the doctor encouraged, talking to the baby, "Come on now." To Peg: "Push, as hard as you can."

"I can't feel it!" she said, a tinge of panic in her voice."

"It's all right. It'll help. Come on now."

Sean looked into the mirror and saw two tiny pale feet, moving, as if they were struggling. If the baby had too little oxygen, what would happen? What? The little feet moved. The doctor's hands probed, turned. *Dear God,* Sean prayed, *bless the work of his hands. Bless Thy servant, Lord. If it be Thy will.* The universe narrowed to a pair of tiny feet, moving, and a man's hands.

"It's too long. It's taking too long." Peg was soaked with sweat, trying to will her numbed body to push.

"I'm here, Peg," Sean said. "It's going to be all right."

He saw the doctor glance up at the clock on the wall, then his eyes went to the tiny feet again, his face set in a grim line. The feet were still and Sean thought, *Dear God, no!* and then they moved again. And suddenly, the baby was free and the doctor held the baby up and an energetic wail came from the mouth of the newborn baby boy.

Peg gave an Indian-like whoop of triumph and she cried out, *"Sean!"*

"You gave us some trouble there, buddy," the doctor said to the squalling baby boy.

"*Sean!*" Peg repeated, her face bathed in sweat and an enormous smile. "*Sean!*"

"Yes, Peg, it's just great! Isn't it great! Oh, it's just great!"

"I mean *that's* Sean!"

"Sean? Megan and Sean?"

"If that's okay."

The nurses were holding both babies now; Megan was wrapped in a blanket and a nurse was gently sponging Sean's tiny body. Their father stared at them, open-mouthed. They were, quite simply, the most beautiful, the most amazing things he had ever seen.

He looked at Peg. "Do you know what you just did? Oh Peg, look at them. Oh God, it's the most wonderful thing I've ever seen in my life. It's just so—wonderful. Oh wow. It's just—wonderful. You are fantastic, oh Peg, fantastic!" He was laughing, like he was drunk.

"You folks want to hold them?" the doctor asked.

"Oh, could we?"

"Why not? They're yours."

He tucked Megan into Peg's arms and gave Sean to his father, saying, "Here's your son, whoever you are."

"Oh, she's so beautiful," Peg cooed. "Megan, Megan, you're beautiful. Oh, look at that beautiful hair."

"He's got hair too," San said, touching little Sean tentatively with his finger. "Oh my gosh."

"They get it from you. You always were hairy."

"His fingers, Peg, they're so *little*. He's beautiful, not wrinkled at all. Sean, you're my *son!* I have a son. And a daughter." He laughed. "Oh God, it's *wonderful!*"

"Are her toes all there? Oh thank God, they are. Oh *Megan! Sean!* They look so intelligent. Don't they look very intelligent, doctor?"

"Regular Ph.D.'s."

"He's got your nose, Peg. And she's so beautiful, look at her. Oh, it's just great!"

"You keep saying that," she laughed.

"It's true. Oh Peg, I'm high as a kite. I've never felt anything like this before. It's a miracle. Oh Peg, *we* did this. It's a miracle."

"Come on you two," the doctor said. "We have other customers."

The nurse wheeled Peg to the recovery room, bathed her, gave her a clean gown, and then Peg slept, for how long she wasn't sure. When she awoke, Sean was leaning over her, stroking her forehead.

"Where are they?" she asked.

"In the nursery. I've been watching them."

"I want to go too."

In front of the nursery window, they watched the two tiny forms in their little cribs. They were silent, awed.

"Two new lives, Peg. It really is a miracle."

"You're thinking of Bill. Don't blame yourself because you couldn't save him."

"I do. But I think I can learn to forgive myself."

"Oh Sean, they're so tiny. What if I drop them? I'm such a klutz."

"You won't, Peg. Look, Megan's worked her fingers out of the little mitt they put on her. She's getting them near her mouth. She's brilliant! She's outwitted the hospital bureaucracy already."

"Look at Sean. All that trouble he gave us, and now he's sacked out as if he hadn't a care in the world. And Megan. Still wiggling. She's going to be the restless one, I think, always in a hurry. Sean, he's not going to be rushed. Look at that sweet little face. He'll do things when he's good and ready."

"They're little people, already, aren't they? I always thought babies were little blobs, but they're *Sean* and *Megan*. They start off right away, being who they are."

"And they're so beautiful. They are clearly the most beautiful babies in the nursery. And I'm not being biased, really I'm not."

"Oh, right, Peg." He smiled and peered trough the nursery window. "Look, I think Megan has her eyes open." He began to wave at her, vigorously. Peg started to wave too.

"Sean, we are making fools of ourselves."

"We are supposed to. Megan, it's *daddy!*"

Then they were quiet again, and he leaned against the nursery window. She looked up at him and saw the tears in his eyes.

"Sean?"

"I'd kill for them, Peg. I'd die for them. How can I love them so much already? I've only known them an hour."

She shook her head. "I never knew they'd be so beautiful. Oh Sean, I wish I was magic. I wish I could wave a wand and cast a spell over them so nothing could hurt them, ever, I wish I was magic."

She reached up and took his hand. He held it, and said, "A little while ago, you reached for me. You said, 'I need you.' You never did that before."

"I never thought I had the right to."

"You were always sending me away. You were so goddamn strong. You have to learn to trust me, Peg. I'm going to be your husband, and I'm the father of Megan and Sean. And I'll take care of them. I always will. And you too, if you'll let me."

"I've always needed you, Sean. Just because I'm strong, that doesn't mean I don't need you. A woman can be strong. I don't want to have to fall apart before you come to me."

"I understand that. But Peg, let me know. Don't keep things inside. Tell me you need me."

"I need you, Sean."

They were quiet again, and she said, "I can't leave them. I'm going to jail, and I can't bear it. It'll kill me, Sean."

"There's a good chance he'll delay the sentence. You told me that yourself."

"But at some point, I'll have to go, I know it."

"I'll be there, Peg. I'll come every day, I'll bring them. They won't keep you away from them."

"Do you promise?"

"I do."

"Oh Sean, I thought I could do it, when they were just— but now that I see them, I couldn't, I—"

"We'll get through it, whatever comes. I'm here. We're a family now. Really."

"You're right. We're strong. We have to be, because of them. It makes a difference, doesn't it? Everything is more important now. Because of Sean and Megan."

He nodded.

"Oh jeez, Sean, are we smart enough, are we good enough to be their parents? I'm so scared, all of a sudden. We'll make mistakes, won't we? Awful ones."

"Probably. But we'll love them, Peg. We'll do our best for them. This is what I'm supposed to do. I know it. I feel it. I'll be there for them. All my life."

She looked up at him and smiled. She knew what kind of a father he would be. He would hover over them the way he had hovered over his tiny patients in their boxes filled with cotton. He would get up twice a night to see if they were breathing. He would suffer the tortures of the damned when their gums ached from getting teeth, and he would drive the pediatrician wild with calls at seven A.M. He would worry that their teeth should be straight and their noses not runny. He would make sure they were dressed properly when it was cold. Or warm. Or in between. He would worry about whether they would go to college. He would be a total pain in the ass about them and she would, she supposed, have to hide all the iodine bottles.

"Where are the nurses?" he asked. "We have been here twenty minutes, and I haven't seen any nurses. What sort of a hospital is this, anyhow? You don't think she could choke on that little mitt, do you?"

"I don't think so."

"Maybe they'll forget to feed them."

"I'm going to feed them, remember?"

"I don't trust hospitals. They lose things."

"They won't lose Sean and Megan. See, they have name tags."

"We're not going to dress them alike and do all those disgusting cutesy-poo things people do with twins. That makes me want to barf."

"Maybe—just one or two stretch suits."

"Peg."

"Okay. No little stretchies."

"Right."

"Maybe—matching snowsuits."

"*Peg!*"

"Socks. Their socks can match, Sean."

"I guess that's okay."

"Little shirts with monograms. They wouldn't even be the same color. And the monograms would be *really* little."

"I can see that I am going to have to keep my eye on you, Peg."

"Yes," she said. "You are."

ACKNOWLEDGMENTS

There are a few people to whom I owe special thanks for their help in getting this book from idea to reality. First, many, many thanks to Elaine Markson, without whose friendship and encouragement the book never would have been possible, and to Geri Thoma and Ron Bernstein for their steadfast help and support.

A special note of thanks to Joyce Engelson, my editor, whose perceptions and guidance were invaluable in the whole process of creating the book.

It's a bit hard to say thanks in an adequate way to Clare Crawford-Mason. It's been a few years since we were both editors on the school paper in the "Immaculate Heart High School," vowing to set the world on fire when we grew up. For this book, I have shamelessly borrowed—or stolen—many of her observations and perceptions about Washington, gleaned from God knows how many conversations in her kitchen and living room. She earned those perceptions the hard way—as a print journalist, a senior producer for NBC, Washington editor of *People* magazine and now head of her own TV production firm, CCM Productions. The Girls Forever Brave and True have come a ways—and it has not been dull.

I wish to express my appreciation, too, to the members of my writers group—Bernice Buresh, Diane Cox, Helen Epstein, Phyllis Karas, Diana Korzenik, Janet Robertson, Carolyn Toll, Sally Steinberg, and Barbara White—for their help and support.

And last but not least, my thanks to Meg Oakman, my graduate assistant, for her help in both research and copyediting.

371